New Swan Shakespeare ADVANCED SERIES

GENERAL EDITOR Bernard Lott M.A., Ph.D.

King Lear

WILLIAM SHAKESPEARE

King Lear

Edited by Bernard Lott M.A., Ph.D.

Longman

Longman Group UK Limited
Longman House, Burnt Mill, Harlow,
Essex CM20 2JE, England
and Associated Companies throughout the world.

This edition © Longman Group Ltd 1974

First published 1974
Seventeenth impression 1992

Produced by Longman Singapore Publishers Pte Ltd
Printed in Singapore

ISBN 0-582-52746-5

Contents

Acknowledgements

WE ARE grateful to the following for permission to reproduce copyright material:

B. T. Batsford Ltd. for an extract from *Prefaces to Shakespeare* by H. Granville-Barker; Cambridge University Press for an extract from 'The Catharsis of *King Lear*' by J. Stampfer in *Shakespeare Survey 13*; the author, Chatto & Windus Ltd. and Stanford University Press for an extract from *Some Shakespearean Themes* by L. C. Knights; and Macmillan, London and Basingstoke and St. Martin's Press, Inc., for an extract from *Shakespearean Tragedy* by A. C. Bradley.

WE ARE grateful to the following for permission to reproduce copyright illustrations:

William Gordon Davis for page xiii top left; Harvard Theatre Collection (photographs by Angus McBean) for pages xiii bottom right, xvii top right, cii, ciii, 50, 51, 88, 89, 126, 127, 170, 171; Raymond Mander & Joe Mitchenson Theatre Collection for page xiii top right and bottom left; National Film Archive for pages xvii bottom, xxiii top right and bottom left; Radio Times Hulton Picture Library for page xli; Sovexportfilm for page xxiii top left; British Library Board for page lxxxi; and John Vickers for page xvii top left.

GENERAL EDITOR's Foreword

THE AIM of this edition of *King Lear* is to ensure that the reader fully understands and appreciates the play itself. It gives detailed explanations of the text: points of difficulty often taken for granted or touched on inconclusively are here treated at length; and besides dealing with such matters as archaic language and allusions to bygone custom, the notes explain briefly certain rare words still current in English which happen to occur in the play (e.g. *fourscore, renege*). Help is also given with complicated syntactical constructions and with patterns of imagery which may not be obvious at first sight. The content of the play, its historical, social and philosophical bases, and the conventions implied in the way characters react to one another may be strange to many readers and are therefore dealt with in detail. Although the subjects treated are sometimes difficult, the explanations are simple in language, and avoid the long expositions to be found in some editions. Again, much space in other editions is sometimes given to alternative readings of the text and to various conjectural explanations of difficult passages. This edition omits almost all such speculation. Where the meaning is doubtful, the editor has chosen the interpretation which seems to fit the context most satisfactorily, and has avoided numerous alternative explanations. If *one* possible alternative serves to make the meaning clearer, this is added. Specific reference is made here and there to variant readings of the original text (the Folios, the Quartos) only where a more helpful explanation of the passage will result.

Some background knowledge is essential to a full understanding of the play. Certain passages can be explained only in the light of some aspect of the 'world view' of Shakespeare's day, or of some piece of information about the region and period in which the action supposedly takes place. A sufficient amount of information is given to clarify the meaning of the passage in question, although there is no attempt at a far-reaching account of the whole subject.

At the back of the book there is an index which glosses and gives the location of all the difficult or unusual words in the text. By reference to the location in the text the student will find a note which will in most instances expand the brief equivalent given in the index. The index will also help him to trace passages in the play, since if he remembers a key word likely to be treated there he can look it up and find a line reference to the text. In this way the glossarial index is also an index to the notes.

The only way to full enjoyment of the play is full understanding of what it means. All the help offered, in the form of notes, glosses, and the introduction, has only this end in view. No attempt has been made to give elaborate criticism of the play, but sources of good criticism are indicated in the bibliography. A study of these sources however can wait until the play is thoroughly known and appreciated for its own sake.

Part One of the Introduction which follows is a general essay on *King Lear*. Part Two contains a series of articles which give more detailed information on certain subjects, as listed on page v. These articles are not essential to an understanding of the play, but include matter which the student of the play may like to have in order to widen his knowledge. The section contains also some extracts from the great critics of *King Lear*.

Introduction

PART ONE

The significance of King Lear today

King Lear is acknowledged as one of the great tragedies in literature. To get to know it is a stimulating and exciting intellectual experience, but the reader can expect to appreciate its greatness only if he becomes really familiar with the text. In the theatre the written word is transformed into speech, carrying the spectator without hesitation through the rush of action and narration. The reader, on the other hand, must bring to his reading a good deal of constructive imagination if he is to appreciate the play's sublimity. And more than at first seems likely, deep acquaintance with the play opens up insights not just into the life and times of Shakespeare but, because of the play's universality, into everyday life here and now.

The old King, wanting to shake off the burdens of ruling his kingdom, proposes to split it up and give a third to each of his three daughters. Before putting this plan into effect he asks each of them in turn to tell him how much she loves him. Two take the safe way, giving fulsome declarations of their love for him; the third, Cordelia, enrages him by speaking only of the love she owes him as a daughter's duty to her father. She loses her share of the kingdom, and this is apportioned between the other two. Quickly Lear finds that his two elder daughters abuse their power and drive him out. After an angry encounter, Lear leaves the dwellings of men and goes out to the desolate heath in the stormy night, and his suffering turns his mind. Cordelia, who has married the King of France, hears of his plight, and comes with a French army to relieve him and nurse him back to sanity. But her army is defeated, and she is hanged by order of Edmund, the leader of the victorious English forces. Lear dies, broken-hearted at the death of the daughter he has wronged.

So runs the main plot of the play. The counterplot deals with the outcome of Edmund's deception of his father, Gloucester.

Edmund, Gloucester's illegitimate son, ousts Gloucester's legitimate son Edgar from their father's favour by deception and misrepresentation. Gloucester remains loyal to Lear in his madness, and pays for this by losing his eyes. Without revealing himself, Edgar is able to help his blind and destitute father, and later kills Edmund in single combat.

A bald summary such as this raises many doubts in the mind. How could an aged king do anything as stupid as Lear does? What makes Gloucester so easily open to deception? Where is it all supposed to happen? – and so on. The only fair answer to such questions is that they do not matter, least of all in a stage presentation of the play. Study of the text gives the reader, as it were, too much time to ponder and look backwards and forwards. Seeing a stage performance, one takes certain things for granted (Lear's sentimental silliness, Gloucester's gullibility). One is asked only to experience with the characters the effects, all those circumstances which go along with these characteristics in these situations. Again, one is sometimes baffled over the matter of location: the action is set vaguely in and around the castles of Gloucester and Albany until all the paths begin to converge on the country near Dover. As with the characters, however, the location is not really a point of difficulty in a stage presentation. The speed and inevitability of movement allow no time for unprofitable questions of this sort.

The great achievement of the play is the fully convincing treatment of the story in spite of the folk-tale improbabilities of the plot. The two worlds of fantasy and reality are brought together by the undoubted, essential truth of the reactions of the characters to the events of the story. If such-and-such can be imagined as happening, then this would be the outcome. And on this, much of the success of a stage play must depend.

A detailed study of the play and its setting is attempted in the remaining sections of this Introduction. Here some of the timeless qualities are touched on because it is these which help us to realise why the play remains important and full of assurance and conviction. It treats with great firmness the results of giving way to foolish emotion. Lear's sentimentality hopelessly impedes his powers of perception. He fails to recognise that all is not well within the structure of his family, that the protestations of his two elder daughters are suspect. He fails to appreciate that the young have their own lives to lead, and are best not treated as if they could be moulded into images to please their parents. Even compared with Lear, Gloucester is easy meat for the same sort of deception: family concord can be wrecked, and in an instant too, by the malevolence of a powerful persuader, and Edmund's trans-parently trumped-up charge against his half-brother finds in Gloucester an amazingly ready listener. Once this is granted, the immensity of their punish-ment is comprehensible: Lear's madness and Gloucester's blindness are the prices they pay to be disillusioned. Before they leave the stage for ever, both of them see life more clearly (a paradox for the blinded Gloucester), and with them we also experience a clarification. With them we must acknowledge that love is not to be confused with flattery, that there is more to life than can be contained in formal pronouncements about it, that the guilty are not necessarily brought to justice within the span of our life on earth, and so on. Much of the play casts sidelong glances at the abstraction of justice; some characters, e.g. Edgar, feel the gods are just in the end, although the play does not leave this as its final impression. Instead of justice, indeed, there is the experience of the ebb and flow of hope, and an enduring appreciation of what is right and what is wrong, despite the absence of obvious reward and punishment to help one tell which is which.

The tragedy is completely satisfying as a stage play because here is shown in little the concept of a creative artist's intellect working on a cosmic scale – the whole universe in its unfathomable relations with a divine cause – together with touches of detail from an acute perception of human ways. The basic Lear story is not treated rigidly. It is manipulated this way and that to accommodate at once the cosmic breadth of the tragedy and the subtle tenderness and strains of joy and grief which place it securely in the here and now.

This treatment of a universal theme leads to an unexpected result which troubled readers during a long period between Shakespeare's age and our own: many could not reconcile themselves to the absence of poetic justice in the working of the main plot, nor accept it in stage performances. Poetic justice is quite simply the convention in literature by which virtue is rewarded and wickedness punished, whether by man or by superhuman agents. One might safely assert that most works of fiction in the literature of the world depend on this principle for their moral message: the good prosper and the bad are in the end brought down. This convention can be seen at work in the sub-plot, the story of Gloucester, Edgar and Edmund, though even here, Gloucester's blinding is a punishment out of all proportion to the fault of his stupid credulity and the act of lust which brought Edmund into the world. In the main plot poetic justice is absent, and we would not have it otherwise, because any neat ascribing of praise or blame as the drama comes to an end could only be facile and unsatisfying.

But to earlier generations the matter appeared differently. About twenty years after the Restoration of the Monarchy in 1660, when the theatres opened again after being closed during the Commonwealth period, Nahum Tate prepared a version of *King Lear* to suit the taste of the age; this called for a romantic love interest and an ending nearer to poetic justice. He makes Cordelia and Edgar secretly in love with one another, and uses this love to explain Cordelia's unemotional answer to Lear's question at the beginning of the play. In this way she loses her chances of getting a dowry, and so avoids having to marry one of her suitors, Burgundy. As in Shakespeare, Albany offers to give the kingdom back to Lear, but in Tate's version he resigns it to Cordelia, now married to Edgar, and she becomes Queen. Lear says that Kent and he will retire from the world and enjoy the calm of the new reign.

Dr. Johnson in 1765 found the death of Cordelia deeply shocking: 'I know not whether I ever endured to read again the last scenes of the play till I undertook to revise them as an editor,' he wrote. And earlier in the same essay: 'Shakespeare has suffered the virtue of Cordelia to perish in a just cause, contrary to the natural ideas of justice, to the hope of the reader, and, what is yet more strange, to the faith of the chronicles.' He therefore tends towards approving what the public had decided: 'Cordelia, from the time of Tate, has always retired with victory and felicity.' Charles Lamb is scathing (1811); he writes ironically: '[The play] is too hard and stony; it must have love-scenes and a happy ending. It is not enough that Cordelia is a daughter, she must shine as a lover too. Tate has put his hook into the nostrils of this Leviathan, for Garrick and his followers to draw the mighty beast about more easily.' So the untameable sea-monster of the play became for many generations a menagerie animal more readily brought to heel. To be fair, one must add that both Johnson and Lamb saw the play as something to be read rather than acted; Lamb went so far as to say that *Lear* could not be represented on a stage.

Yet the play is indeed presented successfully on the modern stage, and very much as Shakespeare wrote it. The impression which a stage presentation leaves behind is life-like and convincing. The sense of reality in the theatre does not come from any simple rounding-off, with justice meted out to the good and the bad according to their deserts. As the play proceeds, the sequence is more one of onsets of consolation for the main sufferers which turn out to be false starts. In the face of the malevolence from which the suffering springs, the corresponding virtues come too late, or turn out to be too weak to counter the wrong done. This wave motion is, if anything, intensified as the play proceeds: in the last few minutes of the drama, from the point where Lear carries Cordelia dead in his arms, we sense a finality. Lear has been punished by loss of worldly power and human faculties and by terrible destitution, but has achieved some enlightenment. And although the swashbuckling King of earlier years shows through momentarily:

> I have seen the day, with my good biting falchion
> I would have made them skip,

(v.iii.276)

the tone is now of clearer vision, a facing-up to reality. Cordelia's death has not offended this but completed it. Yet the final 'false start' is still to come. Albany turns out, perhaps rather unexpectedly, to be one who is in a position to set things to rights in one of those ritual-like speeches which Shakespeare sometimes uses to round off the complexities of a play:

King Lear as portrayed in the theatre:

Henry Irving 1892

Norman McKinnel 1909

Donald Wolfit mid-1940s

John Gielgud 1950

You lords and noble friends, know our intent.
What comfort to this great decay may come
Shall be applied. . . .

(v.iii.276)

He begins this reform programme by reassigning power, absolute power, to
the aged King. The word *absolute* has a ring of foreboding about it. Will the
same sorry process of authoritarian rule begin all over again? The answer is
No; Lear says nothing to show that he has even heard or understood the
offer. His thoughts remain with Cordelia (he calls her affectionately *my poor
fool*), and he dies searching her face for signs that she is still alive.

As drama for the stage, not for reading, the play has much in it to interest
and attract present-day audiences. Lamb found its effect ludicrous because
it did not suit the heightened realism of the romantic stage which was the
fashion of the time. Theatre directors of today do not strive to achieve
'natural' effects in the theatre. The scenery they use is often sparse, sometimes non-existent, and dramatic strength is brought out by other means,
such as due emphasis on the truth and beauty of the language. Among the
critics of the play, Bradley (see the extract on p. lxxxiv) seems to us now to
have been over-concerned with improbabilities in the plot and in the way
events are acted out, on the analogy of everyday experiences in the real
world. The fashion today is much closer to that of Shakespeare's time. The
stage can, if the director so wishes, be virtually empty of visual effects, and
the actors can use styles of speech and mime which are heightened to command the audience's attention, and are not necessarily to be matched against
day-to-day experience at all. The English stage went through a period not
so long ago when even words and gestures were so muted that audiences
were all but left to make their own choice of what was to appear especially
significant. There is currently a return to rather more emphatic styles, but
these do not even approach the vocal projection of nineteenth century
declamatory acting.

In place of the naturalism of the earlier stage, we can now reach towards
a psychological realism better able to represent what in the play might
otherwise seem unattainable: the fantastic, the hideous, the incongruous,
which earlier audiences found it hard to reconcile themselves to, but which
sophisticated audiences now accept without much question. A number of
modern critics (led by G. Wilson Knight – see p. xcviii) have been attracted to
the incompatibilities in the play, which Wilson Knight himself calls grotesque.
In the strange universe of the imagination he finds a potential for comedy,
despite the tragic outcome in the logic of the plot. The clowning of the Fool,
a bridge between the high seriousness of the plot and the madness (real in
Lear, feigned in Kent), attracts particular attention in the modern theatre, as

engaging its own points of sympathy in the modern world. By contrast, people of Shakespeare's time found displays of madness in real life amusing and would watch as a spectacle the behaviour of lunatics in the asylums.

Jan Kott, the Polish critic, in *Shakespeare Our Contemporary* (1964) has pushed the affinity even farther, and sees similarities between *King Lear* and Samuel Beckett's *End Game* (1957) as an example of the 'theatre of the absurd'. Although Kott gives us no more than brilliant flashes illuminating points in one play by reference to the other, he contributes by implication to the contemporary revival of interest in *King Lear*. In the 'theatre of the absurd' an extreme position is reached where to mirror the confusion of ideas and ideals in the modern world there is no rational approach to objectives, no force moving the world of the drama forward to new positions. In Beckett's *Waiting for Godot*, to take a famous example, the two principal characters are encouraged to expect, wait for, hope for the arrival of someone who never comes. There is in *King Lear* a trust in jaded and unsubstantiated philosophies about the benevolence or otherwise of the world order (nature, 'the gods'). In the Beckett plays violent deprivation (the loss of limbs or sight) forces characters to depend on others to act as their 'senses'. The senses are therefore represented separately, so to speak, from those they serve, and are the more easily scrutinised; so Edgar ministers to the blindness of his father Gloucester, and Kent to the madness of Lear when he is destitute. But of course there are important differences between Shakespeare's tragedy and the plays of 'the absurd'. Beckett, Jean Genet, Eugène Ionesco and other modern playwrights who have views on the drama similar to theirs, abandon altogether the rational plot devices of traditional plays in order to reflect in the very formlessness of their own plays the lack of purpose in the world as they experience it around them. In *King Lear* there is 'argument' in the sense of logical progression and sequence, which may be grotesque but is not absurd.

There is too a quality in *King Lear* which makes it suited to the film and television techniques of the packed action point treated by means of close-up filming. The film (1970) which Peter Brook directed and in which Paul Scofield played Lear made good use of the camera to bring the immediacy of personal emotion into an inhospitable, wintry setting. The presentation reached out to universals, but the character revelations and the short, sharp exchanges showed how much more suited the play was to such camera techniques than to the wide picture-stage of the romantic theatre. The play's concern with the human body and its covering, and the subject of the sexual act as a focal point in Lear's rambling thoughts likewise have an unexpectedly contemporary ring about them.

But above all other matter in the play it is the portrayal of madness, real or feigned, which has caught the attention of today's readers and audiences.

The world has moved on from those uncharitable times when madness was looked upon as something at once laughable and somehow caused by faults which could be traced back to the sufferer. The portrayal of madness which has about it a psychological validity now commands respect as, aside from its dramatic significance, a probing into the mystery of the mind. The Fool's chatter, moving erratically from point to point, reference to reference, to the lowest depths of banality or disconcerting incomprehensibility, realises a modern predicament; it comes as no surprise to people who can see the point behind the apparent pointlessness of, say, the circus-clown patter in *Waiting for Godot*. Indeed, the Lear myth itself has been taken up by a living British playwright, Edward Bond. In his play *Lear* (1971) he introduces into the legendary history an altogether different underlying theme. He uses the story to show some of the results, as he sees them, of what he terms today's 'social morality', the system which, as he believes, the leaders of society utilise in order to keep their own power and suppress opposition. People are made by society to feel that opposition to those in power is morally wrong, and the circumstances of aggression are thus created and perpetuated. One can see a number of ways in which the Lear myth could be treated to bring out this theme. Bond uses it to show how modern man is trapped by the 'social morality' into a situation which unavoidably results in violent cruelty, and this is plentifully exemplified in his play. If the play has a moral message, it is a call for the revival of pity which alone can resolve man's predicament as the playwright has identified it. Once more, the terror and the pity of Shakespeare's play are far from alien to the instincts of our own world.

We have so far thought of *King Lear* as primarily a play for the stage. Many however will get to know it as a text for study, and in this guise too the question of its relevance to today's preoccupations calls for our attention. There is certainly one matter which does *not* command the attention it once did in the Western world: the justification of God's ways with men. *King Lear* is a text that generations of readers will have scanned to gain insight into the workings of a Divine Power in the world. The mind tuned to study the text with this aim will need to be imbued with the sense of a personal or personalised God (the 'gods' of the play), whereas today the Western intellectual finds more satisfaction in an on-going existential view of the universe, where man creates his own values as he goes along, and where he finds neither compulsion nor sense in the search for external, objective standards. But at least the hopelessness of the search for this kind of justification, the showing-up in the play that the 'gods' are *not* just in their apportioning of reward and punishment, makes the play more easily acceptable to us than it was to the optimists of eighteenth-century Europe, say, or the Victorians in England, confident in the forward march of material progress. We have become accustomed to delving more deeply than this, questioning as the Fool does the

The Fool as portrayed by:

Alec Guinness 1946

Alan Badel 1950

Oleg Dal 1969

certainty of certainty, the value of values. We are more patient with madmen than previous generations were, not just because humane feelings and personal sympathies are stronger than they used to be, but also because madness may give truer insight into the workings of the human brain than sanity does. Sanity is in Bond's terms now suspect since it can be taken as an all-out concession to social morality. The tables are turned. It might be called madness now to think of the world as rational or just. If there is one absolute to be maintained and developed it is pity, and that remains the proper business of tragedy.

The significance of King Lear to Shakespeare's contemporaries

A special effort of the imagination is called for when we attempt to visualise *King Lear* as people of Shakespeare's time would have seen it. In a number of important ways the play lies outside the established modes of his time, even as he himself used them, and there is some evidence to suggest that it was never among the most popular of his plays. The delay in the intervention of 'justice' to reward the virtuous is one way in which the play defied the conventions. Another is the exclusion of all reference to Christian concepts of morality. Shakespeare's feeling for history is usually sufficient to make him avoid the use of specifically Christian terms in plays which are set in periods before Christianity, but in all except *King Lear* the general morality is Christian. The disgust of the 'good' characters in the early *Titus Andronicus*, for instance, when confronted by the horrors and cruelty of the 'bad' characters shows Christian pity; the imagery and references are often specifically Christian; yet the play is set in some vaguely-defined time during the decline of the Roman Empire, in and near Rome itself. In *Lear*, apart from some verbal echoes from the Bible, the ethos is not that of a Christian writer. (IV.vi.98 may be an exception to this, but the meaning there is not altogether clear.) There is the complexity of the plot as composed by Shakespeare from the detailed suggestions of his sources. (A fuller account of these sources is given below (p. xxxi); here our concern is to sense the attitude of a contemporary audience and see to what extent this attitude depended on their awareness of the sources.)

The story of Lear and his three daughters was very well known; it is told by one after another of the early chroniclers of Britain and was the sole subject of a play, *The True Chronicle History of King Leir*, produced in 1594 but bearing many marks of earlier composition. *Leir* was printed in 1605, at about the same time as *King Lear* was composed. *Leir* must by then have appeared odd and old-fashioned and the reprinting is therefore something of a puzzle. One explanation is that the success of *Lear* aroused a revival of interest in the old piece. Another is that Shakespeare's *Lear* was looked on as being another 'version' of *Leir* or another treatment of the Lear story of the chronicles, so that the *Leir* title-page of 1605, where the play is described as 'sundry times lately acted', refers rather to Shakespeare's play; the printer was perhaps exploiting interest in the *Lear* sequence by bringing out an old play of which he held the copyright.

It is more important to imagine how Shakespeare's contemporaries received the play, and what conventions they assumed.

The interweaving of the Gloucester plot with the Lear plot was evidently original; *Leir* keeps to the story of the King and his three daughters. The addition of the second plot increased the interest and sophistication of the piece, and also its complexity, in a rather special way. Shakespeare's audiences must have noticed that the two plots have much in common (both deal with the wrong done by parents to their children, Cordelia and Edgar have similar parts, both fathers suffer for their lack of shrewdness in dealing with the world), and that putting the two together gave them an opportunity to compare and contrast the almost conventional treatment of the more sophisticated, 'courtly' Gloucester story with the highly individual treatment of the Lear story. *King Lear* has features in the use of language which suggest that the play is close in time to the last plays of Shakespeare (finishing with *The Tempest*); to some extent, then, audiences were prepared and educated for a degree of complexity which outstrips the direct treatment of the earlier chronicle play. Certainly, the motif of parent-children relationships in which there was some viciousness on the parents' side was one which could not well be handled superficially because its attitudes were the opposite of what might have been expected, i.e. the viciousness of children against their parents. This, the more likely sin, counterbalances and outweighs the stupidity of the fathers, but is not the starting-point. A commandment of the Christian church says 'Honour thy father and thy mother', since on this side the command is the more necessary; parents 'honour' their children in the very nature of things.

This partial break with convention exemplifies the questioning spirit of the time. The play contains many references to a real or supposed celestial ordering of life; characters invoke it, often in vain, and probe it, and they show themselves more or less conscious of their bewilderment over the benevolence or otherwise of such an order. We hear of this celestial ordering in such terms as *the gods, heaven(s), Fortune's wheel*:

> Think that the clearest gods, who make them honours
> Of men's impossibilities, have preserved thee.

(IV.vi.74)

> thou mayst shake the superflux to them
> And show the heavens more just.
>
> (III.iv.35)

Fortune, good night. Smile once more; turn thy wheel. (II.ii.164).

Ordinary men in Shakespeare's day continued to assume this divine order-ing of things. One of the best sources for the *Lear* story is the *Mirror for Magistrates* (1586); this collection of stories in verse has as its theme the results of sin, with the reward for evil coming in this world, or, if history does not support this, in the next. *Lear* is of the new world which began to hold in doubt the concept of cosmic justice.

This rationalist confrontation of the divine view of nature was in the air, and beginning to be felt although we should not assume that Shakespeare's audiences were consciously aware of a change of attitude taking place. A modern sceptical world-view was being born, and the stress of these new visions of reality inevitably brought with it strains on the mind; in this play we meet both the true madness of Lear and the feigned madness of Edgar as Poor Tom. Yet any facile view of this transition of thought as being wholly for the common good would be false. We shall see frequently in the com-mentary how a 'reasonable' view does not necessarily come as a comfort to the sufferer. Reason and affection (in the Shakespearian sense of 'emotion, feeling, state of mind towards a thing') are labels which conveniently identify the opposite poles of relationships in society, and the development of the word *affection* to mean 'love' sufficiently indicates which state appeared happier. Lear's daughters reason with him over his requirements when he has renounced his power, and their heartlessness enrages him. When Goneril and Regan, his unkind daughters, try to argue him into agreeing that he does not need any attendants as he moves between his daughters' homes, he says:

> O, reason not the need. Our basest beggars
> Are in the poorest thing superfluous.
> Allow not nature more than nature needs,
> Man's life's as cheap as beast's.
>
> (II.iv.260)

Goneril and Regan may be quite right about their father's knights and the trouble they would cause. But audiences then and now base their judgement on Lear's feelings, not his daughters' rightness. Like us, they must have 'known in their hearts' that concessions would not stop there; the context of the incident had to be felt first and taken into account afterwards. The sympathy of the audiences must always have been with Lear, who did not reason things out and manipulate the frame of nature as Edmund did. For such audiences, as for us, this refusal to depend on any one philosophical position, on either the reason or the emotions, leads beyond the trivialities of ordinary life to a deeper reality. A transparent piece of trickery (Edmund's deception of Gloucester) or an attitude taken at a time of domestic tension (Cordelia's rigid statements of her position) spark off terrible events and finish in tragedy.

The Lear folk-tale seems to have had a special appropriateness at the time the play was written. When James VI of Scotland became James I of England in 1603, he proposed a political union of the two countries, since by acceding to the English throne he had brought them under one ruler. Neither country was ready to accept the proposed union, and during the period 1604-7 the King's speeches frequently referred to the misfortunes which division brought on early Britain. The dividing up of Lear's kingdom would therefore be especially apposite, as exemplifying a misguided attempt to improve the terrestrial order. And the good ordering of nations on earth was no less desirable to Shakespeare and his contemporaries than the ideal celestial order of which 'poetic justice' formed a part.

The nature of the tragedy

We now turn from the immediate impact of the play on audiences today and in Shakespeare's own age to some of its timeless qualities as a tragedy. Little about the sub-plot (the deception of Gloucester) needs to be added to what has already been said: we know that Gloucester, despite youthful misdeeds and his foolish acceptance of flimsy evidence, is basically good, and the blinding is a wickedness which our instincts want to see punished; and punished it is in the swift decline and death of Edmund. Because the evil is plain, regenerative impulses can begin to operate, and the retribution rounds off the plot.

Act III brings together the blinding of Gloucester and Lear's rejection of all shelter and his exposure to the raging storm. He now realises that his 'wits begin to turn'. And his own bewilderment at the onset of suffering in body and mind is a reflection of the observer's perplexity. For, unlike Gloucester, Lear is by no means so obviously in the right. He is suffering, but for what? Foolish pride? A dictatorial attitude to his children? His sentimental view of life? If it is any or all of these things, his punishment looks much too big for the crime. And the end of this suffering, whatever its cause, is the death of Lear himself and his wronged daughter, which at least puts an end to the uncertainties. A 'happy ending' would have given a false impression, a too easy handing-out of praise and blame. It took an actor to restore Shakespeare's text to the stage, and to reason through what readers (Lamb, Hazlitt) were beginning to sense. Kean (1787-1833)

determined to restore the previously rejected text of *King Lear* to the
Fifth Act, thereby saving the audience from the unnatural and impossible recovery of the old king, and the consummation of the
mawkish and improbable loves of Edgar and Cordelia. 'That,' said he
. . . indicating with his finger the last scene in *Lear*, 'is the sacred page
I am yet to expound. . . . The London audience have no notion of what
I can do until they see me over the dead body of Cordelia.'

(Hawkins: *Life of Kean*, ii.212)

When the performance took place, not everyone was convinced that the
change was an improvement; in any case the acting style in Kean's day
would have been too emotional, too highly charged, for present-day audiences
and had we been there we might not have been pleased with what we saw.
But Kean's own performance cannot blur his sensitivity to the play as
supreme tragedy. He understood why Shakespeare rejected for a deeper
truth the victory of the King of France and Cordelia as it appears in the
chronicles.

Cordelia's tragic role is in the ordinary sense complementary to Lear's. In
the exercise of moral judgement we cannot free her of blame, but it is our
awareness of her, rather than the little she says and does, which adds meaning
to her association with her father. The alienation paradoxically brings them
closer and the justice of Cordelia's suffering is much less clear-cut than Lear's.
Hers is the feminine sacrifice; a male character behaving as she does is as
unthinkable today as with Shakespeare. (Celia in T.S. Eliot's *The Cocktail
Party* has qualities in common with Cordelia.) Hers is the tragedy, since she
sacrifices herself to a whim of her father's which brings results exactly as
she would expect them. Knowing that the old man is tetchy and often needs
humouring, she might for reasons of expedience or just peace and quiet have
made a reply which would have pacified him. But it is as if she is here making
a last stand (or is it the first?) to hold her ground. Until the final cataclysm
we see little more of her, and she hardly emerges even then as more than the
instrument of the tragedy. Because of this we must see the incident of her
'reasonable' riposte to her father's question about love as an occasion in
itself, not something led up to by a series of other happenings which the
audience are asked to construct for themselves. Given the fact of the answer,
we are shown what it brings about. Lear fails to appreciate the rightness, the
rational good sense, of the answer, perhaps because of the harsh style in
which it is given, perhaps because he is too old to stomach opinions other
than his own.

Her tending of his consequent suffering brings a kind of solace to Cordelia.
When Lear reawakens to the world, attended by Kent and the Doctor,
Cordelia is not in any ordinary sense brought to be sorry for what she has

King Lear and the cinema:

In recent years, the cinema has added a new dimension to Shakespearan drama. These stills are taken from *Koral Lier* 1969, filmed in Russia and directed by Gregory Kozingsev.

Kent in the stocks (Act II, Scene iv).

Cordelia comforting Lear (Act IV, Scene vii).

Cameras on location in Russia.

done. She is instead a changed person, one who has now learnt some of the reasons of the heart. Her forthrightness has given way to a surprising resilience:

> LEAR I know you do not love me; for your sisters
> Have, as I do remember, done me wrong.
> You have some cause, they have not.
>
> CORDELIA   No cause, no cause.
>
> (IV.vii.74)

There was cause indeed, but now she is prepared to deny it. Sensibility has won over sentimentality. The tragedy has brought a quite surprising and unlooked-for regeneration of the human spirit.

The impact of the drama gathers its strength not only from the under-current of universal abstractions (sentimentality, allegiance, etc.) with which it deals, but also through the heightened reality of everyday affairs in the here and now of the familiar world:

(Lear, mourning the death of Cordelia)

> Thou 'lt come no more,
> Never, never, never, never, never! –
> Pray you, undo this button; thank you, sir.
>
> (v.iii.307)

The old man has a fear of choking, and quickly turns, as old people do, to what they interpret as the immediate needs of the situation. We are reminded of the time when he tore at his clothing for a different reason (III.iv.103):

> Come, unbutton here.

There are places where references look more specific than they are. Dover stands, rather vaguely, for hope, the link between viciousness (Lear's successors) and virtue (France through Cordelia's alliance), and as the tragedy proceeds there is a general drift in its direction. But it remains more a symbol than a location and the best that Regan can wish the blinded Gloucester is that he shall smell his way there (III.vii.92). In this act, Dover begins to emerge as the first of the false starts of consolation. Dover has to Englishmen the ring of 'port in a storm', point of exit and entry, homecoming and so on. Yet in Act V, even Dover as a symbol of hope is destroyed. And we feel the wreck of hope, in this specific case the defeat of France and Cordelia in battle, as much as the vaster conceptions of the storm and the passion of Lear which the storm at once reflects and illuminates.

Shakespeare's chosen device in this tragedy, then, is to look at the universal by means of the particular. Incidents at the periphery of the circle lead us to observe the centre. Lear, as his wits begin to turn, does not see the suffering of his expulsion into the storm as a dominating, universal sorrow; he thinks, on the contrary, that all suffering is rooted in causes similar to his own. Seeing Edgar disguised as a mad beggar Lear asserts, and again and again as some people will do, that Edgar's daughters must have brought him to this pass:

> LEAR Now, all the plagues that in the pendulous air
>   Hang fated o'er men's faults light on thy daughters!
> KENT He hath no daughters, sir.
> LEAR Death, traitor! Nothing could have subdued nature
>   To such a lowness but his unkind daughters.
>
> (III.iv.64)

These instances are keys which may help to unlock the complexities of the tragedy. Nature usually frustrates the human impulse to put it into order or pattern it; the tragedy of Lear offers the fact of experience without plain, straightforward, moral or artistic patterning. Much of this experience is evil and easily overwhelms the palliatives of kindness and love; much of it is just trivial and to all appearances inconsequential. But it is not 'superfluous', any more than clothing is to a human being, whatever those who suffer may protest to the contrary. So in Act II the unkind daughters 'reason' with their father over what his needs really are. And the reasoning-out is mere delusion because it satisfies no one and leads to nothing, just as Cordelia's 'sensible' answer gave her nothing.

> GONERIL (about the retainers Lear wants to keep with him):
>   What need you five-and-twenty, ten, or five,
>   To follow in a house where twice so many
>   Have a command to tend you?
> REGAN   What need one?
> LEAR O, reason not the need. Our basest beggars
>   Are in the poorest thing superfluous.
>   Allow not nature more than nature needs,
>   Man's life's as cheap as beast's.
>
> (II.iv.257)

Lear begins by 'reasoning' well himself, but the immensity of his daughters' cruelty makes him splutter into incoherence and his first twist of fear for his mind

> O fool, I shall go mad!
>
> (II.iv.282)

The structure of the play

One might say for convenience that there are two plots in the play, the Lear plot and the Gloucester plot. To split the play up in this way is, of course, to carry out an operation which the playwright never intended. An account of the structure of the play must not be taken as anything more than a crude skeleton, a lifeless heap of dry bones which need the flesh of artistry to clothe them; but the nature and movement of the whole can be appreciated a little by means of a knowledge of the patterning and framework lying within.

The two plots are, until the beginning of Act V, fairly sharply defined, in the sense that events can be attributed without hesitation to one plot or the other. In Act V, the converging of the plots makes the exercise of allocation to one or the other hardly worth the trouble; they come together, reflecting the clash of forces, basically France against Cornwall, a clash epitomised in the confusion over loyalties which Albany suffers in v.i.

The two plots have the same theme: unfilial behaviour, behaviour between parents and their children which we like to think abnormal. There are obvious parallels in character (Cordelia is to Lear as Edgar is to Gloucester; Kent and Edgar, both using disguise, minister to those who have wronged them). And because of the parallelism, each plot embellishes and deepens the other; as they converge we are able to notice contrasts in the detailed handling of stories which have a basis in common. This is one count on which the play merits close study: the similarities do not simplify the working-out of the plots – on the stage the succession of events in so complex a pattern calls for firm attention and at the same time permits certain improbabilities to go unnoticed – but they add much to the interest of the play as a work of art.

The Gloucester plot is the more conventional. In it are some elements of the 'morality', the tale in which a moral flaw in the central figure brings retribution for those who suffer as a result of that flaw. The play begins almost jokingly with the illegitimacy of Edmund's conception. His malevolence is exposed and displayed for the audience to savour to the full, and it is revealed in the language of the old dramatic style. This plot rapidly becomes humourless and savage, retaining its conventional elements, e.g. the irony in the action of Gloucester revealing his secret intentions to the very man, Edmund, who wishes him ill (III.iii), or being watched over without his knowledge by the very man, Edgar, who wishes him well. Conventional, too, is the long delay in Edgar revealing his relationship to Gloucester, the sufferer who before anyone would benefit from the comfort of such a revelation. Yet from IV.i, when the old tenant leading Gloucester is dismissed and Edgar takes over, through the attempted suicide (IV.vi) and on to Edgar's intervention in Oswald's bloody designs on Gloucester's life (IV.vi.221), the pretence is kept up to Gloucester's great confusion. In the grim guessing-game, however, hope is somehow kept alive, and Gloucester is not to give in, but rather to embrace the times. This is the 'ripeness' that is 'all' (v.ii.11). And then, true to the manipulating of the Gloucester plot type, the protagonist and the antagonist are at long last brought face to face in a ceremonious meeting not far short of ritual; in *King Lear* the pageantry of the champion being publicly called to maintain Edmund's treachery and the revelation of Edgar in such formal surroundings are most appropriate to the denouement of this type of plot. The period of uncertainty is brought to a sudden halt as all is revealed in the hard outlines of near-mechanical design. Yet the language displays a certain softness as the plots converge. Edgar's revelatory account is not the crude outline of misinterpreted events put straight for the record, even though Edmund calls it, not disparagingly, a 'speech' (v.iii.199). On the contrary, it is full of individuality and even the moral scruple is resolved: Has this course of action and deception been the right one? Of course there is no neat answer to this question, but the course Edgar chose is touched with sadness: Gloucester's 'flawed heart . . . burst smilingly' when he had understood the revelation. Like the sunshine and rain together of Cordelia's patience and sorrow (IV.iii.16) when she looks back over recent events and onwards to her meeting with her father, Gloucester's end leads us to relief beyond sorrow.

Some have found in Edgar's continued pretence a precaution he takes against his father destroying himself from remorse. By ministering to him in disguise, Edgar believes he 'saved him from despair'. Would Gloucester have been even more ready to take his own life, whether from remorse or self-pity, if he had known that the man who was caring for him was his son?

The handling of the Lear plot is very unconventional, though the plot itself is not. The unusual qualities of its structure can be brought together under the general one of naturalness in treatment, a naturalness which shows up in contrast with the contrivances of the Gloucester plot. The human urge is, as we have seen, to impose a pattern of order on experience, perhaps partly to wrest it from the unaccountable and make it seem to be under control. Nature resists this urge, and the Lear plot denies it by bringing the spectator several times to a point where resolution is to be expected, only to find that on the brink some set-back swings him away from comfort and fulfilment. Edgar's often-quoted view of poetic justice:

> The gods are just, and of our pleasant vices
> Make instruments to plague us

(v.iii.170)

is his comment on what we have called the Gloucester plot. His involvement with Lear shows the same view discredited in Lear's case. The Lear plot is subjected to subtler and more dynamic treatment than the naive rounding off of the Edmund allegory; Edmund says to Edgar:

> Thou hast spoken right, 'tis true;
> The wheel is come full circle

(v.iii.173)

The 'wave motion' of the Lear plot in Shakespeare's hands is in the rising hopes and falling disappointments of Lear's progress through the world when he is stripped of his power. The end of Act IV, for example, looks as if all is now laid ready for reconciliation: recognition and a battle in which victory can go to the just. But this is not to be . . . And, as we would expect with wave motion, the treatment of the material varies greatly in degrees of intensity. The long, detailed and complex Lear plot has sometimes puzzled readers, though less often spectators, because of stretches in which detail is carefully, almost exhaustively, handled, and adjacent sequences where the barest outline is laid down. The outline style is not uncommon in the expositions at the beginning of Shakespeare's plays, but it is hard to find a parallel to the later treatment in *King Lear* of momentous events. The sketchy presentation of the battle at the beginning of v.ii is a case in point.

The play begins, then (after the joking exchange over Edmund's illegitimacy), in the characteristic Shakespearian mode with the circumstances laid down firmly and in summary form. But there is a difference. Often elsewhere Shakespeare does this by backward glances in the form of references – to a relationship or a historical event, say – whereas in *King Lear* it is a compression of 'real life' action into a tiny compass. Following a preconceived and not very coherent plan, Lear divides his kingdom up, turns in rage against his youngest and truest daughter, banishes the honest Kent, handles with great despatch the marriage of this daughter, and, divested of his kingly powers, leaves. Thus the initial situation is set not by hints and backward glances which the spectator must grasp at but by a highly compressed summary in action of the events themselves.

The scenes from I.iii to the end of the act, being slower in pace, develop the situations already laid down. And because they seize upon that part of the introduction which has especially captured the imagination, the character of Lear himself, it seems natural and unquestionable that this is the aspect selected for the follow-through. The node of this sequence is Goneril's discomfiting of her father and his departure for Regan's home in the hope – vain hope indeed – of better treatment there. Around this node, dramatic incidents take place which provide many aspects of the key event, e.g. Goneril telling Oswald how he is to disregard Lear's orders, the bafflement over loyalties in the heart of Albany.

The modes of summary treatment are reverted to here and there according to pattern. The event selected for treatment is, in the main part of the play, put forth with a good deal of its attendant circumstance. Lear's movements are given scant treatment. He 'turns up' in one or other of the castles with nothing but the vaguest hint as to the time spent on the journey.

Near the centre of the play the treatment of incident and circumstance reaches starkly contrasting styles, until the result is that we measure, as we are desired to do, the importance of one stage in the development of the play against another by the way the language is handled. In II.iv, Lear's hopes in Regan are shown to be ill-founded. Goneril's entrance and her greeting by Regan show that no consolation can be expected of either:

> O Regan, wilt thou take her by the hand?
>
> (II.iv.190)

– and the sorry progress comes to a halt over one contention, the matter of the retainers. Lear makes his stand for many lines (185–282), and when at long last his resistance cracks, then comes the first hint he makes that he fears madness, and almost too promptly the symbol of the storm reinforces this fear:

> LEAR   . . . O fool, I shall go mad!
> CORNWALL Let us withdraw; 'twill be a storm.

The placing of this expository scene next to the following (III.i) compels us to see the conflict in human terms, those of Lear's suffering, not primarily as a power struggle, which of course it also is. Hence the quick sketching-in of events in III.i, necessary to the plot but not vital to the exploitation of character. The invasion of Britain by the King of France is given barely a glance:

> from France there comes a power
> Into this scattered kingdom
>
> (III.i.30)

a power to come out in the open at a sign, for all the world as if only the secret service has yet noticed its presence.

We soon reach the true centre of the play, III.iv, and on the stage we reach it with a miraculous smoothness brought by the quick following-through of incidents which satisfies the spectator although the reader may have reservations about it. In it, Lear seems to reach the nadir of his fortunes, exposing himself to the storm, rejecting Kent's solicitous approaches and allowing his madness to bring his predicament back to its immediate cause, the unkind daughters. Persuaded at last to use the hovel, he finds he may get no shelter even there, since it seems to be inhabited by a spirit, the disguised Edgar, and much is made of his fake madness to check the impact of Lear's. Lear is about to strip off his last covering, and so reduce himself to nothing but the essence of human-kind, when Gloucester, significantly at this centre point in the play, brings to the Lear circle his own cruel sorrow:

> Thou say'st the King grows mad; I'll tell thee, friend,
> I am almost mad myself. I had a son . . .
> The grief hath crazed my wits
>
> (lines 155, 160)

Son and daughters pitted against their parents form the subject which both cast back to.

The most deeply-felt move towards conciliation which turns out to be frustrated is at the end of Act IV. The incentive to pleasurable expectation is the meeting of Kent and Cordelia, each aware of the other's 'goodness' in the lining-up of forces. It is a scene of real or proposed revelation, yet Kent's wish not to reveal himself at this point has an ominous sound about it: even the revelations successfully completed will not bring the desired results, however hopeful they may look. The spirit of reconciliation is abroad:

> CORDELIA   O my dear father! Restoration hang
> Thy medicine on my lips, and let this kiss
> Repair those violent harms that my two sisters
> Have in thy reverence made!
>
> (IV.vii.27)

Lear's rage is over, but there is rage at hand in the impending battle with the cross-play of loyalties in the French and British camps. For Lear this is certainly not 'the worst' because the defeat of his forces in battle is near at hand.

The last scene makes a return to the summary style of the first. In both scenes an enormous amount of ground is covered, and in both the improbability of the events (if projected on a real-life setting) is somehow laid aside. The content of this last scene is set out in the scene synopsis (p. 178), and need not be rehearsed here. The use of language is additional evidence of this type of structural treatment in the play. Some of it is positively backward-looking, recalling Shakespeare's earlier treatment of exposition; Edgar is talking of how he at long last revealed himself to his father, who died of a broken heart, and how Kent then revealed himself:

> Whilst I was big in clamour, came there in a man,
> Who, having seen me in my worst estate,
> Shunned my abhorred society.
>
> (v.iii.208)

Or, to take another instance, there is Albany's handing out of praise and blame and his final despatch of government business. He says to Kent and Edgar:

> Friends of my soul, you twain
> Rule in this realm and the gored state sustain.

(v.iii.320)

The sources of the plots

Shakespeare only very occasionally introduced his own plot material into his plays. Almost everything he wrote for the stage has in subject matter an ancestry in the literature, both cultivated and folk, of the Western world. The sources of the Lear plot are somewhat involved; the source of the Gloucester plot is easy to identify. The former has been traced back to its first written appearance in the *Historia Regum Britanniae* ('History of the Kings of Britain'), compiled about 1136 by the Welsh bishop Geoffrey of Monmouth. The Lear story was taken up and embellished by a number of writers, and all the appearances are that the invention of the writers, not their historical research, has been brought into play and is the cause of variations in the narrative. This fact makes the careful tracing of variants unimportant as a contribution to the study of *King Lear*, provided that Shakespeare's own immediate source can be identified. Unlike some of the legends of King Arthur, which are 'living' today in the sense that most British people know something of them and they continue to appear in children's books, the story of Lear now has no popular currency.

The story appears in a number of chronicles after Geoffrey of Monmouth's, e.g. in the verse-history *Brut* by Layamon (*c.* 1200), in the *Gesta Romanorum* ('Acts of the Romans') (end of the thirteenth century), and in Ralph Holinshed's *Chronicles of England, Scotland and Ireland* (1577). The motive of the earlier chroniclers was to trace British history back to an origin in the classical world of ancient Rome; hence the reference to the Romans, and the name *Brut*, to connect 'Brutus' with 'Britain' and 'British'. This imaginary connection figures less in the later chronicles, e.g. Holinshed, and plays no significant part at all in Shakespeare's play. The Lear story appears in verse in the *Mirror for Magistrates* (1574 and later editions) and in Spenser's *Faerie Queene* (1589–96), and elsewhere.

Shakespeare used Holinshed as the main source for his plays on English history from the times of King John onwards, and one might expect that he would have used it for the 'British' story of Lear also. But internal evidence suggests that he got from Holinshed only a general hint and found elsewhere a work to model his play on. This was the earlier play on the same subject, already mentioned (p. xviii). Its title is entered in the register of the Stationers' Company in London (a process to ensure copyright) in 1594, although no copy of it from that date is known. As we have seen, it appears again in a later entry under 1605, about the same time as Shakespeare's own play was first presented.

Accounts of these early sources, and extracts from them, are readily available for consultation by the specialists who need them in many editions of the play. They add nothing to our appreciation of Shakespeare's work beyond making us admire the way he was able to break with a tradition, and a living tradition, as it seems, bringing a new view to the well-worn story line. It is much more interesting and appreciable to trace out what does not appear in the known sources and must therefore be taken as Shakespeare's own. His freedom in handling the source material strongly suggests that he thought little or nothing of the sources as history, least of all the old-style *King Leir*.

The 'tragic ending' of Shakespeare's *Lear*, with the King's forces routed, Cordelia hanged, and Lear himself dying as his kingly rights are restored to him by the victorious Albany, all this is, as far as we can now tell, Shakespeare's own invention. In *King Leir*, the King himself is a simple, resigned old man, not one to rage against the elements, who is not stirred to retaliation until the King of France arrives with his wife, Cordella, at the head of his army and conquers the British forces. Leir has fled to France in fear of losing his life at the hands of his daughter Ragan, and the victorious King of France restores him to the throne of Britain, as Albany restores Lear's rights to him in Shakespeare's play. But Lear dies before he can enjoy his reinstatement, whereas Leir energetically plans the future according to the needs of the kingdom which has been restored to him.

In all the sources except the old play, *King Leir*, Cordelia (or her prototype) dies by her own hand. In Holinshed, for instance, she is made Queen and reigns for five years. During this time her husband dies, and without his support she cannot defend herself against the attacks of her nephews, the sons of her unkind sisters. In prison she is overcome by grief, and 'being a woman of manly courage', she kills herself.

These are a few instances of variations from the sources which Shakespeare seems to have used in getting to know the folk tale; they illustrate the freedom with which he approached these sources. Even a glance at the sources shows how much more subtle and human Shakespeare made his play. The potentialities of a reconciliation between the old King and his youngest, truest daughter have the fitness and sweetness of propitiation after conflict. This Shakespeare seized upon, unlike the others, as worthy of dramatic intensity. There are, too, the casual images from nature, precisely those matters which the chroniclers would not handle and the writer of the old play had not enough freedom of movement to introduce.

Such instances of detailed visual imagination abound and breathe life into the shell of the old plot. These and the complicated tragic ending must be looked on as Shakespeare's particular contribution to the Lear plot. Many commentators have mentioned the real or feigned madness (Lear, Edgar) in the play as a part of Shakespeare's individual contribution, and with reason. The age in which he lived was harsh and unfeeling; people mocked at physical disabilities in others and crimes were punished with dreadful ferocity. But on the other hand, men's attention was turning towards the sympathetic consideration of such things. It is hard to think of a character in Chaucer who is mad; there were mad people in Chaucer's day as there are in ours, but then they simply did not arouse general sympathy. Renaissance man, aspiring to a different kind of humanity and a more realistic, less romantic and idealised, view of the world, came to look squarely at some of the unpleasantnesses of life. He was distressed by much that he saw going on around him, and his sympathies were engaged. In this way pity rose up the scale of desirable human qualities. One of the unpleasant things was madness, and it called for study because it was part of the human condition. The Senecan tragedy of revenge, which lies behind much Elizabethan tragedy and is associated with the revival of classical learning, often portrays madness in the character whose overpowering wish is to wreak vengeance on the person who has wronged him. Revenge, as Bacon wrote, is a kind of wild justice, and the fantasy of Lear arraigning his daughters in III.vi illustrates this observation.

Studies of true madness (Lear, Ophelia in *Hamlet*), feigned madness (Hamlet), or madness induced (Malvolio in *Twelfth Night*) are spread through Shakespeare's plays. They do not always receive the kind of compassionate treatment we would look for today. Lear's madness does not figure in the sources and was long thought to be a natural product of the handling of the revenge theme in the plot as Shakespeare assembled it for his own purposes. It may indeed be Shakespeare's invention, but there is a parallel from history which may have sparked it off. In 1603 Sir Brian Annesley, a gentleman pensioner of Queen Elizabeth I, was considered unfit to look after himself or his property. Two of his daughters tried to take over his property on the grounds that he was insane, but his youngest daughter, called (almost unbelievably) Cordell, protested to Robert Cecil, Elizabeth's Secretary of State, against her father being designated a lunatic. Five years later this Cordell married Sir William Harvey, the third husband and widower of the Countess of Southampton and step-father of Shakespeare's patron Henry Wriothesley, Earl of Southampton. Shakespeare very possibly knew the story of Cordell's protest and linked it with the Lear plot in his play.

The Gloucester plot is undoubtedly based on a story in Sir Philip Sidney's *Arcadia*, a medley of romances in the pastoral style (1590); it is known as the story of the Paphlagonian king. In it the narrator overhears a blind old man telling a younger man, Leonatus, either to lead him to the top of a rock from which he might throw himself, or to abandon him. Asked to tell their tale, Leonatus explains that the old man is his father, and rightful king of Paphlagonia; he has been driven from his land by another son of his, and now wants to take his own life. The old man fills in the picture: how the son who has driven him out is his by a concubine, and in what evil ways this son contrived to take over all his father's possessions, causing the old man to be ill-treated and eventually blinded. By some vague and unspecified means, the old man is turned against his legitimate son, whose life is saved only through the disobedience of the servants sent out to kill him. Leonatus finds his father and devotes all his time to taking care of him.

Shakespeare's additions to this tale are too obvious to need enumeration in detail: the feigned madness of Edgar which confuses the aged Gloucester, the fake suicide fall at Dover, and so on. As with the Lear plot, however, it is the absence of sharply delineated detail in the sources which most strikes the reader after he has got to know Shakespeare's play. The conventional pastoral moaning and hand-wringing of the *Arcadia* are transformed by the addition of vivid action and detail such as stay in the mind longer, perhaps, than the lightly-sketched outline of the plot.

Shakespeare, of course, moved freely among these sources, gathering and transposing at will. He must have got from the *Arcadia* narrative, for instance, many hints for the portrayal of destitution, but transferred them from the Gloucester plot, which has its source in the *Arcadia*, to the Lear plot.

For the occult language of Edgar when he is feigning madness, Shakespeare is also indebted to an identifiable source. (This matter is treated in the section on the language of the play, below.)

The language of the play

This section deals with the use of language which is particular to the play. Some guidance on problems of reading and understanding Shakespearian English will be found in Part II of this introduction, p. l.

The general impression of the style of *King Lear* is one of variety and appropriateness; it reveals Shakespeare at the peak of his achievement, playing upon the instrument of the English language with easy assurance. To look for a single style is therefore a fruitless task, even though grey, sombre tones predominate. The worthwhile task is to identify the ranges of style he brings into play, and appreciate how the facility subserves the progress of the drama.

The first scene of the play, from the point where the King enters with his train, has been called ritualistic, and the description is a fair one. It sounds as if it has all been prepared, 'coded', beforehand, and, like a service in church, carries much meaning with little spontaneity. The scene is, as we have already noticed, a rehearsing of a series of events which could not conceivably have taken place in real life in such a telescoped fashion; the language of ritual, where one could expect statements to be terse and well-moulded, serves in this way as a fitting vehicle of communication. And there are stylistic features which reflect this treatment when it comes into play again at the end. The special features are compactness and precision of expression, many end-stopped lines which give it something of the tone of Shakespeare's earlier plays, and an unobtrusive balancing-off of words and phrases. The first two features can be illustrated *passim* in the first and last scenes, though in the last there is much interspersion of emotion less obviously controlled. End-stopping is the making of lines correspond with sense-groups of words; e.g.

> The princes, France and Burgundy,
> Great rivals in our youngest daughter's love,
> Long in our court have made their amorous sojourn . . .

> (I.i.41)

These are to be compared with run-on lines such as:

> We have this hour a constant will to publish
> Our daughters' several dowers, that future strife
> May be prevented now

> (I.i.39)

in which the fixed rhythm of the iambic pentameters is rather strictly adhered to, but there is no sense-pause at the end of each line. The third feature can be exemplified from the passage in which the King of France begins his declaration of love for Cordelia free from the taint of worldly gain:

> Fairest Cordelia, that art most rich, being poor;
> Most choice, forsaken, and most loved, despised.

> (I.i.246)

It is all brisk, pointed and factual, and in it Lear looks businesslike and purposeful; this manner contrasts tellingly with his behaviour in the face of mounting suffering. The ritualistic part of the first scene ends with a number of rhymed lines; these give an air of finality to the various arrangements concluded at the discussion on the dynasty.

By giving the first scene a head and tail in a different style, Shakespeare has indicated that the play is not to be taken up with formal exchanges. The talk between Kent and Gloucester about Edmund's origins is in prose, and somewhat casual (in places almost throw-away), but not without occasional carefully-worked contrivances, as in Kent's

> I cannot conceive you
>
> (I.i.10)

or the ominous hint:

> He hath been out nine years, and away he shall again
>
> (I.i.28)

In a play which is structurally an advance towards and withdrawal from positions of hope and retribution, the swing from the formal to the casual and back again brings no surprise; by 'casual' is meant, of course, the attitude of the speakers, not the way Shakespeare approached his task of giving words to those speakers.

There is some correlation between the formal and casual on the one hand and verse and prose on the other. About one third of *King Lear* is in prose, a very high proportion when compared with that in some earlier plays; the earliest in composition, e.g. the three parts of *Henry VI*, have practically none. Various degrees of formality in the verse are to be expected; verse is, after all, by definition more carefully formed than prose and subjected to metrical controls, even though the effect can be informal. In *Lear*, as in all the later plays, these controls are not very strictly adhered to; there is a ground swell of rhythm rather than a steady, monotonous, unbroken beat. Thus the verse is the vehicle for the precise disclosure of the subject matter of the play, as we have already seen with the ritualistic styles. In places it has the feel of carefully thought-out conversation, and is as 'natural' as the needs of the stage permit.

> LEAR I can be patient; I can stay with Regan,
>   I and my hundred knights.
>
> REGAN   Not altogether so:
>   I looked not for you yet, nor am provided
>   For your fit welcome.
>
> (II.iv.226)

Lear sticks to the hundred, and rams his point home by making this reference once more to the number, to ensure there is no misunderstanding. Regan sugars the pill of rebuff by saying, not 'You are mistaken', but, '*Not altogether so*'. Touches like this are the magic through which formal styles flash with mirroring from everyday speech; they come from the evidence of an ear acutely attuned to the ways of everyday language.

And as we move through the play we become conscious of the gamut of its verse styles. At one extreme is the summary style; somewhere near the centre, the common mean, is the style of the snatch above, where the lines retain their clear rhythmic flow but show no contortion to fit the demands of the metre and are enlivened with the touch of common speech. At the other extreme is the language of total simplicity, sunk deep in the rhythms of ordinary everyday speech and drily economical. This last is so sharply apposite that it arrests the attention anywhere, but is most incisive when seen against the overtly contrived speeches of the other language styles of the play. Lear, reawakening to the world around him and at long last becoming aware of the benevolence of his youngest daughter, revives the human sympathies of the play like new blood through the arteries. Cordelia begins formally, asking as a good daughter should for her aged father's blessing:

> O, look upon me, sir,
> And hold your hands in benediction o'er me.
>
> (IV.vii.58)

The full line here is an iambic pentameter without variation from the strict rhythm of stressed and unstressed syllables:

> And hóld|your hánds|in bén|edíct|ion ó'er me.

Lear in his response reflects closely this metrical arrangement:

> Pray, do not mock me:
> I am a very foolish fond old man . . .
>
> (line 60)

But in what follows, the steady beat remains only a point of reference in the mind. And as the lines become less obviously rhythmical, there is a rise in the intensity of complete simplicity, the grammar straightforward and the diction quite without glamour or pretension:

> all the skill I have
> Remembers not these garments, nor I know not
> Where I did lodge last night. Do not laugh at me;
> For, as I am a man, I think this lady
> To be my child Cordelia.
>
> (line 67)

Most of the verse is briskly efficient and precise in tone; it is safe to say that the general style of the verse is firmly-rounded and to the point, giving a feeling of strength and confidence, not only where one would expect it, e.g. in Edmund's self-revelatory speeches:

> To both these sisters have I sworn my love;
> Each jealous of the other, as the stung
> Are of the adder
>
> (v.i.55)

but also with Lear in his vivid flashes of imagination:

> When I do stare, see how the subject quakes!
> I pardon that man's life. What was thy cause?
> Adultery?

(IV.vi.107)

And, most memorable of all, his raging against the elements as images of his daughter's unkindness:

> Rumble thy bellyful! Spit, fire! Spout, rain!
> Nor rain, wind, thunder, fire, are my daughters

(III.ii.14)

Much of the prose is easy, almost casual, in style, a suitable vehicle for the incomplete disclosure of its subject matter compared with the sharp outlines of the verse. A distinctive feature of the prose is the long, rather trailing, sentence. One would not call it imprecise but rather discursive when set against the smart rounding-off of the verse. Scene I.ii after the entry of Gloucester illustrates this point, especially the mock-furtiveness of Edmund's exchanges with Edgar. The Fool's prose – being of the lower social orders, he would be expected to use prose for what he wants to say – is interspersed with jingles which are generally harsh; they use elements of folk-rhymes and nursery verses but are designedly angular and disturbing. Perhaps only in the snatch (III.ii.73) which echoes the Clown's song at the end of *Twelfth Night* does something of the nimbleness of a court fool's rhyming break through:

> He that has and a little tiny wit
> With hey, ho, the wind and the rain. . . .

Harshness and angularity, a fair image of the world which Lear must face, characterise Edgar's speeches in the guise of 'poor mad Tom'. They are in prose, and owe a good deal of their effect to names taken from a traditional demonology – III.vi.29, IV.i.60, with probable references to the same source at II.iv.55, III.iv.57. The names of demons in the two main passages are certainly taken from Samuel Harsnett's *A Declaration of Egregious Popish Impostures* (1603). This book is, or purports to be, evidence taken at the examination of people concerned with or involved in the exorcising of devils. Harsnett, who later became Archbishop of York, collected the evidence in an attempt to prove that the whole operation was rigged, a 'popish imposture'. Forms of Obidicut, Hobbididence, Mahu and the rest, as well as *Hysterica passio* (II.iv.55) occur; and intensive study of Harsnett has revealed many other verbal parallels. There is also the reference in Harsnett to the incident referred to at III.iv.51:

> knives under his pillow and halters in his pew

(see note to this line with the text). Similar parallels can be traced here and there between the play and the plot sources already discussed, but they are not of special interest or significance.

When all is said and done, however, the impression left by the style of *King Lear* is, appropriately enough, lowering with the weight of heavy storm-clouds. One senses little brightness or iridescence in the speeches, little that lingers verbally on the mind with exceptional pleasure. Perhaps because of this one clings gratefully to the touches of common speech, the casual images from nature which have already been noted. *King Lear* has its share of tragic gloom, but so has *Hamlet*, yet long speeches in *Hamlet* have become virtually a part of the language. Lear's speeches at their greatest are transcendental (they are not, as someone said recently, what you would get from a tape-recorder at a death-bed) but their feet are on the earth. The style well befits, as it is designed to do, the bitterness of the themes.

The theatre of Shakespeare's day

We know very little about the early stage history of *King Lear*. Although it has been considered for a long time one of Shakespeare's greatest plays, it was certainly not one of the most popular in the theatre. However, it has a continuous history of stage presentation down to our own day. For more than a century, the text used was far from Shakespeare's own, with (as we have seen) an ending very different from what he intended. But all that is now in the past. Today readers are fortunate in having easily accessible a text of the play probably as close as we shall ever get to what Shakespeare himself wrote for the stage. Charles Lamb, repelled by the confusion of Shakespeare's intentions and the spurious 'happy ending' of performances in his own day, wrote in exasperation that 'the Lear of Shakespeare cannot be acted'. But with the original text now accepted again for the stage, Lamb was wrong in his judgement; rather the contrary: *King Lear* can be read most effectively if its suitability for stage performance lingers in the back of the mind. Of course as we read we visualise both the imagined setting, representing true-to-life situations, and also the stage setting. The compressed treatment of some matters along with the intense dramatic exploitation of others, the patness of cause and effect, can here and there be too contrived for the reader quite to stomach. Yet the mysterious skill of the dramatist makes it all acceptable without question on the stage, and in a fine performance, wonderfully effective. Thus every hint which helps the reader to visualise talk and movement on the stage as well as in real life is valuable and cannot be ignored if the correct impression is to be retained.

From the outset, it seems, *King Lear* was recognised as a play for the court rather than the public theatre. The court's tastes would be more refined than those of the populace; audiences there would not call for slapstick comedy or ranting of a vulgar sort, but would expect to see more sophisticated penetration into matters of fundamental concern such as fate and free will, reason and passion. Indeed, we know on excellent evidence that the play was presented at the Palace of Whitehall in London late in 1606.

The performance referred to is not stated to be the first performance; however, it was plainly a significant event in the history of the play when it was first written.

King James I's palace at Whitehall had a hall which was the setting for many early performances of Shakespeare's plays at the beginning of the King's reign (1603). It may have been on the site of the Banqueting House (completed 1622) which exists today. We must imagine a large room cleared at one end and equipped with a raised platform to make a stage. The royal audience would be small and select, perhaps even taking up less room than the stage. So little is known of the physical conditions for the presentation of plays at court that it is hard to be precise in description. But one thing is certain: the elaborate machinery we are used to in a present-day western theatre, with its drop curtains sharply dividing the audience from the players, its scenery, its realistic sound effects, its quick changes of lighting, and all the other devices which go with the words spoken by the actors and the movements and gestures they make, would not have been possible. At most, only some simple portable machinery could be expected, together with some equally unambitious sound effects, e.g. of the wind and rain of the storm which Lear and Kent suffer together. By contrast, costume was by all accounts considerably more elaborate. Everyday wear in the court and among the rich outside was colourful and fanciful; both men and women took a delight in adorning themselves in unashamedly dazzling colours, and dressing up for stage plays was something which came to them naturally. The usual presentations on the stage today are rather the reverse of this: the settings and stage effects tend to be ambitiously contrived, whereas the clothing of the actors tends to be 'realistic', 'natural'.

The modest conditions under which *King Lear* received its early performance in court very likely account for certain features which critics have commented on. The most revealing is the treatment of troop movements representing the battles between the French and English forces in Act V. The movement of such forces is comparatively easy to represent on the stage; it can be done with few actors in a limited space, their clothing adding to the effect of 'drum and colours'. In the second scene we get only the briefest glimpse of the French forces with Lear and Cordelia, doubtless an image of their hopeless cause. And by Scene iii it is all over, without a struggle or even

The interior of the Swan Theatre as seen in about 1596 (from a sketch by van Buchell after de Witt).

a confrontation on the stage. In the dead hopelessness of their predicament, Lear and Cordelia are led as prisoners across the stage. In the limited area of the court stage there was no opportunity for a more elaborate representation.

Single combat could of course be handled easily in a restricted space. In v.iii the trumpet calls summon the champion, and Edmund and Edgar engage one another in fighting according to a strict code of knightly chivalry, preceded by emblematic exchanges:

> EDMUND   . . . since thy outside looks so fair and warlike . . .
> What safe and nicely I might well delay
> By rule of knighthood, I disdain and spurn
>
> (v.iii.142)

The court stage can fairly be said to have provided the right conditions for action between two or three people, when impact depends on nearness to it of the audience, even to the point of involvement. There are the appalling blinding of Gloucester and the indignity of Kent in the stocks. The effect of both these is inevitably blurred once the distance and the barrier of the proscenium arch are set between players and audience.

If we are right to think of *King Lear* performed initially in these very constrictive circumstances, we have to visualise a setting removed at two degrees from the modern stage (for the public playhouses of Shakespeare's day had little in common with the theatre or cinema of today). His dramatic problem was to put in living, breathing form some profound human emotions. The dramatic poetry he uses is in power and range of experience more than adequate for the purpose. What seems to fall short is the machinery which must have been involved, the representations of the storm on the heath, the trafficking of news by letter, and the soldiers moving to and fro with their trappings. All this might have made the proximity of the stage too immediate. Likewise the scenery. This would have been of the simplest kind, perhaps with a placard now and then announcing where the action was supposed to lie. One can only say that proximity lent its own force to the performance, and the involvement of the audience transcended the more obvious contrivances. It is this point which Lamb must have missed in what he wrote about his reactions to the play, because by his day the separation of the audience from the actors was already becoming marked.

> So to see Lear acted — to see an old man tottering about the stage with a walking-stick, turned out of doors by his daughters in a rainy night — has nothing in it but what is painful and disgusting.*

....

*   A longer quotation from Lamb is given at the end of this Introduction, p. lxxxiii

Lamb goes on to ask, with power in his rhetoric, what looks, or tones, or gestures, or voice, or eye have to do with the timelessness and sublimity of the play's conception; he sees in the play supreme poetry but unactable drama. The whole question is worth dwelling on because *King Lear* does indeed give the reader this impression, and because the urbanity of Lamb's style makes what he says plausible and persuasive. And the charge, if it is one, is levelled against *King Lear* above all other plays of Shakespeare. The best counter-charge is the plain statement that Lamb is not right, that the experience of the playgoer is to the contrary, regardless of his comparative proximity to or remoteness from the stage.

Why this should be so is something of a mystery, at least to the reader, pulled up perhaps by the complications of the plots and the patent improbability of some of the action. Certainly the effects follow quickly and smoothly upon the causes; if this . . . then this . . . The postulates with which the play begins are revealed in action which is concentrated so that the activity on the stage is a summary of what one would expect to extend over a far longer period, with much more preparation, in the real world. The compression of such action on the stage might, as in the present case, reduce it to emblematic displays and for this the Elizabethan love of showy dress was a godsend. Lear in state would rightly appear the powerful monarch, the despot who was crossed at one's peril. The stage was not 'life', and could not pretend to be; it was rather a simplified reality, ideal for the exposition of the poetry. The formalised movement of the sisters' responses to Lear's question:

Which of you shall we say doth love us most?

or the advances and withdrawals of the suitors:

What, in the least,
Will you require in present dower with her,
Or cease your quest of love?

(I.i.47, 188)

conform to this pattern.

As soon as such postulates are set, and irrevocable decisions taken, effects follow inevitably, as if it were fate that is involved; and many of the characters clearly think it is. The audience interest is kept up by such means as this; there is no delay in following through to its consequence a new departure in the ordering of the situation. This fact can be illustrated from many instances in the play. One such can be traced through Act IV, the affair of Gloucester's attempt at suicide. In the first scene, fate, or as we might say coincidence, has put the blinded Gloucester in the hands of the son he has wronged, though Gloucester does not know his identity; this is the scene in which Edgar play-acts poor Tom. It is quietly concluded with Gloucester's wish to be led to Dover, and the portentous sentence of Gloucester's:

> From that place/I shall no leading need.

Three scenes follow, two of which deal with the convergence of Lear and Cordelia, a clear cross-reference to the other pair of wrong-doer and wronged, Gloucester and Edgar. The fifth scene shows Regan in an exchange with Oswald, now altogether too much in her confidence for a manservant; she brings up once more the matter of Gloucester, deploring the unwisdom, as it seems to her, of allowing him to go free after he was blinded:

> where he arrives he moves
> All hearts against us   (IV.v.10)

And in the following scene the Gloucester matter is dealt with by means of coincidences: Gloucester, Lear and Oswald meet at a place near Dover; Gloucester's suicide attempt is immediately followed by Lear's appearance and the beginning of the battle. Gloucester is saved from suicide by a trick which, since there is nothing on the stage to illustrate the supposed contour, must depend for its effect on the poetry of imagination, and this it does, in some much-loved lines:

> How fearful/And dizzy 'tis to cast one's eyes so low!
> . . . Half way down
> Hangs one that gathers sampire, dreadful trade!   (IV.vi.11)

Here it is the enchantment of double illusion: the stage is not real life, nor is the representation on the stage an image of the poetry.

The amount of scenery used in the theatre of Shakespeare's age is doubtful. A little evidence is available to suggest that the halls in court were embellished with some scenery for the occasion, but no contemporary accounts of such presentations in Whitehall are known, although shortly before *King Lear* was being presented there before the King, a tragedy was presented in an Oxford college hall and some notes about preparations for it survive:

> The stage was built close to the upper end of the hall, as it seemed at first sight. But indeed it was but a false wall fair painted and adorned with stately pillars, which pillars would turn about; by reason thereof, with the help of other painted cloths, their stage did vary three times in the acting of one tragedy.*

....

*   Spelling modernised.

One concludes that scenery was not unknown but that its availability could not be relied on. The play therefore did not depend on scenic effects but on the poetry of atmosphere. And when a precise location was to be identified, Shakespeare saw to it that one or other of his characters gave the indication needed: the entry of Lear and his train would be located in the royal palace (i.i); Kent and Oswald meet in front of a great house:

> OSWALD Good dawning to thee, friend. Art of this house?
> KENT Ay.
> OSWALD Where may we set our horses?
> KENT I' the mire.

> (II.ii, beginning)

The country is indicated at once at the beginning of IV.vi:

> GLOUCESTER When shall we come to the top of that same hill?

– and so on.

The public stage appears to have been served less well with scenery, but the fondness for the fine display of costumes was well catered for. Because of the association of *King Lear* with Whitehall, we have first tried to imagine how the play would have been presented there. It was also presented in the public theatre, and something can be surmised from internal evidence about the impression it made.

Watching a play in a modern theatre with its proscenium arch is like looking into a huge picture-frame with living, moving people instead of still figures in the picture. A wide cinema screen or a television set can give a very similar effect, although unlike the theatre these media can direct the spectator's view much more to detail, by taking close-up views, than the producer can do in the theatre. The comparison is not unimportant, since the Shakespearian stage permitted much more close-up viewing than the theatre today. It was round or octagonal, deriving its shape from the 'pits' or arenas used for holding cockfights and bear-baiting. Another influence on the design of the theatre was the inn-yard. The more imposing and elaborate type of Elizabethan inn was an important building, vital to the maintenance of communications when travel was slow and roads, especially in winter, were bad. Such inns consisted of a road-front with an entrance archway in it. This archway led into a courtyard enclosed on all four sides, with galleries round at the levels of the upper floors; access to the rooms was along these galleries. In the inn-yards, travelling troupes of players sometimes set up movable stages, and people would watch their plays either from the galleries or from the ground-level in the inn-yard. The archway must have been closed up during performances of plays, and people were admitted only if they paid either for standing-room at ground-level or for admission to the galleries.

The public theatres, purpose-built on these models, were served by groups of actors. At the turn of the sixteenth century there were no theatres outside the London area, although companies travelled and presented plays on make-shift stages in provincial towns. When *King Lear* was staged in the palace of Whitehall, there were at least four public theatres in London, all used by the company of players which Shakespeare himself was associated with. In 1599 their headquarters became the new theatre on the south side of the River Thames, called the Globe. The entry in the Stationers' Register for *Lear* tells us that the actors who played it before the King in Whitehall were 'His Majesty's servants playing usually at the Globe on the Bankside'. As far as we can tell, the Globe conformed to the traditional pattern of theatre con-struction; only the galleries and part of the stage itself were roofed over, the central area being left open to the sky. This arrangement made artificial lighting unnecessary, since plays were generally presented in the afternoon.

The Elizabethan stage projected far out into the place where the audience sat or stood. Spectators were on three sides of it, and thus in close contact with the players. This 'outer stage' had no curtains, but was covered in part by a projecting roof. At the back, if we can judge accurately from the few extant sketches of Elizabethan theatres, there were two doors, set obliquely, through which actors passed on and off the stage. The absence of any curtain shutting off the whole stage from the audience made for considerable move-ment of this kind. The stage had to be cleared at the changes of scene by actors moving off and others coming on. Between the doors was an 'inner stage', a recess covered with a curtain which could be used to reveal some action going on in a setting remote from the rest. Above the recess was a balcony or *terras* ('terrace') for use when needed as a small upper stage, but possibly for the most part as standing-room for some of the actors and spectators – at least this is the impression given in the drawing of the Swan. Beside the *terras* were the actors' dressing-rooms, reached by stairs from the doors in the main stage.

In the sketch of the Swan, the projecting roof looks as if it covered only the inner stage, the rest being open to the sky, or rather that the inner stage had become merged with the main area, and kept its distinction only by having the roof over it. But since we need not assume any consistency of design among the theatres, elsewhere the roof may well have been a much more important feature. We know that it could project farther out than in the Swan, and could be painted with a dark blue sky and representations of the moon and stars. This contrivance was called 'the heavens', and it had devices in it for letting actors down on to the stage and picking them up from it to 'disappear' in the roof, as well as for other special effects with objects. Right at the top, above 'the heavens', was a room with an opening to the sky where a trumpeter could stand and play flourishes on his trumpet to attract people's attention to the theatre. A flag flew from the roof of this room during performances.

Although some points of detail about the Shakespearian theatre are in doubt, the important effects of the stage arrangement are clear. First, the visual impression was three-dimensional: there was plenty of scope for relative movement, the actors being able to get far away from the audience or at other extremes pass right up among them, virtually mingling with the spectators standing around three sides of the stage. And to add to this in-the-round effect, the balcony made it possible for players to appear well above the stage as a matter of course, not just as a special contrivance. Second, inanimate objects could also be accommodated in a three-dimensional way. *Properties* (easily movable objects for use in plays) are often referred to in contemporary accounts. Indeed, certain effects in *King Lear*, such as the stocks Kent is put into (II.ii and iv, with an interval in iii suggesting that they could be obscured from view, perhaps by drawing a curtain across the inner stage during that time) depend upon suitable properties. Another instance is the weapons carried by the armed forces as they march across the wide area of the stage. Properties tend to be symbols of a situation rather than an attempt at realism. There is extant from Shakespeare's day a list which includes a 'golden sceptre' to indicate a king, a 'bay tree' to indicate a garden, and so on. The signboards, hung up on the stage, if used at all, have had little effect on the plays. Shakespeare wrote without assuming any scenic effects to reinforce the visions evoked by his verse.

The inner stage was used for scenes set away from the main action of the play or placed for some reason differently from the main action. In *King Lear*, the blinding of Gloucester, an incident too painful to be represented in the full view of front stage, would be the kind of action to be staged in the recess. The recess would give the impression of the hovel from which Edgar (as Poor Tom) emerges, and in which Lear at last agrees to take shelter (III.iv). The heath would then be very sufficiently represented by the broad stage. Since different producers would undoubtedly have had different ideas as to how the lay-out of the stage could be put to best use, it is safer to say how the arrangement might have been worked out than to try to be more precise. The open front stage would be in closer touch with the audience and would therefore be suited to intimate exchanges, such as those between Kent and Gloucester at the beginning of the play. When Lear first appears he might move to the inner stage, for the pronouncement of his decisions, which would be more symbolic as heard from a distance, and this is what they must seem to be, a pageant of reality, not reality itself. This counterbalancing is well illustrated in the first scene of the play. Again, in IV.vii, a scene which must be thought of as taking place indoors (the direction reads 'A tent in the French camp'), the inner stage is vital to the representation of a more sheltered

and tender exchange, away from the inclemencies of the open country:
Cordelia and Kent and the Doctor gently whisper their hopes and fears as
the distressed King is carried in.

The use of the *terras*, the small upper stage, is well illustrated in II.i.
Edgar, scared and perplexed at the unjust accusations apparently being made
against him, appears above the main stage, as it were in hiding. His half-
brother Edmund calls him down:

> Brother, a word! Descend! Brother, I say!
>
> (II.i.19)

It is the storm scenes in *King Lear* that people have remembered most
vividly over the ages. On the Shakespearian stage, flashes of lightning and
cracks of thunder could be produced by lighting sulphur or vernis powder,
shaking it from a perforated box into a flame. This would seem to us a poor
contrivance compared with the outburst of rage in Lear's lines, shouted into
the storm:

> You sulphurous and thought-executing fires,
> Vaunt-couriers to oak-cleaving thunderbolts,
> Singe my white head! . . .
> Crack nature's moulds, all germens spill at once,
> That make ingrateful man!
>
> (III.ii.4)

But so it was. And the interest is intensified by the imagery of the storm in
the mind, and the conscious awareness of that imagery:

> KENT   Who's there, besides foul weather?
> GENTLEMAN   One minded like the weather, most unquietly.
>
> (III.i.1)

No women acted on the English stage from Tudor times until the Restoration of the Monarchy in 1660. Women's parts were played by boys, suitably
dressed. Very occasionally, modern productions of Shakespeare have used
boys in the women's parts. The effect is clearly different from what would
normally be expected, but it is not grotesque. One feels that in a play such as
King Lear the passion must have been left to the men. Goneril and Regan,
vicious embodiments of evil, could well be played by clever and inspired
boys. Even Cordelia's part, both tender and guardedly passionate, is not
impossibly demanding for a boy. She is, after all, on the stage for a comparatively small part of the play, and her moments come and go speedily.
She is with the Doctor (IV.iv) and Kent (IV.vii) in sympathetic exchanges

which are nevertheless practical, not unlike the short, sharp interjections at Lear's testing of his daughters' love at the beginning of the play. An actor-boy would have to rise to the height of his powers for the awaking of Lear in IV.vii, yet even here Cordelia is unobtrusive, never patently the centre of action. And so at the beginning of the final scene, when she is seen alive for the last time, her suggestion:

> Shall we not see these daughters and these sisters?
>
> (V.iii.7)

is turned down flatly by her father.

PART TWO

Language difficulties

In this edition, very little space is given to the discussion of textual difficulties, places where the exact nature or meaning of the text is disputed.
Where such difficulties occur, the notes suggest the general meaning of the
passage, taking into consideration the context and the likely meanings of the
doubtful words. Occasionally a single alternative suggestion is made as to
what the passage may mean.

Derivations and other etymological information about words and phrases
are given only rarely, since such notes do not usually add much to the
appreciation of the play. Very occasionally a note includes some reference to
the origin of a word if this is likely to aid the memory and help to bring out a
significant matter, for instance; *interlude* at v.iii.90.

The glossarial index at the end of the book does not give etymological
information. It gives the meanings of all the rare and strange words in the
text, together with line references showing where they can be found. This
arrangement is designed to encourage the student not to learn the words and
their meanings in isolation but to use the index as a means of access to the
relevant passages; the words may thus be read in context and studied as
they actually occur in the play. The index serves also as a useful means of
revision, since through the tracing of individual words it can lead to passages
of particular difficulty.

Set out below is a short list of words which are seldom used today as
Shakespeare used them, but which occur frequently in the play. They have
changed their meanings since Shakespeare used them, or have completely
fallen out of use in current English, or are shortened forms which he used to
capture some special effect, for instance so that they would fit into the
metrical pattern of the lines.

and, an: 'if'; these forms often occur in the earliest editions of Shakespeare,
     and are retained in this text, e.g.

> and thou canst not smile as the wind sits,
> thou'lt catch cold shortly
>   ('if you cannot smile . . .')

                                                  (I.iv.88)

aught: 'anything' (cf. modern English *naught, nought*: nothing)
but: 'only', e.g.

> Thou but rememberest me
>   ('You only remind me')

                                                  (I.iv.58)

do: This and its derived forms are often used as an auxiliary verb without any separate meaning, whereas in modern English *do* gives special emphasis to the main verb, e.g.

> I do beseech you/To understand my purposes aright
>
> (I.iv.221)

> I did commend your highness' letters to them
>
> (II.iv.27)

Conversely, *do* and its derived forms are often not used in positions where we would expect them in modern English, as in questions and negative sentences:

> Mak'st thou this shame thy pastime?
>
> (II.iv.6)

> Nay, I know not.
>
> (II.i.6)

Cf. modern English 'Do you make . . . ?' and 'I do not know.'

durst: 'dare', 'would dare'.

else: otherwise.

ere: 'before', e.g. I.i.12

Occasionally *ere* is linked with *or*, the phrase *or ere* giving the same meaning, e.g. II.iv.282.

fain: 'glad', 'gladly', 'pleased', especially as an adverb with *would*, e.g.

> in respect of that, I would fain think it were not.
>
> (I.ii.61)

for: 'as', 'as for', especially at the beginning of a sentence, e.g.

> For you, great King, I would not . . .
>   ('As for you, great King . . .')
>
> (I.i.204)

get: 'beget'.

how now: 'what is it' (said by a speaker as he turns his attention to a particular person).

late: 'recent'; *of late*: 'recently', e.g.

> These late eclipses in the sun and moon
>
> (I.ii.96)

mark: 'take note of', 'notice'.

methinks: 'it seems to me (that)', merging into 'I think' (past tense, *methought*).

on: 'of'.

power: 'army', 'military force'.

practice: 'intrigue', 'cunning', 'trickery', 'evil design'. Cf. modern English *underhand practices*.

presently: 'immediately', 'at once', 'at the present moment'.

purpose: 'plan', 'proposal', 'determination', 'decision to act', e.g.

> Know of the duke if his last purpose hold
>
> (v.i.1)

> 'Find out from the duke whether his most recent decision [on what to do] still holds good'.

sirrah: 'sir'. This is the form of address most frequently used by speakers to their social inferiors; its origin must lie in the irony of calling an inferior, not a superior, by the title 'Sir'. Through double irony, Lear reduced to the status of a private citizen, is called 'Sirrah' by his Fool.

> FOOL   Sirrah, I'll teach thee a speech.
> LEAR   Do.
> FOOL   Mark it, nuncle.
>
> (I.iv.102)

sway (n.): 'rule', 'sovereignty'.

't: 'it'; this clipped form occurs frequently where the rhythmic pattern of the line does not demand a full syllable:

> Thou think'st 'tis much that this contentious storm
>
> (III.iv.6)

(Occasionally other words are shortened for the same purpose, e.g. *above* is reduced to *'bove* in:

> Or swell the curléed waters 'bove the main
>
> (III.i.6)

-th: Some frequently used verbs take this ending instead of *-s* in the third person singular (*he, she, it,* etc.) of the simple present tense. The style was becoming archaic by the time *King Lear* was written, and is restricted for the most part to the appropriate forms of *have* and *do*:

> The shame itself doth speak/For instant remedy
>
> (I.iv.229)

> anger hath a privilege
>
> (II.ii.62)

thou, thee, thy, thine: 'you', 'your', 'yours'. Both these sets of forms are used as second person singular pronouns in the play, and the use of one or other often indicates something of the attitude of one speaker to

another at that point. The *thou*-forms are used in addressing
(a) social inferiors:

> LEAR (to the disguised Kent)
>   I thank thee, fellow; thou servest me, and I'll love thee.
>
> (I.iv.76)

(b) members of one's family in normal, cordial terms of relationship:

> LEAR (to Goneril, at the parcelling out of the kingdom, and when he
> has gone beyond the formal style of his first announcements)
>   Of all these bounds, even from this line to this . . .
>   We make thee lady.
>
> (I.i.59)

(c) supernatural beings, as in most Christian prayers in modern English

> Thou, nature, art my goddess
>
> (I.ii.1)

The *you*-forms are colder, more formal and respectful. At the beginning
of the play Lear uses them until he warms to his task, and his daughters
respond in the same mode. The reversion to coldness at Cordelia's reply
is marked at once by Lear's return to the *you*-forms, showing how his
displeasure has been aroused:

> How how, Cordelia! mend your speech a little,
> Lest it may mar your fortunes
>
> (I.i.90)

Later in this scene, the King of France, immediately affectionate and
understanding with Cordelia, talks directly to her and breaks through
the coldness of his exchanges with Lear (in which *you* is the second-
person equivalent of the royal *we*):

> Thee and thy virtues here I seize upon
>
> (I.i.248)

Just as he uses 'sirrah', the Fool, 'all-licensed', uses *thou*-forms to
address the King:

> All thy other titles thou hast given away; *that* thou wast born with
>
> (I.iv.134)

The patterning of these sets of forms in *King Lear* is for the most part
consistent and used with some subtlety. It is therefore a valuable indication of the relationships between characters.
Verb forms associated with *thou* regularly end in *-st*, but there are
some irregularities: *art* and *wilt* are examples.

twixt, betwixt: 'between'.

use: 'treat', 'deal with'.

we, us, our, ours: When the King refers to himself he normally uses these forms, not *I, me*, etc. They were probably thought of as sounding grander, though originally they may have indicated simply that the sovereign was speaking both of himself and of his subjects, as the body of the state. Lear significantly begins to use *I, me*, etc. when his authority shows signs of cracking:

> Why came not the slave back to me when I called him?
>
> (I.iv.47)

Cf.

> Ourself, by monthly course . . .
>   shall our abode
> Make with you by due turns.
>
> (I.i.130)

would: takes on a variety of meanings according to the context: 'want', 'wish', 'should', 'I wish'.

Conditional clauses which in modern English would begin with a conjunction such as *if* are sometimes expressed by inverting the position of the verb and the subject:

> Be it lawful . . .
>   ('If it is lawful')
>
> (I.i.249)

> stood I within his grace
>   ('if I stood . . .')
>
> (I.i.269)

The uses in the play of the terms *nature, natural* and *unnatural* need special mention; they depend on various views of the world and the ways of God and man in it. For convenience, the uses of *nature* etc. can be divided into three blocks of meanings, though of course the philosophical concepts involved are not simple enough for each instance of usage to be assigned unhesitatingly to one or other of these blocks. As Albany says of Goneril:

> That nature which contemns it origin
> Cannot be bordered certain in itself.
>
> (IV.ii.32)

Nor can we expect all the words Shakespeare puts into the mouths of the characters to be in adherence to a precise philosophical system. But we can gather together instances of the words in use and see how their meanings form a pattern.

As we would expect, at the back of them all lies man's idea of the uncontrolled mass of phenomena which the universe seems to be made up of. These phenomena have inherent qualities, not necessarily good and benevolent or the opposite. Of people, *nature* is sometimes used as we would use it today, as in, say, 'He's a good-natured fellow':

> Natures of such deep trust we shall much need
>
> (II.i.117)
>
> Thy tender-hefted nature
>
> (II.iv.167)

The elements which went to make up this universe were thought of as being in chaotic disorder unless some supreme power, God, arranged them in order and pattern; disaster came from cracking up the forms into which the atoms of creation were cast, disrupting the shaping of what was shapeless. Lear makes a terrible threat when he says:

> Crack nature's moulds, all germens spill at once,
> That make ingrateful man!
>
> (III.ii.8)

If this arrangement or shaping into order is assumed, nature can be thought of as essentially good, kind, beneficent. To act according to nature is to be one's true self, taking one's rightful place among the well-shaped forms or norms of the world. Lear says hopefully to Regan:

> Thou better know'st
> The offices of nature, bond of childhood . . .
>
> (II.iv.173)

accepting without question that put in this way the offices are *good* offices, and the bond with the parents a healthy one. The use of the negative *unnatural* seems everywhere in the play to depend on this same use of *natural*: to act unnaturally is to go against the good order and shaping of established nature, to act unkindly, not in accordance with one's true nature. At the beginning of III.iii, Gloucester tells Edmund about the way he has been treated as a punishment for his adherence to the King's cause. He says:

> Alack, alack, Edmund, I like not this unnatural dealing.

In line 6, Edmund echoes the word in feigned sympathy:

> Most savage and unnatural!

The word *disnatured* relates to this range of meanings (I.iv.268).

In this view of the universe there is a rational optimism which is not borne out by the adversities which man has to contend with, symbolised in the storm and thunder of the play. *King Lear* can indeed be seen as a critique of this optimistic world view, since man's nature is shown in it to be precarious and needing to be 'accommodated' if it is to retain its humanity at all. The King demands that nature should be good, and puzzles over events which show conclusively that his expectations will not be met. His ill-treatment of Cordelia he calls:

> O most small fault . . .
> That, like an engine, wrenched my frame of nature
> From the fixed place.
>
> (I.iv.253)

A fallen part of the ideal nature is therefore acknowledged, the 'bias of nature' which Gloucester cites as a cause of his own distress (I.ii.103). And since every earth-born creature is part good and part evil, there must be in nature some lack of form and order. Gloucester in the speech before he throws himself forward in the belief that he is on the cliff-edge says that if he could resign himself to fate, to 'the gods':

> My snuff and loathéd part of nature should
> Burn itself out.
>
> (IV.vi.40)

The good man is the man whose good parts predominate over the bad ones. The play is about the good, well-ordered man in a bad, disordered society; he can be played on by both good and ill in the universe, but in his fallen state must admit that all in the world is not for good.

When Edmund invokes nature as his goddess (I.ii.1) he uses the term in yet another sense. He is rejecting the concept of nature as a preordained system, ruled according to a fate which cannot be manipulated by man. He is taking the scientific, rationalist view of the 'modern man', unencumbered by old wives' tales of the stars in the heavens fixing the future whatever men's efforts to change it. Edmund binds his services to the law of the nature he recognises, which is no law at all but an acknowledgement that much can be done by man to change the natural world to suit his own ends. Gloucester attributes the troubles of the times to strange appearances in nature (the eclipses) which reflect disturbances in the order of the universe:

> 'machinations, hollowness, treachery, and all ruinous disorders',
>
> (I.ii.104)

despite anything man does in his attempts to reason himself out of them:

> Though the wisdom of nature can reason it thus and thus, yet nature
> finds itself scourged by the sequent effects.
>
> (I.ii.97)

Lear fails to understand the conflict between these views of nature as fate, and nature as a universe over which man can exercise some free will. Regan's heart, he sees, is not shaped according to the benevolence of 'true' nature, and some other, rational explanation of her evil is therefore called for:

> let them anatomize Regan; see what breeds about her heart. Is there any cause in nature that makes these hard hearts?
>
> (III.vi.72)

There is of course no final solution to the problem of reconciling good with evil, but Lear triumphs over the predicament in the sense that he never wavers from his assumption that the universe, 'nature', should by right deal justly with human beings.

The principal characters in King Lear

LEAR. When we think of Lear on the stage, our imagination goes first to a white-haired, white-bearded old man dressed as artists have drawn Old Testament prophets, exposed to the wind and thunder of a dreadful storm. This view of him is one that naturally predominates because it is the quintessence of his part in the play named after him: the trappings of reverence and respect are no use to this archetypal man when nature has turned against him. The storm around him is at one with the bewilderment in his being. He has been stripped of dignities which look permanent but prove to be as precarious as the balance of his mind. And it is right, too, to associate him with clothing because the changes in his fortunes are reflected in his attitude to clothing.

In him, evil is put to good use, for how else could he be made to feel with humanity? Of human suffering he says:

> O, I have ta'en
> Too little care of this! Take physic, pomp;
> Expose thyself to feel what wretches feel.
>
> (III.iv.32)

What the homeless and destitute feel is, as likely as not, none of their own doing. The rich and powerful must not blame the poor for their poverty, nor accept it without question or sympathy. Lear made a sinful mistake, and the play sweeps us on through this to its consequences. From a position of acceptance, Lear is compelled to question cause and effect, to try to decide what the role of kingship means and what it carries with it in the way of duty and obligation. At the beginning of the play, the forthright tone of his speeches shows that no experience has led him so far to hesitate over the significance and duties of kingship.

His relations with those closest to him mirror the ambivalence of his own attitudes. He inspires in Kent a strong and durable loyalty. Banished for plain speaking, Kent in disguise is quickly by the King's side, telling himself that he will work well for the master he loves. Lear, characteristically impetuous, hires him, and Kent, evidently fulfilled in his abasement to the kingship, sees fit to allow his deception to run out beyond all possible needs as far as the King is concerned. At the start of this servant-master relationship, the middle-aged nobleman Kent adopts attitudes more appropriate to the Fool, but Lear sees this as a recommendation rather than otherwise, perhaps because wordplay is a release from reality:

> LEAR   How old art thou?
> KENT   Not so young, sir, to love a woman for singing, nor so old to dote on her for anything: I have years on my back forty-eight.
>
> (I.iv.33)

Kent's boundless loyalty to the King shows there are qualities in Lear which are hardly apparent in his relations with others who associate with him. Lear has inspired in Kent a devotion lying beyond the duty of a subject to serve the power thought to be invested by divine right in a king. Kent feels both love and respect for Lear as man and as King, such that he can contemplate no future for himself when Lear has died:

> I have a journey, sir, shortly to go;
> My master calls me; I must not say no.
>
> (v.iii.322)

The King commands in the Fool the reactions of a more conventional devotion than Kent's, but of course this is what he pays his Fool to give him. Lear needs his Fool to show him some of the realities below the surface of what is happening, even when the demonstration is beyond the reach of words. The Fool pines away after Cordelia leaves, and when the knight draws attention to this, Lear's response is illuminating:

> No more of that; I have noted it well.
>
> (I.iv.65)

He needs but does not want to be reminded of the unhappiness mounting up in the train of his arbitrary decisions. He tries to explain away the 'most faint neglect' of the servants, and when he fails to do so, his inclination is to handle it as a bureaucrat would:

> I will look further into 't
>
> (I.iv.61)

presumably in the hope that it will go away.

This vessel of kingly power and human weakness baffles those who do not know him with his peremptory changes of attitude. The King of France is sorely puzzled:

> This is most strange,
> That she, who even but now was your best object,
> ... should in this trice of time
> Commit a thing so monstrous, to dismantle
> So many folds of favour.

(I.i.209)

Lear's character is revealed fully by the end of Act I. His exchanges with the Fool in I.v settle once for all the flaws in the King, and the omens are not good. In little, this scene shows the King to be a strange amalgam of the sharp giver of orders, the musing player with words, and the caster-back to events whose causes he does not understand and whose consequences rankle. Fittingly at the end of the scene he prays he shall not go mad.

It would be pointless here to go over the decline in Lear's fortunes, since that is the core of the whole play. Rejected by Goneril, despite the hesitantly sympathetic advances of her husband Albany, and rejected too by Regan, he determines to face adversity without the advantages of comfort and respect which would be expected to go along with his status. The challenge proves too demanding. Brought down to the essentials of human life, the constitution of necessity remains to him as cloudy as ever:

> O, reason not the need. Our basest beggars
> Are in the poorest thing superfluous

(II.iv.260)

His attempts to 'anatomize' Regan are an instance of this intellectual determination to fathom what had been obscured by the trappings and shelterings of the kingly image. Lear has by this point reached an awareness of the only thing that can bring him ultimate reconciliation with the realities of the human condition, a deeper search for what is essential in mankind. There is a long gap between this, the end of Act III, and Lear's next appearance, fantastically dressed with wild flowers. This appearance marks the onset of the acute disturbance of mind from which he is recalled when Cordelia, by simply being her natural self, brings him back to consciousness of the life he has known. He accepts prison in the British camp, preferring it to having to face up to unconfined nature. We become aware that his reason has returned, for his choice makes sense. When he brings in on to the stage the dead Cordelia, his rage is towering, his grief bitter and harrowing, but they are not the cries of a madman. His passing is a loss not of mind but of consciousness.

Lear's character is, then, many-faceted. But this is not to say that it is inconsistent. There are, on the contrary, many consistencies. Perhaps the most important is the relief he gets at moments of tension by indulging in threats and spiteful fantasy. This release of tension is linked with weakness of mind but is at the same time a human failing which we all know something about: an urge to verbalise powerful antipathies. He splutters when the threats are too ill-formulated to specify:

> No, you unnatural hags,
> I will have such revenges on you both
> That all the world shall – I will do such things –
> What they are, yet I know not, but they shall be
> The terrors of the earth.
>
> (II.iv.274)

When he rages against the wind and weather, his unkind daughters seem somehow always involved:

> Nor rain, wind, thunder, fire are my daughters;
> I tax not you, you elements, with unkindness;
> I never gave you kingdom, called you children
>
> (III.ii.15)

Edgar as Poor Tom he thinks of as cast down for the same causes as his own:

> What, have his daughters brought him to this pass?
>
> (III.iv.60)

With the Fool and his own fantasy, Lear can let himself go:

> To have a thousand with red burning spits
> Come hissing in upon 'em –
>
> (III.vi.13)

Dressed with wild flowers, he takes on mad pretensions of authority – he calls Gloucester 'Goneril with a white beard' – and is to the eyeless Gloucester immediately recognisable. And, his sanity restored, he puts into words his desire for retribution, even in the presence of the dead Cordelia whose true worth he now understands. He looks back to the days of his daring youth, when he would have made skip those 'murderers, traitors all'.

CORDELIA. After Lear one naturally goes on to think of Cordelia because her relations with her father, crystallised in her views on the right apportionment of filial love, set off the tragedy. Although her appearances are few in number and what she actually says and does when she is on the stage is very small in quantity, she is never far from our minds as the play proceeds, and the trail of fire she has fused will need to burn home. We as spectators are never in doubt of this, and her long absence, from the time she goes as wife to the King of France, the only bidder for her hand, to her part in the restoration of Lear, is dramatically of great importance, maintaining the suspense of the play clean and clear of its complexities.

Her style of speech has a hard, brittle quality, compact and self-confident even in emotion, very different from that of Kent with whom she feels so many bonds of compatibility. Is she essentially soft-voiced but tough-centred, admitting emotion in its proper place, but as if under scrutiny all the while? The answer is probably yes. In many ways she is like Portia in *The Merchant of Venice* – they are not aliens to emotion, but do not allow it to run away with them. As with Portia, her role is an impressive one because she seems always in command of it, simple, sincere, natural yet bravely facing temptation and falsehood when forms of words savouring of these qualities are placed invitingly before her.

Her appearances break down into three episodes.

In the first she is the truth-sayer, the implacable enemy of hypocrisy. Her directness and sincerity of purpose lead her to say things which she knows perfectly well her father will misinterpret, in the sense that he will fail to recognise the source from which they spring. Lear's autocracy begins to slide away from the moment she refuses the pretence of saying all her love is directed to him. It is quickly eroded by her sisters' subsequent rejection of his person and train. She looks ahead unflinchingly, knowing her directness will do her no good, but refusing to modify it:

> I love your Majesty
> According to my bond; nor more nor less.
>
> (I.i.88)

and her reasoning is incontestable:

> Why have my sisters husbands, if they say
> They love you all?
>
> (I.i.95)

This is all too forthright and outspoken to be taken as unwitting. Cordelia is in no doubt whatever about the results of her frankness, and she evinces no surprise when she loses her father's blessing and the dowry, a loss which would, if it were not for the sympathetic King of France, have made it impossible for her to marry as a princess was expected to do. This episode closes with a barbed remark to the sisters who must in reason take over her share in the care of their father:

> stood I within his grace,
> I would prefer him to a better place.
>
> (I.i.269)

The senselessness of the whole situation, of Lear's desire to extract from his daughters their conventional protestations of filial love, is cut through with the biting precision of this closing and fittingly rhymed couplet of lines.

The second episode does not occur until Lear's suffering has passed and his deranged mind stands in need of the comfort his affectionate daughter can give. Cordelia's long absence from the stage marks her inevitable allegiance to the French faction, with which the rejected Lear eventually associates himself. And it is, of course, her allegiance to her father, not the invading forces of France, which persuades her to seek him out (IV.iv). She is perturbed at the compromising position she finds herself in, but political considerations are put aside in her longing to see her father again. Of her forces she says:

> No blown ambition doth our arms incite,
> But love, dear love, and our aged father's right.
>
> (IV.iv.27)

On his side, Lear's shame at his misjudgement keeps him from approaching Cordelia, as Kent says in the previous scene. Indeed, Kent, whose fate is so similar to her own, has given her the help she needed, as she readily acknowledges in the scene (IV.vii) which contains Lear's restoration to consciousness and sanity. She is tender to the point of falsehood, much against the nature she showed in the first scene of the play:

> LEAR I know you do not love me; for your sisters
> Have, as I do remember, done me wrong.
> You have some cause, they have not.
>
> CORDELIA No cause, no cause.
>
> (IV.vii.74)

In a way her own position and her father's are now reversed: he in his turn can now look at effects, if not causes, with her own scrupulous eye. He says to her:

> Pray you now, forget and forgive; I am old and foolish.
>
> (IV.vii.85)

They can both, then, in their own way share in Cordelia's aphorism:

> We are not the first
> Who with best meaning have incurred the worst.
>
> (V.iii.3)

She believes her father wants to see his other daughters, but this is not so. He is content to accept confinement in prison so long as she can be with him, and to conjure up a fantasy of the fate which will befall her sisters. Cordelia can only weep. Yet Lear's restoration is her victory.

In her final appearance she is brought in dead in Lear's arms. She was hanged on Edmund's orders, countermanded too late to save her. We are left with Lear's lament for her:

> Her voice was ever soft,
> Gentle and low, an excellent thing in woman.

(v.iii.272)

ALBANY attracts attention on the stage mostly because we see him growing in spiritual stature. Even at the beginning of the play there are one or two hints that he is a man to be reckoned with, but we see no proof of this until the general moral decline around him throws up a situation in which he can shine and over which he can take control. His part in the plot is many-sided: his moral advance is seen as a counter-swing to the degradation of Edmund, with whom he is politically involved. Yet the power of his personality has to be taken on trust until he releases himself from the stranglehold of his wife Goneril, for up to that point he is in a sense in disguise, and his role in the plot subtly reflects back and forward the other more obvious disguises in the play, those of Edgar and Kent. Significantly he depends to a considerable degree on their support at the end of the play.

He is the first person mentioned in the play, and is identified as the King's favourite, evidently with the matter of succession uppermost in Lear's mind. We can safely assume that qualities of statesmanship and moral leadership have become inert as Goneril has come to show herself in her true colours as a heartless and domineering wife. The change subserves the demands of the plot, but must properly be seen independently of these. His unspectacular appearances early in the play are meant to show his present plight. His character develops morally and spiritually in changed circumstances, as another's would do.

Albany does not himself play any significant part until the main lines of the plots have been laid down, and his wife has shown her malice towards Lear her father. When Lear challenges him about this, he does no more than recommend patience and, even more weakly, profess (or feign?) ignorance of the reasons for the disturbance in his palace (I.iv). He ends the scene by making himself appear intentionally imperceptive in his attempt to counter his wife's criticism of him:

GONERIL   No, no, my lord,
           This milky gentleness and course of yours
           Though I condemn not, yet, under pardon,
           You are much more at task for want of wisdom
           Than praised for harmful mildness.
ALBANY   How far your eyes may pierce I cannot tell.
           Striving to better, oft we mar what's well.

                                                    (I.iv.326)

This does not sound like the talk of a man who has just inherited half a kingdom, even though through his wife.

When we see him again the fearful changes of fortune have taken place, Lear rejected and exposed to the storm and Gloucester blinded. Albany's change of personality is a general consequence of the worsening of the world in which he lives, although his tougher manner develops before he knows of Gloucester's blinding and the death of Cornwall, his brother-in-law, as a direct result. Unexpectedly, some good comes out of the pervading evil of vicious cruelty and inhumanity: Oswald, Goneril's servant, finds him 'never man so changed', and detects the conflict which is to be peculiar to Albany, that of political against moral right. Kent has indeed foretold this event, though somewhat obscurely:

           There is division,
       Although as yet the face of it is covered
       With mutual cunning, 'twixt Albany and Cornwall;
           . . . from France there comes a power
       Into this scattered kingdom.

                                                    (III.i.19, 30)

Kent goes on to hint at the eventuality of those loyal to the old King going over to France, but such treasonable talk has of course to be imprecise for safety's sake. No one could doubt that Albany is morally on the King's side, yet if he is to side with the King he will be collaborating with an invader, and thus threatening the good order of the state.

However, the state of the realm is for the moment in anything but good order, so that Albany's conflict of allegiance does not need to be brought to a head. As Act V begins, we hear from Edmund, now mustering forces in the British camp near Dover, that Albany is an uncertain quantity: 'He's full of alteration/And self-reproving.' Yet when he enters, Albany shows that his mind is made up. Only the language in which he expresses his decision retains vestiges of the indirectness and uncertainty which once pervaded his mind:

> For this business,
> It touches us, as France invades our land,
> Not bolds the King, with others, whom, I fear,
> Most just and heavy causes make oppose.   (v.i.24)

– a very devious way of saying that he will side with his wife's faction because to do otherwise would be to abet a foreign enemy of the state. In the last scene Albany, redeemed and transformed, acquires even a firmness of speech and gesture. A clash with Edmund is inevitable. It turns out to be over captives when the battle is finished and the French forces routed. And if only because Lear and Cordelia under guard have just left the stage, it is they among the captives who are uppermost in our thoughts. Edmund wants to put off discussing their future, although Albany has demanded they should be handed over. Albany, in reasserting his position, assumes his full stature:

> Sir, by your patience,
> I hold you but a subject of this war,
> Not as a brother.   (v.iii.60)

And after Edmund's arrest (v.iii.83), Albany is in control, a grim master-of-ceremonies when Edgar and Edmund face one another. He falters over Lear and Cordelia, and their fate is doubly sealed by delay on delay in sending their reprieve.

Like Albany, GLOUCESTER is transformed and redeemed in the play, but Gloucester's treatment at the hands of his antagonists is infinitely more violent, and the nature of his redemption consequently more extreme. By his own suffering he comes in the end to know that adversity can bring spiritual rewards. After he is blinded he says of himself:

> I stumbled when I saw. Full oft 'tis seen,
> Our means secure us, and our mere defects
> Prove our commodities.   (IV.i.20)

His fall from power is the result of this stumbling. He stumbles because of his vanity, his violence of temperament, and his conventional, unrewarding ideas on the world and fate.

Some but not all of the qualities he reveals in himself early in the play have counterparts after the blinding. This event, appalling to a degree that many have found unforgivable in the dramatist, is a watershed and the personal qualities we come to recognise in Gloucester sustain the most intense changes at this point. The blinding is a marker of change in that it breaks up the long, almost continuous appearances of Gloucester on the stage – he is second only to Lear in the way his presence controls the course of the play. The many-sidedness of Gloucester's character and its readiness to change keep him in our thoughts even when he is not physically before our eyes, so that Lear's particular sorrows are not allowed to blot out the sorrows of others.

Gloucester's vanity in the power he gets from his social status has at the start a blind heartlessness about it. His pride and self-confidence make him gullible enough to believe Edmund's tales about Edgar. The demands of the Gloucester plot require the deception to be carried through with rough-and-ready efficiency, and Gloucester is too puffed-up with his own importance to question for a moment what Edmund tells him or wonder about Edmund's motives for saying what he does. Gloucester orders the apprehension of the fugitive Edgar and then turns to licking his own imaginary wounds:

> – to his father, that so tenderly and entirely loves him. Heaven and earth! Edmund, seek him out; wind me into him, I pray you.
>
> (I.ii.90)

Aside from the King (whom he treats with exaggerated respect) he is at first considerate only to Cornwall, whom he sees as his 'arch and patron'. To Cornwall he is positively deferential. Yet it is in his dealings with Cornwall that the first traces of feeling for other human beings begin to appear: Gloucester pleads that Kent should not be put in the stocks, and even gives a thought to the effect this action of his will have on the perpetrator of the punishment, Cornwall.

From this point on his powers to feel for others grow quickly. They are the benignant outcome of the web of intrigue which is closing in on him, the strong man who turns out to be vulnerable after all. He tells Edmund:

> When I desired their leave that I might pity [the King], they took from me the use of mine own house; charged me, on pain of their perpetual displeasure, neither to speak of him, entreat for him, nor any way sustain him.
>
> (III.iii.2)

By the following scene Gloucester has thrown in his lot entirely with the outcast King on the heath. He deplores the unjust treatment of Kent, whose honest dealing he understands, but he still fails to penetrate the deception Edmund has worked on him, and therefore laments his own fate at the hands of the son who of all people is the best disposed to him.

After the blinding he starts noticing details of other people's behaviour. On two occasions he remarks on the way people are speaking: Edgar's altered manner of speech when he is intent on the trick of the imaginary cliff-top near Dover (IV.vi); and Lear's raging words, about which Gloucester says:

The trick of that voice I do well remember.
Is 't not the King?

(IV.vi.105)

The second occasion has also the dramatic significance of re-emphasising his blindness. He must now recognise others by their voices.

His faith in astrology and other superstitions is not subjected to any startling transformation. Looked at in one way, this superstition is a body of beliefs yielding conventional responses, stereotyped expectations of the outcome of situations in the natural world or explanations of the causes of events which have already taken place. Gloucester's reactions to his own predicament, caused as he supposes by his son Edgar, would have seemed to Shakespeare's audience less stupid than they do to us. Edmund, pouring scorn on the astrology his father professes, is the radical, the man of the new world. Gloucester's conventional adherence to popular beliefs is a retreat into the comfort of the old world. His trusting simple-mindedness brings him to giving Edmund information about the assembling of the King's supporters which, interpreted by Cornwall's faction as disloyalty, leads Gloucester to his blinding.

Dover cliff is the place of his greatest despair. He remains puzzled, and his most often quoted words:

As flies to wanton boys are we to the gods;
They kill us for their sport

(IV.i.37)

are about the hopelessness of any effort to change fate, not a turning-back to the reading of signs to account for events when they have taken place. This too represents a change of attitude, one which is born of self-questioning in the face of suffering. And he dislikes the newly acquired sensitivity he becomes conscious of as he thinks back on what he and the King have both suffered:

Better I were distract.
So should my thoughts be severed from my griefs,
And woes by wrong imaginations lose
The knowledge of themselves.

(IV.vi.274)

Recent commentators on the play have perhaps made too much of Gloucester's fault in the begetting of Edmund. True, Edgar links it and the blinding as crime and punishment; he says to Edmund:

The dark and vicious place where thee he got
Cost him his eyes.

(V.iii.172)

But this sin never seems to play any important part in Gloucester's thinking. It sticks in the mind because he brings it in casually and jokingly at the beginning of the play. On the other hand, Edmund makes full play of it to account for his own disillusioned view of the world. He has suffered too much because of his bastardy for anyone to deceive him. Gloucester from appearing irredeemable is made ready and ripe for redemption when he is blinded and Regan shows him in a flash that Edmund is his evil genius, and his thoughts turn to the wronged son, the son of his marriage. He is drawn back from despair, but continues to the end in need of a sensible, practical mentor to keep up his spirits. This mentor at last reveals himself as Edgar, and only then does Gloucester's heart

> 'Twixt two extremes of passion, joy and grief,
> Burst smilingly.
>
> (v.iii.198)

GONERIL. It is small wonder that Goneril makes inroads into her father's weak brain, as at the mock trial (III.vi.44). Of the two sisters, she is the one who initiates evil courses, even from the beginning:

> GONERIL Pray you, let's hit together: if our father carry authority with such dispositions as he bears, this last surrender of his will but offend us.
> REGAN We shall further think on't.
> GONERIL We must do something, and i' the heat.
>
> (I.i.296)

She has ready to hand various stratagems which will at once provoke the situation she wishes to develop and keep her clear of the immediate consequences. She proposes to feign sickness, and she orders her servants to treat the King and his train with 'weary negligence'. It is all part of a carefully worked plan in which the malevolence is blatant. She tells her steward, Oswald:

> I would breed from hence occasions, and I shall,
> That I may speak.
>
> (I.iii.25)

If anything Goneril is tougher than her sister Regan in 'breeding occasions', more cruel and heartless, lusting after the infliction of agony on others. She provokes the blinding of Gloucester (beginning of III.vii). All these terrible things in her mental make-up give grounds for the curses which Lear heaps on her, the madness which he feels overwhelming him when her full battery of evil has yet to be revealed:

I prithee, daughter, do not make me mad.
I will not trouble thee, my child; farewell.   (II.iv.214)

But Goneril cannot be touched. The harm she has caused to her father's mind
makes him turn naturally to her case when he stages the mock trial as he
shelters from the storm with Edgar, Kent and the Fool (III.vi).

She is, however, touched by the jealous and illicit love she conceives for
Edmund. Her love-talk with him grows more intense as she comes to know
of Albany's transformation. These feelings are deepened still further when
Cornwall dies and his widow shows herself infatuated by Edmund. Goneril
takes direct action by poisoning Regan to open up her own way to Edmund.
But this course goes awry, and she characteristically detects trickery in others
as the cause: Edmund need not have accepted from an unidentified assailant
the challenge to fight. Someone else has now bred an occasion:

> This is practice, Gloucester.
> By the law of arms thou wast not bound to answer
> An unknown opposite; thou art not vanquished,
> But cozened and beguiled.   (v.iii.151)

Her husband confronts her with the letter she has addressed in secret to
Edmund, and she leaves, desperate but defiant. She takes her own life,
perhaps in despair at Edmund's death, confessing that she poisoned Regan.

For CORNWALL we expect no redemption, and none is forthcoming. Even Lear
himself, a bad judge of people, preferred Albany to Cornwall. His role is
wicked through and through, and shows a decline from subservience under
Regan's iron will to independent malevolence and blood-lust.

Cornwall's involvement is with the Gloucester plot. His own vicious behaviour represents the contrast with Gloucester's too-trusting spirit. Near the
beginning of Act II some sort of relationship between them seems to be developing, one of spurious sympathy between a man in power and one who has
been wronged. Out of this relationship, so brittle and so quickly to be destroyed, springs the 'adoption' of Edmund by Cornwall (II.i.114). The contact
with Gloucester is pursued in the next scene, when both are seen taking
vigorous action against Kent, whose attitudes to Oswald puzzle them and
prompt an almost naive attempt on Cornwall's part to explain things away.
He finds no nature of deep trust in Kent:

> This is some fellow
> Who, having been praised for bluntness, doth affect
> A saucy roughness, and constrains the garb
> Quite from his nature.   (II.ii.87)

– and he pursues this theme at some length, counterbalancing Kent's invective against Oswald which has closely preceded it.

Later in Act II, Cornwall is carried along by the tide of events more than induced by them to take positive action. The women, not he, are positive over turning Lear out of doors into the storm. But he is not difficult to persuade. To Gloucester at the end of Act II he says:

> My Regan counsels well. Come out o' the storm.

Cornwall's most positive action is his loathsome turning on Gloucester which ends in the blinding. The pursuit of this vile end, the lust for blood, give him the confidence which he has so far lacked, especially in the presence of Regan. He even interrupts her, at the point where both question Gloucester about the activities in Dover. When he has blinded one of Gloucester's eyes, a servant tries to restrain him. The servant is killed, but not before he has given Cornwall a fatal wound. These are the first and most ignominious of the deaths in the tragedy.

REGAN brings to the play unrelieved wickedness so virulent that it breeds strife in others around her. Because, perhaps, of this consistency of evil, we are not conscious of the frequency of her appearances until we begin to assess it. Unlike Goneril, she is on the stage for a large part of the play, not perhaps controlling much, and sometimes indeed almost unobtrusive, an evil genius all too often at hand but not in the centre of the arena. We have nevertheless an uneasy feeling that she is always likely to be found at the heart of the plotting, as the person who precipitates the thoughts and secret ambitions of others into action, even if she is not herself in the end the one to make the final move.

She is very much herself at the blinding of Gloucester (III.vii). She starts off the witch-hunt by calling for him to be hanged. Others, especially Goneril, push the matter to more horrible depths. She subjects him to the gross indignity of pulling his beard, and is at the forefront of the questioning of his alleged treachery. She races on and has to be checked:

> REGAN   Wherefore to Dover? Wast thou not charged at peril –
> CORNWALL   Wherefore to Dover? Let him first answer that.   (III.vii.51)

All darkness and wickedness as she is, Shakespeare gives her touches of naturalism which remain in the mind. It is not just that nothing in the big scale, however appalling to the eye or ear, moves her. She can equally manipulate her words over smaller matters to ensure that she carries people along with her and gets what she wants. In II.iv, Lear, driven by Goneril from her home, curses her and goes far towards satisfying himself that he will be received by Regan as a father should be. Goneril and Regan each have their special ways of ramming home the point they wish to make (II.iv.226–232). Each retains the shreds of diplomacy, but each is determined to drive the contention to a point of conclusion. Plainly Lear is to suffer.

Her sordid involvement with Edmund we hear more about from her than from her rival Goneril. Oswald, the carrier of Goneril's letter to Edmund (IV.v) is not persuaded by Regan's imperious manner to hand it over to her. She finds herself presenting her case to Oswald for her marriage with Edmund, so moved is she by the passion of desire. Her jealousy knows no bounds. Their squabble flashes up and in the plain, bold lines of the tragedy Regan is poisoned by her sister, though not before she has proclaimed a sort of marriage contract between herself and Edmund (v.iii.78). This is a desperate promise of marriage before she dies and Edmund has to face the forces of truth and honour in the person of Edgar.

EDMUND is a realist, astonishingly adept in deceiving others. The play really begins with an account of his illegitimacy, rather a joke and at the same time ominously serious. Yet there is no inkling in Gloucester's jocular tone of the price he is going to have to pay for the lustful pleasure which resulted in Edmund's birth. It is sufficient to accept that Edmund's status has given him the means of mixing with the highest in the land (the nobles surrounding the King) and also motives for action of a man slighted and looked down on for something which cannot possibly be interpreted as a fault of his own. He has suffered much, and has become adept in posturing and displaying his evil intentions to further his own ends. The impression he leaves on the spectator is of a man whose personality glows through the conventions of what he says. He is, after all, a consummate deceiver, driven to underhandedness by disparagement and neglect at the hands of his kin and his acquaintances:

He hath been out nine years, and away he shall again

his father says of him when, at the beginning of the play, he introduces him to Kent. (The device is as much dramatic, a way of introducing characters to the audience, as an element in the plot.) Kent turns out to be gentle and long-suffering, the last man to penetrate the machinations of another as a patron should be able to do.

Edmund's villainy is displayed in his declarations to the audience, made according to the dramatic conventions of the time. And whereas the disguise of others (Kent, Edgar) is physical, Edmund relies on the subtler exercise of acting out of character when he sees advantage in doing so. And we must accept, again within the dramatic convention, that his victims can often be totally deceived over his good faith. He dupes his father into believing a trumped-up charge of evil designs in his half-brother Edgar which long family associations should have made inconceivable. Against this, Edmund's bastardy – or rather the treatment he has received because of it – has produced the causes of his wickedness. His handling of the life-long predicament makes him for the play a ,dominant personality, well shown in the vigorous way he deals with clap-trap about supernatural causes for earthly disasters:

> This is the excellent foppery of the world, that when we are sick in fortune – often the surfeit of our own behaviour – we make guilty of our disasters the sun, the moon and the stars; as if we were villains by necessity, fools by natural compulsion.

(I.ii.109)

Edgar is surprised when he overhears, as he is meant to, a comment of Edmund's about ominous portents in eclipses:

> Do you busy yourself about *that*?

(I.ii.131)

he asks. Edmund does. His deceptions are at the heart of his 'practices', and Edgar is carried along by him without more than an occasional incredulous question.

Edmund's is a resourceful personality. Little things are brought in to help along the big design. He accuses Edgar of speaking against Cornwall, and of himself being influenced by astrology. This brings Cornwall firmly in on his side against Edgar.

He then (III.iii) discusses with his father the plight of Lear, and, with the sure knowledge of his father's sympathies, prepares to inform against him as a traitor to the ruling power. Cornwall is persuaded to take steps to apprehend Gloucester, and as he is hunted down Edmund says nothing. When the blinding of Gloucester is near, Cornwall tells Edmund the deed is 'not fit for your beholding' (III.vii). Typically, the instigator is silent and absent when the results of his plotting are to come about.

Both Regan and Goneril fall in love with him, and each very naturally suspects the designs of the other. The experience seems to add, if anything, to his resourcefulness, for, as he reveals at the end, he appreciates that, despised and feared as he has been, there were those who loved him. In the self-revelatory soliloquy at the end of v.i, he is the grim puppet-master manoeuvring the others into positions which will be to his advantage. His words show him at the height of his power, commanding and scheming in pursuance of a grand design.

Edmund negotiates with the officer and then with Albany over Lear and Cordelia, doubtless with the idea that absolute power to do as he pleases will soon be in his hands. Yet he goes in good heart into single combat with an unidentified challenger, although the code of chivalry would have justified a refusal to do so, and is defeated. He admits to the crimes recounted, or more properly hinted at, by Edgar as he reveals himself, and knows 'The wheel is come full circle'. His fall from the heights is quick and complete.

EDGAR. Like Albany, Edgar finds 'himself' as the drama of the play unfolds. When we first see him, the impression is of a modest, open and unsuspicious character without the special qualities which would single him out as vital to the piece, and not noticeably endowed with much native wit. Yet vital he is, for the stresses he is subjected to bring out in him impressive resources and great fortitude. The resourcefulness is easily seen, for example, in the changes of style when Edgar speaks, and the neutral and unpromising beginnings give no indication of the power and energy he calls up when under the stress of the action.

Edmund wants to see him disinherited so that he can get the lands which would otherwise go to the legitimate heir. Edgar is totally duped by Edmund's ploy. Taking his cue from his father's harassed forebodings over eclipses, Edmund pretends to be worried over them too and Edgar breezily enquires about his troubled thoughts. Edmund quickly works him into a state of genuine perturbation. He is alleged to have furthered the differences between Cornwall and Albany. Edmund goes his individual way, clouding the issue further: was it Cornwall or Albany that Edgar is supposed to have 'spoken 'gainst'? (II.i.20–27). There is then the pretence of the sword-play, and the friendly and trusting Edgar is banished by his undiscriminating father. Under such stress as this he begins to reveal himself for what he can really be. Paradoxically, the prospect of disguise opens the way to the realisation of his true potentialities. Primarily for self-protection, he takes on the guise of a Bedlam beggar, and in the stage traditions of the time such disguise is assumed to be impenetrable, so that even his own father does not recognise him:

> [I] am bethought
> To take the basest and most poorest shape
> That ever penury, in contempt of man,
> Brought near to beast. (II.iii.6)

Lear detects that his wits are in danger of turning, so that when the disguised Edgar, feigning madness, appears before him in front of the hovel, he assimilates Edgar's role of madness and destitution, stripping off his own clothes to be like him. In this way a rapport is established between Lear and Edgar such as the Fool had failed to achieve, and Lear calls Edgar his philosopher. Edgar is able and willing to maintain the part he has assumed.

By the end of Act III he has become to Lear 'most learned justicer', and is prepared to go through the mockery of an imaginary trial involving the unkind daughters and their father. Moreover, to keep the complications of the drama in check, Edgar at the end of III.vi soliloquises on human suffering, his own guise, and Lear's plight.

> How light and portable my pain seems now,
> When that which makes me bend makes the king bow.
> He childed as I fathered!
>
> (III.vi.104)

From about this point Edgar begins to harbour doubts about the course of action he has adopted. 'I cannot daub it further' he says, but yet he does, even when he sees his father blind and destitute. Of course, Edmund would make every effort to apprehend him if he revealed himself, but that consideration does not seem quite enough to justify him in keeping up the disguise. However, the pattern and convention of the drama fittingly accommodate the long disguise of Edgar, reflecting back and forth with Kent's disguise in banishment. We are to see Edgar, then, as an honourable person adept at deceiving and misleading others when the cause is morally right.

He settles on a scheme of deception when he meets his father and discovers that Gloucester's dejection has left him only thoughts of suicide. The episode of the imaginary cliff shows Edgar breaking through his assumed role and willy-nilly speaking with something like his inbred authority. Gloucester notices this change of tone:

> Methinks thy voice is altered, and thou speak'st
> In better phrase and matter than thou didst.
>
> (IV.vi.7)

and is not put off when Edgar denies it. So that although the pretended falling off the cliff is physically improbable and unconvincing, and its aftermath spills over into fantasy and the supernatural, Edgar and Gloucester, on whom the attention is fixed, react to one another in essentially human ways, and provide a sort of assurance that even in a world of crazed suffering humanity is not destroyed. Edgar's description of the 'thing' he pretends he saw standing with Gloucester on the imagined cliff-top:

> methought his eyes
> Were two full moons; he had a thousand noses,
> Horns welked and waved like the enridgéd sea
>
> (IV.vi.70)

is counterbalanced by the veiled but felt authority of the way he handles the Gentleman he questions about the approaching battle:

> I thank you, sir; that's all.
>
> (IV.vi.209)

Edgar retains the essential qualities of a human being, and never slips out of the dramatist's control.

Again, the same scene shows him in the impersonation of a country bump-kin, complete with a rural accent this time, a pretence which he maintains only until Oswald is felled in an instant and dies. Events then heap on to Edgar's shoulders: he has Goneril's damning letter which affirms Albany's change of attitude, he gives his father new heart after the defeat of the Lear faction in the battle, and reveals himself almost in story-book fashion after he has fought in single combat the half-brother who has brought him so much sorrow. Once more, the fanciful and the down-to-earth are equally rep-resented.

The complexity of his involvement might lead us to expect that he will dominate the play, or share with a few others this domination. The truth is different: he emerges more as one bound up in various involved ways with the activities of others. This view of him emerges in the recital of his personal revelation ('List a brief tale . . .' v.iii.181), apposite and touching but some-how not at the heart of the action. His unhappiness at having held so long to his disguise may be meant as an instance of more general dissatisfaction with himself: his share in the events of the play does not give him the influence over them which one would expect. Describing the help he gave his father, he says:

> Led him, begged for him, saved him from despair;
> Never – O fault! – revealed myself unto him,
> Until some half-hour past, when I was armed;
> Not sure, though hoping, of this good success,
> I asked his blessing   (v.iii.191)

He goes on to say that when he had finished this account his father was too stricken in heart to survive. Perhaps he thinks that an earlier revelation of himself would have given Gloucester a better chance of survival. He is too late to save Lear and Cordelia from the sentence passed on them by Edmund and accepts the authority over the realm which Albany gives him and which Kent, possible fellow in authority as he had been fellow in disguise, rejects as the play closes. From what we have come to know of Edgar's character, it is no real surprise that he is ready to accept responsibility in the end.

The play has many appearances of KENT and references to him. Vivid, dramatic action does not fall to him, he is not the loud-mouthed protagonist or antagonist in any particular cause, but his presence is felt and his qualities of steadfastness and quiet reliability are a yardstick against which the evil of the play's action can be measured. An actor taking the part is likely to be

surprised at the length of time he spends on the stage: Kent, with his unfalter-
ing devotion to the majesty and kingship of Lear, acts out by his almost
continuous presence on the stage the role of ministration to Lear which he
has taken upon himself. This is the side he shows, too, to Cordelia, who
knows about his disguise and values his friendship and care for the King at its
true worth, ignoring the political consequences of his allegiance to what can
only be called a foreign faction:

> CORDELIA O thou good Kent, how shall I live and work
> To match thy goodness? My life will be too short,
> And every measure fail me.
> KENT To be acknowledged, madam, is o'erpaid.
> All my reports go with the modest truth;
> Nor more nor clipped, but so.
>
> (IV.vii.1)

His courteous, formal manner here can be traced back to his philosophy: he
attributes disaster to astrological causes rather than the evil inherent in
humanity, and has no cause therefore to abuse people for their failings. It is
not difficult to be courteous to people if one is sure that, without evil
influences which are none of their doing, they are essentially kind and honourable. Before Kent chooses to go into disguise deeper than that of Caius the
King's servant, he shows where he is in the old world of astrology. When the
Gentleman with whom he talks, and who brings him and us up to date on
the political situation, tells of Cordelia's disgust at her sisters' behaviour to
their father, Kent declares his belief:

> It is the stars,
> The stars above us, govern our conditions;
> Else one self mate and make could not beget
> Such different issues.

– referring to the natures of the three sisters (IV.iii.32). The Machiavellian
workings of an Edmund are not for him. The best he can do is to disguise
himself so that the King, who has banished him to vindicate his own majesty
when affronted by Kent's sensible awareness of the situation, will not
recognise him as an intruder and will take him on as a servant. After two
brushes with Goneril's steward Oswald, Kent assumes with his true peers a
direct style of ding-dong exchanges 'tis my occupation to be plain', he says,
(II.ii.84), and, mocking his own disguise, embarks on a piece of spurious
rhetoric which baffles the assembled company, and which Cornwall cuts
short. At this point he suffers the indignity of the stocks, and, a man of
many styles, he moves into a philosophic mood at the end of the scene
which seems to come easily to him, and which is nearer to the familiar

Shakespeare poetry of the more romantic plays than *King Lear* gets elsewhere. Of the letter he says:

> I know 'tis from Cordelia,
> Who hath most fortunately been informed
> Of my obscuréd course . . .
>   All weary and o'erwatched,
> Take vantage, heavy eyes, not to behold
> This shameful lodging.
>
> (II.ii.157)

The veiled confidence of his plain speaking is to be compared with that of the Fool. His disguise associates him with Edgar in the complex of the drama. This interplay with other characters is made possible because Kent is master of many moods; indeed, his involvement in so much that is happening makes him a complicated character, difficult to pin down. We have seen him speaking plain and then philosophising; we have insight into another pattern of behaviour when Gloucester, disobeying Regan and Goneril's directions, sets out to find Lear in the storm. In Kent's presence, though Gloucester does not know this, Gloucester calls him

> that good Kent!
> He said it would be thus, poor banished man!
>
> (III.iv.153)

From this point until the end of the play it is Kent's 'correctness' of attitude, the appropriateness of his reactions to the changing circumstances around him, which are most memorable. Although he quickly becomes deeply implicated in the politics and the plotting (by the end of III.iv he has thrown in his lot with Lear completely), he keeps his head.

A way of showing this 'correctness' is to notice the various verbal attitudes he adopts according to who he is with. The brisk discussion between him and the Gentleman (IV.iii, end of IV.vii) brings us up to date on the political situation, and shows the man of affairs, with the added mystery of the deeper disguise (end of IV.iii). With Cordelia, who alone knows his true identity, he is all kindness and tenderness, yet he maintains a courtly distance from her, as befits a subject talking to a member of the royal house:

> Pardon me, dear madam;
> Yet to be known shortens my made intent.
> My boon I make it that you know me not
> Till time and I think meet.
>
> (IV.vii.8)

He continues to be kind and deferential to her and helpful in an unosten-
tatious way when, in the same scene, Lear is brought back to consciousness.
Kent's unobtrusive manner fits well the continued disguise, which is important to him because it is to enable him to be involved in the final catastrophe without being hounded down as an outlaw who has broken the edict
of his banishment.

He reveals himself just before the time of the challenge, as Edgar tells us
(v.iii.208–18). But Kent's heart can bear no more, and again as Edgar observed,
'the strings of life/Began to crack', so that when he returns to the stage it is
to say farewell to the King. Lear, still alive, gets a glimmering of Kent's
identity (he knows his name) but wanders off into the byways of his own
grief and humiliation, never quite grasping the significance of Kent's devotion to him. The devotion is absolute – Kent will not stay alive while his
master is dying:

> I have a journey, sir, shortly to go;
> My master calls me; I must not say no. (v.iii.322)

This neat couplet is virtually the end of the play. At least Kent will not be
involved in the political settlement which Albany has instituted.

The FOOL does not have much in common with the light-hearted tricksters
of Shakespeare's comedies, such as Feste in *Twelfth Night*. Yet there are
essences which remain the same. In *King Lear* the traditional fool's gaiety is
tart and soured, not because the Fool has a paucity of true wit but because in
the play he must assimilate the high tragedy of the situation and not vulgarise
it. For as long as his presence is felt he is so preoccupied with the sufferings
of others, so ready, in verbal terms, to pick up their cues, that it is hard to
associate him with any particular personality traits of his own. But looked at
in another way, that is precisely the role a fool is hired to fulfil. He is paid to
minister to the needs of his master in a specially sensitive way, to recognise
his various moods and play up to them. Only the Fool dares to confront Lear
with the root of his folly; and Lear in his turn is prepared to take this only
from the Fool. Kent's quiet demur results in immediate banishment. The Fool,
true to the tradition, uses in such circumstances the rhyming adage, his stock-
in-trade, which however sharp its cutting edge remains at a distance from
the actual and the immediate by means of its style of age-old wisdom.

He turns to this soon after we first see him, after he has lamented the lot of
the court fool who ventured to speak plain, without rhyme or generalisation:

> *Have more than thou showest,*
> *Speak less than thou knowest,*
> *Lend less than thou owest,*
> *Ride more than thou goest . . .* (I.iv.105)

Some of the rhymes are evidently 'spontaneous' adaptations of traditional verses adjusted to suit the particular circumstances. They are interspersed with prose repartee, often not in very good taste (taste was not his business), often near to the wind, and sometimes curiously naïve (e.g. the business of the egg-crowns, I.iv.140–144). All this talk deliberately avoids facing up to facts. It makes its effect by dealing with situations analagous to those which other characters find themselves in. People are left to work out the connection for themselves.

In I.v the Fool is seen in the full flight of his particular expertise, asking Lear inane questions to distract him from his sorrows. The success of this is, however, only partial.

Despite this appearance of glossy slickness, the Fool has his own world of private feeling, and as Lear's sorrows heap up on him, the Fool turns serious from time to time, and especially when he discovers Edgar, feigning madness and grimly playing the fool as the 'spirit' in the hovel. At the end of this scene (III.ii) there is the oddly incongruous Merlin-joke, so out of character and so dependent on an historical sense which Shakespearian audiences knew little of.

When he disappears from the play he leaves a memory more of his private world than of his public fooling. Compared with Lear and Edgar, the Fool stands very obviously for common sense and worldly wisdom. He joins half-heartedly in the mock court-scene (III.vi.18–53) contrived by Lear as an outlet for his spitting fury, and finishes by catching up a word in what is said to round off his own contribution:

> LEAR . . . We'll go to supper i' the morning. So, so, so.
> FOOL And I'll go to bed at noon.

> (III.vi.79)

(The trick harks back to 'down' in Lear's mouth bringing up the anecdote of the cockney and the eels:

> she . . . cried, 'Down, wantons, down!'

> (II.iv.120)

Lear does not, as some have thought, take over the fooling at this point. Rather, he evinces genuine distraction, 'matter and impertinency mixed', and no fooling is needed as a substitute for it.

The provenance of King Lear; the extant texts

There is no single and completely reliable source for a text of the play, and this is the cause of doubt in places as to exactly what Shakespeare wrote and intended should be spoken by the actors on the stage. Today a playwright has his plays published in printed form in enough copies for actors and other readers to be quite certain of what he intends should be said and done on the stage. Shakespeare and his contemporaries on the other hand seem to have shown little or no interest in the publication of their plays, or indeed in what happened to the manuscripts after they had been copied out in parts for the actors to work to.

One reason for this casual attitude to the dissemination of the plays was the size of the current demand for entertainment. Shakespeare at the height of his powers wrote plays for his own company of players in answer to insistent demands for new work. Compared with today, the theatre-going population was in his time very small, and a position could quickly be reached in which, say, everyone in London likely to be interested could have seen a new play and would then call for something even newer. We can imagine with some justice therefore that Shakespeare's main concern, and that of his contemporary playwrights, was to get plays out as quickly as possible. There was little time to follow up what happened to the printed versions afterwards. These facts must in part account for the great number and diversity of the plays he wrote during his busiest years (1591–1611) as well as for the obvious imperfection of the texts as we now have them.

At that time plays were probably staged on the basis of manuscript copies of the texts, including copies of the entire play for the use of prompters and managers, and actors' parts, with cues and other directions. It has been suggested with good reason that the Folio edition (F) of 1623 represents versions of the plays close to those actually used in the theatres rather than those printed for private reading, the Quartos (Q).

King Lear was first published in a Quarto dated 1608 (*quarto* means having pages about the same size as those of this *New Swan Shakespeare* edition). It is poorly printed and contains many obvious inaccuracies. It bears all the marks of having been hastily put out to meet the public desire for a printed version of the play. A second Quarto, also dated 1608, contains only very minor differences from Q1; it was in all probability published eleven years later, retaining the date of Q1. The play was registered for publication in the Stationers' Company on 26th November of the previous year (part of the entry is given on p. xlvi above). This London Company or 'guild' maintained a register of all published books as they appeared for the purposes of ensuring copyright.

The day of the performance referred to in the Stationers' Register was 26th December, 1606, and the play can therefore only have been written some time before then.

It must have been written after the publication of Samuel Harsnett's book *A Declaration of Egregious Popish Impostures*; the connection between the play and this book is discussed above (p. xxxviii).

M. William Shak-ſpeare:

HIS
True Chronicle Hiſtorie of the life and
death of King LEAR and his three
Daughters.

With the vnfortunate life of Edgar, *ſonne*
and heire to the Earle of Gloſter, and his
ſullen and aſſumed humor of
TOM of Bedlam :

As it was played before the Kings Maieſtie at Whitehall vpon
S. Stephans *night in Chriſtmas Hollidayes.*

By his Maieſties ſeruants playing vſually at the Gloabe
on the Bancke-ſide.

LONDON,
Printed for *Nathaniel Butter,* and are to be ſold at his ſhop in *Pauls*
Church-yard at the ſigne of the Pide Bull neere
S^t. *Auſtins* Gate. 1 6 0 8

The title page of the First Quarto of King Lear (1608).

King Lear has certain similarities with the later plays of Shakespeare, a consideration which suggests the latter part of the period between the appearance of Harsnett's book and the Stationers' Register entry. The date 1605–6 appears very likely.

In 1623 two of Shakespeare's associates brought out a large collection of his plays as a memorial to him after his death (he died in 1616), and to meet the needs of an interested body of readers now appreciating the permanent value of the dramatist's work. This collection became known as the First Folio (*folio* means with pages about twice the size of *quarto* ones). The plays in it seem to be close to actors' versions, as is to be expected from editors who were fellow-workers with Shakespeare in the company of players. The version of *King Lear* in F is substantially different from the Qs. F omits about 300 lines of the Q versions, yet is close enough to reproduce some obvious errors. It contains about 110 lines which do not appear in the Qs. Possibly the compilers of F used a Q copy and altered it by comparing it with a prompter's manuscript so as to shorten it and accelerate the progress of the action. The passages which F omits are to some extent of a more philosophical nature such as might be cut from a stage version, and might in any case not be so readily remembered by anyone preparing a manuscript from a stage production.

The text of the play given here contains the passages unique to both Qs and F, and selects readings according to which give the better general sense. Occasionally readings from both F and Qs are mentioned in the notes.

A few passages of literary criticism relating to King Lear

Critics who have written about *King Lear* tend to derive from the play a complexity and profundity of thought which sometimes makes their criticism hard reading. A number of threads can be detected running through this criticism; two are the matter of Lear's and Cordelia's deaths, and the stage-worthiness of the play. Each of these is illustrated in the extracts which follow.

(a) *Dr Johnson* considered both these matters and gave a sensitive, personal view of each.

> My learned friend Mr. Warton [Joseph Warton, a contemporary poet and critic] who has, in *The Adventurer* [a periodical, 1752–4], very minutely criticized this play, remarks that the instances of cruelty are too savage and shocking, and that the intervention of Edmund destroys the simplicity of the story. These objections may, I think, be answered by repeating that the cruelty of the daughters is an historical fact, to which the poet has added little, having only drawn it into a series by

dialogue and action. But I am not able to apologize with equal plausibility for the extrusion of Gloucester's eyes, which seems an act too horrid to be endured in dramatic exhibition, and such as must always compel the mind to relieve its distress by incredulity. Yet let it be remembered that our author well knew what would please the audience for which he wrote.

The injury done by Edmund to the simplicity of the action is abundantly recompensed by the addition of variety by the art with which he is made to co-operate with the chief design, and the opportunity which he gives the poet of combining perfidy with perfidy, and connecting the wicked son with the wicked daughters, to impress this important moral, that villainy is never at a stop, that crimes lead to crimes, and at last terminate in ruin. But, though this moral be incidentally enforced, Shakespeare has suffered the virtue of Cordelia to perish in a just cause, contrary to the natural ideas of justice, to the hope of the reader, and, what is yet more strange, to the faith of chronicles. . . . A play in which the wicked prosper and the virtuous miscarry may doubtless be good, because it is a just representation of the common events of human life; but, since all reasonable beings naturally love justice, I cannot easily be persuaded that the observation of justice makes a play worse; or that, if other excellencies are equal, the audience will not always rise better pleased from the final triumph of persecuted virtue.

In the present case the public has decided. Cordelia, from the time of Tate, has always retired with victory and felicity. And, if my sensations could add anything to the general suffrage, I might relate that I was many years ago so shocked by Cordelia's death, that I know not whether I ever endured to read again the last scenes of the play till I undertook to revise them as an editor.

Samuel Johnson: *The Plays of William Shakespeare*, 1765.

(b) *Lamb* writes as follows on the same two themes:

So to see Lear acted, – to see an old man tottering about the stage with a walking-stick, turned out of doors by his daughters in a rainy night – has nothing in it but what is painful and disgusting. We want to take him into shelter and relieve him. That is all the feeling which the acting of Lear ever produced in me. But the Lear of Shakespeare cannot be acted. The contemptible machinery by which they mimic the storm which he goes out in, is not more inadequate to represent the horrors of the real elements than any actor can be to represent Lear; they might more easily propose to personate the Satan of Milton upon a stage, or one of Michael Angelo's terrible figures. The greatness of Lear is not in corporal dimension, but in intellectual: the explosions of his passion are terrible as a volcano: they are storms turning up and disclosing to the bottom that sea, his mind, with all its vast riches. It is his mind which is laid bare. This case of flesh and blood seems too insignificant to be thought on; even as he himself neglects it. On the stage we see nothing but corporal infirmities and weakness, the impotence of rage; while we read it, we see not Lear, but we are Lear, – we are in his mind, we are sustained by a grandeur which baffles the malice of daughters and storms; in the aberrations of his reason, we discover a mighty irregular power of reasoning, immethodized from the ordinary purposes of life, but exerting its powers, as the wind blows where it listeth, at will upon the corruptions and abuses of mankind. What have looks, or tones, to do with that sublime identification of his age with that of the *heavens themselves*, when, in his reproaches to them for conniving at the injustice of his children, he reminds them that 'they themselves are old'? What gesture shall we appropriate to this? What has the voice or the eye to do with such things? But the play is beyond all art, as the tamperings with it show; it is too hard and stony; it must have love-scenes and a happy ending. It is not enough that Cordelia is a daughter, she must shine as a lover too. Tate has put his hook into the nostrils of this Leviathan, for Garrick and his followers, the showmen of the scene, to draw the mighty beast about more easily. A happy ending! – as if the living martyrdom that Lear had gone through, – the flaying of his feelings alive, did not make a fair dismissal from the stage of life the only decorous thing for him. If he is to live and be happy after, if he could sustain this world's burden after, why all this pudder and preparation, – why torment us with all this unnecessary sympathy? As if the childish pleasure of getting his gilt robes and sceptre again could tempt him to act over again his misused station, – as if at his years, and with his experience, anything was left but to die.

Lear is essentially impossible to be represented on a stage.

Charles Lamb: 'On the Tragedies of Shakespeare,
considered with reference to their
fitness for Stage Representation,' 1811

(c) *A. C. Bradley*, Professor of Poetry at Oxford, published two famous lectures on *King Lear*. In them he tries to resolve certain difficulties arising from the complexity of the play and the evident injustice of its conclusion; to him it seems 'Shakespeare's greatest work, but . . . not . . . the best of his plays'.

On the one hand we see a world which generates terrible evil in profusion. Further, the beings in whom this evil appears at its strongest are able, to a certain extent, to thrive. They are not unhappy, and they have power to spread misery and destruction around them. All this is undeniable fact.

On the other hand this evil is merely destructive: it founds nothing, and seems capable of existing only on foundations laid by its opposite. It is also self-destructive: it sets those beings at enmity; they can scarcely unite against a common and pressing danger; if it were averted they would be at each other's throats in a moment; the sisters do not even wait till it is past. Finally, these beings, all five of them, are dead a few weeks after we see them first; three at least die young; the outburst of their evil is fatal to them. These also are undeniable facts; and, in face of them, it seems odd to describe King Lear as 'a play in which the wicked prosper' (Johnson).

Thus the world in which evil appears seems to be at heart unfriendly to it. And this impression is confirmed by the fact that the convulsion of this world is due to evil, mainly in the worst forms here considered, partly in the milder forms which we call the errors or defects of the better characters. Good, in the widest sense, seems thus to be the principle of life and health in the world; evil, at least in these worst forms, to be a poison. The world reacts against it violently, and, in the struggle to expel it, is driven to devastate itself.

If we ask why the world should generate that which convulses and wastes it, the tragedy gives no answer, and we are trying to go beyond tragedy in seeking one. But the world, in this tragic picture, is convulsed by evil, and rejects it.

And if here there is 'very Night herself,' she comes 'with stars in her raiment.' Cordelia, Kent, Edgar, the Fool – these form a group not less remarkable than that which we have just left. There is in the world of King Lear the same abundance of extreme good as of extreme evil. It generates in profusion selfless devotion and unconquerable love. And the strange thing is that neither Shakespeare nor we are surprised. We approve these characters, admire them, love them; but we feel no mystery. We do not ask in bewilderment, Is there any cause in nature that makes these kind hearts? Such hardened optimists are we, and Shakespeare, – and those who find the darkness of revelation in a tragedy which reveals Cordelia. Yet surely, if we condemn the universe for Cordelia's death, we ought also to remember that it gave her birth. The fact that Socrates was executed does not remove the fact that he lived, and the inference thence to be drawn about the world that produced him.

A. C. Bradley: *Shakespearean Tragedy*, 1904

(d) *Harley Granville-Barker*, a playwright and man of the theatre who was also a penetrating critic, considers the play's stage-worthiness from the point of view of a professional actor.

> Bradley and Lamb may be right in their conclusions. It is possible that this most practical and loyal of dramatists did for once – despite himself, driven to it by his unpremeditating genius – break his promise and betray his trust by presenting to his fellows a play, the capital parts of which they simply could not act. Happily for them, they and their audiences never found him out. But if Bradley is right, not the most perfect performance can be a fulfilment, can be aught but a betrayal of King Lear. There is the issue. The thing is, of course, incapable of proof. The best that imperfect human actors can give must come short of perfection, and the critic can always retort to their best that his imagination betters it. Bradley's argument is weighty. Yet – with all deference to a great critic – I protest that, as it stands, it is not valid. He is contending that a practical and practised dramatist has here written a largely impracticable play. Before condemning these 'Storm-scenes' he should surely consider their stagecraft – their mere stagecraft. For may not 'the mere dramatist' have his answer hidden there? But this – starting from his standpoint of imaginative reader – he quite neglects to do.
>
> Ought we, moreover, to assume – as Bradley seems to – that a play must necessarily make all its points and its full effect, point by point, clearly and completely, scene by scene, as the performance goes along? Not every play, I think. For the appreciation of such a work as King Lear one might even demand the second or third hearing of the whole, which the alertest critic would need to give to (say) a piece of music of like calibre. But leave that aside. No condoning of an ultimate obscurity is involved. And comedy, it can be admitted, demands an immediate clarity. Nor is the dramatist ever to be dispensed from making his story currently clear and at least provisionally significant. But he has so much more than that to do. He must produce a constant illusion of life. To do this he must, among other things, win us to something of a fellow-feeling with his characters; and even, at the play's critical moments, to identifying their emotions with our own.
>
> Now the significance of their emotions may well not be clear to the characters themselves for the moment, their only certainty be[ing] of the intensity of the emotions themselves. There are devices enough by which, if the dramatist wishes, this significance can be kept currently clear to the audience. There is the Greek chorus; the earlier Elizabethans turned Prologue and Presenters to account; the raisonneur of nineteenth century comedy has a respectable ancestry. Shakespeare was

the raisonneur in varying guises. In this very play we detect him in the Fool, and in Edgar turned Poor Tom. But note that both they and their 'reasoning' are blended not only into the action but into the moral scheme, and are never allowed to lower its emotional temperature by didactics – indeed they stimulate it. For here will be the difficulty in preserving that 'dramatic clearness' which Bradley demands; it would cost – and repeatedly be costing – dramatist and actors their emotional, their illusionary, hold upon their audience. Lear's progress – dramatic and spiritual – lies through a dissipation of egoism; submission to the cruelty of an indifferent Nature, less cruel to him than are his own kin; to ultimate loss of himself in madness. Consider the effect of this – of the battling of storm without and storm within, of the final breaking of that Titan spirit – if Shakespeare merely let us look on, critically observant. From such a standpoint, Lear is an intolerable tyrant, and Regan and Goneril have a case against him. We should not side with them; but our onlooker's sympathy might hardly be warmer than, say, the kindly Albany's.* And Shakespeare needs to give us more than sympathy with Lear, and something deeper than understanding. If the verity of his ordeal is really to be brought home to us, we must, in as full a sense as may be, pass through it with him, must make the experience and its overwhelming emotions momentarily our own.

Shakespeare may (it can be argued) have set himself an impossible task; but if he is to succeed it will only be by these means. In this mid-crisis of the play he must never relax his emotional hold on us. And all these things of which Bradley complains, the confusion of pathos, humour and sublime imagination, the vastness of the convulsion, the vagueness of the scene and the movements of the characters, the strange atmosphere and the half-realized suggestions – all this he needs as material for Lear's experience, and ours. Personally, I do not find quite so much vagueness and confusion. To whatever metaphysical heights Lear himself may rise, some character (Kent and Gloucester through the storm and in the hovel, Edgar for the meeting with the blinded Gloucester), some circumstance, or a few salient and explicit phrases will always be found pointing the action on its way. And if we become so at one with Lear in his agony that for the time its full significance escapes us, may not memory still make this clear? For that is very often true of our own emotional experiences. We are in confusion of suffering or joy at the time; only later do we realize, as we say, 'what it

....

* Whom Shakespeare carefully keeps out of the angry scenes which lead to Lear's self-banishment to the wild and the storm. (Granville-Barker's note.)

all meant to us.' It is, I suggest, this natural bent which Shakespeare turns to his account in these larger passages of King Lear. In the acting they move us profoundly. The impression they make remains. And when the play is over they, with the rest of it, should cohere in the memory, and clarify; and the meaning of the whole should be plain. Shakespeare, I protest, has not failed; he has – to the degree of his endeavour – triumphantly succeeded. But to appreciate the success and give effect to it in the play's performance we must master and conform to the stagecraft on which it depends.

In this hardest of tasks – the showing of Lear's agony, his spiritual death and resurrection – we find Shakespeare relying very naturally upon his strongest weapon, which by experiment and practice he has now, indeed, forged to an extraordinary strength, and to a suppleness besides: the weapon of dramatic poetry. He has, truly, few others of any account. In the storm-scenes the shaking of a thunder-sheet will not greatly stir us. A modern playwright might seek help in music – but the music of Shakespeare's day is not of that sort; in impressive scenery – he has none. He has, in compensation, the fluidity of move-ment which the negative background of his stage allows him. For the rest, he has his actors, their acting and the power of their speech. It is not a mere rhetorical power, nor are the characters lifted from the commonplace simply by being given verse to speak instead of con-versational prose. All method of expression apart, they are poetically conceived; they exist in those dimensions, in that freedom, and are endowed with that peculiar power. They are dramatic poetry incarnate.

Thus it is that Shakespeare can make such calls upon them as here he must. In the storm-scenes they not only carry forward the story, revealing and developing themselves as they do so, they must – in default of other means – create the storm besides. Not by detachedly describing it; if they 'lose themselves' in its description, they will for that while lose something of their own hold on us. The storm is not in itself, moreover, dramatically important, only in its effect upon Lear. How, then, to give it enough magnificence to impress him, yet keep it from rivalling him? Why, by identifying the storm with him, setting the actor to impersonate both Lear and – reflected in Lear – the storm. That, approximately, is the effect made when – the Fool cowering, drenched and pitiful, at his side – he launches into the tremendous:

> Blow, winds, and crack your cheeks! rage! blow!
> You cataracts and hurricanoes, spout
> Till you have drenched our steeples, drowned the cocks!
> You sulphurous and thought-executing fires,

> Vaunt-couriers to oak-cleaving thunderbolts,
> Singe my white head! And thou, all-shaking thunder,
> Smite flat the thick rotundity o' the world!
> Crack nature's moulds, all germens spill at once,
> That make ingrateful man!

This is no mere description of a storm, but in music and imaginative suggestion a dramatic creating of the storm itself; and there is Lear – and here are we, if we yield ourselves – in the midst of it, almost a part of it, yet Lear himself, in his Promethean defiance, still dominates the scene.

But clearly the effect cannot be made by Lamb's 'old man tottering about the stage with a walking-stick'; and by any such competitive machinery for thunder and lightning as Bradley quite needlessly assumes to be an inevitable part of the play's staging it will be largely spoiled. What actor in his senses, however, would attempt to act the scene 'realistically'? (I much doubt if any one of Lamb's detested barn-stormers ever did.) And as to the thunder and lightning, Shakespeare uses the modicum to his hand; but it is of no dramatic consequence, and his stagecraft takes no account of it.* Yet if the human Lear seems lost for a moment in the symbolic figure, here is the Fool to remind us of him:

> O nuncle, court holy-water in a dry house is better than this rain-water out o'door. Good nuncle, in, and ask thy daughters' bless-ing. Here's a night pities neither wise man nor fool.

– and to keep the scene in touch with reality. Yet note that the fantasy of the Fool only mitigates the contrast, and the spell is held unbroken. It is not till later – when Lear's defiant rage, having painted us the raging of the storm, has subsided – that Kent's sound most 'realistic' common sense, persuading him to the shelter of the hovel, is admitted.

> H. Granville-Barker: *Prefaces to Shakespeare*, 1946 edition.

(e) *L. C. Knights* sees the play as of essential significance in the civilisation which produced it, yet having the timelessness and universality of the greatest

....

* Bradley argues in a footnote that because Shakespeare's 'means of imitating a storm were so greatly inferior to ours' he could not have 'had the stage-performance only or chiefly in view in composing these scenes'. But this is surely to view Shakespeare's theatre and its craft with modern eyes. The contemporary critic would have found it easier to agree that just because your imitation storm was such a poor affair you must somehow make your stage effect without relying on it. (Granville-Barker's note.)

works of art. His arguments can only be exemplified, not followed through, in a short extract. That given here deals with the revelation of Lear's true nature and the nature of the world about him.

> Lear, at the opening of the play, is the embodiment of perverse self-will. Surrounded by obsequious flattery ('They told me I was everything'), he knows neither himself nor the nature of things. It is his human self-will that is stressed, and we need not fuss very much about the apparent absurdity of his public test of his daughters' affections in the division of the kingdom. It is a dramatically heightened example of something not uncommon – the attempt to manipulate affection which can only be freely given.

> > Which of you shall we say doth love us most?
> > That we our largest bounty may extend
> > Where nature doth with merit challenge.*

> > > > > > > > (I.i.47)

> To a demand of this kind the only honest reply is Cordelia's 'Nothing'. Now one result of perverse demands is a distorted view of the actual, and one way of discovering that your own lanthorn gives no light is, as Swift put it, by running your head into a post – something that is unquestionably there. Because Lear is perverse he is deceived by appearances; and because he allows himself to be deceived by appearances he sets in motion a sequence of events that finally brings him face to face with an actuality that can be neither denied nor disguised.

> The subsequent action of the play is designed not only to force the hidden conflict in Lear into consciousness, and, with the fullest possible knowledge of the relevant facts, to compel a choice, but to force each one of us to confront directly the question put by Lear as Everyman, 'Who is it that can tell me who I am?' One answer to that question is embodied in the group of characters who are most directly opposed to Lear. Edmund, Goneril, and Regan take their stand on the unrestrained self-seeking of natural impulse. The two daughters, by their actions, by what they say, and by the imagery of beasts of prey so consistently associated with them, represent a ferocious animality. Their indifference to all claims but those of their own egotism is made explicit by Edmund,

....

* Lear's habit of arithmetical computation of degrees of affection – Coleridge's 'debtor and creditor principles of virtue' – is amusingly illustrated in Act II, scene iv, when, after he has been rebuffed by Regan, he turns to Goneril:

> I'll go with thee:
> Thy fifty yet doth double five and twenty,
> And thou art twice her love. (Knight's note.)

who brings into the play conceptions of Nature and human nature, radically opposed to the traditional conceptions, that were beginning to emerge in the consciousness of the age. For Edmund, man is merely a part of the morally indifferent world of nature, and his business is simply to assert himself with all the force and cunning at his command: 'Thou, Nature, art my goddess' (I.ii.1); 'All with me's meet that I can fashion fit' (I.ii.169). It is into the world of indifferent natural forces, so glibly invoked by Edmund, that Lear is precipitated by a perversity of self-will that clung to the forms of human affection whilst denying the reality.

We can now see how the play at the personal or psychological level is able to bring to a focus far wider issues. Lear goes mad because he is a mind in conflict; because his conscious view of himself, to which he clings with the whole force of his personality, is irreconcilably opposed to what are in fact his basic attitudes. '"Ay" and "no" too was no good divinity' (IV.vi.99), and from the start there is 'division' in his 'kingdom'. His talk is of love and paternal care, but both his action in casting off Cordelia and – those infallible signs of what a man truly is – his assumptions as they appear in moments of emotional stress, together with his whole tone and manner, reveal a ferocious egotism. Early in the play the contrast is more than once starkly enforced.

> Here I disclaim all my paternal care,
> Propinquity and property of blood,
> And as a stranger to my heart and me
> Hold thee from this for ever. The barbarous Scythian,
> Or he that makes his generation messes
> To gorge his appetite, shall to my bosom
> Be as well neighboured, pitied, and relieved,
> As thou my sometime daughter.
>
> (I.i.109)

> Yea, is it come to this?
> Let it be so: yet have I left a daughter,
> Who, I am sure, is kind and comfortable:
> When she shall hear this of thee, with her nails
> She'll flay thy wolvish visage.
>
> (I.iv.289)

In each of these passages the implications of the opening lines collide sharply with what follows. Whatever Lear thinks of himself, one side of his nature is already committed – even before he is thrust into it – to the world that Edmund, Goneril, and Regan take for granted, a

world where everything that might conceivably be regarded as mere
sentimental illusion or the product of wishful thinking is absent, where
neither 'humane statute', custom nor religion checks the free play of
brute natural force. If Lear is ever, as Kent bids him, to 'see better',
this is the world he must see and feel in its full impact.

The storm scenes, and the scenes immediately following, represent
a twofold process of discovery – of the 'nature' without and within. No
summary can attempt to do them justice, and perhaps the best way of
indicating what goes on in them is to revert to what has been said of
Shakespeare's superb and daring technique. The effect is analogous to
that of a symphony in which themes are given out, developed, varied,
and combined. And since one of the characters goes mad, one is an
assumed madman, and one is a Fool, there is a freedom without precedent in the history of the drama – a freedom only limited by the controlling purpose of the play – to press into service all that is relevant
to the full development of the main themes.

The storm itself is vividly presented in all its power to harm; but this
is far from being the only way in which the action of Nature is brought
home to us. Part of the dramatic function of Edgar is to reinforce the
message of the storm. Disguised as one of the lowest creatures to be
found in rural England in the sixteenth century (and therefore, for the
purpose of the play, becoming one), a wandering madman and beggar,

> the basest and most poorest shape
> That ever penury, in contempt of man,
> Brought near to beast,

he brings with him continual reminders of rural life at its most exposed
and precarious – 'the winds and persecution of the sky', 'low farms,
Poor pelting villages, sheep-cotes and mills' (II.iii). When Lear with
Kent and the Fool surprises him in the hovel, he at once strikes the note
of the familiar indifference of Nature – familiar, that is, to those who
live close to nature, though not to those who, like Edmund, invoke an
abstraction that suits their bent. His talk is of cold and fire, of whirl-
pool, whirlwind and quagmire, of natural calamity and disease. Nothing
he says but has this far-reaching yet precise suggestiveness.

> Poor Tom, that eats the swimming frog, the toad, the tadpole,
> the wall-newt, and the water; that in the fury of his heart, when
> the foul fiend rages, eats cow-dung for sallets; swallows the old rat
> and the ditch-dog; drinks the green mantle of the standing pool . . .
> (III.iv.121)

This is more than a mad fantasy of an extremity of deprivation. The effect is as though the evolutionary process had been reversed to show where man as mere earth-bred creature belongs. One recalls Timon's invocation of the earth:

> Common mother, thou,
> Whose womb unmeasurable, and infinite breast,
> Teems, and feeds all; whose self-same mettle,
> Whereof thy proud child, arrogant man, is puffed
> Engenders the black toad and adder blue,
> The gilded newt and eyeless venomed worm,
> With all the abhorréd births below crisp heaven
> Whereon Hyperion's quickening fire doth shine . . .
>
> (*Timon of Athens*, IV.iii.176)

Man may indeed pride himself on the achievements of civilisation, riding 'proud of heart . . . on a bay trotting-horse over four-inched bridges' (III.iv.53), but the structure is frail; it is Tom's world that endures. 'You talk of Nature', Shakespeare seems to say, 'well, take a good look at her.' 'Still through the hawthorn blows the cold wind.'

This then is the Nature 'outside'. What of human nature, the nature within? Here too the direct revelation of the action is extended and reinforced – almost overwhelmingly so – by the poetry of allusion. A long catalogue of sins – ranging from the adulteration of beer to usury, slander, perjury, and murder – could be collected from the exchanges of Lear, Edgar, and the Fool, and as they accumulate they give a sorry enough picture of man in his meanness. But the recurring themes are lust and cruelty. Lust and cruelty are demonstrated in the action of the play; they are harped on in Edgar's 'mad' talk; they are the horrible realities that Lear discovers beneath appearances. In the great speech beginning,

> Thou rascal beadle, hold thy bloody hand!
> Why dost thou lash that whore? Strip thine own back . . .
>
> (IV.vi.154)

Lust and sadism are – with superb insight – identified. The world of appearances is based on artificial and unreal distinctions – 'Robes and furred gowns hide all'. Strip them off and you find what Lear found in the storm.

> Is man no more than this? Consider him well. Thou owest the worm no silk, the beast no hide, the sheep no wool, the cat no perfume. Ha! here 's three on 's are sophisticated. Thou art the

> thing itself; unaccommodated man is no more but such a poor,
> bare, forked animal as thou art. Off, off, you lendings! Come,
> unbutton here.
>
> (III.iv.97)

The 'thou' of that speech, the 'thing itself', is – we have just heard –
'one that slept in the contriving of lust, and waked to do it . . . false
of heart, light of ear, bloody of hand; hog in sloth, fox in stealth, wolf
in greediness, dog in madness, lion in prey' (III.iv.85). This, we may
say, is the Edmund philosophy, though presented with a violence of
realization quite foreign to the Edmund of the play. 'Lechery?' says
Lear in his madness when finally broken by the storm, 'the world of
nature is completely lustful. Let us admit it. Anything else is mere
pretence.' 'To 't, luxury, pell-mell. For I lack soldiers' (IV.vi.115).

L. C. Knights: 'King Lear', in *Some Shakespearean Themes*, 1960

(f) *J. Stampfer* wrote 'The Catharsis of *King Lear*' to show that the problem
of the play's ending is one of philosophic order as well as dramatic effect.

> . . . the ending is decisive in resolving the plethora of attitudes presented
> in the play concerning the relationship between God and man. Set side
> by side, out of context, and unrelated to the denouement, these atti-
> tudes, and their religious frames of reference, can be made to appear
> an absolute chaos. Certainly almost every possible point of view on
> the gods and cosmic justice is expressed, from a malevolent, wanton
> polytheism (IV.i.37) to an astrological determinism (IV.iii.32), from an
> amoral, personified Nature-goddess (I.ii.1) to 'high-judging Jove'
> (II.iv.224). But the very multitude, concern, and contradictory character
> of these references do not cancel each other out, but rather show how
> precarious is the concept of cosmic justice. Surely if the play's ending
> is an ending, and cosmic justice has hung in the balance with such
> matters as Goneril's cruelty (IV.ii.40–44), Gloucester's blinding
> (III.vii.67), and Edmund's death (V.iii.150), it collapses with Lear's
> ultimate question: 'Why should a dog, a horse, a rat, have life, And
> thou no breath at all?' Despite the pagan setting, the problem of
> theodicy, the justification of God's way with man, is invoked by so
> many characters, and with such concern, that it emerges as a key issue
> in the play. As such, either the denouement vindicates it, or its integrity
> is universally destroyed. In point of fact, this is implied in the deaths
> of Lear and Cordelia.
>
> The force of evil, perhaps the most dynamic element in the Christian
> tragedies, is extended to wide dimensions in *King Lear*, where two
> distinct modes of evil emerge, evil as animalism, in Goneril and Regan,

and evil as doctrinaire atheism, in Edmund. These modes are not to be confused. Goneril, in particular, is, from the point of view of conscience, an animal or beast of prey. She and Regan never discuss doctrine, as does Edmund, or offer motives, as does Iago. Their actions have the immediacy of animals, to whom consideration never interposes between appetite and deed. It is in this spirit that Lear compares Goneril, in a single scene (I.iv), to a sea-monster, a detested kite, a serpent and a wolf, and Albany, in another (IV.ii), to a tiger, a bear, a monster of the deep, and a fiend, as though, through them, animalism were bursting through civil society.

Edmund, on the other hand, is a doctrinaire atheist, with regard not only to God, but also to the traditional, organic universe, a heterodoxy equally horrifying to the Elizabethans. This doctrinaire atheism involves an issue as basic in *King Lear* as that of a retributive justice, and that is the bond between man, society and nature. Here, there is no plethora of attitudes, but two positions, essentially, that of Cordelia, and that of Edmund. Cordelia's position is perhaps best expressed by Albany, after he learns of Goneril's treatment of Lear:

> That nature which contemns its origin
> Cannot be bordered certain in itself;
> She that herself will sliver and disbranch
> From her material' sap, perforce must wither
> And come to deadly use.

> (IV.ii.32)

According to Albany, an invisible bond of sympathy binds human beings like twigs to the branches of a tree. This bond is no vague universal principle, but closely rooted in one's immediate family and society. This is natural law in its most elemental possible sense, not a moral code, but almost a biochemical reaction. Hierarchical propriety is a necessity for life, like sunlight and water, its violation an act of suicide or perversion. It is Cordelia, in response to this law, who says firmly, 'I love your Majesty According to my bond; nor more nor less' (I.i.88). This bond, the central concept of the play, is the bond of nature, made up at once of propriety and charity.

In contrast to this concept of Nature is Edmund's soliloquy affirming his doctrinaire atheism (I.ii.1–15), where natural law is summed up in two phrases, 'the plague of custom', and 'the curiosity of nations'. The bond of human relations, as understood by Cordelia and Albany, is a tissue of extraneous, artificial constraints. Edmund recognizes a hierarchy, but rather than growing out of society, this hierarchy goes wholly against its grain. This is the hierarchy of animal vitality, by 'the lusty stealth of nature', even in the act of adultery, creates more worthy issue than the 'dull, stale, tired bed' of marriage. And in response to Gloucester's superstitious references to the larger concept of the organic universe, Edmund repudiates any relationship between the 'orbs from whom we do exist' and his own destiny (I.ii.109–122).

Strangely enough, however, while the denouement seems to destroy any basis for providential justice, it would seem to vindicate Cordelia with regard to the bond of human nature. Thus, the deaths of Cornwall, Goneril, and Regan are, as Albany prophesied, the swift and monstrous preying of humanity upon itself. Cornwall is killed by his own servant; Regan is poisoned by her sister; and Goneril finally commits suicide. Even more is Cordelia vindicated in Edmund, who is mortally wounded by his brother, and then goes through a complete, and, to this reader, sincere repentance before his death. Critics have expressed bewilderment at Edmund's delay in attempting to save Lear and Cordelia. They do not, however, remark the significance of the point at which Edmund acts. For it is not until Goneril confesses the poisoning of Regan and commits suicide, thus persuading Edmund that he was loved, that he bestirs himself to save Lear and Cordelia if it is not too late. Intellectual assent is not sufficient. Only to those wholly caught up in the bond of love is charity possible:

EDMUND   Yet Edmund was beloved:
　　　　　The one the other poisoned for my sake,
　　　　　And after slew herself.
ALBANY   Even so. Cover their faces.
EDMUND   I pant for life. Some good I mean to do,
　　　　　Despite of mine own nature.

(v.iii.239)

Herein, however, lies a sardonic paradox; for Edmund deceived himself. He was the object of lust, but was not encompassed by love. Goneril slew Regan for his sake, but it was out of lust and ambition; she was incapable of that love which brings to self-transcendence, such as Cordelia's love of Lear, or his own act of 'good', in spite of his 'own nature'. And far from killing herself for Edmund's sake, she committed suicide, utterly alone, at the implicit threat of arrest for treason. Edmund, ever the doctrinaire logician, took false evidence of the bond of love at face value, and died as isolated as he lived. The two forms of evil in King Lear were ultimately opaque to one another.

But an even more sardonic paradox is implicit in Edmund's death. For Edmund, by abandoning his atheistic faith and acknowledging the power of love, accepts Cordelia's instinctual affirmation of natural law. But the denouement itself, with the gratuitous, harrowing deaths of Cordelia and Lear, controverts any justice in the universe. Chance kills, in despite of the maidenly stars. It would seem, then, by the denouement, that the universe belongs to Edmund, but mankind belongs to Cordelia. In a palsied cosmos, orphan man must either live by the moral law, which is the bond of love, or swiftly destroy himself. To this paradox, too, Shakespeare offers no mitigation in *King Lear*. The human condition is as inescapable as it is unendurable.

To so paradoxical an ending, what catharsis is possible? This question can be answered only by re-examining the structure of the plot. There can be observed, in *Hamlet*, a radical break from the mode of redemption in such earlier plays as *Romeo and Juliet*. In *Romeo and Juliet*, redemption comes when the tragic hero affirms the traditional frame of values of society, love, an appropriate marriage, peace, and the like, though society has, in practice, ceased to follow them. The result is to enhance the *sancta* of society by the sacrifice of life itself. In *Hamlet*, redemption only comes, finally, when the tragic hero spurns and transcends the *sancta* of society, and appeals to a religious mysticism into which human wisdom can have no entry, and in which, at most, 'the readiness is all'. The final result, however, is none the less the redemption of society and the reconciliation of the tragic hero to it; for Hamlet's last act is to cast a decisive vote for the next king of Denmark. Even *Othello*, domestic tragedy though it is, ends with the reconciliation of the tragic hero and society; and Othello's last act is an affirmation of loyalty to Venice and the execution of judgement upon himself. *King Lear* is Shakespeare's first tragedy in which the tragic hero dies unreconciled and indifferent to society.

J. Stampfer: 'The Catharsis of *King Lear*',
in *Shakespeare Survey 13*, 1960.

Bibliography

(1)   General Criticism; helps to the study of Shakespeare, with special
reference to *King Lear*.

Bradley, A. C.: *Shakespearean Tragedy: Lectures on 'Hamlet', 'Othello', 'King
Lear', and 'Macbeth'*, 1904. (See extract (c) in the preceding section.)

Brooke, N.: *Shakespeare: King Lear,* 1963.

Danby, J. F.: *Shakespeare's Doctrine of Nature: A Study of King Lear, 1949*.

Granville-Barker, H.: *Prefaces to Shakespeare*, 1930, 1946. (The preface on
King Lear, from which extract (d) in the preceding section is taken,
should be read from the later editions, 1946 (US) or 1958 (UK); important
changes have been introduced in these.)

Halliday, F. E.: *A Shakespeare Companion: 1564-1964*, 1964.

Halliday, F. E.: *Shakespeare and his Critics*, 1958. A survey of trends in
Shakespeare criticism.

James, D. G.: *The Dream of Learning*, 1951.

Knight, G. Wilson: *The Wheel of Fire*, 1930, 1949. Contains '*King Lear* and the
Comedy of the Grotesque'.

Leech, C.: *Shakespeare's Tragedies and other Studies in Seventeenth Century
Drama*, 1950.

Raleigh, W.: *Shakespeare*, 1907. Remains one of the best introductions to the
plays.

Ridler, A. (ed.): *Shakespeare Criticism 1919-35*, 1936.

Shakespeare Survey 13, Cambridge, 1960. This number is devoted mainly to
King Lear.

Smith, D. N. (ed.): *Shakespeare Criticism: Heminge and Condell to Carlyle*,
Oxford, 1916.

Spencer, T.: *Shakespeare and the Nature of Man*, Cambridge, 1943.

(2)   Shakespeare's Language and Imagery.

Hulme, H. M.: *Explorations in Shakespeare's Language*, 1962.

Onions, C. T.: *A Shakespeare Glossary*, Oxford, 1911, 1958.

Spurgeon, C. F. E.: *Shakespeare's Imagery and what it tells us*, Cambridge, 1935.

(3)   Sources.

Muir, K.: *Shakespeare's Sources*, vol. 1, 1957. The sources of *King Lear* are
discussed on pp. 141 ff.

(4)   The Texts of the Play.

Duthie, G. I.: *Shakespeare's King Lear*, 1949. A detailed study of the early texts. General information on the Quartos and Folios can be found in a 'companion', as in list (1) above.

(5)   The Age of Shakespeare.

Craig, H.: *The Enchanted Glass: The Elizabethan Mind in Literature*, 1936 (New York), 1950 (Oxford).
Ford, B. (ed.): *The Age of Shakespeare*, 1955 (Vol. 2 of *A Guide to English Literature*). Essays for more advanced students on many aspects of Shakespeare's age.
Lee, S. and Onions, C. T. (eds.): *Shakespeare's England: An Account of the Life and Manners of his Age*, Oxford, 2 vols., 1916.
Tillyard, E. M. W.: *The Elizabethan World Picture*, 1943.

(6)   The Theatre of Shakespeare's day.

Adams, J. C.: *The Globe Playhouse: its Design and Equipment*, Cambridge, U.S.A., 1942.
Bradbrook, M. C.: *Elizabethan Stage Conditions: A Study of their Place in the Interpretation of Shakespeare's Plays*, Cambridge, 1932.
Hodges, C. W.: *The Globe Restored: A Study of the Elizabethan Theatre*, 1953.
Shakespeare Survey 12, Cambridge, 1959. Devoted to the theatre of Shakespeare's day.

(7)   Shakespeare's Life.

Halliday, F. E.: *Shakespeare: A Pictorial Biography*, 1956.

THE TRAGEDY OF
King Lear

Dramatis Personae

LEAR, *King of Britain*
The KING OF FRANCE
The DUKE OF BURGUNDY
The DUKE OF CORNWALL, *Regan's husband*
The DUKE OF ALBANY, *Goneril's husband*
The EARL OF KENT
The EARL OF GLOUCESTER
EDGAR, *Gloucester's son*
EDMUND, *Gloucester's bastard son*
CURAN, *a courtier*
OSWALD, *Goneril's steward*
AN OLD MAN, *Gloucester's tenant*
A DOCTOR
A FOOL
AN OFFICER, *employed by Edmund*
A GENTLEMAN, *attending on Cordelia*
A HERALD
Cornwall's SERVANTS
GONERIL
REGAN   *Lear's daughters*
CORDELIA
KNIGHTS *attending on* LEAR, OFFICERS, MESSENGERS, SOLDIERS *and* ATTENDANTS

SCENE: *Britain*

The illustrations which run through the text are taken from the 1950 production of the Royal Shakespeare Company at Stratford-upon-Avon.

Lear with his daughters Goneril (left) and Regan (Act I, Scene i).

Cordelia addressing her father, King Lear (Act I, Scene i).

Gloucester discussing Edgar with Edmund (Act I, Scene ii).

I.i   After a hint about the division of the kingdom, Edmund and his origins are discussed. Then the King in audience announces that he wishes to apportion the kingdom among his three daughters. Two are married and by flattery secure their portions for themselves and their husbands. The third, Cordelia, unmarried, is too frank to earn her portion. Kent intervenes and is summarily banished. Cordelia's two suitors are summoned; one rejects her because she has lost her dowry; the other, the King of France, accepts her nevertheless. Her sisters, alone, discuss the King's imminent departure on giving up his power.

     This prologue to the play combines exposition and action: the problem is posed by a miniature representation of the events leading up to the properly extended action of the play. The squeezing of this preliminary action into small compass – too much happens in too short a time – is acceptable on the stage because the audience is aware that these close-packed events are not the tragedy but the point of departure from which the tragedy springs. And it *does* happen *Upon the gad*, as Gloucester says (I.ii.26).

1   *had more affected:* had more affection for. – The first words of the play introduce its main subject, the precariousness of Lear's decisions and the uncertainty of action springing from them.

1   *Albany,* a traditional name for the northernmost part of Britain; it has not survived in everyday use. Cornwall, the south-western part, survives in the name of a county. Dukes were given the names of the part of the kingdom they held and ruled under the King.

3   *the division of the kingdom* – Lear has evidently discussed this matter in private with Gloucester and Kent. Only later in the scene (line 32ff.) does he make a general announcement of his determination to divide the kingdom up into three parts.

5   *equalities . . . moiety:* the shares (*equalities*) are so carefully balanced (*weighed*) that close examination (*curiosity*) reveals nothing which would persuade one [duke] to prefer the other's share (*moiety*).

8   *breeding . . . charge* – He means that Edmund has been his responsibility; Edmund is Gloucester's illegitimate son.

9   *brazed:* hardened (as if covered with brass).

10   *conceive:* understand. – Gloucester picks up the word and puns on it, using it to mean 'become pregnant'.

13   *smell a fault:* suspect that there was sin. – The idea that sin has a bad smell occurs again (I.v.19, II.iv.68, and IV.vi.131, where the smell is of *mortality*).

15   *proper:* fine, good-looking.

16   *by order of law:* in the course of law, by legal means.

17   *account:* estimation.

17   *knave:* fellow – not in any bad sense but somewhat jokingly, since this is usually a word for addressing a servant.

18   *something saucily:* rather wantonly – i.e. as a result of conception out of wedlock.

20   *whoreson:* fellow – not literally 'son of a whore', although there is some play on this interpretation here.

23   *My Lord of Kent* – i.e. the Earl of Kent. Gloucester is telling Edmund his name and title.

25   *My services . . . lordship:* I am your servant, my lord.

26   *sue:* beg.

27   *study deserving:* try to deserve [your love].

28   *out:* abroad. – This explains why he has never before met so important a man as the Earl of Kent. It is also to be taken as a reason for the villainy in Edmund's character; he has not had long association with his father and brother, and his feelings of bitterness at his origins have not been checked. Worse, his father intends to send him away again.

28   *The King is coming* – The more important scenes in Shakespeare's plays often, as here, begin quietly with conversation between a small number of people and lead up to a big event; there are references to the current situation (here to the temperament of the King) which prepare for an important focal incident (here the King's announcement that he is determined to divide his kingdom).

SD   *Sennet:* a fixed set of notes played on the trumpet to announce the arrival or departure of high-ranking people.

     a coronet – This symbol of kingly power is later (I.i.134) thought of as being divided between the dukes when Lear appoints them regents. The Fool tells Lear (I.iv.144): *thou clovest thy crown i' the middle.*

30   *Attend:* Go and wait on.

King Lear ACT I scene i

A state room in King Lear's palace.

Enter KENT, GLOUCESTER, *and* EDMUND.

KENT I thought the King had more affected* the Duke of Albany* than Cornwall.

GLOUCESTER It did always seem so to us. But now, in the division* of the kingdom, it appears not which of the dukes he values most; for equalities* are so weighed that curiosity in neither can make choice of either's moiety. 5

KENT Is not this your son, my lord?

GLOUCESTER His breeding,* sir, hath been at my charge. I have so often blushed to acknowledge him that now I am brazed* to it.

KENT I cannot conceive* you. 10

GLOUCESTER Sir, this young fellow's mother could; whereupon she grew round-wombed, and had indeed, sir, a son for her cradle ere she had a husband for her bed. Do you smell a fault?*

KENT I cannot wish the fault undone, the issue of it being so proper.* 15

GLOUCESTER But I have a son, sir, by order of law,* some year elder than this, who yet is no dearer in my account.* Though this knave* came something saucily* into the world before he was sent for, yet was his mother fair. There was good sport at his making, and the whoreson* must be acknowledged. Do you 20 know this noble gentleman, Edmund?

EDMUND No, my lord.

GLOUCESTER My Lord of Kent.* Remember him hereafter as my honourable friend.

EDMUND My services* to your lordship.* 25

KENT I must love you, and sue* to know you better.

EDMUND Sir, I shall study deserving.*

GLOUCESTER He hath been out* nine years, and away he shall again. The King is coming.*

Sennet. Enter a servant bearing a coronet,* KING LEAR, CORN-WALL, ALBANY, GONERIL, REGAN, CORDELIA, *and* ATTENDANTS.

LEAR Attend* the Lords of France and Burgundy, Gloucester. 30

31   *my liege:* my sovereign lord – a title commonly used when addressing a king. The name implies an overlord to whom allegiance is to be paid.

32   *we* – an instance of the 'royal *we*' (see Introduction, p. iv).

32   *our darker purpose:* my more secret intention. – This is to give the best share of the kingdom to the daughter who loves him best. His intention to divide the kingdom is already generally known, and Goneril and Regan know what shares they can expect.

34   *fast:* fixed.

37   *Unburthened,* an old form of *unburdened.*

37   *son* – i.e. son-in-law.

39   *constant will . . . dowers:* firm intention to announce publicly (*publish*) the dowry of each of my daughters. – He hopes that by doing this he will have forestalled quarrelling over the succession and inheritance of the kingdom after his death.

41   *prevented:* forestalled.

42   *in:* for.

43   *amorous sojourn:* stay for the purpose of wooing – a rather pompous phrase which nevertheless packs a lot of meaning into a small space.

45   *us:* ourselves (i.e. 'I want to dispossess myself'). – The following word, *both,* refers to all three burdens.

46   *Interest of territory:* right to the possession of [my] lands.

49   *Where nature . . . challenge:* where the natural relationship (*nature,* that between father and child) and also merit (the affection a child should in common morality have for a parent) lay claim to (*challenge*) it (the largest division of the kingdom). – Lear has already decided to divide up his kingdom and give a third share to each of his daughters; he has even made up his mind that the most profitable share should go to Cordelia (line 82). Yet now, almost as an afterthought, he decides that merit among his daughters shall be assessed according to how much they profess to love him. We are to understand that his capriciousness and vanity have made him ask for these professions of love to justify decisions he has already made, to demonstrate that the partitioning he has planned is just and fair; he says, in effect: 'I will give the best share to the daughter who has a claim to it on her own merits as well as by right of her birth.' The merits he judges by protestations of love which he now invites from each of his daughters.

51   *wield the matter:* express. – The substance of her love is too great for the matter to be expressed in words.

52   *eye-sight, space, and liberty:* sight, the whole world of external appearances (*space*), and the freedom to enjoy it. – This is the most likely explanation, but it is hard to pin down such exaggeration to precise meanings.

54   *with* – i.e. endowed with.

55   *found:* experienced.

56   *unable:* weak – i.e. too weak for the task.

57   *all manner . . . much:* all the qualities of everything I have said (*so much*).

59   *these bounds:* this territory.

60   *shadowy:* shady. – The forests are full of trees and therefore rich in timber.

60   *champains:* open plains; *riched:* enriched.

61   *wide-skirted meads:* extensive meadows.

62   *We make thee lady:* I make you mistress, owner of all these lands (linking with *Of* at the beginning of the speech).

62   *issue:* descendants.

65   *that self metal:* the same stuff. – Metaphorical uses of the word *metal* are now normally spelt *mettle,* meaning in modern English 'quality of mind, character, courage'.

66   *prize . . . worth:* estimate myself to be her equal [in love for you].

67   *names my very . . . love:* gives expression to my own love as it really is.

68   *Only . . . profess:* except that she falls short [of my own feelings] because I profess. – Regan's language when she makes her profession of filial love is even more grotesque and exaggerated than Goneril's.

GLOUCESTER I shall, my liege.*

                                [Exeunt GLOUCESTER *and* EDMUND

LEAR Meantime we* shall express our darker* purpose.
Give me the map there. Know that we have divided
In three our kingdom; and 'tis our fast* intent
To shake all cares and business from our age,   35
Conferring them on younger strengths, while we
Unburthened* crawl toward death. Our son* of Cornwall,
And you, our no less loving son of Albany,
We have this hour a constant* will to publish
Our daughters' several dowers, that future strife   40
May be prevented* now. The princes, France and
Burgundy,
Great rivals in* our youngest daughter's love,
Long in our court have made their amorous sojourn,*
And here are to be answered. Tell me, my daughters –
Since now we will divest us* both of rule,   45
Interest* of territory, cares of state –
Which of you shall we say doth love us most?
That we our largest bounty may extend
Where nature* doth with merit challenge. Goneril,
Our eldest-born, speak first.   50

GONERIL Sir, I love you more than word can wield* the matter,
Dearer than eye-sight, space,* and liberty,
Beyond what can be valued, rich or rare;
No less than life, with* grace, health, beauty, honour,
As much as child e'er loved or father found,*   55
A love that makes breath poor and speech unable;*
Beyond all manner* of so much I love you.

CORDELIA *[Aside]* What shall Cordelia do? Love, and be silent.

LEAR *[Pointing out an area on the map]* Of all these bounds,*
even from this line to this,
With shadowy* forests and with champains* riched,   60
With plenteous rivers and wide-skirted* meads,
We make thee lady.* To thine and Albany's issue*
Be this perpetual. What says our second daughter,
Our dearest Regan, wife of Cornwall? Speak.

REGAN I am made of that self metal* as my sister,   65
And prize* me at her worth. In my true heart
I find she names* my very deed of love;
Only* she comes too short, that I profess
Myself an enemy to all other joys

70   *the most precious . . . sense:* my sensibility at its peak of perfection. – The *square* here may refer to the carpenter's set-square which is used to judge the perfection of a right angle; or it may refer to a square as a perfect geometrical figure.

71   *alone felicitate . . . love:* made happy only by loving you, my dear lord.

74   *More richer* – The 'double comparative' is not uncommon in Shakespeare, and this, the Quarto reading, may well be the correct one. It connects easily with *precious* in line 70. But the Folios read *More ponderous* ('greater in weight') here, possibly linking with *metal* in line 65.

75   *hereditary:* descendants.

76   *Remain:* let . . . remain.

77   *validity:* value; *pleasure:* delightfulness.

79   *Although . . . least* – This, the Q (Quarto) reading, is a form of a common English phrase, *last but not least,* meaning 'dealt with last but not to be taken as the least in importance because of that'.

80   *milk* – i.e. the pastures from which milk comes, as wine comes from the vineyards.

81   *to whose . . . interested* – The rulers of France and Burgundy are striving with one another to be involved in (*interested to*) Cordelia's love.

83   *Nothing* – This word is echoed in many places in the play. Cordelia is disgusted by the extravagance of her sisters' replies, and has nothing to say but this. But because she does not explain her position, her curt reply to her father sounds sullen and unfriendly; by saying it she adopts a fighting posture, confronting her sisters rather than her father. Many dramatic effects in the play depend on the impact of simple, direct language, often (as here) contrasting with fulsome exaggeration.

88   *My heart . . . mouth* – i.e. she cannot say what is in her heart, even though she is nearly choked with unhappiness.

89   *bond* – i.e. duty as a daughter to her father. She fully understands the world's moral code in this respect; it is her duty to return to her parent the affection and well-being she has received from him.

90   *mend:* amend, improve – contrasting with *mar* in the following line.

93   *Return . . . fit:* repay you by fulfilling those duties which are right and proper. – And she goes on to enumerate them; *as:* which (although in modern English *as* goes with *such* as a relative, e.g. 'These are *such* things *as* cannot be seen elsewhere').

96   *all:* entirely, only. – See also line 100 below.

96   *Haply:* Perhaps.

97   *plight:* promise, as an engagement to marry, by the holding of hands.

98   *care:* concern, attention. – See also line 109.

100   *all:* only. – Cordelia, who started speaking with one blunt word, has now shown up the hollow absurdity of her sisters' avowals of love. Did they marry so as to go on loving only their father?

104   *thy truth . . . dower:* then your truthfulness shall be your [only] dowry.

105   *the sun, The mysteries . . .* – Lear solemnly swears that all family ties between him and Cordelia are broken. He has acted in a fit of violent passion and has not paused even for a moment to consider the cool assurance and essential truth of what Cordelia has just said. The mysterious sources of nature that he mentions represent his passion in revolt against Cordelia's control. Although these passionate oaths are grandiloquent and reach beyond the reasonable limits of the situations, they sound grand and proper on the stage, his rhetoric contrasting with the simplicity and directness of Cordelia's speech. The deities he swears by also have historical propriety: the sun (Apollo) and the night (*Hecate*) were deities worshipped by the Druids, the priests of ancient Britain, Gaul and Ireland. The *mysteries of Hecate* (line 106) are the rites of that goddess, which are especially associated with ghosts, magic and witchcraft, and hence with the darkness of night.

107   *the operation of the orbs* – i.e. the influence on earthly people of the heavenly bodies in their courses. Astrology taught that the relative positions of the heavenly bodies had a meaning and gave an indication of future events; they even ruled the fate of the world and the people who lived in it.

	Which the most precious square* of sense possesses,	70
	And find I am alone felicitate*	
	In your dear highness' love.	

CORDELIA   [*Aside*] Then poor Cordelia!
And yet not so, since I am sure my love's
More richer* than my tongue.

LEAR To thee and thine hereditary* ever   75
Remain* this ample third of our fair kingdom,
No less in space, validity* and pleasure,
Than that conferred on Goneril. [*To* CORDELIA] Now, our joy,
Although the last, not least,* to whose young love
The vines of France and milk* of Burgundy   80
Strive to be interessed;* what can you say to draw
A third more opulent than your sisters? Speak.

CORDELIA Nothing,* my lord.

LEAR Nothing?

CORDELIA Nothing.   85

LEAR Nothing will come of nothing. Speak again.

CORDELIA Unhappy that I am, I cannot heave
My heart into my mouth.* I love your Majesty
According to my bond;* nor more nor less.

LEAR How, how, Cordelia! mend* your speech a little,   90
Lest it may mar your fortunes.

CORDELIA   Good my lord,
You have begot me, bred me, loved me. I
Return* those duties back as are right fit,
Obey you, love you, and most honour you.
Why have my sisters husbands, if they say   95
They love you all?* Haply,* when I shall wed,
That lord whose hand must take my plight* shall carry
Half my love with him, half my care* and duty.
Sure, I shall never marry like my sisters,
To love my father all.*   100

LEAR But goes thy heart with this?

CORDELIA   Ay, good my lord.

LEAR So young, and so untender?

CORDELIA So young, my lord, and true.

LEAR Let it be so; thy truth then be thy dower;*
For, by the sacred radiance of the sun,*   105
The mysteries of Hecate, and the night;
By all the operation of the orbs*
From whom we do exist and cease to be;

110   *Propinquity:* close relationship.
110   *property:* complete identity – even closer than relationship.
112   *Hold . . . this:* regard you from this time – connecting with *as* in the previous line.
       The barbarous . . . appetite – Latin writers use the name *Scythian* to denote the wandering tribes of people who lived north of the Black Sea in the great plains stretching to the Baltic. With them were associated acts of great barbarity. Lear also speaks of the cannibal, 'he who, to indulge his appetite, makes dishes of food (*messes*) out of his own flesh and blood (*generation*)'. It is uncertain whether *generation* means 'offspring' or 'parents' in this passage; the usual meaning is the former, but the Scythians themselves were reputed to kill and eat their parents. However, *he* in this passage does not refer to Scythians but just to cannibals in general.
116   *sometime:* former.
       The first episode is now over: Cordelia is banished from her family, and Lear's other daughters have established their rights to parts of the kingdom. Attention on the stage now moves to Kent, who pleads for Cordelia, and is himself banished from the kingdom.
117   *wrath* – i.e. the object of its wrath.
118   *set my rest:* stake everything I have – as in a card game called primero, and also: 'make my resting place'.
119   *kind nursery:* loving tender care. – *kind* implies 'loving' and also 'natural', i.e. what would be expected of relationships between members of the same family.
119   *Hence . . . sight!:* Go away, out of my sight! – This appears to be addressed to Kent, who, despite Lear's warnings, boldly moves up to him on the stage.
120   *So be . . . from her:* As my grave (i.e. death) shall be my peace, so here I take from her her father's heart. – He swears by his peace in death that he withdraws his special love from Cordelia.
121   *France* – i.e. the King of France.
121   *Who stirs:* Is no one going to move? – The courtiers are struck motionless with horror at the oath that Lear has sworn. This is the first of a number of occasions on which Lear's authority does not get him the speedy obedience he thinks he should have.
123   *digest:* amalgamate. – The share set apart for Cordelia is now going to be divided between the other two sisters.
124   *marry her:* get her a husband.
125   *invest:* endow.
126   *large effects . . . majesty:* grand things that follow in the train of (*troop with*) kingly state. But he retains (*reservation*, line 128) a hundred knights who will be at the expense of (*sustained by*) his sons-in-law when he is the guest of each for one month (*by monthly course*) by turns.
131   *additions to a king:* titles belonging to a king.
132   *sway:* control; *execution:* exercise of powers.
134   *part betwixt you:* divide between you. – The *coronet* is evidently not the King's own. The dukes make no acknowledgement of the gift, and all the attention is turned towards Kent and the King's displeasure with him.
137   *patron . . . prayers* – Those who depended on patronage for their living were expected, especially in the medieval church, to pray for the people who supported them.
138   *make from the shaft:* keep clear of the arrow – i.e. keep away; do not interfere with what I intend to do. Kent takes up Lear's image of the arrow.
139   *though . . . invade:* even though the arrow enters – Some arrows had points sticking forwards instead of barbs; these were called 'fork-heads'.
140   *be Kent . . . mad* – i.e. Kent will never be disrespectful (*unmannerly*) until Lear is mad. He implies that this will never happen, but ironically the play as it proceeds is about Lear's oncoming madness. Kent shows himself bound by his allegiance to the King, as Cordelia has revealed her belief and trust in the bond of the family (line 89).
141   *What wouldst thou do:* What are you trying to do. – Kent uses *thou, thee, thy* instead of the more respectful *you* etc. because he is speaking bluntly as an old friend.
142   *have dread:* be frightened. – Kent's *duty* is not frightened to speak when the King's power stoops (*bows*) low in the face of flattery.
144   *Reverse thy doom:* Change your judgement. – He is thinking in particular of Lear's rejection of Cordelia.

Here I disclaim all my paternal care,
Propinquity* and property* of blood,   110
And as a stranger to my heart and me
Hold* thee from this for ever. The barbarous Scythian,*
Or he that makes his generation messes
To gorge his appetite, shall to my bosom
Be as well neighboured, pitied and relieved,   115
As thou my sometime* daughter.

KENT   Good my liege –
LEAR   Peace, Kent!
Come not between the dragon and his wrath.*
I loved her most, and thought to set my rest*
On her kind nursery.* Hence,* and avoid my sight!
So be* my grave my peace, as here I give   120
Her father's heart from her! Call France.* Who stirs?*
Call Burgundy. Cornwall and Albany,
With my two daughters' dowers digest* this third.
Let pride, which she calls plainness, marry her.*
I do invest* you jointly with my power,   125
Pre-eminence, and all the large effects*
That troop with majesty. Ourself, by monthly course,
With reservation of an hundred knights
By you to be sustained, shall our abode
Make with you by due turns. Only we still retain   130
The name and all the additions* to a king;
The sway,* revénue, execution* of the rest,
Belovéd sons, be yours; which to confirm,
This coronet part betwixt you.*
KENT   Royal Lear,
Whom I have ever honoured as my King,   135
Loved as my father, as my master followed,
As my great patron* thought on in my prayers –
LEAR The bow is bent and drawn; make from the shaft.*
KENT Let it fall rather, though the fork* invade
The region of my heart; be Kent unmannerly,*   140
When Lear is mad. What wouldst thou* do, old man?
Think'st thou that duty shall have dread* to speak,
When power to flattery bows? To plainness honour's
bound,
When majesty stoops to folly. Reverse thy doom;*

145   *in thy best consideration:* in the light of your better judgement, reasoning – the opposite of the *hideous rashness.*

146   *Answer . . . judgement:* I will stake my life that I am right in my belief that . . .

149   *Reverbs no hollowness:* does not reverberate because of being hollow. – The proverb 'Empty vessels make the most noise' suggests that the greatest talkers are those with the least that is worth saying. The word *hollowness,* then, has two meanings here: (i) the literal meaning, the quality of having a thin covering with an empty space inside, like a drum, which reverberates because of its hollowness; and (ii) insincerity, the paying of empty compliments.

150   *never held . . . enemies:* never considered except as a stake to wager in contests with your enemies. – The word *wage* also suggests waging war. Kent asserts that he will always risk his life in the service of his King.

153   *still:* for ever.

154   *The true blank:* the real centre of the target. – The blank is the white spot in the centre of the target, and therefore the point to aim at; Lear should always look to Kent (for advice).

155   *Apollo* – Lear begins to swear by this pagan god of the sun, of poetry, music and healing, and Kent interrupts him. Shakespeare is concerned to give the play a pagan setting; Apollo is specifically mentioned in his sources.

156   *swear'st:* swear by.

156   *vassal:* wretch; *miscreant* may be used here in its original sense, 'unbeliever', since Kent has referred to the gods contemptuously.

161   *vent clamour:* utter noise.

162   *recreant:* traitor (cf. *miscreant,* line 156). – In the following line Lear appeals to Kent's *allegiance* to him.

165   *we durst never yet:* I have never dared to do before.

165   *strained:* excessive.

166   *our power* – i.e. his power to carry out this sentence.

167   *nor . . . nor:* neither . . . nor.

167   *place:* position as a king.

168   *Our potency made good:* (i) with my regal power still maintained; or (ii) with the power I have resigned, backed up by those to whom it has been given (i.e. Cornwall and Albany). – The first explanation is the more likely, since the theme of the speech, indeed the theme of much of this scene, is Lear's impetuousness, his readiness to do or say things without wishing to be bound by the consequences. Since he is still talking about his power (line 166) and how he cannot bear to have it compromised (line 167), he is unlikely to give his sentence (*reward*) on the basis of power which he has formally resigned.

170   *diseases:* troubles. – F has *disasters* here, but that is too strong a word for the immediate troubles that Kent will have to face. The image of sickness has already been used by Kent (lines 159–60).

173   *trunk:* body – literally the body without head or limbs, and therefore a disparaging term.

174   *Jupiter,* in Roman mythology, lord of heaven, the god who determined the course of human affairs.

177   *Freedom lives hence* – i.e. the home of freedom is elsewhere. Kent turns Lear's sentence into a paradox; it is not banishment which is elsewhere but freedom. He has kept his mind steady despite the passionate outbursts of the King; his lines from here to 183 are in rhyming couplets, a style which shows control and regularity of thought.

178   *dear:* loving.

        And in thy best consideration* check   145
        This hideous rashness. Answer my life my judgement,*
        Thy youngest daughter does not love thee least;
        Nor are those empty-hearted whose low sound
        Reverbs* no hollowness.

LEAR   Kent, on thy life, no more.

KENT My life I never held* but as a pawn   150
        To wage against thy enemies, nor fear to lose it,
        Thy safety being the motive.

LEAR   Out of my sight!

KENT See better, Lear, and let me still* remain
        The true blank* of thine eye.

LEAR Now, by Apollo —

KENT   Now, by Apollo,* King,   155
        Thou swear'st* thy gods in vain.

LEAR   O, vassal!*miscreant!*
                     [*Laying his hand on his sword*

ALBANY   }
CORNWALL } Dear sir, forbear.

KENT Do;
        Kill thy physician, and the fee bestow
        Upon the foul disease. Revoke thy doom;   160
        Or, whilst I can vent clamour* from my throat,
        I'll tell thee thou dost evil.

LEAR   Hear me, recreant!*
        On thy allegiance, hear me!
        Since thou hast sought to make us break our vow,
        Which we durst* never yet, and with strained* pride 165
        To come between our sentence and our power,*
        Which nor* our nature nor our place* can bear,
        Our potency* made good, take thy reward.
        Five days we do allot thee, for provision
        To shield thee from diseases* of the world,   170
        And on the sixth to turn thy hated back
        Upon our kingdom. If on the tenth day following
        Thy banished trunk* be found in our dominions,
        The moment is thy death. Away! By Jupiter,*
        This shall not be revoked.   175

KENT Fare thee well, King. Since thus thou wilt appear,
        Freedom* lives hence, and banishment is here.
        [*To* CORDELIA] The gods to their dear* shelter take thee, maid,
        That justly think'st and hast most rightly said!

180   *large:* grand. – May their deeds, he says, prove the sincerity of their grand speeches.
181   *effects:* realisation – contrasted with [empty] *words of love.*
183   *shape his old course:* carry on his usual way of life – presumably with special reference to
                    speaking plainly what he thinks. Kent rounds off his neat couplets with an
                    antithesis: *old course . . . country new.*
SD   *Flourish,* like the *sennet* (page 1), a passage of music blown on a trumpet to announce the
                    approach of a procession or of some important person or people.
186   *We first address:* I address myself first.
187   *rivalled:* competed – especially as between suitors for a woman.
187   *What . . . least* – i.e. What is the lowest amount you will accept as an immediate payment
                    of dowry?
190   *crave:* ask.
191   *tender:* offer, put down.
192   *hold:* esteem; *so* – i.e. dear, but with the other meaning of the word, 'of great value';
                    'while she was dear to me I took her to be worth a high dowry'.
194   *If aught . . . your grace* (line 196): [Possibly] If anything (*aught*) within that body, which
                    looks so deceptively small, or all of it, with my displeasure added to it (*pieced*)
                    and nothing more, can please (*like*) your grace by its fitness . . . – The phrase
                    little-seeming substance is difficult. It probably means 'creature which looks
                    deceptively little' and refers to Cordelia's small size and the contrast between
                    this and the monster which Lear makes her out to be. Lines 208–9 pursue the
                    hint that in Lear's eyes she is 'unnatural', not the product of benevolent
                    Nature; cf. also line 213. Elsewhere in Shakespeare, *substance* is used to apply
                    to the human body (*Macbeth* I.v.47), and it also frequently contrasts with the
                    ideas of shadow or appearance; this latter aspect links with *seeming* in the
                    present text, and we are almost certainly right in looking for an explanation
                    which brings out the antithesis of reality and appearance. Lear explains that
                    Cordelia is there as she stands, looking little but, because of her outspokenness,
                    monstrously lacking in normal filial love; nothing else can be expected of her
                    by a husband; there will be no 'dowry' except the King's displeasure. But
                    some think that the phrase refers to the *substance* of what Cordelia has said;
                    Lear then is ironically calling it *little-seeming,* i.e. trivial.
198   *owes:* has.
200   *Dowered . . . strangered:* endowed . . . disowned. – The three measured phrases, beginning
                    in the previous line, themselves sound like an imprecation.
202   *Election . . . conditions:* one [I] cannot make a choice (*Election*) on such terms.
204   *tell you:* give you an account of. – He swears by the gods (*the power that made me*) that
                    she has nothing more to give.
204   *For:* As for.
205   *I would not . . . I hate:* I do not want to stray so far away from my love of you as to give
                    you a marriage partner whom I hate. – Despite his anger, Lear again uses
                    balanced and carefully worded utterances (cf. lines 199–200 above): *your love
                    . . . I hate;* the use of *match,* literally 'find a mate, an equal', gives the sense that
                    his love for the French king would be ill-matched with his hatred of Cordelia.
206   *beseech:* I beseech.
207   *To avert your liking:* to turn your affections.
210   *your best object:* the greatest object of your love.
211   *argument:* subject.
212   *trice:* moment.

[*To* REGAN *and* GONERIL] And your large* speeches may your
deeds approve,   180
That good effects* may spring from words of love.
Thus Kent, O princes, bids you all adieu.
He'll shape* his old course in a country new.   [*Exit*

Flourish. *Re-enter* GLOUCESTER *with* FRANCE, BURGUNDY, *and*
ATTENDANTS.

GLOUCESTER Here's France and Burgundy, my noble lord.
LEAR My lord of Burgundy,   185
    We first address* towards you, who with this king
    Hath rivalled* for our daughter. What, in the least,*
    Will you require in present dower with her,
    Or cease your quest of love?
BURGUNDY   Most royal Majesty,
    I crave* no more than what your highness offered,   190
    Nor will you tender* less.
LEAR   Right noble Burgundy,
    When she was dear to us, we did hold* her so*;
    But now her price is fallen. Sir, there she stands;
    If aught* within that little-seeming substance,
    Or all of it, with our displeasure pieced,   195
    And nothing more, may fitly like your grace,
    She's there, and she is yours.
BURGUNDY   I know no answer.
LEAR Will you, with those infirmities she owes,*
    Unfriended, new adopted to our hate,
    Dowered* with our curse, and strangered with our oath,   200
    Take her, or leave her?
BURGUNDY   Pardon me, royal sir;
    Election* makes not up on such conditions.
LEAR Then leave her, sir; for, by the power that made me,
    I tell* you all her wealth. [*To* FRANCE] For* you, great king,
    I would not* from your love make such a stray,   205
    To match you where I hate; therefore beseech* you
    To avert* your liking a more worthier way
    Than on a wretch whom nature is ashamed
    Almost to acknowledge hers.
FRANCE   This is most strange,
    That she, who even but now was your best object,*   210
    The argument* of your praise, balm of your age,
    The best, the dearest, should in this trice* of time

213   *a thing . . . favour:* something so unnatural as to strip off (*dismantle*) so many layers of your favour. – The image is of a robe of honour being stripped from someone formerly loved and respected. The idea behind *monstrous* is something un-natural and forbidding; it contrasts with nature, who, Lear says, almost disclaims Cordelia as her own (lines 208–9).

214   *her offence . . . monsters it:* this offence of hers which makes it (the *thing,* line 213) appear monstrous (*monsters*) must be so grossly contrary to nature.

216   *your fore-vouched . . . taint:* the love you asserted just now must have decayed.

217   *which* – refers back to the idea that she could commit such an offence.

218   *faith:* article of faith. – He could never believe such evil of Cordelia unless it were miracu-lously revealed to him. This and the following line use the imagery of religion (*faith, reason, miracle*) to make Lear's change of attitude sound vastly impor-tant, like a conversion in religious faith. There may also be a reference here to contemporary discussions about natural religion, a Christianity depending on reasoning rather than revelation. France's hyperbole approaches very near to irony.

219   *I yet beseech . . . known* (line 222): Yet I beg your Majesty, if it (i.e. the fact that you no longer love me) is because (*If for*) I lack (*want*) the gift of glib and subtle speech to utter insincere promises (since I do what I firmly intend to do and speak afterwards), to let it be known that . . . – Compared with the confident measures of the King of France's last speech, Cordelia is cautious, even hesitant; her sentence is complex because she wants to state her case fully.

222   *that* – following on from *beseech* (line 219): I beg your Majesty . . . to let it be known that . . .

224   *dishonoured:* dishonourable.

226   *But even . . . richer:* but (I am deprived of them) just for the lack of those things without which I am the richer. – She is all the better for not having a *still-soliciting eye* (line 227), i.e. one constantly entreating, always begging for something.

229   *lost . . . liking:* ruined me in your affections.

231   *Is it but . . . to do?* (line 233): Is the case (of Cordelia's disgrace) only this, a natural holding-back (*tardiness*) which often makes no promises about (*leaves . . . unspoke*) what one intends to do?

234   *What . . . lady:* What do you think about the lady? – i.e. Will you have the lady?

235   *regards:* considerations.

236   *éntire:* essential. – This line will scan only if *entire* is stressed on the first syllable, as was common in Shakespeare's time:

Alŏof|from the ĕn|tĭre point.|Will yŏu|have hĕr?

244   *respects:* considerations (like *regards* in line 235). – Burgundy insists on the promised *portion* (line 238).

246   *Fairest . . .* – The King of France takes Cordelia when her father has rejected her as a daughter and Burgundy has refused her as a wife. The situation is paradoxical: a loved child no longer loved and a princess without inheritance. France ex-ploits this situation in his speech by playing on its contrasts in his measured lines: *rich* (to France) – *poor* (cut off by Lear); *choice* (chosen by France) – *for-saken* (rejected by the others); *loved – despised* (both these last pairs reflect the theme 'accepted – rejected'); *take – cast away; cold'st – inflamed;* and so on.

249   *Be it lawful:* if it is lawful that . . . – Perhaps he fears there may be some restraint on a suitor immediately following another.

250   *their cold'st neglect:* the coldest disregard of them (i.e. Cordelia's notices).

Commit a thing so monstrous,* to dismantle
So many folds of favour. Sure, her offence*
Must be of such unnatural degree   215
That monsters it, or your fore-vouched* affection
Fall'n into taint – which* to believe of her
Must be a faith* that reason without miracle
Could never plant in me.

CORDELIA   I yet beseech* your majesty,
If for I want that glib and oily art,   220
To speak and purpose not, since what I well intend
I'll do 't before I speak – that* you make known
It is no vicious blot, murder, or foulness,
No unchaste action, or dishonoured* step,
That hath deprived me of your grace and favour;   225
But even for want of that for which I am richer,*
A still-soliciting eye, and such a tongue
As I am glad I have not, though not to have it
Hath lost* me in your liking.

LEAR   Better thou
Hadst not been born than not to have pleased me better.   230

FRANCE   Is it but this? a tardiness* in nature
Which often leaves the history* unspoke
That it intends* to do? My Lord of Burgundy,
What say* you to the lady? Love's not love
When it is mingled with regards* that stand   235
Aloof from the éntire* point. Will you have her?
She is herself a dowry.

BURGUNDY   Royal Lear,
Give but that portion which yourself proposed,
And here I take Cordelia by the hand,
Duchess of Burgundy.   240

LEAR   Nothing; I have sworn, I am firm.

BURGUNDY   [To CORDELIA] I am sorry then you have so lost a father
That you must lose a husband.

CORDELIA   Peace be with Burgundy!
Since that respects* of fortune are his love,
I shall not be his wife.   245

FRANCE   Fairest* Cordelia, that art most rich, being poor;
Most choice, forsaken, and most loved, despised;
Thee and thy virtues here I seize upon.
Be it lawful* I take up what's cast away.
Gods, gods! 'tis strange that from their cold'st neglect*   250

251 *inflamed respect:* passionate liking. – The word *inflamed* links with *kindle*.
252 *thrown to my chance:* fallen to my lot.
254 *waterish* – both (i) well-watered, abounding in rivers, and (ii) poor in spirit; the word
        therefore plays on Burgundy as the name of a place and the name of a person.
255 *unprized precious:* unappreciated by others but precious to me. – Placing these two
        epithets together brings France to the crowning paradox.
256 *though unkind:* even though [they think you] unnaturally cruel. – France tells her to wish
        her relatives well (*Bid them farewell*) despite what they think of her. Or
        perhaps he means simply 'although they are so unkind to you'. The former
        interpretation seems closer to his ironic tone.
257 *here . . . where:* this place . . . place elsewhere.
261 *benison:* blessing.
264 *The jewels . . . you:* Cordelia, her eyes full of tears, leaves you, the jewels of our father. –
        She calls her sisters *jewels* of their father because they are so high in his esteem.
265 *what:* for what.
267 *as they are named:* by their proper names (which would be too abusive).
267 *Use:* Treat.
268 *your professèd bosoms:* the tenderness you claim to feel towards him. – She would not
        want to commit him to their true feelings.
269 *stood I:* if I stood – see Introduction, page liv.
270 *prefer:* advance – or possibly 'commend'.
272 *study:* concern, endeavour.
274 *At fortune's alms:* with an insufficient allowance of money (from fortune). – Fortune is
        not giving big rewards by way of dowry but only small amounts like alms for
        charity.
274 *scanted:* withheld.
275 *well are . . . wanted:* well deserve to go without what you have not got. – This must refer
        to the love and blessing she would have expected from her father (line 261).
276 *plighted:* folded – and therefore concealed, dissembling. (*Plight* and *pleat* are related
        forms.)
277 *Who:* those who.
277 *them derides:* laughs them to scorn. – In the end shame laughs to scorn those who try to
        hide their faults by dissimulation.
280 *appertains to:* concerns.
280 *hence:* move away. – Goneril turns without compunction to the practical problem of their
        father's accommodation.
285 *too grossly:* very obviously.

My love should kindle to inflamed* respect.
Thy dowerless daughter, King, thrown to my chance,*
Is queen of us, of ours, and our fair France.
Not all the dukes of waterish* Burgundy
Can buy this unprized* precious maid of me.   255
Bid them farewell, Cordelia, though unkind;*
Thou losest here, a better where* to find.

LEAR   Thou hast her, France; let her be thine, for we
Have no such daughter, nor shall ever see
That face of hers again. Therefore be gone   260
Without our grace, our love, our benison.*
Come, noble Burgundy.

[*Flourish. Exeunt all but* FRANCE, GONERIL, REGAN, *and*
CORDELIA

FRANCE   Bid farewell to your sisters.
CORDELIA   The jewels* of our father, with washed eyes
Cordelia leaves you. I know you what* you are;   265
And, like a sister, am most loath to call
Your faults as they are named.* Use* well our father;
To your professéd* bosoms I commit him;
But yet, alas, stood* I within his grace,
I would prefer* him to a better place.   270
So farewell to you both.

REGAN   Prescribe not us our duties.
GONERIL   Let your study*
Be to content your lord, who hath received you
At fortune's alms.* You have obedience scanted,*
And well are worth the want* that you have wanted.   275
CORDELIA   Time shall unfold what plighted* cunning hides;
Who* covers faults, at last shame them derides.*
Well may you prosper!

FRANCE   Come, my fair Cordelia.
[*Exeunt* FRANCE *and* CORDELIA

GONERIL   Sister, it is not a little I have to say of what most nearly
appertains* to us both. I think our father will hence* tonight.   280
REGAN   That's most certain, and with you; next month with us.
GONERIL   You see how full of changes his age is; the observation we
have made of it hath not been little. He always loved our
sister most; and with what poor judgement he hath now
cast her off appears too grossly.*   285

286   *he hath . . . himself:* he has always (*ever*) understood his own nature only (*but*) superficially.

288   *his time:* the years of his life; *rash:* hot-headed.

289   *look:* expect; *alone:* just.

290   *long . . . condition:* deeply rooted habits of mind; *therewithal:* along with it.

293   *unconstant starts:* unexpected impulses; *like:* likely.

295   *compliment:* ceremony, formality.

296   *hit:* come to an agreement.

297   *carry authority . . . bears:* continues to exercise his authority with the sort of temperament (*dispositions*) he has [just now] shown. – He has supposedly abdicated, yet he has exercised total authority over his youngest daughter.

298   *last surrender:* recent renunciation [of his kingly power]; *offend us:* do us harm. – Goneril is afraid that, if the King's capriciousness continues, what looked like good fortune to them – a half share each of the kingdom – might bring nothing but trouble.

300   *i' the heat:* at once, 'while the iron is hot'. – It is characteristic of Goneril to press for action; throughout the scene she has dominated Regan.

I.ii   Gloucester finds Edmund reading a fake letter supposedly written by Edgar and threatening their father's life. Edmund persuades his father that Edgar is plotting to kill him. And he also deceives Edgar into thinking he must take shelter from his father's anger.
  Here the Gloucester plot starts in real earnest. It is loosely linked with the Lear plot, and is in the play to give it variety and complexity of interest which the Lear plot alone would inevitably lack. More important, it and the Lear plot illuminate each other, the Gloucester plot being a somewhat conventional display of villainy and gullibility, the Lear plot a tragic view of the consequences of a capricious and ill-judged action, unrelieved by the balancing conventions of justice and retribution. The improbabilities of the action in this scene do not merit separate study: why does Edgar supposedly write to Edmund, since they live together? Where is the *lodging* of Edmund which Edgar is to hide in?

1   *nature* – In committing himself to nature, not God, Edmund is preparing the audience for his villainy; 'you see as soon as a man cannot reconcile himself to reason, how his conscience flies off by way of appeal to Nature' (Coleridge). Also Edmund is a 'natural' son, i.e. born of parents who were not married.

2   *bound:* under obligation – as a servant was *bound* to his master.

2   *Wherefore . . . custom:* Why should I be subject to the curse of custom. – This is the custom by which the elder son takes precedence over the younger; even if Edmund were legitimate, he would not inherit from his father because he is a younger son.

4   *curiosity of nations:* people's over-fussiness in matters of detail; *deprive me:* keep from me what I should otherwise have.

5   *For that:* because; *moonshines:* months.

6   *Lag of:* behind (in years).

6   *bastard . . . base* – An illegitimate child was assumed to be low and vile; Edmund speaks as if the word *base* were connected etymologically with *bastard* (see also line 10).

7   *dimensions:* bodily parts; *compact:* put together.

8   *generous:* high-born, gallant; *true:* well proportioned.

9   *honest madam's issue:* the children of a chaste woman (born only to her husband). – The use of *madam* is ironic.

9   *Why . . . With base:* Why do people call us [bastards] base? – The use of *brand* recalls the marking of men and animals with a sign on their skins.

11   *in the lusty . . . nature:* in the secrecy of full-blooded nature. – The idea once again is of the 'natural' child being born to secret, passionate lovers.

12   *More composition . . . quality:* better physique and greater energy. – He implies that the strains are mixed but the mixture is better.

13   *doth, within . . . Go . . . –* The subjects are *composition* and *quality*; the words *dull, stale, tired* refer to the occupants of the marriage bed.

14   *fops:* fools.

15   *Got:* begotten.

16   *I must:* I am determined to.

REGAN 'Tis the infirmity of his age; yet he hath ever* but slenderly
known himself.

GONERIL The best and soundest of his time* hath been but rash;* then
must we look* to receive from his age not alone* the imper-
fections of long ingrafted condition,* but therewithal* the   290
unruly waywardness that infirm and choleric years bring
with them.

REGAN Such unconstant starts* are we like* to have from him as this
of Kent's banishment.

GONERIL There is further compliment* of leave-taking between France   295
and him. Pray you, let's hit* together: if our father carry
authority* with such dispositions as he bears, this last surrender* of his will but offend us.

REGAN We shall further think on 't.

GONERIL We must do something, and i' the heat.*   300

[Exeunt

scene ii

The Earl of Gloucester's castle.

Enter EDMUND, *with a letter.*

EDMUND Thou, nature,* art my goddess; to thy law
My services are bound.* Wherefore should I
Stand in the plague of custom,* and permit
The curiosity* of nations to deprive* me,
For that* I am some twelve or fourteen moonshines*   5
Lag* of a brother? Why bastard?* wherefore base?
When my dimensions* are as well compact,
My mind as generous* and my shape as true,
As honest madam's issue?* Why* brand they us
With base? with baseness? bastardy? base, base?   10
Who in the lusty* stealth of nature take
More composition* and fierce quality
Than doth,* within a dull, stale, tired bed
Go to the creating a whole tribe of fops*
Got* 'tween asleep and wake? Well then,   15
Legitimate Edgar, I must* have your land.

17   *is to:* is the same towards.
19   *speed:* is successful.
20   *my invention thrive:* my device succeed.
21   *top the* – The earliest editions have other words here which do not make good sense (Q – *tooth'*; F – *to'th'*); *top*, 'get the better of', is likely in view of the contrast with *base* in the preceding line and the extension to *grow* in this line.

For the villain to finish a self-revelatory speech with such ejaculations as *I grow; I prosper* is in the tradition of tragic drama. There is an English saying: 'Pride comes before a fall'.

23   *in choler parted:* left in anger. – *Choler* originally meant stomach bile, one of the four principal fluids in animal bodies. A person's disposition was said to be dependent upon the relative proportions of these fluids in the body; a superfluity of choler made a person quick to anger. Hence *choler* and *anger* came to be nearly synonymous.

The King of France was evidently angry because of some further insult to Cordelia. Although he is later reported to be *hot-blooded* (II.iv.208), he was calm and controlled when he last appeared; but we know he met Lear again before he left with Cordelia (I.i.295).

24   *tonight:* last night; *subscribed:* given up.
25   *Confined to exhibition:* restricted to an allowance of money [for his personal expenses]. – He has given all his possessions to his sons-in-law and will have only an allowance to live on. (A minor scholarship in some British schools and universities is still called an *exhibition*.)
26   *Upon the gad:* on the spur of the moment. – A gad, like a spur, is a sharp point; to act suddenly is to act as if pricked by a sharp point.
26   *how now:* how are things. – He has taken some time to notice Edmund, time enough to give his summary of the situation.
32   *dispatch:* quick putting away. – There is also a possible play of words on *dispatch* associated with the sending of letters. The whole of Gloucester's speech here has an ironic tone.
33   *nothing* – There has already been considerable use of the word *nothing* after Cordelia's declaration (I.i.83).
37   *o'er-read:* read through.
37   *for so much as:* as far as.
38   *o'erlooking:* reading through.
39   *sir* – Gloucester calls his son 'sir' in an attempt to exert his authority.
40   *to detain or give it:* by keeping it back or giving it up.
41   *to blame:* blameworthy, objectionable.
44   *essay or taste:* trial, test. – The image of tasting is furthered with *bitter* (45) and *relish* (47) below.
45   *This policy . . . age:* The policy of paying great respect to old age. – The word *policy* suggests that it is all a trick played by old people to win respect.
46   *the best of our times:* the best years of our lives.
47   *relish:* enjoy; *idle and fond:* unprofitable and foolish.
48   *of aged tyranny:* by a tyrannical old man – i.e. their father, Gloucester himself.
48   *who sways . . . suffered:* who rules not by the strength it (*the oppression*) has, but by the way we tolerate it.
50   *sleep till I waked him* – i.e. sleep to eternity, die. The viciousness of this remark and indeed the whole letter may seem almost melodramatic to us today; but bitter struggles to the death between members of a family, arising from dynastic quarrels, were not uncommon in Shakespeare's day and later. They are a feature of medieval European history.
51   *should:* would.

Our father's love is to* the bastard Edmund
As to the legitimate; fine word, 'legitimate'!
Well, my legitimate, if this letter speed*
And my invention* thrive, Edmund the base   20
Shall top* the legitimate. I grow; I prosper.
Now, gods, stand up for bastards!

Enter GLOUCESTER.

GLOUCESTER Kent banished thus! and France in choler* parted!
And the king gone tonight!* subscribed his power!
Confined to exhibition!* All this done   25
Upon the gad!* – [*He notices* EDMUND] Edmund, how now!*
what news?

EDMUND So please your lordship, none.
                              [*Pocketing the letter ostentatiously*

GLOUCESTER Why so earnestly seek you to put up that letter?

EDMUND I know no news, my lord.

GLOUCESTER What paper were you reading?   30

EDMUND Nothing, my lord.

GLOUCESTER No? What needed then that terrible dispatch* of it into your
pocket? The quality of nothing* hath not such need to hide
itself. Let's see; come, if it be nothing, I shall not need
spectacles.   35

EDMUND I beseech you, sir, pardon me. It is a letter from my brother,
that I have not all o'er-read;* and for so much* as I have
perused, I find it not fit for your o'erlooking.*

GLOUCESTER Give me the letter, sir.*

EDMUND I shall offend, either to detain* or give it. The contents, as   40
in part I understand them, are to blame.*

GLOUCESTER Let's see, let's see.

EDMUND I hope, for my brother's justification, he wrote this but as
an essay* or taste of my virtue.

GLOUCESTER [*Reads*] *This policy* and reverence of age makes the world bitter*   45
to the best of our times; keeps our fortunes from us till our*
oldness cannot relish them. I begin to find an idle and fond*
bondage in the oppression of aged tyranny; who sways,* not*
as it hath power, but as it is suffered. Come to me, that of
this I may speak more. If our father would sleep till I waked*   50
him, you should enjoy half his revenue for ever, and live*
the beloved of your brother, EDGAR. Hum! Conspiracy! –
'Sleep till I waked him, you should enjoy half his revenue!'
– My son Edgar! Had he a hand to write this? a heart

58   *casement:* window; *closet:* private room.
59   *character:* handwriting.
60   *matter:* subject-matter.
60   *durst:* would dare.
61   *that* – i.e. the matter.
61   *fain:* gladly – see Introduction, p. li.
65   *heretofore sounded you in:* approached you before now about . . . – Gloucester, like the
        worried man he is, alternates questions with statements of opinion; Edmund's
        pretence is carried through faultlessly.
68   *the father . . . son* – i.e. instead of the son being *ward* to his father, an adolescent still under
        the care of a guardian.
71   *Unnatural* – Gloucester calls Edgar 'unnatural' because it was commonly held in Shake-
        speare's day that the course of nature was beneficial. See Introduction, p. liv,
        for a more detailed account of the concept of nature in the play.
72   *sirrah* – see Introduction, p. lii.
72   *apprehend:* seize, arrest.
74   *If it shall please you:* If you would kindly agree.
76   *you should . . . course:* you would be taking a safe course. – Edmund understandably does
        not want Edgar and Gloucester to meet at this stage in his plot.
77   *where:* whereas.
80   *pawn down:* stake (in a wager).
80   *wrote,* for *written; feel:* try out, test.
81   *pretence of danger:* dangerous intention.
84   *meet:* fitting. – To gain his ends, Edmund now speaks to his father with the greatest
        deference, using ingratiating forms of address: *your honour,* etc.
85   *auricular:* aural, perceived by the ear. – Edmund's pompous phraseology contributes to
        the deferential manner.
91   *wind me into him:* worm your way into his confidence on my behalf [so that you can inform
        against him].
92   *frame . . . after:* manage the affair according to . . .
93   *unstate . . . resolution:* (even) give up my rank in order to be quite certain about this.
94   *presently* – see Introduction, p. lii; *convey the business:* manage the matter in secret.
95   *withal:* with it.
96   *These late eclipses . . . (late:* recent) – In Shakespeare's day it was very commonly thought
        that the positions of the stars and planets in the sky indicated good or bad
        fortune on earth. Eclipses were considered to be particularly unlucky. The
        reasoning behind this firm belief in astrology was associated with the contem-
        porary concept of order. The orderly movement of the heavenly bodies
        reflected and was reflected by the orderly structure of things in nature on
        earth: the sequence of day and night and of the seasons, the social order by
        which the great, in successive ranks, ruled over the less, and so on; all these
        things were taken as manifestations of an ordered creation. An eclipse of the
        sun resulted in the 'confusion' of day and night, and therefore evidently broke
        the natural order of things; it could only be a reflection of other confusions in
        the order of nature, Gloucester begins to consider the father-son relationship,
        where, in the natural order of things, the son should honour his father; it is
        on this point that Edmund has sown the seeds of grave suspicion in Gloucester's
        mind. Gloucester is aware (line 97) that there may be a good scientific explana-
        tion for eclipses, but his fears nevertheless abound.
        There was an eclipse of the sun in October 1605, but reasons for connecting
        it with this passage (as some editors do) are unconvincing; the practice of
        astrology was universally current, and phenomena in the skies were recorded
        from early times.

and brain to breed it in? When came this to you? Who   55
brought it?

EDMUND   It was not brought me, my lord; there's the cunning of it;
I found it thrown in at the casement* of my closet.*

GLOUCESTER   You know the character* to be your brother's?

EDMUND   If the matter* were good, my lord, I durst* swear it were his;   60
but, in respect of that,* I would fain* think it were not.

GLOUCESTER   It is his.

EDMUND   It is his hand, my lord; but I hope his heart is not in the
contents.

GLOUCESTER   Has he never heretofore* sounded you in this business?   65

EDMUND   Never, my lord. But I have heard him oft maintain it to be
fit that, sons at perfect age, and fathers declined, the father
should be as ward to the son,* and the son manage his
revenue.

GLOUCESTER   O villain, villain! His very opinion in the letter! Abhorred   70
villain! Unnatural,* detested, brutish villain! worse than
brutish! Go, sirrah,* seek him; I'll apprehend* him; abomin-
able villain! Where is he?

EDMUND   I do not well know, my lord. If it shall please* you to suspend
your indignation against my brother till you can derive from   75
him better testimony of his intent, you should run a certain
course;* where,* if you violently proceed against him, mis-
taking his purpose, it would make a great gap in your own
honour and shake in pieces the heart of his obedience. I dare
pawn down* my life for him that he hath wrote* this to feel*   80
my affection to your honour and to no further pretence* of
danger.

GLOUCESTER   Think you so?

EDMUND   If your honour judge it meet,* I will place you where you
shall hear us confer of this, and by an auricular* assurance   85
have your satisfaction; and that without any further delay
than this very evening.

GLOUCESTER   He cannot be such a monster –

EDMUND   Nor is not, sure.

GLOUCESTER   – to his father, that so tenderly and entirely loves him.   90
Heaven and earth! Edmund, seek him out; wind* me into
him, I pray you: frame* the business after your own wisdom.
I would unstate* myself to be in a due resolution.

EDMUND   I will seek him, sir, presently,* convey* the business as I
shall find means, and acquaint you withal.*   95

GLOUCESTER   These late eclipses* in the sun and moon portend no good to

97   *the wisdom . . . thus:* rational scientific knowledge can give various reasons for it (the
                phenomenon).
98   *yet nature . . . effects:* yet the natural world, mankind, is afflicted with the results that
                follow (*sequent*). – In other words, the rational explanation of eclipses does not
                prevent disasters from happening (in Gloucester's belief) as a result.
99   *friendship falls off:* the bonds of friendship are weakened.
99   *brothers divide* – The order in the state itself reflects and is reflected by the order in the
                family. Both the phrases in this declaration end with a mention of the family;
                the second is fittingly a reference to the filial bond.
100   *mutinies:* discord, civil strife.
103   *falls . . . nature:* betrays his natural instincts; *bias:* bent, the way something normally
                tends to move. – The image is taken from the game of bowls: to make the game
                interesting, bowls were unevenly weighted so that the player had to take into
                account a tendency of the bowl to swing to the right or left as it moved along
                the ground. Gloucester is very clear-headed about the King's *bias of nature*
                but fails to see similar tendencies in himself; through superstitious beliefs he
                condemns his son without any sort of trial.
104   *hollowness:* insincerity.
105   *disorders:* disorderly practice. – The image of physical sickness here is extended to the end
                of the sentence; but just as important is its reference to nature. Nature is by
                rights orderly and works for good; but 'unnatural' events, such as eclipses,
                symbolise a violation of the natural order and bring disasters with them, and
                even the grave seems to promise no peace (*disquietly*).
106   *Find out:* Expose.
109   *foppery:* stupidity.
110   *sick in fortune:* in trouble.
110   *surfeit:* natural unhappy outcome. – Our behaviour in excess (*surfeit*) 'spills over' into
                unhappy results.
111   *make guilty . . . sun:* put the blame for our troubles on the sun. – Edmund is here criticising
                astrology, the study of the ways in which stars are supposed to influence
                human life on the earth. But there is irony in his use of the word *disaster:* this
                comes from Latin *dis astre*, meaning 'unfavourable star', so that despite what
                he is saying he is implying a link between stars and human calamity.
113   *treachers:* traitors.
114   *spherical predominance:* the ascendancy of a planet. – Astrologers paid special attention
                to the constellations which were most evident at a man's birth. It was thought
                that much could be read of his character and the way he would develop from
                looking at the stars and planets in this way. The system drew heavily on the
                symbolism of the Zodiac, which people thought had a great influence on their
                lives.
115   *of:* to.
116   *a divine thrusting-on:* supernatural impulse.
117   *of whoremaster man:* by man the fornicator.
117   *goatish:* lustful. – Edmund is saying satirically: it is a fine evasion by man, with all his
                sexual desires, to blame (*lay . . . to the charge of*) his lustful disposition on a star.
118   *compounded:* made terms.
119   *the dragon's tail* – People born when the constellation Draco is high in the sky were thought
                to be especially rough.
120   *Ursa major*, the sign of the Great Bear, a constellation in the northern sky. – Its influence
                was thought of as making people especially lustful.
120   *Fut:* Pooh! – an expression of contempt.
121   *that:* what.
122   *bastardizing:* conception outside marriage.
123   *pat:* just at the right moment. – In the 'catastrophes' of the old-style comedies something
                happened to solve a difficulty at the moment it was most needed. The reference
                to old comedies is a measure of the subtlety and sophistication of Shakespeare's
                own plays; *Lear* is an example of a play in which tragic complications are not
                resolved by events taking place at the 'right' moment.
124   *cue:* hint as to how to act [in this situation]. – *Cue* is a theatrical term and thus links with
                the reference to *comedy*. Edmund's pose is to be the mood of melancholy, i.e.
                pensive sadness; *villainous* is a pun: (i) 'extreme' and (ii) 'evil', connecting
                with Edmund's self-revelation earlier in the scene (I.ii.1–22).

us. Though the wisdom of nature* can reason it thus and
thus, yet nature finds itself scourged* by the sequent effects:
love cools, friendship falls off,* brothers divide;* in cities,
mutinies;* in countries, discord; in palaces, treason; and the   100
bond cracked 'twixt son and father. This villain of mine
comes under the prediction; there's son against father. The
King falls from bias of nature;* there's father against child.
We have seen the best of our time: machinations, hollowness,* treachery and all ruinous disorders* follow us dis-   105
quietly to our graves. Find out* this villain, Edmund; it shall
lose thee nothing; do it carefully. And the noble and true-
hearted Kent banished! his offence, honesty! 'Tis strange.   '
                                                          [*Exit*

EDMUND This is the excellent foppery* of the world, that when we
are sick in fortune* – often the surfeit* of our own behaviour –   110
we make guilty* of our disasters the sun, the moon and the
stars; as if we were villains by necessity, fools by heavenly
compulsion; knaves, thieves and treachers* by spherical
predominance;* drunkards, liars and adulterers by an
enforced obedience of* planetary influence; and all that we   115
are evil in, by a divine thrusting-on.* An admirable evasion
of whoremaster man,* to lay his goatish* disposition to the
charge of a star! My father compounded* with my mother
under the dragon's tail,* and my nativity was under *Ursa
major*;* so that it follows I am rough and lecherous. Fut!*   120
I should have been that* I am, had the maidenliest star in the
firmament twinkled on my bastardizing.* Edgar –

Enter EDGAR.

[*Aside*] And pat* he comes like the catastrophe of the old
comedy. My cue* is villainous melancholy, with a sigh like

125 *Tom o' Bedlam:* madman. – *Bedlam* comes from *Bethlehem*; the London hospital for
        lunatics began in the priory of St Mary of Bethlehem. It seems that some of the
        beggars in the London streets were lunatics released from Bedlam, or pre-
        tended to be so. Here the reference is to the sighing of such a beggar, which
        catches the attention of passers-by. Later (II.iii) Edgar himself assumes the
        disguise of a Bedlam beggar.

126 *fa, sol . . .* – Notes in the musical scale; he sings to give the impression that he has not
        heard Edgar coming. He may also be punning on the word *divisions*: (i) cleav-
        ages in families, and so on (as in lines 99ff.), and (ii) embellished melodies in
        music. The use of the word may have suggested to him that singing would
        help cover up his wicked plans.

129 *this other day:* the other day. – He is determined to exploit to the full the supposed implica-
        tions of eclipses, which he has been ridiculing.

132 *he writ of:* he [the writer of the alleged prediction] wrote about.

132 *succeed unhappily:* are coming true with terrible results.

133 *unnaturalness* – See the note on line 71 above.

134 *dissolutions . . . amities:* the breaking up of old-established ties of friendship.

136 *diffidences:* suspicions.

136 *dissipation of cohorts:* (perhaps) wastage of personnel in the army divisions, e.g. by deser-
        tion. – But since the subject seems out of place here, the text as we have it is
        probably faulty.

138 *sectary astronomical:* student of astrology. Astronomy seems not to have been studied
        independently of the supposed influence of the stars on human affairs. Edgar's
        question is slightly barbed, and Edmund now turns to attack.

141 *Spake you:* Did you speak. – Cf. *Parted you* (line 143): Did you part; *Found you:* Did you find.
        See Introduction, p. li.

142 *two hours together:* for a full two hours.

146 *Bethink yourself wherein:* Try to think in what way.

147 *forbear his presence:* keep out of his way.

148 *qualified:* moderated.

149 *with the mischief . . . allay:* it would hardly stop at actual bodily injury (*mischief*) to you.

152 *have a continent forbearance:* restrain yourself and keep out of his way. Cf. *forbear,* line 147.

153 *as I say:* my advice to you is.

154 *lodging* – In a large castle-like building, wings containing the private apartments of the
        family could be very much apart from the main military area, and self-
        contained.

154 *fitly:* at the right time.

155 *Pray ye:* I beg you.

156 *stir abroad:* move about away from home.

159 *meaning:* intention.

160 *faintly . . . horror of it:* toned down, not approaching the horror of a full description of it.

162 *anon:* shortly. – Edgar is now really worried.

Tom o' Bedlam.* [*Aloud*] O, these eclipses do portend these   125
divisions! fa, sol, la, mi.*

EDGAR   How now, brother Edmund! What serious contemplation
are *you* in?

EDMUND   I am thinking, brother, of a prediction I read this other day,*
what should follow these eclipses.   130

EDGAR   Do you busy yourself about *that*?

EDMUND   I promise you, the effects he writ of* succeed unhappily;* as
of unnaturalness* between the child and the parent; death,
dearth, dissolutions of ancient amities;* divisions in state;
menaces and maledictions against king and nobles; needless   135
diffidences,* banishment of friends, dissipation of cohorts,*
nuptial breaches, and I know not what.

EDGAR   How long have you been a sectary astronomical?*

EDMUND   Come, come; when saw you my father last?

EDGAR   Why, the night gone by.   140

EDMUND   Spake you* with him?

EDGAR   Ay, two hours together.*

EDMUND   Parted you in good terms? Found you no displeasure in him
by word or countenance?

EDGAR   None at all.   145

EDMUND   Bethink* yourself wherein you may have offended him; and
at my entreaty forbear his presence* till some little time hath
qualified* the heat of his displeasure, which at this instant
so rageth in him that with the mischief* of your person it
would scarcely allay.   150

EDGAR   Some villain hath done me wrong.

EDMUND   That's my fear. I pray you, have a continent forbearance* till
the speed of his rage goes slower, and, as I say,* retire with
me to my lodging,* from whence I will fitly* bring you to
hear my lord speak. Pray ye,* go; there's my key; if you do   155
stir abroad,* go armed.

EDGAR   Armed, brother!

EDMUND   Brother, I advise you to the best. Go armed. I am no honest
man if there be any good meaning* towards you. I have told
you what I have seen and heard – but faintly,*nothing like   160
the image and horror of it. Pray you, away.

EDGAR   Shall I hear from you anon*?

EDMUND   I do serve you in this business.   [*Exit* EDGAR
A credulous father, and a brother noble,
Whose nature is so far from doing harms   165
That he suspects none; on whose foolish honesty

167   *practices:* evil designs. *ride.* – He thinks of Edgar as a patient horse.
167   *I see the business:* I have it all planned [in my mind].
168   *wit:* cunning.
169   *All with me . . . fit:* everything that suits my purposes (*can fashion fit*) is justified (*meet*). –
         This is another declaration of evil intent, winding up the scene in a rhymed
         couplet on a theme with which it began.

I.iii.   Goneril, who now has Lear staying with her, tells her steward to make him and his
         retainers increasingly unwelcome and uncomfortable; for Lear wants to continue to
         exercise kingly power even though he says he has relinquished it.
           The first two scenes of the play launched the Lear and the Gloucester plots by giving a
         concentrated form of action serving the purpose of exposition. In this scene the proper
         action of the play begins; it is a close-up view of a trivial incident for which the motivation
         has been clear in the summary action of scene i.

1   *for chiding . . . fool:* because he [the gentleman] scolded his [Lear's] clown, the Fool. – The
            Fool must have made some caustic remark which offended Goneril's attendant.
5   *sets . . . odds:* causes strife amongst us all.
6   *himself:* he himself.
9   *come slack . . . services:* become less efficient as a servant to him than you have been.
10   *answer:* be responsible for.
11 SD   *within* – i.e. at the back of the stage. Horns were blown to signal the approach of a hunt;
            their sound here shows that the King is returning from hunting, and will there-
            fore be tired and in need of good service.
12   *Put on:* Assume.
13   *I'd . . . question:* I want it [the negligence] to come to the point where it is noticed and
            discussed.
14   *distaste:* dislikes; *let him:* let him go.
16   *Idle:* Foolish – because he wants to continue to wield the power he has given up.
19   *must be used . . . abused:* must be treated with reproofs (*checks*) just as much as gestures of
            flattering kindness, when these [gestures of kindness] are plainly being
            abused. – But *they* may refer to *Old fools*, in which case the sentence would
            mean: . . . 'when these old fools are obviously being deluded'. The general
            drift is that Goneril is finding excuses to get her father out of the way, and is
            trying to justify to herself the acts of harshness she contemplates towards him.
24   *grows:* comes.
25   *occasions . . . speak:* opportunities . . . for speaking out. – She wants situations to arise in
            which she can give vent before others to the feelings she has already expressed
            in private.
26   *straight:* at once.
27   *To hold . . . course:* [telling her] to keep to the same course as I do, to do exactly as I do.

My practices* ride easy. I see the business.*
Let me, if not by birth, have lands by wit;*
All with me*'s meet that I can fashion fit.

[*Exit*

scene iii

A room in the Duke of Albany's palace.

Enter GONERIL *and* OSWALD, *her steward.*

GONERIL   Did my father strike my gentleman for chiding* of his fool?
OSWALD   Yes, madam.
GONERIL   By day and night he wrongs me; every hour
He flashes into one gross crime or other
That sets us all at odds.* I'll not endure it.   5
His knights grow riotous, and himself* upbraids us
On every trifle. When he returns from hunting,
I will not speak with him. Say I am sick.
If you come slack* of former services,
You shall do well; the fault of it I'll answer.*   10
OSWALD   He's coming, madam; I hear him.   [*Horns within**
GONERIL   Put on* what weary negligence you please,
You and your fellows; I'd have it come to question.*
If he distaste* it, let him* to our sister,
Whose mind and mine, I know, in that are one,   15
Not to be over-ruled. Idle* old man,
That still would manage those authorities
That he hath given away! Now, by my life,
Old fools are babes again, and must be used*
With checks as flatteries, when they are seen abused.   20
Remember what I tell you.
OSWALD   Very well, madam.
GONERIL   And let his knights have colder looks among you;
What grows* of it, no matter; advise your fellows so.
I would breed from hence occasions,* and I shall,   25
That I may speak. I'll write straight* to my sister,
To hold my very course.* Prepare for dinner.

[*Exeunt*

I.iv   The banished Kent returns in disguise, brushes with Oswald, and is hired for service by
Lear. The Fool shows Lear something of his own stupidity and Goneril complains at having
to entertain her father and his retinue. Lear curses her and sets out with his Fool.
    The balance between the summary action of scenes i and ii and the close-up look at a
comparatively unimportant incident, scene iii, is now achieved. With the motivation of
the key characters properly revealed, the full importance of the events in this scene
can be appreciated. For instance, Albany in a few words at the end reveals serious mis-
givings over his wife's attitude.

1   *but:* only – see Introduction, p. 1.
1   *as well* – i.e. in addition to the disguise, which is apparent as he comes on to the stage.
            Later in this speech, Kent uses a 'stage declaration' to make clear to the audience
            who he is and what he proposes to do.
1   *other accents borrow:* take on a different style of speech.
2   *defuse* – i.e. *diffuse:* make unrecognisable.
3   *issue:* consequence.
4   *razed my likeness:* disguised myself – literally: wiped out my [former] appearance.
5   *serve* – He plans to act in disguise as a servant to the King, from whose presence he has been
            banished.
6   *So may it come:* either (i) 'I hope it may come about', or (ii) 'it may so happen (that)'.
7   *full of labours:* most industrious [in serving the King].
8   *stay a jot:* [have to] wait a single moment.
10   *A man* – Kent takes Lear's question literally in order to give a pert answer.
11   *What . . . profess:* What work do you do? – Kent pretends to misunderstand him, and
            answers as if *profess* meant 'assert, affirm'.
11   *What . . . with us:* What do you want with me? What is your business?
13   *that will . . . trust:* who will entrust affairs to me.
13   *converse:* associate.
14   *judgement* – apparently both God's and man's.
15   *when I cannot choose:* when I have no choice, when I must.
15   *eat no fish* – (i) Perhaps he professes not to eat fish because a fish meal on Fridays was a
            custom among Roman Catholic families. (At the time the play was written,
            Catholics were considered by many to be disloyal to the state.) (ii) But he may
            mean simply to contrast fish with meat; meat, not fish, was looked upon as the
            food which gave bodily strength. (iii) Possibly the remark is just inconsequen-
            tial, a third, alliterative item in a series: *fear – fight – fish.*
17   *as poor as the King* – An ironic remark, it seems; although Kent already has some concep-
            tion of the King's sorry state, he is being deliberately provocative in linking
            together kingship and poverty. Lear's riposte is as one would expect.
24   *countenance:* bearing.
29   *keep honest counsel:* keep secrets of an honourable kind.
29   *curious:* elaborate. – An old joke about servants was their inability to carry messages
            correctly.

scene iv

A hall in the Duke of Albany's palace.

Enter KENT, *disguised.*

KENT If but* as well* I other accents borrow*
That can my speech defuse,* my good intent
May carry through itself to that full issue*
For which I razed* my likeness. Now, banished Kent,
If thou canst serve* where thou dost stand condemned,   5
So may it come,* thy master whom thou lov'st
Shall find thee full of labours.*

Horns within. Enter LEAR, KNIGHTS, *and* ATTENDANTS.

LEAR Let me not stay a jot* for dinner; go get it ready. [*Exit an*
ATTENDANT.] How now! what art thou?

KENT A man,* sir.   10

LEAR What dost thou profess?* What wouldst thou with us?*

KENT I do profess to be no less than I seem; to serve him truly that
will put me in trust;* to love him that is honest; to converse*
with him that is wise and says little; to fear judgement,* to
fight when I cannot choose,* and to eat no fish.*   15

LEAR What art thou?

KENT A very honest-hearted fellow, and as poor as the King.*

LEAR If thou be as poor for a subject as he is for a king, thou art
poor enough. What wouldst thou?

KENT Service.   20

LEAR Who wouldst thou serve?

KENT You.

LEAR Dost thou know me, fellow?

KENT No, sir; but you have that in your countenance* which I
would fain call master.   25

LEAR What's that?

KENT Authority.

LEAR What services canst thou do?

KENT I can keep honest counsel,* ride, run, mar a curious* tale in
telling it, and deliver a plain message bluntly. That which   30
ordinary men are fit for, I am qualified in, and the best of
me is diligence.

LEAR How old art thou?

34   *to love . . . singing:* that I would fall in love with a woman because of her singing.

38   *yet:* for the present.

39   *knave:* servant – i.e. the Fool. By Shakespeare's day the word was beginning to take on a more pejorative meaning: 'rogue', as in II.ii.80, 81.

43   *clotpoll,* 'clot'. – Lear tries to pretend to himself that Oswald has been too stupid to answer his question. Oswald has pretended to be busy carrying out other instructions, and in this way obeys Goneril's orders (I.iii.9ff.).

48   *roundest:* most frank, to the point of rudeness.

51   *entertained:* treated.

52   *that ceremonious . . . wont:* the same well-ordered devotion that you were once accustomed (*wont*) to. – *Ceremonious* does not carry with it any suggestion of sham or hollow affection; proper ceremonies were symbols of genuine respect for a person in authority.

52   *abatement . . . as well:* falling-off of kindness which appears both . . .

53   *general dependants:* ordinary people – e.g. the servants.

58   *Thou but rememberest me:* You do no more than remind me.

58   *conception:* thoughts.

59   *a most faint neglect:* very poor service – from the attendants (the *weary negligence* of I.iii.12); *faint:* inactive, lazy.

60   *jealous curiosity:* jealously guarded politeness – over the way the servants should attend to his needs, service which he is reluctant to give up. The overtones of meaning of the word *curiosity* can be studied here and at I.i.5 and I.ii.4: precision, care for accuracy over detail, leading to excessive scrupulousness in one's affairs. In the present passage Lear's modesty is significant; at this stage he tries to give others the benefit of the doubt in the matter of the neglect he notices.

61   *a very pretence:* a definite intention.

68   *sir* – Masters calling their servants *sir* or *sirrah* are common in Shakespeare's plays. The repetition of *sir* in this line suggests that Lear is using the term of address ironically. See Introduction, p. ii.

KENT   Not so young, sir, to love a woman for singing,* nor so old
        to dote on her for anything: I have years on my back   35
        forty-eight.

LEAR   Follow me; thou shalt serve me; if I like thee no worse after
        dinner, I will not part from thee yet.* Dinner, ho, dinner!
        Where's my knave?* my fool? Go you, and call my fool
        hither.   [*Exit an* ATTENDANT   40

        Enter OSWALD.

        You, you, sirrah, where's my daughter?

OSWALD So please you –   [*Exit*

LEAR   What says the fellow there? Call the clotpoll* back. [*Exit a*
        KNIGHT.] Where's my fool, ho? I think the world's asleep.

        Re-enter KNIGHT.

        How now! where's that mongrel?   45

KNIGHT He says, my lord, your daughter is not well.

LEAR   Why came not the slave back to me when I called him?

KNIGHT Sir, he answered me in the roundest* manner, he would not.

LEAR   He would not!

KNIGHT My lord, I know not what the matter is; but, to my judgement, 50
        your highness is not entertained* with that ceremonious
        affection as you were wont;* there's a great abatement* of
        kindness appears as well in the general dependants* as in
        the duke himself also and your daughter.

LEAR   Ha! sayest thou so?   55

KNIGHT I beseech you, pardon me, my lord, if I be mistaken; for my
        duty cannot be silent when I think your highness wronged.

LEAR   Thou but rememberest* me of mine own conception:* I have
        perceived a most faint neglect* of late which I have rather
        blamed as mine own jealous curiosity* than as a very pre-   60
        tence* and purpose of unkindness. I will look further into 't.
        But where 's my fool? I have not seen him this two days.

KNIGHT Since my young lady's going into France, sir, the fool hath
        much pined away.

LEAR   No more of that; I have noted it well. Go you, and tell my   65
        daughter I would speak with her.   [*Exit an* ATTENDANT
        Go you, call hither my fool.   [*Exit an* ATTENDANT

        Re-enter OSWALD.

        O, you sir,* you, come you hither, sir: who am I, sir?

OSWALD My lady's father.

72   *I beseech your pardon* – Oswald in his turn is now ironical with the King; he uses a polite
           phrase without any intention of politeness.
73   *bandy*: exchange, throw or hit to and fro as in a ball game. – They are bandying attitudes
           (*looks*) with the irony of their words. The phrase *to bandy words* survives in
           modern English.
75   *foot-ball* was looked upon as a game for the lower orders of society.
78   *arise*: get up.
79   *differences*: distinctions [of class] – i.e. Oswald's social position as against the King's.
80   *If you . . . tarry*: If you want to go down again, wait. – More literally: 'If you, you rascal
           (*lubber*), want to stretch out your own length [on the ground] again, wait.'
80   *go to*: away with you – expressing disgust.
80   *have you wisdom*: (perhaps) haven't you the good sense to go away.
81   *earnest . . . service* – i.e. an instalment of the pay he will get for his service. An *earnest* is
           a small payment made to secure a bargain.
83   *coxcomb*: cap in the form of a cock's crest, the symbol of a professional fool. – His play
           with this coxcomb depends on his use of it to indicate who is acting foolishly;
           he who is invited to wear a coxcomb has been singled out as a fool.
84   *pretty knave*: clever rogue.
85   *you were best*: you had better.
87   *taking . . . favour*: being on the side of someone who is out of favour. – There follows the
           first long sequence by the Fool. It is characteristically a series of amusing
           remarks which carry with them some deeper philosophical implications.
87   *and*: if – see Introduction, p. 1.
88   *as the wind sits*: according to the direction of the wind – i.e. in support of the side at the
           moment in favour. The wind's direction is unpredictable; so is fortune with its
           favours. The metaphor is continued in *catch cold*, i.e. succumb to the ill favour.
90   *on 's*: of his (see Introduction p. li). – The Fool's account of recent events is the reverse of
           the literal truth (Lear banished his third daughter and raised the first two in
           his favour) but has an inner meaning: Cordelia is in fact lucky to be out of
           Lear's way, and has become Queen of France.
92   *nuncle*: (mine) uncle. – Fools seem commonly to have used this term in addressing their
           masters.
92   *Would I had*: I wish I had.
95   *living*: possessions. – He is saying, 'If I had given *my* daughters all my possessions, I would
           certainly need to keep the marks of being a fool', since the act would be a very
           foolish one. He now offers his cap to Lear, telling him to beg another one from
           his daughters, thus making him appear doubly foolish.
98   *the whip* – a warning. Fools could be whipped if their satire became too personal.
99   *must*: that must go.
99   *out* – i.e. out of the house.
100   *Lady the brach*: the bitch called Lady. – Evidently the bitch is the flatterer, following the
           scent of favour, whereas truth is the male dog which is driven out of doors to
           the kennel. *Lady the brach* must stand for Goneril and Regan.
101   *A pestilent . . . to me!* – Apparently said about the Fool because of his bitter jibes: 'You
           are a pestilent . . .'; *gall*: sore.
104   *Mark it*: Take good notice of it. – The jingle which follows is a typical composition of a
           court fool. It is a series of genuine or invented proverbs in rhyme, the rhyme
           and rhythm intended to make the advice of the proverbs easily memorable.
           See Introduction, p.lxxviii.

LEAR   'My lady's father!' My lord's knave; you whoreson dog!   70
       you slave! you cur!

OSWALD I am none of these, my lord; I beseech your pardon.*

LEAR   Do you bandy* looks with me, you rascal?   [*Hitting him*

OSWALD I'll not be struck, my lord.

KENT   Nor tripped neither, you base foot-ball* player.   75

              [*Tripping up his heels so that he falls down*

LEAR   [*To* KENT] I thank thee, fellow; thou servest me, and I'll love
       thee.

KENT   [*To* OSWALD] Come, sir, arise,* away! I'll teach you differ-
       ences.* Away, away! If you will measure your lubber's
       length again, tarry.* But away! go to;* have you wisdom?* so.   80

                        [*Pushes* OSWALD *out*

LEAR   Now, my friendly knave, I thank thee. There's earnest* of
       thy service.   [*Giving* KENT *money*

       Enter FOOL.

FOOL   Let me hire him too; here's my coxcomb.*

                        [*Offering* KENT *his cap*

LEAR   How now, my pretty knave!* how dost thou?

FOOL   [*To* KENT] Sirrah, you were best* take my coxcomb.   85

KENT   Why, fool?

FOOL   Why, for taking one's part that's out of favour.* Nay, and*
       thou canst not smile as the wind sits,* thou'lt catch cold
       shortly. There, take my coxcomb. Why, this fellow has
       banished two on 's* daughters, and done the third a blessing   90
       against his will. If thou follow him, thou must needs wear
       my coxcomb. How now, nuncle!* Would I had* two cox-
       combs and two daughters!

LEAR   Why, my boy?

FOOL   If I gave them all my living,* I'd keep my coxcombs myself.   95
       [*Offers him his cap.*] There's mine; beg another of thy
       daughters.

LEAR   Take heed, sirrah; the whip.*

FOOL   Truth's a dog must* to kennel; he must be whipped out,*
       when Lady the brach* may stand by the fire and stink.   100

LEAR   A pestilent gall* to me!

FOOL   Sirrah, I'll teach thee a speech.

LEAR   Do.

FOOL   Mark* it, nuncle:

105   *Have . . . showest* – i.e. Don't display everything you have.
107   *owest:* own.
108   *goest:* walk
109   *trowest:* believe – i.e. don't believe everything you hear.
110   *Set . . . throwest:* don't stake all that you have to gamble with.
112   *in-a-door:* indoors.
114   *two tens . . . score* – This phrase is spoken evidently to complete the rhyme and round off the jingle with some semblance of meaning; perhaps, 'every score [of pieces of money] you have will be worth more than twenty to you'.
115   *nothing:* nonsense. – For the use of the word *nothing* in the play, see note to I.i.83.
116   *an unfee'd lawyer* – i.e. a lawyer who has not been paid any fee, and will therefore not talk on behalf of his client.
119   *the rent* – This comes to nothing, because he has given away the entire source of it.
121   *bitter:* sarcastic.
125   *That lord* – The Fool is probably inventing an imaginary counsellor who, in his opinion, misled the King into giving up his possessions. This counsellor is the bitter fool of the jingle; the professional fool is sweet by comparison. In the older play of *Leir* there is in fact such a lord; the reference here may hark back to this older character. The jibe is made worse by the King himself standing for the counsellor (line 128, 133), as the Fool tells him to.
128   *Do thou . . . appear* (line 130): stand for him [the counsellor], and [then] the *sweet and* [the] *bitter fool* will be seen at once [side by side].
135   *born with* – He was a 'born fool'.
136   *fool:* foolishness.
137   *let me* – i.e. let me have all the foolishness to myself.
138   *a monopoly out:* a monopoly granted to me – in trading foolishness. In Shakespeare's day the monarch sometimes gave the sole right in trading in a certain commodity to an individual. This led to artificially high prices for even the commonest necessities of life and caused great outcry among the public. The Fool says that he could not keep all the foolishness in the world to himself even if he were given a monopoly to trade in it.
141   *crowns:* the ends of the egg, and also [the source of the Fool's riddle] symbols of kingship. – The riddle is childishly simple, but Lear 'feeds' the Fool with the questions he needs to carry on the comedy.
143   *eat,* for *eaten.*
144   *clovest:* split in two (past tense of *cleave*).

> *Have more than thou showest,** 105
> *Speak less than thou knowest,*
> *Lend less than thou owest,**
> *Ride more than thou goest,**
> *Learn more than thou trowest,**
> *Set less than thou throwest.** 110
> *Leave thy drink and thy whore,*
> *And keep in-a-door,**
> *And thou shalt have more*
> *Than two tens* to a score.*

KENT This is nothing,* fool. 115

FOOL Then 'tis like the breath of an unfee'd* lawyer – you gave me nothing for 't. Can you make no use of nothing, nuncle?

LEAR Why, no, boy; nothing can be made out of nothing.

FOOL [*To* KENT] Prithee, tell him, so much the rent* of his land comes to. He will not believe a fool. 120

LEAR A bitter* fool!

FOOL Dost thou know the difference, my boy, between a bitter fool and a sweet fool?

LEAR No, lad; teach me.

FOOL
> *That lord* that counselled thee* 125
> *To give away thy land,*
> *Come place him here by me;*
> *Do thou* for him stand:-*
> *The sweet and bitter fool*
> *Will presently appear;* 130
> *The one in motley here,*
> *The other found out there.*

                              [*He points to* LEAR

LEAR Dost thou call me fool, boy?

FOOL All thy other titles thou hast given away; *that* thou wast born* with. 135

KENT This is not altogether fool,* my lord.

FOOL No, faith, lords and great men will not let* me; if I had a monopoly out,* they would have part on 't. And ladies too, they will not let me have all the fool to myself; they'll be snatching. Give me an egg, nuncle, and I'll give thee two 140 crowns.*

LEAR What two crowns shall they be?

FOOL Why, after I have cut the egg in the middle and eat* up the meat, the two crowns of the egg. When thou clovest* thy

146 *borest . . . ass . . . dirt* – This refers to Aesop's fable of the man who carried his two sons over a muddy patch in the road and then carried his donkey over too.
146 *wit:* good sense.
148 *like myself* – i.e. foolishly, as a fool is expected to speak.
149 *so* – i.e. foolish. He means that he is not now fooling, but talking good sense. If anyone takes the good sense to be fooling, he, not the fool, deserves to be whipped for it.
150 *Fools . . . year:* There never was a time when fools were less in favour than now.
151 *foppish:* foolish. – Since wise men have become foolish, there is no need for fools.
152 *wear:* use.
153 *apish:* silly.
155 *used it:* made a practice of it.
160 *play bo-peep:* act stupidly, or possibly, hide himself or blindfold himself as children do when they play hide-and-seek. – The quatrain is an adaptation of an old song. Its purpose is to bring home to the audience the balance and contrast of the situation: the balance of the King and the Fool pitted against one another is reflected in the strict rhythm and rhyme of the lines; the contrasts are everywhere: weeping for joy; singing for sorrow; the king among fools; all these contribute to the confusion of roles which is a major theme of the play: *thou madest thy daughters thy mother*, etc. (line 155).
162 *Prithee:* I pray you, please.
164 *whipped* – Corporal punishment was so readily used in Shakespeare's time that it was looked upon as an unavoidable part of education; a birch was the sign of the schoolmaster's profession.
165 *kin:* [sort of] family.
167 *holding my peace:* remaining silent.
169 *pared thy wit:* cut away your good sense.
171 *what makes . . . on:* what is that frown doing on your face. – A *frontlet* was a band of cloth worn across the forehead; the wrinkles of a frown look like a frontlet.
171 *Methinks:* It seems to me. – See Introduction, p. li.
173 *pretty:* fine.
174 *care for:* worry about.
174 *an 0 . . . figure:* nothing. – A figure before 0 is necessary to make it a number.
176 *forsooth:* indeed (*sooth:* truth).
178 *Mum:* Quiet. – The rhyme means: The man who keeps nothing at all for himself, having become tired of everything, will find himself in want.
181 *shealed peascod:* pea-pod which has been shelled – i.e. with all the peas taken out; a hollow with nothing inside.

crown i' the middle and gavest away both parts, thou borest   145
thine ass on thy back o'er the dirt.* Thou hadst little wit* in
thy bald crown when thou gavest thy golden one away. If I
speak like myself* in this, let him be whipped that first finds
it so.*

> [*Singing*] *Fools had ne'er less grace in a year;*   150
>> *For wise men are grown foppish,*
>> *And know not how their wits to wear,*
>> *Their manners are so apish.*

LEAR   When were you wont to be so full of songs, sirrah?
FOOL   I have used it,* nuncle, ever since thou madest thy daughters   155
thy mother. For when thou gavest them the rod and puttest
down thine own breeches,

> [*Singing*] *Then they for sudden joy did weep,*
>> *And I for sorrow sung,*
>> *That such a king should play bo-peep,*   160
>> *And go the fools among.*

Prithee,* nuncle, keep a schoolmaster that can teach thy fool
to lie; I would fain learn to lie.
LEAR   And you lie, sirrah, we'll have you whipped.*
FOOL   I marvel what kin* thou and thy daughters are: they'll have   165
me whipped for speaking true, thou'lt have me whipped for
lying, and sometimes I am whipped for holding my peace.*
I had rather be any kind o' thing than a fool. And yet I would
not be thee, nuncle; thou hast pared thy wit* o' both sides
and left nothing i' the middle. Here comes one o' the parings.   170

Enter GONERIL.

LEAR   How now, daughter! what makes that frontlet* on? Methinks* you are too much of late i' the frown.
FOOL   Thou wast a pretty* fellow when thou hadst no need to care
for* her frowning; now thou art an O* without a figure. I am
better than thou art now; I am a fool, thou art nothing.   175
[*To* GONERIL] Yes, forsooth,* I will hold my tongue; so your
face bids me, though you say nothing.

> *Mum,* mum:*
> *He that keeps nor crust nor crumb,*
> *Weary of all, shall want some.*   180

[*Pointing to* LEAR] That's a shealed peascod.*

182   *all-licensed:* permitted to do all he wants, to take any liberty. – In this formal speech Goneril begins the attack on her father and his band of retainers. Lear being powerless in the land and insensitive to the feelings of others, we are to believe there is some justification in Goneril's complaints about his retainers. But that does not excuse the cruelty and heartlessness of her attack, which, as the tone of the poetry shows, comes from a combination of careful consideration and pent-up emotion. Cf. I.iii.25.

183   *other:* others.

185   *rank:* gross.

187   *safe:* sure.

187   *fearful:* afraid.

188   *yourself . . . done:* you yourself have just now spoken and done. – The phrase *too late*, 'just now, very recently', evidently carries no meaning of excessive delay; Goneril may be referring to the clash with Oswald and that earlier with her gentleman.

189   *protect:* condone.

189   *put it on:* encourage it.

190   *allowance:* approval.

190   *which . . . proceeding* (line 195): and if you do this (i.e. condone and encourage the unruly behaviour), the fault will be blamed [on you] (*not 'scape censure:* line 191); and in order to put things right, it will be necessary to take active measures (*redresses*) which, in our earnest desire (*tender*) for a healthy state (*wholesome weal*), may offend you in the way they work out, and would otherwise be thought shameful (*Which else were shame*), but which the needs of the situation show to be the action of good sense (*discreet proceeding*). – Goneril's speech rises to a climax of carefully phrased complexity. She is shown choosing her words carefully and at the same time wrapping them in the obscurity of so complex a sentence that she avoids a direct confrontation with her father. It seems that whenever possible she uses impersonal forms: *the fault, the redresses*.

198   *it . . . it:* its . . . its. – The couplet has the ring of a proverbial saying. It refers to the mother-cuckoo's action of placing her egg among those of the hedge-sparrow. The sparrow hatches the cuckoo's egg and feeds the cuckoo chick until it gets so big that it pushes all the other eggs and nestlings out of the nest and bites off its foster-parent's head. Goneril is beginning to treat her father as cruelly.

199   *darkling:* in the dark. – The lighted candle is the King's power.

200   *our:* my. – Lear's use of the 'royal plural' shows how he continues to think of himself as exercising the rights of a king.

202   *I would:* I wish.

203   *fraught:* filled, plentifully supplied.

204   *dispositions:* moody fits.

206   *May . . . horse:* Can't even a fool see when the cart is pulling the horse? – The daughter is dominating her father, the King, instead of the King his daughter.

207   *Whoop . . . thee* – This is perhaps the cry of the carter to his mare Jug (a nickname for Joan). Some editors have taken it to be a quotation from an old song, now lost; it plainly refers to 'putting the cart before the horse'.

211   *notion:* understanding. – In this speech Lear goes a long way towards admitting that he is transformed for the worse, and the transformation surprises and puzzles him. Who am I? he wants to know.

211   *his discernings . . . lethargied:* his powers of discernment are blunted.

212   *waking:* Am I awake? – *Ha!* is an exclamation of anger and bewilderment. It breaks off the sentence before ever he reaches the *or* that one would expect to follow *Either*.

215   *I would learn that:* I want to find that out. – He has ignored the Fool's remark and refers back to his last question.

215   *sovereignty:* supreme power.

216   *false persuaded:* persuaded falsely. – Since he is no longer sure of his own nature and kingly powers, how can he be honestly persuaded to recognise his daughters as his own, despite the evidence of his senses?

218   *Which,* referring back to *Lear's shadow* (line 214), or perhaps to *I* in what Lear has just said.

220   *admiration:* pretended surprise. – Lear's concern is genuine enough, but it suits Goneril's purpose to make people believe she takes Lear's behaviour to be mere affectation.

221   *is much . . . pranks:* is of the same sort as your other recent silly actions; *savour:* kind, quality.

GONERIL Not only, sir, this your all-licensed* fool,
　　　　But other* of your insolent retinue
　　　　Do hourly carp and quarrel, breaking forth
　　　　In rank* and not-to-be-endured riots. Sir,　　　　　　　185
　　　　I had thought, by making this well known unto you,
　　　　To have found a safe* redress; but now grow fearful,*
　　　　By what yourself* too late have spoke and done,
　　　　That you protect* this course, and put it on*
　　　　By your allowance;* which* if you should, the fault　　190
　　　　Would not 'scape censure,* nor the redresses sleep,
　　　　Which, in the tender of a wholesome weal,
　　　　Might in their working do you that offence,
　　　　Which else were shame, that then necessity
　　　　Will call discreet proceeding.　　　　　　　　　　　195
　　FOOL For, you know, nuncle,

　　　　　　　The hedge-sparrow fed the cuckoo so long,
　　　　　　　That it had it* head bit off by it young.

　　　　So out went the candle, and we were left darkling.*
　　LEAR Are you our* daughter?　　　　　　　　　　　200
GONERIL Come, sir,
　　　　I would* you would make use of that good wisdom
　　　　Whereof I know you are fraught,* and put away
　　　　These dispositions* that of late transform you
　　　　From what you rightly are.　　　　　　　　　205
　　FOOL May not an ass* know when the cart draws the horse?
　　　　　　　Whoop,* Jug!
　　　　　　　I love thee.
　　LEAR Doth any here know me? This is not Lear.
　　　　Doth Lear walk thus? Speak thus? Where are his eyes?　210
　　　　Either his notion* weakens, his discernings*
　　　　Are lethargied – Ha! waking?* 'tis not so.
　　　　Who is it that can tell me who I am?
　　FOOL Lear's shadow.
　　LEAR I would learn that;* for, by the marks of sovereignty,*　215
　　　　knowledge, and reason, I should be false persuaded* I had
　　　　daughters.
　　FOOL Which* they will make an obedient father.
　　LEAR Your name, fair gentlewoman?
GONERIL This admiration,* sir, is much o' the savour　　　220
　　　　Of other your new pranks.* I do beseech you
　　　　To understand my purposes aright:

224   *squires*, gentlemen next below a knight in rank; they were originally shield-bearers.
225   *deboshed*: depraved, debauched.
227   *Shows*: looks.
227   *epicurism*: riotous living. – The Greek thinker Epicurus taught a rigorous philosophy of
          the pursuit of virtue, but after his death some who professed to be his followers
          gave themselves up to sensual enjoyment, misinterpreting his doctrine that
          truth could be perceived only through the senses.
229   *speak*: call out.
230   *desired*: requested.
232   *disquantity your train*: reduce the number of your attendants.
233   *still depend*: continue to be your dependants.
234   *besort*: befit.
238   *left a daughter*: one daughter left.
241   *Woe, that*: Woe to him who . . . – Lear is talking about himself.
243   *Is it your will?*: Is this what you want? – As they are in Albany's palace, he is properly
          their host, and should be able to overrule his wife. His entry gives Lear some
          faint hope of this.
245   *thou show'st thee*: you show yourself.
246   *the sea-monster* – No special monster seems to be referred to here, though *the* may indicate
          a type of hideous creature which is the ugliest thing Lear can think of. (Some
          have thought that the reference is to a hippopotamus or a whale or to a sea
          monster in classical mythology, e.g. the one killed by Perseus after he had
          rescued Andromeda from it.)
248   *choice and rarest parts*: the choicest and rarest qualities.
249   *That . . . know*: who know their duty down to the smallest detail.
250   *And in . . . name*: and live up to their good reputation (*worships of their name*) with the
          greatest care (*in the most exact regard*).
251   *O most small fault* – This fault is lack of gratitude.
253   *That, like . . . place*: [this small fault] which, like an instrument of torture (*engine*),
          wrenched my frame out of its proper shape. – The phrase *From the fixed place*
          must refer to the rightness in the nature of things of the properly constituted
          body as part of the general order of the universe; the *fault* has twisted this
          awry, violating natural order.
255   *gall* – the symbol of hatred and bitterness.
257   *dear*: precious. – The image of the *gate* brings together his head (his intelligence) and the
          gate of his son-in-law's home, which is shut to him.

As you are old and reverend, you should be wise.
Here do you keep a hundred knights and squires,*
Men so disordered, so deboshed* and bold,   225
That this our court, infected with their manners,
Shows* like a riotous inn: epicurism* and lust
Make it more like a tavern or a brothel
Than a graced palace. The shame itself doth speak*
For instant remedy. Be then desired*   230
By her that else will take the thing she begs
A little to disquantity* your train;
And the remainder that shall still depend,*
To be such men as may besort* your age,
Which know themselves and you.

LEAR   Darkness and devils!   235
Saddle my horses; call my train together.
Degenerate bastard! I'll not trouble thee.
Yet have I left a daughter.*

GONERIL You strike my people, and your disordered rabble
Make servants of their betters.   240

Enter ALBANY.

LEAR Woe, that* too late repents – [*To* ALBANY] O, sir, are you
come?
Is it your will?* Speak, sir. Prepare my horses.
Ingratitude, thou marble-hearted fiend,
More hideous when thou show'st* thee in a child   245
Than the sea-monster!*

ALBANY   Pray, sir, be patient.

LEAR [*To* GONERIL] Detested kite! thou liest.
My train are men of choice and rarest parts,*
That all particulars* of duty know,
And in the most exact regard* support   250
The worships of their name. O most small fault,*
How ugly didst thou in Cordelia show!
That, like an engine,* wrenched my frame of nature
From the fixed place, drew from my heart all love
And added to the gall.* O Lear, Lear, Lear!   255
Beat at this gate, that let thy folly in,   [*Beating his head*
And thy dear* judgement out! Go, go, my people.

ALBANY My lord, I am guiltless, as I am ignorant
Of what hath moved you.

LEAR   It may be so, my lord.

265   *derogate:* degraded. – Lear's cursing of Goneril strikes at the root of her womanhood; she can pass it off only as a result of his dotage (line 277).

266   *teem:* bear children.

267   *spleen:* malice. – The organ of the body called the spleen was thought to be the seat of malice and bad temper.

268   *thwart, disnatured:* perverse, lacking in natural affection.

269   *brow of youth:* youthful forehead.

270   *cadent:* falling; *fret:* wear.

271   *her mother's . . . benefits:* the troubles and joys of her (Goneril's) motherhood. – The curse is pitiless: her child will mock and despise her.

276   *Never afflict:* Do not worry.

277   *disposition:* mood. – Goneril uses Lear's brief absence from the stage – in his fury he has left the others for a moment or two – to make light of the power of his curse; she makes it sound like an old man's inconsequent fit of temper.

279   *at a clap:* at one stroke. – Goneril has already asked him (lines 230–2) to reduce the number of knights in his retinue; since she takes up the matter of *A hundred knights* later in the scene (line 308), we must assume that at this point Lear has been told off-stage to get rid of fifty knights within the next fortnight. At line 308 Goneril is harking back to her insistence that a hundred is too many.

284   *make thee worth them:* should have you as their cause, and thus attribute to you more importance than you deserve.

285   *untented:* either (i) too deep to be cleaned, or (ii) not cleaned out and therefore liable to fester. – A *tent* was a small roll of cloth used in cleaning out a wound.

286   *Old fond eyes:* Foolish old eyes (his own).

287   *Beweep:* if you weep over.

288   *loose:* release.

289   *temper:* moisten. – He would debase his eyes by throwing them on the hard earth.

291   *comfortable:* helpful.

294   *resume the shape –* Cf. *my frame of nature,* line 253.

296   *mark that:* notice that – i.e. Lear's threat to take back the power (*the shape*) he has given up. Goneril knows in her heart that her husband cannot approve of what is happening; she therefore draws his attention to this potential threat to Albany's newly acquired power. He begins to remonstrate but her powerful personality enables her quickly to brush him aside.

297   *partial:* favourably disposed. – He wants to say something about his love for her not blinding him to the wickedness of her actions, but she interrupts him.

	Hear, nature, hear; dear goddess, hear!	260
	Suspend thy purpose, if thou didst intend	
	To make this creature fruitful!	
	Into her womb convey sterility!	
	Dry up in her the organs of increase,	
	And from her derogate* body never spring	265
	A babe to honour her! If she must teem,*	
	Create her child of spleen,* that it may live	
	And be a thwart, disnatured* torment to her!	
	Let it stamp wrinkles in her brow of youth,*	
	With cadent* tears fret channels in her cheeks,	270
	Turn all her mother's pains and benefits*	
	To laughter and contempt, that she may feel	
	How sharper than a serpent's tooth it is	
	To have a thankless child! Away, away! [*Exit*	

ALBANY Now, gods that we adore, whereof comes this?   275
GONERIL Never afflict* yourself to know the cause,
But let his disposition* have that scope
That dotage gives it.

Re-enter LEAR.

LEAR What, fifty of my followers at a clap!*
Within a fortnight!
ALBANY   What's the matter, sir?   280
LEAR I'll tell thee. [*To* GONERIL] Life and death! I am ashamed
That thou hast power to shake my manhood thus,
That these hot tears, which break from me perforce,
Should make thee worth them.* Blasts and fogs upon thee!
The untented* woundings of a father's curse   285
Pierce every sense about thee! Old fond eyes,*
Beweep* this cause again, I'll pluck ye out
And cast you with the waters that you loose*
To temper* clay. Yea, is it come to this?
Let it be so. Yet have I left a daughter,   290
Who, I am sure, is kind and comfortable.*
When she shall hear this of thee, with her nails
She'll flay thy wolvish visage. Thou shalt find
That I'll resume the shape* which thou dost think
I have cast off for ever; thou shalt, I warrant thee.   295
                    [*Exeunt* LEAR, KENT, *and* ATTENDANTS
GONERIL Do you mark that,* my lord?
ALBANY I cannot be so partial,* Goneril,

300   *after:* follow.
301   *tarry:* wait.
303   *A fox . . .* – This jingle has all the signs of a verse made up on the spur of the moment. The last two lines could perhaps have rhymed in Shakespearian English: /ˈhaːtə – ˈaːtə/.
305   *Should sure:* should surely go.
306   *cap . . . halter* – His fool's cap is the mark of his trade, but he would give up even this in exchange for a rope to hang them with.
308   *This man* – i.e. her father, the King, whom she can now refer to in this disparaging way. She is a powerful persuader, and with irony (*'Tis politic*) and the piling-on of instances (*dream – buzz – fancy – complaint*) she quickly demolishes all opposition. And her calling for Oswald is a constant distraction in her speeches at this point.
310   *At point:* ready.
311   *buzz:* rumour.
312   *enguard:* protect.
313   *in mercy:* absolutely in his power.
315, 316   *still:* always.
316   *Not fear . . . taken:* and not live in constant fear of being overtaken [by the harms, dangers].
318   *sustain:* maintain.
319   *unfitness* – She interrupts herself in saying something about what will happen if Regan takes her father in.
323   *full:* in full; *particular:* personal, own.
325   *compact:* confirm.
327   *milky . . . course:* mild and generous course of action.
328   *under pardon:* if you will forgive me for saying so.
329   *at task:* open to criticism. – His attitude to life, his *milky gentleness* earns him little praise, whereas he is blamed for lack of wisdom.
334   *the event:* let us see how things turn out.

To the great love I bear you –

GONERIL   Pray you, content. What, Oswald, ho!

[*To the* FOOL] You, sir, more knave than fool, after* your   300
master.

FOOL   Nuncle Lear, nuncle Lear, tarry;* take the fool with thee.

> *A fox,* when one has caught her,*
> *And such a daughter,*
> *Should sure* to the slaughter,*   305
> *If my cap would buy a halter;**
> *So the fool follows after.*   [*Exit*

GONERIL   This man* hath had good counsel. A hundred knights!
'Tis politic and safe to let him keep
At point* a hundred knights; yes, that on every dream,   310
Each buzz,* each fancy, each complaint, dislike,
He may enguard* his dotage with their powers
And hold our lives in mercy.* Oswald, I say!

ALBANY   Well, you may fear too far.

GONERIL   Safer than *trust* too far:
Let me still* take away the harms I fear,   315
Not fear still to be taken.* I know his heart.
What he hath uttered I have writ my sister.
If she sustain* him and his hundred knights
When I have showed the unfitness* –

Re-enter OSWALD.

                          How now, Oswald!
What, have you writ that letter to my sister?   320

OSWALD   Yes, madam.

GONERIL   Take you some company, and away to horse.
Inform her full* of my particular fear,
And thereto add such reasons of your own
As may compact* it more. Get you gone,   325
And hasten your return. [*Exit* OSWALD] No, no, my lord,
This milky gentleness and course* of yours
Though I condemn not, yet, under pardon,*
You are much more at task* for want of wisdom
Than praised for harmful mildness.   330

ALBANY   How far your eyes may pierce I cannot tell.
Striving to better, oft we mar what's well.

GONERIL   Nay, then –

ALBANY   Well, well; the event.*   [*Exeunt*

I.v   Lear sends Kent to give forewarning of his arrival. There follow exchanges with the Fool who at once comforts and tortures Lear with his scraps of conversation; Lear's mind touches on the rising fear of madness at the treatment he has received.

The Fool dominates this scene; the apparent inconsequence of what he says is a symbol of the threat in Lear's mind to his own belief in the propriety and justice of the natural order. Two minds, both in some ways abnormal, are matched at the time of Lear's first rebuff.

1   *Go . . . letters:* Go ahead of me to the town of Gloucester with this letter (*letters*). – We are to assume that the Earl of Gloucester's home is near the town of that name.

3   *her demand . . . letter:* what she may question in connection with the letter. – He is to tell her nothing except on this condition.

3   *If . . . afore you:* If you do not travel quickly I shall arrive before you; *diligence:* despatch, speed (as of the post).

6   *If a man's . . . kibes:* If a man had his brain in his heels, would it not be liable to get chilblains (*kibes*)? – This question conforms to the pattern of conventional fooling: a condition is postulated which sounds nonsense, and the listener, granting the condition for the moment, is led into a proposition which he must agree to.

9   *go slip-shod:* walk in slippers. – His wit, or brain, would never need to walk in slippers because it does not exist; if it did, Lear would never have acted as he has done.

11   *use:* treat.

11   *kindly:* (i) affectionately, and also (ii) according to her true nature. – The two meanings derive from the same origin (cf. line 27, where Lear says: *I will forget my nature,* i.e. I will no longer be the kind father).

12   *this:* this one – i.e. Goneril.

12   *crab:* crab-apple, a wild apple which looks rather like the ordinary apple but is bitter to the taste.

16   *on 's:* of one's.

18   *of either side 's nose:* on either side of one's nose.

19   *spy:* look closely.

20   *I did her wrong* – Lear acknowledges for the first time that he has misjudged Cordelia.

26   *horns* – i.e. the eye-stalks of the snail, which are delicate and can be retracted into the shell for protection.

26   *case:* covering. – The word is used to mean eye-sockets at IV.vi.143.

27   *kind* – See note to line 11.

29   *asses:* idiots (contrasting with horses). – The Fool pursues the time-honoured routine of raillery, introducing a subject apparently new (in this case the stars) but linked by imagery with the situation in hand, and intended to illuminate it by apt, amusing (*pretty*, line 30) remarks.

29   *about 'em:* to see about them.

30   *seven stars:* the Pleiades, a cluster of stars, seven of which are readily visible to the naked eye. – Lear gives an answer to the naive riddle which is typical of the style of humour associated with fools, and thus invites the remark that he could be a fool himself. But the insult slips away unheeded, and his mind turns back to the unkindness of his daughter.

33   *To take . . . perforce!:* To take it back (*again*) by constraint! – He is evidently thinking of the right granted him (to have a hundred knights and squires in his retinue) being withdrawn by Goneril. When this happened he thought first of his daughter's ingratitude to him (I.iv.244), and so here also. *Monster* probably means 'monstrous', though it may be a noun to signify Goneril.

scene v

A court in front of the Duke of Albany's palace.

Enter LEAR, KENT, *and* FOOL.

LEAR   Go you before to Gloucester with these letters.* Acquaint my
daughter no further with anything you know than comes
from her demand* out of the letter. If your diligence* be not
speedy, I shall be there afore you.

KENT   I will not sleep, my lord, till I have delivered your letter.   5

                                                                    [*Exit*

FOOL   If a man's brains were in 's heels,* were 't not in danger of
kibes?

LEAR   Ay, boy.

FOOL   Then, I prithee, be merry; thy wit shall ne'er go slip-shod.*

LEAR   Ha, ha, ha!   10

FOOL   Shalt see thy other daughter will use* thee kindly;* for
though she's as like this* as a crab* 's like an apple, yet I can
tell what I can tell.

LEAR   Why, what canst tell, my boy?

FOOL   She will taste as like this as a crab does to a crab. Thou canst   15
tell why one's nose stands i' the middle on 's* face?

LEAR   No.

FOOL   Why, to keep one's eyes of either side 's nose,* that what a
man cannot smell out he may spy* into.

LEAR   I did her wrong* –   20

FOOL   Canst tell how an oyster makes his shell?

LEAR   No.

FOOL   Nor I neither; but I can tell why a snail has a house.

LEAR   Why?

FOOL   Why, to put 's head in; not to give it away to his daughters,   25
and leave his horns* without a case.*

LEAR   I will forget my nature. – So kind* a father! – Be my horses
ready?

FOOL   Thy asses* are gone about* 'em. The reason why the seven
stars* are no more than seven is a pretty reason.   30

LEAR   Because they are not eight?

FOOL   Yes, indeed; thou wouldst make a good fool.

LEAR   To take 't again perforce!* Monster ingratitude!

FOOL   If thou wert my fool, nuncle, I'd have thee beaten for being
old before thy time.   35

38   *mad* – The first intimation of his madness coming on is given by Lear himself.
39   *in temper:* in my right mind.
43   *She that's . . . shorter* – This final couplet of the scene probably means that the girls in the
     audience who are so simple as to see only the comic side of the Fool's words,
     and not the impending tragedy, will certainly not have wit enough to keep
     their virginity for long; *departure* means perhaps (i) departure from the stage
     and (ii) verbal manipulations; *departure* and *shorter* rhymed in Shakespearian
     English.

LEAR How's that.

FOOL Thou shouldst not have been old till thou hadst been wise.

LEAR O, let me not be mad,* not mad, sweet heaven!
Keep me in temper;* I would not be mad.

Enter GENTLEMAN.

How now! are the horses ready?   40

GENTLEMAN Ready, my lord.

LEAR. Come, boy.

FOOL [*To the audience*] She that's a maid now,* and laughs at my
departure,
Shall not be a maid long, unless things be cut shorter.   45

[*Exeunt*

Lear accompanied by the Fool, discovering Kent in the stocks (Act II, Scene iv).

Regan greeting Lear after Kent is set free (Act II, Scene iv).

II.i   Edmund hears that Cornwall and Regan are on their way to Gloucester's castle (they apparently live near by; at least Lear addresses a letter to them in Gloucester, I.v.i); there is talk of war breaking out between Albany and Cornwall. In a contrived scuffle to impress Gloucester, Edmund pretends Edgar wounds him, and Edgar flees. Cornwall and Regan arrive; they tell Gloucester they are resolved not to receive Lear.

This scene follows, despite certain time difficulties (e.g., the *fortnight* of I.iv.280), very close upon I.ii; Edgar has been in hiding and now flees. Goneril and Albany's treatment of Lear is seen against Regan and Cornwall's; both the latter are shown here involved in the Gloucester plot. The hints of emnity between Cornwall and Albany come to nothing.

1   *Save thee:* May God save you – a standard greeting.
6   *the news abroad:* the rumours going about. – In what follows, *news* is treated as a plural noun, not a singular as in modern English.
7   *ear-kissing arguments:* matters passed around discreetly (the speaker 'kissing' the listener's ear as he whispers them). – Q has *ear-bussing,* with the same meaning, except that *bussing* may incorporate word-play with *buzzing,* passing rumours (cf. I.iv.311).
10   *toward:* about to take place.
14   *be* – The form of the verb shows that Edmund is reporting what he has heard: 'will be'.
14   *The better!:* So much the better!
15   *This weaves . . .* – Edmund at once considers the news in the light of his plotting (*business*); it quickly becomes incorporated into the schemes.
16   *set guard:* sent out guards.
17   *of a queasy question:* of a difficult nature.
18   *act:* do.
18   *Briefness:* Speed, prompt action.
SD   *Enter* EDGAR – Q places this entry four lines earlier, and in doing so may refer to an appearance on the upper stage, where Edgar could be seen by the audience but not immediately noticed by Edmund.
20   *fly this place:* go away very quickly.
21   *Intelligence is given:* It is known [through secret informers].
22   *the night* – Shakespeare thought of the events in this scene as following immediately on those in I.ii: *without any further delay than this very evening* (I.ii.86–7). In any case there is a stage tradition that the working out of an evil scheme or plot takes place as soon as possible after that scheme is hatched. Here the night has this dramatic significance of swift fulfilment and cover for evil deeds.
23   *spoken 'gainst* – Edmund confuses Edgar by hinting at accusations of treasonable acts which may be levelled against him: he asks Edgar whether he has said anything against Cornwall or, two lines later, against Albany. It is all done so quickly, and one injustice mounts so fast on another, that Edgar fails to take even the most elementary measures to clear himself of the charges, and is caught in the compromising situation of a fight as Gloucester enters.
26   *Upon his party:* on his [Cornwall's] side – i.e. contradicting what he has just said so as to confuse Edgar utterly.
27   *Advise yourself:* Think carefully.
29   *In cunning:* In pretence [of a fight]. – Edmund wants to avoid giving Gloucester the impression that he and Edgar are conniving together against their father. It is hard to say what Edmund wants Edgar to think; most probably he wants Edgar to react without thinking at all. Edgar's natural response is to defend himself from attack.
29   *upon:* against.
30   *quit you well:* acquit yourself well in action, fight well.
31   *Light, ho* – Edmund makes it seem that they are fighting in the dark. Cf. line 38.
33   *Some blood . . . endeavour:* If I draw some of my own blood, it will give people the impression (*beget opinion*) that I have had a fierce encounter (with him).

ACT II scene i

The Earl of Gloucester's castle.

Enter EDMUND *and* CURAN, *meeting.*

EDMUND Save thee,* Curan.

CURAN And you, sir. I have been with your father, and given him
notice that the Duke of Cornwall and Regan his duchess will
be here with him this night.

EDMUND How comes that?   5

CURAN Nay, I know not. You have heard of the news abroad,* I mean
the whispered ones, for they are yet but ear-kissing arguments?*

EDMUND Not I. Pray you, what are they?

CURAN Have you heard of no likely wars toward,* 'twixt the Dukes   10
of Cornwall and Albany?

EDMUND Not a word.

CURAN You may do then in time. Fare you well, sir.   [*Exit*

EDMUND The duke be* here tonight? The better!* best!
This weaves* itself perforce into my business.   15
My father hath set guard* to take my brother;
And I have one thing, of a queasy question,*
Which I must act.* Briefness* and fortune, work!
[*He calls out.*] Brother, a word! Descend! Brother, I say!
Enter EDGAR.
My father watches. O sir, fly* this place.   20
Intelligence is given* where you are hid.
You have now the good advantage of the night.*
Have you not spoken 'gainst* the Duke of Cornwall?
He's coming hither, now, i' the night, i' the haste,
And Regan with him. Have you nothing said   25
Upon his party* 'gainst the Duke of Albany?
Advise yourself.*

EDGAR I am sure on 't, not a word.

EDMUND I hear my father coming. Pardon me.
In cunning* I must draw my sword upon* you.
Draw! Seem to defend yourself! Now quit you well.*   30
[*Shouts*] Yield! Come before my father. Light, ho,* here!
Fly, brother. Torches, torches! So farewell.   [*Exit* EDGAR
Some blood drawn on me would beget opinion*
                                                      [*Wounds his arm*

53

39   *conjuring . . . mistress:* calling upon the moon goddess to be his benevolent mistress. – Such incantations will capture Gloucester's attention since he has shown himself to be easily influenced by superstitions (I.ii.96ff.).

41   *Look, sir . . .* – Edmund plays for time by talking and giving the wrong direction, since he does not want Edgar caught before he has himself had time to convince Gloucester of Edgar's guilt. The repetition at line 44 serves to highlight the enormity of Edmund's treachery.

47   *But that . . .* – The clauses of Edmund's speech are linked together loosely and without clear grammatical conjunction. He is deliberately speaking in starts to give the impression of confusion. The drift of the passage is, however, on the whole clear enough: he is giving an account of what he wants Gloucester to think has happened. His sentence beginning *When by no means* (line 42) comes to a halt at the end of line 46, as if what was intended to be an introductory clause has inadvertently been turned into a final clause. *But that* ('But') starts a new sentence, and *Spoke* (line 49) begins a new clause, with conjunction *and* understood. At *sir, in fine* (line 50) he makes as if to pull himself together and make a clear statement of fact; but even now the sentences grow complex and straighten out only at the end of the speech: *Full suddenly he fled* (line 58). He cunningly slips into the present tense at one point in his account (*he charges home,* line 53), to give immediacy to his fabricated report.

48   *'Gainst parricides . . .* – The killing of a father was considered the most heinous of all crimes; the gods rained down all their thunder on such a murderer.

50   *in fine:* to sum up.

51   *loathly opposite:* bitterly opposed.

52   *fell motion:* fierce, well-trained thrust (*motion* was a technical term in fencing), his sword drawn and at the ready for this (*preparéd*).

53   *he charges . . . body:* he makes a thrust at my unprotected (*unprovided*) body.

54   *lanced:* pierced.

55   *best alarumed spirits:* spirits thoroughly aroused [as if by a trumpet-call to arms].

57   *Or whether* – The sentence takes a new turn at this point, as if the construction had been on the model: '. . . whether he saw my spirits aroused . . . or whether he was frightened by the noise . . . I do not know, but he very suddenly fled.'

57   *gasted:* frightened.

58   *Full:* very.

58   *Let him fly far:* He had better fly a long way. – There is a touch of dramatic irony here, since Gloucester is unwittingly saying exactly what Edmund wishes him to. The audience knows what Gloucester does not, that he is playing straight into Edmund's hands.

60   *And found – dispatch:* and when he is found, kill him.

61   *My worthy . . . patron:* my honourable chief and patron [Cornwall]. – Cornwall is evidently superior to Gloucester in status, despite Gloucester's age. This perhaps because Cornwall's wife is a princess.

64   *caitiff:* wretch; *to the stake:* to the place of execution.

66   *dissuaded:* discouraged, tried to dissuade.

67   *pight:* determined (past participle of *pitch*); *curst:* fierce.

68   *discover:* expose.

69   *unpossessing:* without possessions – since, being illegitimate, he is unable to inherit property.

70   *would:* should. – The sense of what follows is: 'If I should set myself up against you, do you think that the placing of any trust in you, or your own virtue or worth, could make people believe your words?' The speech which Edmund puts into the mouth of Edgar is sharply ironic in the setting of the dramatic situation, since most of it applies aptly to Edmund's own machinations; note especially lines 74–5.

70   *reposure:* placing.

Of my more fierce endeavour. I have seen drunkards
Do more than this in sport. Father, father!   35
Stop, stop! No help?

Enter GLOUCESTER, *and* SERVANTS *with torches.*

GLOUCESTER Now, Edmund, where's the villain?
EDMUND Here stood he in the dark, his sharp sword out,
Mumbling of wicked charms, conjuring* the moon
To stand 's auspicious mistress.
GLOUCESTER   But where is he?   40
EDMUND Look, sir,* I bleed.
GLOUCESTER   Where is the villain, Edmund?
EDMUND Fled this way, sir. [*He points in the wrong direction.*] When
by no means he could –
GLOUCESTER Pursue him, ho! – Go after.   [*Exeunt some* SERVANTS
'By no means' what?   45
EDMUND Persuade me to the murder of your lordship –
But that* I told him the revenging gods
'Gainst parricides* did all their thunders bend,
Spoke with how manifold and strong a bond
The child was bound to the father – sir, in fine,*   50
Seeing how loathly opposite* I stood
To his unnatural purpose, in fell motion,*
With his preparéd sword, he charges* home
My unprovided body, lanced* mine arm.
But when he saw my best alarumed spirits*   55
Bold in the quarrel's right, roused to the encounter,
Or whether* gasted* by the noise I made,
Full* suddenly he fled.
GLOUCESTER   Let him fly far.*
Not in this land shall he remain uncaught;
And found – dispatch.* The noble duke my master,   60
My worthy arch and patron,* comes tonight.
By his authority I will proclaim it,
That he which finds him shall deserve our thanks,
Bringing the murderous caitiff* to the stake;*
He that conceals him, death.   65
EDMUND When I dissuaded* him from his intent
And found him pight* to do it, with curst speech
I threatened to discover* him. He replied,
'Thou unpossessing* bastard! dost thou think,
If I would* stand against thee, could the resposure*   70

72	*faithed:* credited, believed.
73	*though:* even though.
73	*didst . . . character:* showed me my own handwriting.
74	*it all* – refers back to *what* (line 72).
75	*suggestion:* wicked prompting; *plot:* plotting; *practice:* intrigue.
76	*thou must . . . thought:* you would have to assume everyone to be stupid if they did not think (*not thought*) that . . .
78	*pregnant and potential:* ready and powerful.
79	*Strong* – This is the Q reading; F has *O strange.* If *Strong* is correct, it must refer to the strength of the alleged villainy; if *O strange* is correct, it must link with *I never got him* in the following line, the implication being: How can I have begotten a son so strangely unlike me? The Q reading is usually preferred.
79	*fastened:* hardened.
SD	*Tucket:* a trumpet-call associated with a particular distinguished person and blown to announce his arrival. – Gloucester recognises it at once as announcing Cornwall. *within* – i.e. at the back of the stage.
82	*ports:* gates, or possibly seaports.
86	*Loyal . . . boy* – The irony of *Loyal* as applied to Edmund is matched with Gloucester's pun on the word *natural:* he means (i) reflecting what is good in nature, natural filial affection, and (ii) illegitimate, bastard. In this short phrase he implies that, contrary to the belief of the time, his bastard son has natural affection for him, and his legitimate son is without this affection.
87	*capable (of my land,* line 85) – i.e. entitled to inherit (my lands); cf. I.ii.16.
90	*comes too short:* falls short.
91	*How dost:* How are you.
94	*named* – i.e. gave a name, the godfather naming his godchild.
96	*Was he not . . .* – Regan's role in the drama is to follow up and intensify the more tentative approaches made by her husband. She quickly dominates the situation on the stage, and Cornwall can only agree (line 106) with what she says.
99	*consort:* company – with stress on the second syllable.
100	*No marvel . . . affected:* It is not surprising then, that he was intent on evil.
101	*they have . . . on:* they who have incited him to . . .
102	*the expense . . . revénues:* the right to spend and squander all his property.

Of any trust, virtue, or worth in thee
Make thy words faithed?* No; what I should deny –
As this I would; ay, though* thou didst produce*
My very character – I'd turn it all*
To thy suggestion,* plot, and damnéd practice.   75
And thou must make a dullard* of the world,
If they not thought the profits of my death
Were very pregnant and potential* spurs
To make thee seek it.'

GLOUCESTER   Strong* and fastened* villain!
Would he deny his letter? I never got him. [*Tucket* within* 80
Hark, the duke's trumpets! I know not why he comes.
All ports* I'll bar; the villain shall not 'scape;
The duke must grant me that. Besides, his picture
I will send far and near, that all the kingdom
May have due note of him. And of my land,   85
Loyal and natural boy,* I'll work the means
To make thee capable.*

Enter CORNWALL, REGAN, *and* ATTENDANTS.

CORNWALL How now, my noble friend! since I came hither,
Which I can call but now, I have heard strange news.
REGAN If it be true, all vengeance comes too short*   90
Which can pursue the offender. How dost,* my lord?
GLOUCESTER O, madam, my old heart is cracked, is cracked!
REGAN What, did my father's godson seek your life?
He whom my father named?* Your Edgar?
GLOUCESTER O, lady, lady, shame would have it hid!   95
REGAN Was he not companion* with the riotous knights
That tend upon my father?
GLOUCESTER I know not, madam; 'tis too bad, too bad.
EDMUND Yes, madam, he was of that consórt.*
REGAN No marvel* then, though he were ill affected.   100
'Tis they have put him on* the old man's death,
To have the expense and waste of his revénues.*
I have this present evening from my sister
Been well informed of them; and with such cautions,
That if they come to sojourn at my house,   105
I'll not be there.
CORNWALL   Nor I, assure thee, Regan.
Edmund, I hear that you have shown your father

108   *A child-like office:* a service arising from filial duty.
109   *did bewray his practice:* uncovered his wicked designs.
110   *apprehend:* seize.
113   *Make . . . please:* Make your own plans [for carrying this out, i.e. the seizure of Edgar], using my resources in any way you please. – This and the previous sentence are in a brisk, close-packed style which shows Cornwall's agitation. There follows the irony of a change of tone to deep, confident trust when Cornwall turns to Edmund. This new style is short-lived, for as soon as Cornwall turns to practical affairs, his wife, the dominant partner, interrupts (line 121) and takes over.
121   *threading . . . night:* making our way with difficulty through the darkness. – In this metaphor there is a pun on the dark eyes of night and the eye of a needle.
122   *Occasions:* [it is because of] matters.
122   *poise:* weight, importance. – F and the uncorrected Qs have *prize* here, which is probably an incorrect reading, although it may mean 'worth', 'value' in this context.
125   *differences:* quarrels.
125   *which* – i.e. in a letter which.
126   *from:* away from. – She will not send a letter from her own home since she does not want to give her father the impression that she is there to receive him. She wishes first to consult Goneril, who is also coming to Gloucester's castle (II.iv.184).
127   *From hence . . . dispatch:* are waiting to be sent off from here. – The separate (*several*) messengers are Kent and Oswald.
129   *bestow . . . counsel:* give the advice we need.
130   *craves . . . use:* demands to be carried out at once.

II.ii   Oswald and Kent, both acting as messengers, meet at Gloucester's castle. Kent picks a quarrel with Oswald, and when Cornwall demands an explanation, it is Oswald's which he accepts. Kent is put in the stocks.
    This scene brings us closer to the main theme of the play; it requires the apportionment of our sympathy as well as the exercise of our reason in the discrimination of right and wrong. Kent's bluntness may be 'wrong' – it is indeed he who has picked the quarrel with Oswald; Cornwall's concern for state order may be 'right', and so on. But our sympathies remain with Kent, with the unhappy King and with Cordelia, who is now shown to be in contact with Kent (line 157).

SD   *severally:* separately – i.e. from different directions.
1   *dawning* — The whole of the scene takes place before sunrise; the darkness before dawn presages the gloom of the unkind treatment of Lear.
1   *Art . . . house:* Are you of this house? Do you belong [as a servant] to this place?

	A child-like office.*	
EDMUND	'Twas my duty, sir.	
GLOUCESTER	He did bewray* his practice, and received	
	This hurt you see, striving to apprehend* him.	110
CORNWALL	Is he pursued?	
GLOUCESTER	Ay, my good lord.	
CORNWALL	If he be taken, he shall never more	

CORNWALL If he be taken, he shall never more
Be feared of doing harm. Make your own purpose,
How in my strength you please.* For you, Edmund,
Whose virtue and obedience doth this instant   115
So much commend itself, you shall be ours.
Natures of such deep trust we shall much need;
You we first seize on.

EDMUND   I shall serve you, sir,
Truly, however else.

GLOUCESTER   For him I thank your grace.

CORNWALL You know not why we came to visit you –   120

REGAN Thus out of season, threading dark-eyed night* –
Occasions,* noble Gloucester, of some poise,*
Wherein we must have use of your advice.
Our father he hath writ, so hath our sister,
Of differences,* which* I best thought it fit   125
To answer from* our home; the several messengers
From hence attend dispatch.* Our good old friend,
Lay comforts to your bosom, and bestow
Your needful counsel* to our businesses,
Which craves the instant use.*

GLOUCESTER   I serve you, madam;   130
Your graces are right welcome.

                                        [*Flourish. Exeunt*

scene ii

In front of Gloucester's castle.

Enter KENT *and* OSWALD, *severally.**

OSWALD Good dawning* to thee, friend. Art of this house?*
KENT Ay.

3   *set:* tie up, stable. – Kent's reply shows that he wilfully misunderstands.
5   *Prithee:* I pray you; please.
8   *Lipsbury pinfold* – Perhaps a particular enclosed space which cannot now be identified;
       a *pinfold* (or pound) is an enclosure for keeping stray cattle in. It has been
       suggested that Lipsbury is a joking name for lips (like Bedfordshire for bed),
       giving a meaning 'in between my teeth, in my grasp', but this interpretation
       seems rather far-fetched.
10   *use:* treat.
12   *for:* as. – Kent answers assuming the introduction, 'I know you as . . .' Instead of accusing
       Oswald directly, he attacks him as a serving-man who has given himself the
       airs of a gentleman. This confusion is an example in a small way of a theme
       which is vital to the whole play, the disordering of social classes. Lear is to
       fall from being the highest in the land to being the lowest.
13   *broken meats:* scraps of food left over by others.
14   *three-suited* – i.e. with three suits, such as servants were fitted out with annually. Cf.
       III.iv.126: *Poor Tom . . . who hath had three suits to his back.*
14   *hundred-pound:* (presumably) with assets of [only] one hundred pounds – but the intended
       abuse is hard to explain since this would be a substantial sum in Shakespeare's
       day. Perhaps this was the smallest amount of property which would qualify a
       man to call himself a gentleman.
15   *worsted-stocking* – Worsted is woollen yarn, whereas true gentlemen wore silk stockings.
15   *lily-livered:* cowardly. – The liver was thought to be the seat of courage, and therefore a
       bloodless liver argued lack of courage.
15   *action-taking:* litigious – more ready to go to law over a quarrel than to fight it out.
16   *glass-gazing:* vain, for ever gazing into the looking-glass.
16   *superserviceable:* (perhaps) over-attentive, officious, obsequious as a servant.
16   *finical:* overfastidious.
17   *one-trunk inheriting:* owning only one trunkful of possessions.
18   *bawd . . . service* – i.e. one who prostitutes his duties as a servant by being overobsequious.
18   *composition:* compound.
19   *pander:* a go-between who furthers evil designs between people, especially in illicit love.
       – Pandarus plays this part in Chaucer's *Troilus and Criseyde.*
21   *thy addition:* the names I have just given you.
23   *of thee:* to you.
26   *Draw:* Draw your sword.
27   *a sop . . . moonshine* – The idea of moonshine is caught up from the previous sentence and
       suggests here that Kent will beat Oswald into such a bloody mess that he will
       float in a pool of moonshine like a piece of solid food, such as toast, floating in a
       drink.
28   *cullionly:* base (from *cullion:* rascal).
28   *barber-monger:* fop, one going too frequently to the barber's shop. – The accusation of
       vanity is taken up again in lines 31 and 35.
31   *Vanity the puppet's part* – He refers to Goneril in this way, likening her to the personifi-
       cation of vanity in the puppet shows of Morality plays. In such plays the
       characters were personifications of virtues and vices, and the way they fared
       in the play was a token of the likely end of people with such qualities in
       real life.
32   *carbonado:* cut crosswise – as meat was cut before broiling or grilling.
32   *shanks:* legs – used contemptuously.
33   *Come your ways:* Come on.
35   *Stand:* Don't run away.
35   *neat:* foppish. – The adjective could refer also to something praiseworthy, 'elegant', but
       not here.
38   *Part:* Disengage, separate.
39   *With you* – i.e. The quarrel is with you; defend yourself.
39   *goodman boy* – a mockingly respectful form of address. Kent in disguise plays with Edmund
       like an old servant talking to a disrespectful young master.
39   *flesh:* initiate [with the first experience of bloodshed]. – Dogs and hawks were *fleshed* with
       meat from the game killed so as to make them more fierce and therefore better
       hunters.

OSWALD Where may we set* our horses?

KENT I' the mire.

OSWALD Prithee, if thou lovest me, tell me.   5

KENT I love thee not.

OSWALD Why then, I care not for thee.

KENT If I had thee in Lipsbury pinfold,* I would make thee care
for me.

OSWALD Why dost thou use* me thus? I know thee not.   10

KENT Fellow, I know thee.

OSWALD What dost thou know me for?*

KENT A knave, a rascal, an eater of broken meats;* a base, proud,
shallow, beggarly, three-suited,* hundred-pound,* filthy,
worsted-stocking* knave; a lily-livered,* action-taking*   15
whoreson, a glass-gazing,* superserviceable,* finical* rogue;
one-trunk inheriting* slave; one that wouldst be a bawd in
way of good service,* and art nothing but the composition*
of a knave, beggar, coward, pander,* and the son and heir of
a mongrel bitch; one whom I will beat into clamorous whin-   20
ing, if thou deniest the least syllable of thy addition.*

OSWALD Why, what a monstrous fellow art thou, thus to rail on one
that is neither known of thee* nor knows thee!

KENT What a brazen-faced varlet art thou, to deny thou knowest
me! Is it two days ago since I tripped up thy heels and beat   25
thee before the King? Draw,* you rogue, for, though it be
night, yet the moon shines. I'll make a sop o' the moonshine*
of you. Draw, you whoreson cullionly* barber-monger,* draw.

[Drawing his sword

OSWALD Away! I have nothing to do with thee.

KENT Draw, you rascal. You come with letters against the King, and 30
take Vanity* the puppet's part against the royalty of her
father. Draw, you rogue, or I'll so carbonado* your shanks!*
Draw, you rascal! Come your ways.*

[He beats him

OSWALD Help, ho! murder! help!

KENT Strike, you slave. Stand,* rogue. Stand, you neat* slave,   35
strike.

OSWALD Help, ho! murder! murder!

Enter EDMUND, *with his rapier drawn.*

EDMUND How now! What's the matter? Part!*

KENT With* you, goodman boy,* if you please. Come, I'll flesh* ye;
come on, young master.   40

45	*difference:* quarrel.
47	*No marvel:* I am not surprised.
48	*disclaims in thee:* disowns you, renounces any claim to have produced you.
48	*a tailor –* 'The tailor makes the man' was a proverbial expression. Tailors were thought of as rather low in the social scale. There may also be a reference here to the contrast between outward appearance and inward reality: 'without your fine clothes you are nothing'. This contrast is an important part of Lear's attitude to the storm in III.iv, especially lines 96–103.
51	*ill:* badly.
54	*at suit of:* at the pleading of. – Oswald pretends he refrained from killing Kent because of his age, as shown by his grey beard. A dramatic joke on *suit* and *tailor* in the previous lines is probably intended.
56	*zed –* The letter Z was generally ignored as a heading in dictionaries of Shakespeare's time, possibly because it was felt to be un-English, an unnecessary substitute for S.
57	*unbolted –* literally 'unsifted', so that the metaphorical meaning is 'unrefined', but Kent's attack has suggested that Oswald is over-refined: *a tailor made thee* (line 48). Perhaps it means simply 'natural', since lime and sand in their natural state had to be trodden with water to make *mortar* (line 58).
58	*jakes:* latrine.
59	*wagtail –* This bird struts about on well-kept lawns, and because of the quick movements of its head and tail looks very pleased with itself.
65	*should wear . . . honesty –* The unwritten code of chivalry implied that men who bore arms carried them for honest ends and did not use them for evil.
66	*holy cords –* The cords referred to are evidently those which bind members of a family together, perhaps here the 'bonds' between husband and wife. Those who cause dissension between members of a family are compared with rats which can eat away cords too well tied to be undone. The theme of what follows is the wretchedness of sinking one's own sense of justice and right into the wishes of one's superiors. The nature of this tirade is hardly what could be expected of a (presumed) serving man, and Cornwall and Gloucester are understandably baffled.
66	*a-twain:* in two.
67	*intrinse:* intricately tied; *unloose:* undo; *smooth:* flatter, encourage.
68	*rebel,* for *rebels.*
69	*oil to fire –* The flatterer adds fuel to the flame of his master's passions; or if the master is melancholy, he feeds that mood instead, bringing *snow* to his coldness of mind.
70	*Renege:* deny.
70	*halcyon:* [a classical name for] the kingfisher. – It was believed that a kingfisher hung up would turn its beak into the direction of the wind.
71	*gale and vary:* varying wind – i.e. passing mood.
72	*nought:* nothing. – The only thing dogs can do, he asserts, is follow their master.
73	*epileptic:* like a man with epilepsy, pale and twisted.
74	*Smile you:* Do you mock at. – The *epileptic visage* takes on the look of inane smiling.
74	*as . . . fool:* as if I were a jester.
75	*Sarum Plain . . . Camelot –* Sarum is the old name of Salisbury; Camelot is the name given to the capital city – often identified with Winchester – of the legendary King Arthur. The southern edge of Salisbury Plain is not very far from Winchester, but beyond this fact no particular significance seems to be attached to these place-names. They are ancient, and would be associated by the audience with the legendary history of Britain, and therefore with King Lear. *Camelot* may have been suggested because of its assonance and alliteration with *cackling.*
79	*antipathy:* opposition in feeling or character.

Enter CORNWALL, REGAN, GLOUCESTER *and* SERVANTS.

GLOUCESTER	Weapons! arms! What's the matter here?
CORNWALL	Keep peace, upon your lives.
	He dies that strikes again. What is the matter?
REGAN	The messengers from our sister and the King.
CORNWALL	What is your difference?* Speak.
OSWALD	I am scarce in breath, my lord.
KENT	No marvel,* you have so bestirred your valour. You cowardly rascal, nature disclaims* in thee; a tailor* made thee.
CORNWALL	Thou art a strange fellow. A tailor make a man?
KENT	Ay, a tailor, sir; a stone-cutter or a painter could not have made him so ill,* though he had been but two years at the trade.
CORNWALL	Speak yet, how grew your quarrel?
OSWALD	This ancient ruffian, sir, whose life I have spared at suit* of his grey beard –
KENT	Thou whoreson zed!* thou unnecessary letter! My lord, if you will give me leave, I will tread this unbolted* villain into mortar, and daub the walls of a jakes* with him. Spare my grey beard, you wagtail?*
CORNWALL	Peace, sirrah!
	You beastly knave, know you no reverence?
KENT	Yes, sir; but anger hath a privilege.
CORNWALL	Why art thou angry?
KENT	That such a slave as this should wear a sword,
	Who wears no honesty.* Such smiling rogues as these,
	Like rats, oft bite the holy cords* a-twain*
	Which are too intrinse* to unloose, smooth every passion
	That in the natures of their lords rebel;*
	Bring oil to fire,* snow to their colder moods;
	Renege,* affirm, and turn their halcyon* beaks
	With every gale and vary* of their masters,
	Knowing nought,* like dogs, but following.
	A plague upon your epileptic* visage!
	Smile* you my speeches, as I were a fool?*
	Goose, if I had you upon Sarum Plain,*
	I'd drive ye cackling home to Camelot.
CORNWALL	What, art thou mad, old fellow?
GLOUCESTER	How fell you out? Say that.
KENT	No contraries hold more antipathy*
	Than I and such a knave.

45

50

55

60

65

70

75

80

82   *likes:* pleases.
86   *shoulder* – i.e. the part of the body lying between the shoulders.
90   *constrains . . . nature:* assumes a manner (*garb*) quite different from his real character.
92   *And they . . . plain* – The literal meaning of this line may be something like: If they accept [that he speaks the truth], let it be so; if not, [at least] he speaks his mind. More freely interpreted, this perhaps means: Either they admit that he speaks the truth, or, at least, they must admit that he speaks plainly. But *plain* may appear here incorrectly, caught up from the previous line in place of a word now lost.
95   *silly duckling . . . nicely:* poor attendants bobbing up and down in their anxiety to please, who strain to carry out their duties in every detail. – Here *nicely* means 'scrupulously, with great attention to detail'.
98   *the allowance . . . influence:* with the approval (*allowance*) of your powerful glances (*aspéct*), the influence of which. – Kent is making fun of Cornwall by adopting a different style of speech (*To go out of my dialect*, line 101), involving grandiloquent flattery instead of bluntness. The words *aspect* and *influence* are terms from astrology: the *aspect* of a heavenly body is its position in relation to other heavenly bodies as they appear to the observer on earth; its *influence* is the power and control it is supposed to have, by reason of this position, over events in the world. Kent makes Cornwall sound like a heavenly body; the image is further exploited in the following lines. Although the flattery sounds absurd, and is a deliberate parody, the contemporary style of dedication of books, works of art, etc., was not very different from this.
100   *flickering Phoebus' front:* the forehead of Phoebus the sun god, shining with unsteady light. – The alliteration is in keeping with the new style of speaking that Kent has assumed; *flickering* is designedly inappropriate, forced in for the sake of the alliteration.
100   *mean'st:* do you mean.
101   *To go . . . dialect* – In addition to changing his tone by reverting to his frank manner, he now talks in prose, a suitable vehicle for direct communication; *dialect:* way of speaking.
101   *discommend:* disapprove of.
103   *He that . . . knave* – Kent is talking about the kind of speaker Cornwall has already described, the blunt man who is nevertheless a deceiver.
104   *though . . . to 't* – It is impossible to be certain of what this means. The general drift of the passage suggests: I refuse to be a 'plain knave' even if I should displease you to such an extent as to make you entreat me to be one.
108   *upon his misconstruction:* because he [the King] misinterpreted my actions. – Oswald is trying to pretend that he was not in fact treating the King disrespectfully (L.iv.69ff.).
109   *conjunct:* closely in league [with the King].
109   *flattering:* encouraging. – Oswald pretends that he suffered from Kent encouraging the King to be displeased with him.
110   *being down, insulted:* I being down, he insulted me.
112   *put upon . . . worthied him:* made himself out to be such a hero that he won a reputation for excellence (*worthied:* gave a reputation for excellence).
113   *For him . . . subdued:* for setting upon someone who had suppressed his own animosity. – Oswald makes out that he took no action to retaliate when the King hit him.
114   *fleshment:* excitement at a first success [in a fight]; literally, the contact of the sword with flesh. – Oswald makes a further unjust accusation against Kent. Cf. II.ii.39.
115   *None of . . . fool:* All these rogues and cowards think even Ajax is a fool [compared with them]. – Ajax, in Homer's *Odyssey* and in Shakespeare's *Troilus and Cressida*, appears as a true warrior but also a boaster; he boasted that he would be saved from shipwreck in spite of the gods. Oswald is the sort of person who in his own estimation appears superior even to this.
116   *stocks* – See illustration, p. 50. The use of the stocks was a common form of punishment for insubordinate servants.
117   *stubborn:* rough; *reverend:* aged.

CORNWALL Why dost thou call him knave? What is his fault?

KENT His countenance likes* me not.

CORNWALL No more perchance does mine, nor his, nor hers.

                       [*He indicates* EDMUND *and* REGAN

KENT Sir, 'tis my occupation to be plain:

      I have seen better faces in my time   85

      Than stands on any shoulder* that I see

      Before me at this instant.

CORNWALL   This is some fellow

      Who, having been praised for bluntness, doth affect

      A saucy roughness, and constrains the garb

      Quite from his nature;* he cannot flatter, he –   90

      An honest mind and plain, he must speak truth!

      And they will take it, so; if not, he's plain.*

      These kind of knaves I know, which in this plainness

      Harbour more craft and more corrupter ends

      Than twenty silly ducking observants*   95

      That stretch their duties nicely.

KENT Sir, in good faith, in sincere verity,

      Under the allowance* of your great aspéct,

      Whose influence, like the wreath of radiant fire

      On flickering Phoebus' front* –

CORNWALL   What mean'st* by this?   100

KENT To go out of my dialect,* which you discommend* so much.

      I know, sir, I am no flatterer. He that beguiled you in a plain

      accent was a plain knave,* which, for my part, I will not be,

      though I should win your displeasure to entreat me to 't.*

CORNWALL What was the offence you gave him?   105

OSWALD I never gave him any.

      It pleased the King his master very late

      To strike at me, upon his misconstruction;*

      When he, conjunct,* and flattering* his displeasure,

      Tripped me behind; being down, insulted,* railed,   110

      And put upon him such a deal of man,

      That worthied him,* got praises of the King

      For him attempting who was self-subdued,*

      And in the fleshment* of this dread exploit

      Drew on me here again.

KENT   None of these rogues and cowards   115

      But Ajax is their fool.*

CORNWALL   Fetch forth the stocks!*

      You stubborn* ancient knave, you reverend braggart,

122   *grace . . . master* – i.e. the honour of the crown and of the King as a person.
127   *should not use:* would not treat.
128   *colour:* kind.
129   *bring away:* bring along. – The stage direction indicates how the stocks were brought out
          from the back on to the open stage. They would be set up as a focal point for
          the audience's attention, and so symbolise Kent's humiliation.
132   *check:* reprove.
132   *Your . . . correction:* The humiliating punishment you propose.
133   *contemnéd'st:* most damnable.
135   *must:* will [inevitably].
136   *so slightly valued:* so little respected, valued at so little.
137   *answer:* be responsible for.
142   *pleasure:* will.
144   *rubbed:* thwarted. – The term is taken from the game of bowls, in which the bowl *rubs*
          when it comes up against an obstacle which hinders it or diverts it from its
          proper course. Shakespeare uses the image in a number of places elsewhere,
          the most famous being in *Hamlet* (III.i.65): *Ay, there's the rub*.
145   *I have . . . hard:* I have gone without sleep (*watched*) and travelled in discomfort.
146   *sleep out:* spend sleeping.
147   *grow out at heels:* become threadbare – perhaps with a joke on his heels and feet being in
          the stocks.
148   *Give:* May God give.
149   *ill taken:* badly received.
150   *must approve:* cannot help showing to be true. – The gist of Kent's speech to the end of the
          scene is: He sees coming to Lear exposure to the unkinder side of life. By the
          fading light of day he tries to read a letter from Cordelia, who seems almost
          miraculously to know what his plans are and what is happening. She knows
          about the terrible injustices in the kingdom and is preparing to deal with them.
          But Kent's eyes are tired, and he closes them, shutting out the sight of the
          stocks and leaving the future to fortune.
151   *Thou out . . . sun:* you come out of good fortune, heaven's blessing, into the hot sunshine –
          i.e. (perhaps) your luck has gone from better to worse. The saying is known
          from other sources, but it has not been satisfactorily explained; in England
          sunshine is associated with well-being, not adversity. But it may nevertheless
          refer to being driven out of shelter, away from house and home. The mention
          of the sun is certainly taken literally in what follows.

We'll teach you –

KENT   Sir, I am too old to learn.
Call not your stocks for me; I serve the King,
On whose employment I was sent to you;   120
You shall do small respect, show too bold malice
Against the grace and person of my master,*
Stocking his messenger.

CORNWALL   Fetch forth the stocks!
As I have life and honour, there shall he sit till noon.

REGAN   Till noon! till night, my Lord; and all night too.   125

KENT   Why, madam, if I were your father's dog,
You should not use* me so.

REGAN   Sir, being his knave, I will.

CORNWALL   This is a fellow of the self-same colour*
Our sister speaks of. Come, bring away* the stocks!

[Stocks brought out

GLOUCESTER   Let me beseech your grace not to do so.   130
His fault is much, and the good King his master
Will check* him for 't. Your purposed low correction*
Is such as basest and contemnéd'st* wretches
For pilferings and most common trespasses
Are punished with. The King must* take it ill,   135
That he, so slightly valued* in his messenger,
Should have him thus restrained.

CORNWALL   I'll answer* that.

REGAN   My sister may receive it much more worse,
To have her gentleman abused, assaulted,
For following her affairs. Put in his legs.   140

[KENT is put in the stocks

CORNWALL   Come, my good lord, away.

[Exeunt all but GLOUCESTER and KENT

GLOUCESTER   I am sorry for thee, friend; 'tis the duke's pleasure,*
Whose disposition, all the world well knows,
Will not be rubbed* nor stopped. I'll entreat for thee.

KENT   Pray, do not, sir. I have watched and travelled hard.*   145
Some time I shall sleep out,* the rest I'll whistle.
A good man's fortune may grow out at heels.*
Give* you good morrow!

GLOUCESTER   [<i>Aside</i>] The duke's to blame in this; 'twill be ill taken.*   [<i>Exit</i>

KENT   Good King, that must approve* the common saw,   150
Thou out of heaven's benediction comest
To the warm sun!*

153   *this under globe* – i.e. this 'world below', the world under heaven.
154   *comfortable*: helpful.
155   *Nothing almost . . . misery*: (literally) hardly anything but misery sees miracles, i.e.
         miracles hardly ever happen except to those in the greatest distress. – Perhaps
         he means that in the eyes of the distressed any change may look like miraculous
         help. But the text as we have it may be faulty here, with an accidental and
         misleading link between *misery* and *miracles*.
159   *obscuréd course*: action taken in disguise.
161   *and shall . . . remedies*: (evidently) and will find time away from this disordered (*enormous*)
         state of things to redress the grievous treatment suffered by Lear and the
         country. – The letter must say something about the invasion of Britain which
         France is planning (III.i.30). But the meaning of the passage is obscure, prob-
         ably because the text as we have it is faulty; *enormous* means literally 'not
         having the normal pattern or standard'.
161   *o'erwatched*: tired from keeping awake for too long (cf. line 145).
162   *vantage*: advantage. – Sleep will give him the advantage of not seeing the stocks he is
         imprisoned in (*This shameful lodging*).
164   *thy wheel* – The wheel was a symbol of fortune since, after it has turned, it is a matter of
         chance which part is high and which low. A man's luck will change like this
         with no more reason than the chance turn of events. Here fortune is personified
         as a goddess with the wheel as her symbol.

II.iii   Edgar reveals to the audience his plan for disguise. Two key characters in disguise are
          now near one another, though they do not know it. There is contrast as well as similarity;
          the pathetic beauty of Edgar's lines on the Bedlam beggars is very different from Kent's
          forthrightness. Kent's indignity and Edgar's simulation foreshadow the true nakedness
          and madness which is to be Lear's fate. Thus the point of Lear's arrival is prepared for.

1   *proclaimed*: publicly announced as a wanted person (cf. II.i.59).
2   *happy*: opportune. – He was lucky enough to find a hollow tree to hide in.
3   *port*: place of exit. – Cf. II.i.82, where *ports* may refer specifically to seaports.
5   *attend my taking*: wait to catch me.
6   *am bethought*: have made up my mind.
8   *in contempt of man*: showing how despicable a creature man is.
9   *Brought near to*: brought down almost to the level of. – Penury is personified as deliber-
         ately reducing *man* to the level of the *beast* so as to show contempt for him.
10   *elf*: tangle. – Neglected masses of knotted hair were supposed to be caused by elves.
11   *presented*: exposed.
13   *proof*: proof of the existence of, experience.
14   *Bedlam beggars*: men who came from, or who pretended to come from, the Hospital of
         'Bedlam' (i.e. Bethlehem) in London, where the insane were gathered to-
         gether. – They begged in the streets and stuck sharp objects into their flesh
         to attract attention. Such a beggar was known as Tom 'o Bedlam (cf. I.ii.125)
         and called out 'Poor Tom's a-cold' to passers-by (cf. line 20 and III.iv.55).
15   *mortified*: deadened, without feeling.
16   *pricks*: skewers.
17   *with . . . object*: by means of this horrible spectacle.
18   *pelting*: petty; *sheep-cotes*: enclosures for sheep.
19   *bans*: curses.
20   *Enforce their charity* – i.e. compel others to show them charity.
20   *Poor . . . Tom* – Edgar begins to act the part of a Bedlam beggar. *Turlygod*, another name
         for a beggar, is otherwise unknown.
21   *That's . . . nothing am*: Something remains to me [as Poor Tom]; as Edgar I am nothing. –
         The fear of disappearance and annihilation runs through the play. The
         exchange between Lear and Cordelia (I.i.86ff.) sets the theme: *Nothing will
         come of nothing*. But there is also a possibility that here the second clause refers
         to his disguise, so that the meaning is simply: 'I am no longer Edgar in any way;
         nothing about me is Edgar.'

Approach, thou beacon to this under globe,*
That by thy comfortable* beams I may
Peruse this letter! [*He takes out a letter.*] Nothing almost   155
sees miracles
But misery.* I know 'tis from Cordelia,
Who hath most fortunately been informed
Of my obscuréd course;* and shall find time
From this enormous state, seeking to give   160
Losses their remedies.* All weary and o'erwatched,*
Take vantage,* heavy eyes, not to behold
This shameful lodging.
Fortune, good night. Smile once more; turn thy wheel!*
                                                          [*Sleeps*

scene iii

A Wood.

Enter EDGAR.

EDGAR   I heard myself proclaimed,*
And by the happy* hollow of a tree
Escaped the hunt. No port* is free, no place,
That guard and most unusual vigilance
Does not attend my taking.* Whiles I may 'scape   5
I will preserve myself, and am bethought*
To take the basest and most poorest shape
That ever penury, in contempt of man,*
Brought near to* beast. My face I'll grime with filth,
Blanket my loins, elf* all my hair in knots,   10
And with presented* nakedness outface
The winds and persecutions of the sky.
The country gives me proof* and precedent
Of Bedlam beggars,* who with roaring voices
Strike in their numbed and mortified* bare arms   15
Pins, wooden pricks,* nails, sprigs of rosemary;
And with this horrible object,* from low farms,
Poor pelting* villages, sheep-cotes and mills,
Sometimes with lunatic bans,* sometimes with prayers,
Enforce their charity.* Poor Turlygod!* poor Tom!   20
That's something yet; Edgar I nothing am.*   [*Exit*

II.iv   Lear now arrives with the Fool, and is enraged to find Kent in the stocks. He goes off to look for Gloucester, and returns with him. Regan and Cornwall also come, but Lear finds he can expect no sympathy from Regan. When Goneril arrives, the problem of the retainers dominates the discussion. Lear's anger and the storm together begin to be felt. Lear leaves, no one knows where for.

The structure of this scene achieves a balance of action and exposition. As in his anger he cursed Goneril in I.iv, Lear is now near to cursing Regan, but forbears. The problem of the retainers is treated at sufficient length to indicate it has some validity, although the reasoning is doubtful. The shattering of Lear's reasonable faith in the natural order is symbolised in the onset of the storm, and man's *needs* in nature seem not to distinguish him from the animal. Has Lear discovered that what he wants lies beyond basic necessity?

1   *they* – i.e. Cornwall and Regan, who are with Gloucester, and to whom Lear sent Kent as his messenger (I.v.1–4). Lear has apparently been to Cornwall's castle already. Regan has received the letter that Goneril sent through Oswald (II.i.124–6 and notes).

3   *there was . . . remove:* they had no plans for making a move.

7   *cruel* – a pun on the more usual sense and on the word *crewel*, thin yarn such as was used for making garters. The Fool is of course referring to the stocks which encase Kent's legs.

9   *over-lusty at legs:* too much inclined to jump about – with perhaps an allusion to Kent as a messenger who has used his legs in a lost cause.

10   *nether-stocks:* stockings – fitting below the *upper-stocks*, i.e. knee-breeches, and with a pun on the wooden stocks Kent is confined in.

11   *What's he . . . thee here:* Who is it that has misunderstood (*mistook*) your rank [as royal messenger] so badly as to put you here?

21   *durst not:* would not dare to.

23   *upon respect:* upon the respect due to [my messenger].

24   *Resolve:* Tell; *modest:* fitting.

24   *which way . . . deserve:* in what way you could have deserved.

26   *Coming from us* – This refers to Kent coming as messenger from the King.

27   *commend:* hand over.

28   *Ere . . . risen:* before I had got up. – Kent is at pains to show that he treated Regan and Cornwall with fitting respect, presenting Lear's letter on his knees.

29   *a reeking post:* a sweating messenger. – The idea of emitting hot moisture is continued in *Stewed* in the following line.

scene iv

In front of Gloucester's castle. Kent in the stocks.

Enter LEAR, FOOL, *and* GENTLEMAN.

LEAR 'Tis strange that they* should so depart from home,
And not send back my messenger.
GENTLEMAN   As I learned,
The night before there was no purpose in them
Of this remove.*
KENT   Hail to thee, noble master!   5
LEAR Ha!
Mak'st thou this shame thy pastime?
KENT   No, my lord.
FOOL Ha, ha! he wears cruel* garters. Horses are tied by the heads,
dogs and bears by the neck, monkeys by the loins, and men
by the legs. When a man's over-lusty at legs,* then he wears
wooden nether-stocks.*   10
LEAR What's* he that hath so much thy place mistook
To set thee here?
KENT   It is both he and she:
Your son and daughter.
LEAR No.
KENT Yes.   15
LEAR No, I say.
KENT I say, yea.
LEAR No, no, they would not.
KENT Yes, they have.
LEAR By Jupiter, I swear, no.   20
KENT By Juno, I swear, ay.
LEAR   They durst* not do 't;
They could not, would not do 't; 'tis worse than murder,
To do upon respect* such violent outrage.
Resolve* me with all modest haste which way
Thou might'st deserve,* or they impose, this usage,   25
Coming from us.*
KENT   My lord, when at their home
I did commend* your highness' letters to them,
Ere I was risen* from the place that showed
My duty kneeling, came there a reeking post,*

32	*spite of intermission:* regardless of the delay [to my own business with them].
33	*on whose contents:* and having read the contents.
34	*meiny:* body of servants.
40	*Displayed:* behaved ostentatiously, 'showed off'.
41	*more . . . wit:* more courage than good sense.
41	*drew:* I drew my sword. – Kent is referring to himself also in *Having* in this line and *meeting* in line 37.
43	*trespass worth:* crime earning.
45	*wild geese* – Flocks of wild geese in the sky were taken as a sign of bad weather to come; they would be flying south to escape the cold of the northern winter. The punishment of Kent is an indication of more trouble for the King. The verse which follows is about fortune following fortune and misfortune following misfortune.
47	*blind* – i.e. blind to their fathers' needs, unkind to them.
48	*bags* – i.e. money bags.
49	*kind:* loving, affectionate – in contrast to *blind* in the sense 'unfeeling, unkind'.
51	*turns the key:* opens the door. – The Fool calls Fortune an utter (*arrant*) harlot because her favours are available only to those who have money.
52	*as many . . . year:* as many sorrows on account of (*for*) your daughters as you can recount (*tell*) in a year. – But the Fool, despite the gravity of what he has to say, seizes the opportunity to make a pun on *dolours* with *dollars* and on *tell* meaning 'count up'.
54	*this mother . . . Hysterica passio* – These were both common names for hysteria, a condition thought to originate in the pit of the stomach and to rise up through the body, affecting one part after another. The term *mother* was popularly associated with the womb of a woman's body, but it may be akin to the by-names of various dreaded diseases in other parts of the world, e.g. smallpox, called 'the goddess' or 'the lady'.
56	*Thy element's below:* your proper place is low down in the body – see preceding note.
61	*How chance:* How does it come about that . . .
65	*We'll set . . . ant:* We'll send you to the ant's school. – The Fool seems to mean that Kent could learn from the ant the answer to his question about Lear's train of attendants (line 61): the King is in the winter of fortune, which is no time for people to work for him, any more than the ant will work in winter when there is no food to be had. Perhaps he is encouraging Kent himself to abandon the King's cause now that the King's fortunes are so low. If so the Fool's own position as set out in the verses in lines 74ff. shows that he is speaking ironically, giving mock advice which is not really advice at all, but a description of the world as it is. This would be characteristic of the Fool's attitude.
67	*but:* except – i.e. if one is not blind, one's eyes give evidence enough of what is to be done: abandon the man in adversity.
68	*stinking* – i.e. reeking of fortune's displeasure, which even a blind man can smell out. The image of the *wheel* which follows is appropriate to fortune (cf. II.ii.164).

Stewed in his haste, half breathless, panting forth   30
From Goneril his mistress salutations;
Delivered letters, spite of intermission,*
Which presently they read; on whose contents*
They summoned up their meiny,* straight took horse,
Commanded me to follow and attend   35
The leisure of their answer; gave me cold looks.
And meeting here the other messenger,
Whose welcome, I perceived, had poisoned mine –
Being the very fellow that of late
Displayed* so saucily against your highness –   40
Having more man than wit* about me, drew.*
He raised the house with loud and coward cries.
Your son and daughter found this trespass worth*
The shame which here it suffers.

FOOL Winter's not gone yet, if the wild geese* fly that way.   45

      Fathers that wear rags
        *Do make their children blind;**
      *But fathers that bear bags**
        *Shall see their children kind.**
      Fortune, that arrant whore,   50
      Ne'er turns the key to the poor.*

But, for all this, thou shalt have as many dolours* for thy
daughters as thou canst tell in a year.

LEAR O, how this mother swells up toward my heart!
    *Hysterica passio,** down, thou climbing sorrow,   55
    Thy element's below!* Where is this daughter?

KENT With the earl, sir, here within.

LEAR Follow me not; stay here.   [*Exit*

GENTLEMAN Made you no more offence but what you speak of?

KENT None.   60
    How chance* the King comes with so small a train?

FOOL And thou hadst been set i' the stocks for that question, thou
hadst well deserved it.

KENT Why, fool?

FOOL We'll set thee to school to an ant,* to teach thee there's no   65
labouring i' the winter. All that follow their noses are led by
their eyes but* blind men; and there's not a nose among
twenty but can smell him that's stinking.* Let go thy hold
when a great wheel runs down a hill, lest it break thy neck
with following it. But the great one that goes up the hill,   70

72   *again:* back.

74   *That sir which:* The man who . . . – It is very much in the Fool's style to break out into these
      verse adages.

75   *for form:* for the sake of appearance – i.e. not from true feelings of loyalty.

76   *pack:* pack up and go. – The mention of the storm is prophetic.

80   *The knave . . . away:* The knave who runs away does what a fool would do. – In these lines
           good sense has in part been sacrificed to verbal play on the contrast between
           knave and *fool* and between the various senses of *fool*. The Fool in the play
           seems to be observing that the *wise* (i.e. prudent) *man* can yet be a fool in that
           there is a wisdom still finer than prudence, the wisdom shown by the fidelity
           of attendant to master. The dilemma is between judgement or shallow realism
           on the one hand and feeling or more profound realism on the other.

81   *perdy:* by God (French: *par Dieu*).

SD   *Re-enter* LEAR – Lear's return at this point is fitting, since the talk has turned to allegiance
           to powerful men, such as he once was, and has reached an impasse.

84   *Deny:* Refuse. – Lear is repeating what Gloucester has been telling him about the refusal
           of Cornwall and Regan to see him.

85   *fetches:* tricks – hence excuses, tricks to get out of an awkward situation.

86   *images:* indications.

87   *Fetch* – an angry pun on *fetches* in line 85.

88   *quality:* character.

90   *course:* course of action – with reference perhaps to stars in their courses (cf. *fiery*).

97   *would:* wants to. – For a moment Lear speaks with mock politeness where he would expect
           to command.

100   *hot:* hot-tempered – catching up the idea of *fiery*, which he has just scorned.

102   *still:* always; *office:* duty.

103   *Whereto:* to which [*office*].

106   *am fall'n . . . will:* am no longer in sympathy with my rasher impulse.

107   *fit:* bout of illness – here extended to mean the sick man in contrast to *the sound man*,
           strong in body and mind, in the next line.

108   *Death . . . state:* May my royal power pass away! – an oath which has a significance he
           does not appreciate.

let him draw thee after. When a wise man gives thee better
counsel, give me mine again.* I would have none but knaves
follow it, since a fool gives it.

> That sir* which serves and seeks for gain,
> And follows but for form,*   75
> Will pack* when it begins to rain,
> And leave thee in the storm.
> But I will tarry; the fool will stay,
> And let the wise man fly.
> The knave turns fool that runs away;*   80
> The fool no knave, perdy.*

KENT Where learned you this, fool?

FOOL Not i' the stocks, fool.

Re-enter LEAR,* *with* GLOUCESTER.

LEAR Deny* to speak with me? They are sick? They are weary?
They have travelled all the night? Mere fetches;*   85
The images* of revolt and flying off.
Fetch* me a better answer.

GLOUCESTER   My dear lord,
You know the fiery quality* of the duke,
How unremovable and fixed he is
In his own course.*   90

LEAR Vengeance! plague! death! confusion!
'Fiery'? what 'quality'? Why, Gloucester, Gloucester,
I'd speak with the Duke of Cornwall and his wife.

GLOUCESTER Well, my good lord, I have informed them so.

LEAR Informed them! Dost thou understand me, man?   95

GLOUCESTER Ay, my good lord.

LEAR The King would* speak with Cornwall; the dear father
Would with his daughter speak, commands her service.
Are they informed of this? My breath and blood!
'Fiery'? 'the fiery duke'? Tell the hot* duke that –   100
No, but not yet; may be he is not well;
Infirmity doth still* neglect all office
Whereto* our health is bound; we are not ourselves
When nature being oppressed commands the mind
To suffer with the body. I'll forbear;   105
And am fall'n out with my more headier will,*
To take the indisposed and sickly fit*
For the sound man. [*Looking at* KENT] Death on my state!*

108   *Wherefore:* Why. – As he looks at Kent in the stocks, his anger is directed once more at Cornwall.
110   *remotion:* remoteness, holding themselves aloof.
111   *practice:* cunning; *forth* – i.e. out of the stocks.
114   *chamber:* private apartment.
115   *it cry . . . death:* it [the noise of the drum] has put sleep to death, made them give up all attempts to sleep.
116   *would:* want to.
117   *rising heart* – Cf. line 55: *Hysterica passio . . . thou climbing sorrow.*
118   *as the cockney . . . alive:* as the woman did to the eels when she put them still alive into the pastry. – *cockney,* then as now, referred to a Londoner, but was also used to mean an affected woman or a cook. All or any of these meanings would make sense here; a comic London woman is probably meant. She and her brother show the same misguided tender-heartedness. She cannot bring herself to kill the eels before putting them into the pie, and only hits them on the head when they wriggle. Her brother buttered his horse's hay. Lear's heart has been foolishly tender towards his daughters, but it is now too late to cry 'down' to it.
119   *knapped:* hit with a smart blow.
119   *coxcombs:* heads. – The word is used ludicrously.
120   *wantons:* you playful creatures.
121   *buttered his hay* – The hero of this story (introduced for convenience as the cockney's brother) thought he was being kind to his horse by putting butter on its hay. Horses in fact dislike grease, as every man in Shakespeare's audience knew.
122   *Good morrow:* Good morning, good day. – Since it is evening, Lear is speaking cuttingly to Cornwall and Regan, who should have been with him earlier in the day.
125   *thou . . . glad:* you were not glad.
126   *I would . . . adulteress:* I would dissociate myself from your mother's tomb, as being the burial place of an adulteress. – If Regan were not glad to see her father, he could surmise only that her mother had not been a faithful wife to him.
128   *Some other time* – Lear means he will take up later the wrongful seizing of Kent.
129   *naught:* wicked.
130   *like a vulture* – This is probably a reference to the classical story of Prometheus, who stole fire from heaven and was punished by Zeus by being chained to a rock where every day an eagle consumed his liver, while every night a new liver grew in his body. But the general meaning is that Goneril's unkindness is eating into Lear's heart.
132   *quality:* manner. – Overwhelming grief prevents him from finishing the sentence.
133   *I have hope . . . duty* (line 135): I am inclined to believe that you are undervaluing her rather than that she is being undutiful to you.
138   *riots* – These were the pretext for a reduction in the size of Lear's train (I.iv.232 etc.); *have:* may have.
139   *ground:* grounds, reason; *wholesome:* beneficial.

Wherefore*
Should he sit here? This act persuades me
That this remotion* of the duke and her   110
Is practice* only. Give me my servant forth.
Go tell the duke and 's wife I'd speak with them,
Now, presently. Bid them come forth and hear me,
Or at their chamber* door I'll beat the drum
Till it cry sleep* to death.   115

GLOUCESTER I would* have all well betwixt you.   [Exit

LEAR O me, my heart, my rising heart!* But down!

FOOL Cry to it, nuncle, as the cockney did to the eels* when she
put 'em i' the paste alive: she knapped* 'em o' the coxcombs*
with a stick, and cried 'Down, wantons,* down!' 'Twas her   120
brother that, in pure kindness to his horse, buttered his hay.*

Re-enter GLOUCESTER, *with* CORNWALL, REGAN, *and* SERVANTS.

LEAR Good morrow* to you both.

CORNWALL   Hail to your grace!
                                                    [KENT *is set free*

REGAN I am glad to see your highness.

LEAR Regan, I think you are; I know what reason
I have to think so: if thou shouldst not be glad,*   125
I would divorce me from thy mother's tomb,
Sepulchring an adult'ress.* [*To* KENT] O, are you free?
Some other time* for that. [*Exit* KENT] Belovéd Regan,
Thy sister's naught.* O Regan, she hath tied
Sharp-toothed unkindness, like a vulture,* here.   130
                                          [*Points to his heart*
I can scarce speak to thee; thou'lt not believe
With how depraved a quality* – O Regan!

REGAN I pray you, sir, take patience. I have hope*
You less know how to value her desert
Than she to scant her duty.

LEAR   Say, how is that?   135

REGAN I cannot think my sister in the least
Would fail her obligation. If, sir, perchance
She have restrained the riots* of your followers,
'Tis on such ground* and to such wholesome end
As clears her from all blame.   140

LEAR My curses on her!

REGAN   O, sir, you are old.
Nature in you stands on the very verge

143   *confine:* assigned limit.
144   *discretion:* discreet person; *state:* condition.
148   *mark . . . house:* notice how this befits our family, the royal house. – This remark leads into
          the irony of the lines that follow: the parent is a suppliant to his child, not vice
          versa.
150   *Age is unnecessary:* Old people are useless.
151   *vouchsafe:* deign to give; *raiment:* clothes.
154   *abated:* deprived.
155   *struck . . . tongue:* chastised me with words. – The metaphor of the tongue is continued
          with *serpent-like* in the next line.
158   *ingrateful top:* ungrateful head.
158   *young bones* – This presumably refers to Goneril's own bones, but a passage in the analogue,
          King Leir, has the phrase in the sense 'unborn children'. Shakespeare may have
          recalled the phrase but given it a more literal meaning.
159   *taking:* infecting – with an implication of supernatural causes.
162   *fen-sucked:* sucked up from the marshes. – Mists seemed to be sucked up out of the un-
          healthy marshes by the action of the sun.
163   *To fall . . . pride* – This line is difficult to interpret, and the version we have now seems to
          be corrupt; the F reading finishes . . . *blister;* the Q is as given here. The general
          meaning is clear enough: he curses her beauty and the pride she takes in it.
          Literally the line may mean: so that it [her beauty] should fall away and wither
          her pride.
167   *tender-hefted* – The context suggests that this means 'tender-hearted, gentle'. *Heft* or *haft*
          are forms of a word meaning 'handle', and it has been suggested that the com-
          pound may mean 'set in a tender handle or bodily frame', but the notion is
          far-fetched, and the reading may be incorrect.
171   *scant my sizes:* cut down my allowances.
172   *oppose . . . coming in:* prevent me from coming in by bolting the door.
174   *offices of nature:* natural duties [that a child owes to its parent].
174   *bond of childhood:* a child's obligations to its parents.
175   *Effects:* forms.
177   *Wherein:* with which.
177   *to the purpose:* get to the point. – What he is saying, she means, is irrelevant.
SD   *Tucket,* a trumpet call, the 'signature tune' of an important person, used to announce his
          arrival. Regan recognises this one as her sister's.
179   *this approves . . . here:* she said in her letter that she would soon be here, and this confirms
          (*approves*) it.

Of her confine.* You should be ruled and led
By some discretion* that discerns your state
Better than you yourself. Therefore I pray you   145
That to our sister you do make return;
Say you have wronged her, sir.

LEAR   Ask her forgiveness?
Do you but mark* how this becomes the house:
[Kneeling] 'Dear daughter, I confess that I am old.
Age is unnecessary.* On my knees I beg   150
That you'll vouchsafe* me raiment, bed and food.'

REGAN   Good sir, no more; these are unsightly tricks.
Return you to my sister.

LEAR   [Rising]   Never, Regan.
She hath abated* me of half my train;
Looked black upon me; struck me with her tongue,*   155
Most serpent-like, upon the very heart.
All the stored vengeances of heaven fall
On her ingrateful* top! Strike her young bones,*
You taking* airs, with lameness.

CORNWALL   Fie, sir, fie!

LEAR   You nimble lightnings, dart your blinding flames   160
Into her scornful eyes. Infect her beauty,
You fen-sucked* fogs, drawn by the powerful sun,
To fall and blast her pride.*

REGAN   O the blest gods! so will you wish on me,
When the rash mood is on.   165

LEAR   No, Regan, thou shalt never have my curse.
Thy tender-hefted* nature shall not give
Thee o'er to harshness. Her eyes are fierce, but thine
Do comfort and not burn. 'Tis not in thee
To grudge my pleasures, to cut off my train,   170
To bandy hasty words, to scant my sizes,*
And in conclusion to oppose the bolt*
Against my coming in. Thou better know'st
The offices of nature,* bond of childhood,
Effects* of courtesy, dues of gratitude;   175
Thy half o' the kingdom hast thou not forgot,
Wherein* I thee endowed.

REGAN   Good sir, to the purpose.*

LEAR   Who put my man i' the stocks?   [Tucket* within

CORNWALL   What trumpet's that?

REGAN   I know 't; my sister's; this approves* her letter,

181   *easy-borrowed*: taken on without justification. – This pride, which has nothing to justify
       it, springs from the uncertain favour (*fickle grace*) of his mistress. Lear has
       found Goneril's favour towards himself uncertain, and so, he suggests, will
       Oswald.
184   *on 't*: of it.
186   *you* – i.e. *Heavens*, the gods.
186   *your sweet . . . obedience*: your kindly rule approves of obedience.
187   *yourselves*: you yourselves – still referring to the *Heavens*.
188   *send down* – i.e. send me help.
189   *this beard* – as a symbol of old age. With his daughters both together before him he first
       watches their reactions to one another in the increasing tension of the situation.
190   *wilt . . . hand*: you are taking her by the hand! – i.e. a cry of protest rather than a question.
192   *All's not . . . terms so*: Everything is not offensive which [an old man's] lack of judgement
       (*indiscretion*) considers to be an offence and [his] dotage calls offensive.
193   *O sides . . .* – Lear is referring to the sides of his body, which seem too strong to allow
       his heart to break in his paroxysm of sorrow.
195   *disorders*: disorderly acts.
196   *advancement*: honour.
197   *being weak, seem so* – i.e. behave in a way that suits a weak old man.
201   *from*: away from.
205   *wage*: contend – as in 'to wage war'.
207   *Necessity's sharp pinch* – i.e. to accept these things as hardships brought on by necessity
       (the need to avoid at all costs a return to Goneril).
210   *knee*: kneel before.
210   *squire-like*: like a personal servant.
210   *pension . . . afoot*: beg for a small allowance (*pension*) to keep me in the humblest condition
       of life.
212   *sumpter*: drudge – literally : 'pack-horse'.

That she would soon be here.

Enter OSWALD.

                                   Is your lady come?   180
LEAR This is a slave whose easy-borrowed* pride
Dwells in the fickle grace of her he follows.
Out, varlet, from my sight!
CORNWALL   What means your grace?
LEAR Who stocked my servant? Regan, I have good hope
Thou didst not know on 't.* Who comes here?

Enter GONERIL.

                                   O Heavens,   185
If you* do love old men, if your sweet sway
Allow obedience,* if yourselves* are old,
Make it your cause; send down,* and take my part!
[*To* GONERIL] Art not ashamed to look upon this beard?*
O Regan, wilt thou take her by the hand?*   190
GONERIL Why not by the hand, sir? How have I offended?
All's not offence that indiscretion* finds
And dotage terms so.
LEAR   O sides, you are too tough.*
Will you yet hold? How came my man i' the stocks?
CORNWALL I set him there, sir; but his own disorders*   195
Deserved much less advancement.*
LEAR   You! did you?
REGAN I pray you, father, being weak, seem so.*
If, till the expiration of your month,
You will return and sojourn with my sister,
Dismissing half your train, come then to me.   200
I am now from* home, and out of that provision
Which shall be needful for your entertainment.
LEAR Return to her, and fifty men dismissed?
No, rather I abjure all roofs, and choose
To wage* against the enmity o' the air,   205
To be a comrade with the wolf and owl –
Necessity's sharp pinch!* Return with her?
Why, the hot-blooded France, that dowerless took
Our youngest born, I could as well be brought
To knee* his throne, and squire-like,* pension beg   210
To keep base life afoot.* Return with her?
Persuade me rather to be slave and sumpter*

220   *embossed:* swollen.

223   *the thunder-bearer* – Jupiter, the god in classical mythology who was armed with thunder-bolts as weapons. People in distress called on him to avenge them.

224   *high-judging:* judging from on high, or supreme judge. – *Jove* is another name for Jupiter.

225   *Mend:* Reform, improve yourself.

225   *be better . . . leisure* – This is another way of saying what is in the first half of the line: 'improve when it is convenient for you to do so'.

230   *that mingle . . . passion:* who bring some common sense to bear on your passionate out-bursts. – Lear has, on the contrary, shown some amount of sense in the ordering of his appeals; he has with reasoned patience turned to Regan when Goneril argued against accommodating him, and deftly introduced his condition that he should bring his hundred knights with him (line 227).

235   *sith that:* since; *charge:* expense.

241   *slack you:* be inattentive in their duties to you.

246   *gave,* caught up from *give* in the preceding line.

246   *And in . . .gave it:* And not a moment too soon [because you were becoming totally in-competent to manage your own affairs.

247   *my guardians, my depositaries:* people who looked after my property, my trustees.

248   *reservation to be:* reserved right that I should be . . . – Cf. I.i.128. The question of the atten-dants now takes on giant proportions; it is becoming a test case of the amount of true power left in the King's hands. The numbers of followers mentioned in the succeeding lines give Lear a second opportunity to think of filial love meted out in specific quantities. Cf. I.i.97–8, where Cordelia says:

> *That lord whose hand must take my plight shall carry*
> *Half my love with him, half my care and duty.*

To this detested groom.   [*Pointing at* OSWALD

GONERIL   At your choice, sir.

LEAR [*To* GONERIL] I prithee, daughter, do not make me mad.
I will not trouble thee, my child; farewell.   215
We'll no more meet, no more see one another –
But yet thou art my flesh, my blood, my daughter;
Or rather a disease that's in my flesh,
Which I must needs call mine. Thou art a boil,
A plague-sore, an embosséd* carbuncle,   220
In my corrupted blood. But I'll not chide thee;
Let shame come when it will, I do not call it.
I do not bid the thunder-bearer* shoot,
Nor tell tales of thee to high-judging* Jove.
Mend* when thou canst; be better at thy leisure.*   225
I can be patient; I can stay with Regan,
I and my hundred knights.

REGAN   Not altogether so:
I looked not for you yet, nor am provided
For your fit welcome. Give ear, sir, to my sister;
For those that mingle reason with your passion*   230
Must be content to think you old, and so –
But she knows what she does.

LEAR   Is this well spoken?

REGAN I dare avouch it, sir. What, fifty followers?
Is it not well? What should you need of more?
Yea, or so many, sith* that both charge and danger   235
Speak 'gainst so great a number? How in one house
Should many people under two commands
Hold amity? 'Tis hard, almost impossible.

GONERIL Why might not you, my lord, receive attendance
From those that she calls servants or from mine?   240

REGAN Why not, my lord? If then they chanced to slack* you,
We could control them. If you will come to me,
For now I spy a danger, I entreat you
To bring but five-and-twenty; to no more
Will I give place or notice.   245

LEAR I gave* you all –

REGAN   And in good time you gave it.*

LEAR Made you my guardians, my depositaries,*
But kept a reservation to be* followed
With such a number. What, must I come to you
With five-and-twenty? Regan, said you so?   250

252   *Those wicked . . . wicked:* Even wicked people's appearance improves when [you find that] others are still more wicked. – The twenty-five Regan says she will allow is even harsher than Goneril's fifty (line 203); Goneril is therefore not so bad after all. Lear turns to her.

258   *follow:* attend.

260   *reason not:* do not argue about. – Lear realises that he has been let down, since quantitative reasoning can be no measure for love, only for judgement.

261   *Are in . . . superfluous* – i.e. however poor they are, they have something more than is absolutely necessary for survival. If they were totally reduced to bare necessity, they would not be distinguishable from animals.

262   *Allow not:* If you do not allow.

264   *If only . . . warm* (line 266): if it were gorgeous merely to keep oneself warm you would not need to wear the gorgeous apparel you have now got on, which [being fashionably scanty] hardly keeps you warm in any case. – This is a further illustration of varying notions of what constitutes necessity, and foreshadows the cold terrors of the storm.

266   *for true need:* as for true necessity. – Lear breaks off here, turning his attention to what he most needs in the present predicament: patience. And in a few touching lines he gives a shrewd description of his own condition. But this soon degenerates into a string of futile threats.

271   *fool . . . much:* do not make me such a fool as . . .

281   *flaws:* fragments.

283   *storm* – The foreboding storm symbolises the smouldering passion in Lear's brain, soon to burst into flames.

285   *bestowed:* lodged.

286   *hath . . . rest:* he has estranged himself from peace of mind.

288   *For his particular:* As far as he himself is concerned.

REGAN   And speak 't again, my lord; no more with me.

LEAR   Those wicked* creatures yet do look well-favoured,
When others are more wicked; not being the worst
Stands in some rank of praise. [*To* GONERIL] I'll go with
thee:
Thy fifty yet doth double five-and-twenty,   255
And thou art twice her love.

GONERIL   Hear me, my lord:
What need you five-and-twenty, ten, or five,
To follow* in a house where twice so many
Have a command to tend you?

REGAN   What need one?

LEAR   O, reason not* the need. Our basest beggars   260
Are in the poorest thing superfluous.*
Allow not* nature more than nature needs,
Man's life 's as cheap as beast's. Thou art a lady;
If only to go warm were gorgeous,*
Why, nature needs not what thou gorgeous wear'st,   265
Which scarcely keeps thee warm. But for true need* –
You heavens, give me that patience, patience I need!
You see me here, you gods, a poor old man,
As full of grief as age, wretched in both.
If it be you that stirs these daughters' hearts   270
Against their father, fool me not so much*
To bear it tamely. Touch me with noble anger,
And let not women's weapons, water-drops,
Stain my man's cheeks! No, you unnatural hags,
I will have such revenges on you both   275
That all the world shall – I will do such things –
What they are, yet I know not, but they shall be
The terrors of the earth. You think I'll weep;
No, I'll not weep; [*Storm heard at a distance.*]
I have full cause of weeping. But this heart   280
Shall break into a hundred thousand flaws*
Or ere I'll weep. O fool, I shall go mad!
          [*Exeunt* LEAR, GLOUCESTER, GENTLEMAN *and* FOOL

CORNWALL   Let us withdraw; 'twill be a storm.*   [*Storm and tempest*

REGAN   This house is little. The old man and his people
Cannot be well bestowed.*   285

GONERIL   'Tis his own blame; hath put himself from rest,*
And must needs taste his folly.

REGAN   For his particular,* I'll receive him gladly,

289   *purposed:* resolved.
293   *calls to horse* – i.e. calls his people to mount their horses; *will:* will go.
294   *give him way:* let him go his own way.
295   *entreat . . . stay:* do not do anything to try to persuade him to stay (*by no means* modifies
        entreat).
297   *ruffle:* bluster.
301   *with:* by. – The *desperate train* are evidently the few followers who did not desert the
        King (cf. line 61); saying that they are *desperate* (enraged and reckless), Regan
        makes them an excuse for shutting up the doors.
302   *incense:* incite; *apt:* ready, willing.
303   *wisdom:* common sense.
304   *my lord* – i.e. Gloucester, who seems to hesitate out of feelings of pity for Lear.

But not one follower.

GONERIL   So am I purposed.*

Where is my Lord of Gloucester?   290

CORNWALL Followed the old man forth. He is returned.

Re-enter GLOUCESTER.

GLOUCESTER The King is in high rage.

CORNWALL   Whither is he going?

GLOUCESTER He calls to horse,* but will I know not whither.

CORNWALL 'Tis best to give him way;* he leads himself.

GONERIL My lord, entreat him by no means to stay.*   295

GLOUCESTER Alack, the night comes on, and the bleak winds
Do sorely ruffle.* For many miles about
There's scarce a bush.

REGAN   O, sir, to wilful men
The injuries that they themselves procure
Must be their schoolmasters. Shut up your doors.   300
He is attended with* a desperate train,
And what they may incense* him to, being apt
To have his ear abused, wisdom* bids fear.

CORNWALL Shut up your doors, my lord.* 'Tis a wild night.
My Regan counsels well. Come out o' the storm.   305

[*Exeunt*

Kent, Lear, Fool and Edgar as poor Tom (Act III, Scene vi).

Cornwall blinding Gloucester, with Regan looking on (Act III, Scene vii).

III.i   The rumour of dissent between Cornwall and Albany (II.i) is now seen as a possible source of comfort, since it looks as if it will be at least a pretext for a French invasion. This is revealed by Kent when he meets a gentleman of the King's retinue in the height of the storm.

2   *One minded*: Someone whose mind is engaged. – The gentleman opens his mind to Kent, and in this way furnishes descriptions of the King's plight which could not be realised in action on the stage.

4   *fretful elements*: tempestuous wind and rain. – The word *fretful* would usually be applied to a person, 'ill-tempered', and may therefore extend here the train of thought in *minded . . . unquietly* (line 2). The *elements* are the heavens and the wind and rain beneath the sky. Cf. also *impetuous* (line 8).

6   *curléd* – i.e. with great waves; *main*: land.

7   *things*: the state of the world in general.

8   *eyeless*: blind.

9   *make nothing of*: treat without respect.

10   *his little . . . man* – In Shakespeare's day a popular view of man was to imagine him as a miniature representation of the world or the universe. Man was sometimes referred to as the *microcosm* ('little world') as against the great world about us (the *macrocosm*). Both were looked upon as systems having some interrelation with the whole of creation. Lear's *little world* here is weak in contention with the storm of the world about him.

12   *cub-drawn*: ferocious and hungry, having been sucked dry of milk by its cubs; *couch*: take cover.

13   *belly-pinchéd*: starving, pinched in the stomach.

14   *unbonneted*: with head uncovered.

15   *take all* – i.e. he is prepared to part with everything.

16   *out-jest . . . injuries*: drive out with jokes the ill-usage which has pierced him to the heart.

18   *upon . . . note*: on the strength of what I know about you; *note*: knowledge, information.

19   *Commend . . . thing*: entrust an important matter.

19   *division*: angry disagreement.

22   *Who have . . .* – The talk is of people who seem merely servants in a great household but are in fact spies. All high-born people are likely to have them.

22   *that . . . high*: who have been exalted and placed high by the auspicious stars of their fortune.

24   *speculations*: watchers.

25   *Intelligent*: giving information. – This mention of 'intelligence' contributes to the picture being built up of a state of war between Britain and France.

26   *snuffs and packings*: quarrels and plotting.

27   *the hard . . . borne*: the cruel way in which both of them have acted. – A rider who is cruel to the horse's mouth is said to *bear a hard rein*.

29   *furnishings*: unimportant externals, trimmings.

30   *from France* – Kent is disturbed over the whole situation and rushes ahead with sentences which are not properly shaped. (The punctuation given here assumes that the clauses following *state* in line 25 give the kind of information referred to in *Intelligent*: '. . . giving information about our state [on such matters as] what has been seen . . .') Shakespeare is skating quickly over some rather difficult features of his plot: France would take some time to muster forces to deal with the traitorous daughters and their husbands, and must be made to seem disinterested in doing so (one does not plant spies in an unoffending friendly country or prepare to invade it without clear evidence of offences).

30   *power*: army – see Introduction, p. ii.

31   *scattered*: distracted, disunited; *who* – refers to *power*.

32   *Wise . . . negligence*: taking wise advantage of our lack of preparedness.

32   *secret feet*: a secret foothold.

33   *at point*: ready. – They are confident enough to be ready to reveal themselves by displaying their military colours (*open banner*).

ACT III scene i

A heath.

Storm still. Enter KENT *and a* GENTLEMAN, *meeting.*

KENT   Who's there, besides foul weather?

GENTLEMAN   One minded* like the weather, most unquietly.

KENT   I know you. Where's the King?

GENTLEMAN   Contending with the fretful elements;*
Bids the wind blow the earth into the sea,   5
Or swell the curléd* waters 'bove the main,
That things* might change or cease; tears his white hair,
Which the impetuous blasts, with eyeless* rage,
Catch in their fury, and make nothing of;*
Strives in his little world of man* to out-scorn   10
The to-and-fro-conflicting wind and rain.
This night, wherein the cub-drawn* bear would couch,*
The lion and the belly-pinchéd* wolf
Keep their fur dry, unbonneted* he runs,
And bids what will take all.*

KENT   But who is with him?   15

GENTLEMAN   None but the fool, who labours to out-jest*
His heart-struck injuries.

KENT   Sir, I do know you,
And dare, upon the warrant,* of my note
Commend a dear thing* to you. There is division,*
Although as yet the face of it is covered   20
With mutual cunning, 'twixt Albany and Cornwall;
Who have* – as who have not, that their great stars
Throned and set high?* – servants, who seem no less,
Which are to France the spies and speculations*
Intelligent* of our state: what hath been seen,   25
Either in snuffs* and packings of the dukes,
Or the hard rein* which both of them have borne
Against the old kind King; or something deeper,
Whereof perchance these are but furnishings* –
But true it is, from France* there comes a power*   30
Into this scattered* kingdom; who already,
Wise in our negligence,* have secret feet*
In some of our best ports, and are at point*

34   *Now to you:* Now this is where you become concerned.
35   *on my credit:* on the strength of what I say.
35   *build –* i.e. place your confidence.
36   *To:* as to.
37   *making just report:* for making an accurate report.
38   *how:* how much; *bemadding:* maddening.
39   *plain:* complain of.
41   *assurance:* confidence [in my information].
42   *office:* task, opportunity for service.
45   *out-wall:* outward appearance. – Kent's appearance makes the gentleman doubt his
         authority, and at first he wants to delay making a decision. But the contents of
         Kent's purse convince him; to prove his good faith Kent has a ring Cordelia
         will recognise.
48   *fellow:* companion [in what is to be done]. – Kent is referring to himself.
49   *Fie on:* A curse on.
52   *to effect:* in importance.
53   *in which . . . this:* in which task it is for you (*your pain*) to go that way, while I go this.
55   *Holla:* call out to.

III.ii   Like the gusts in the storm, Lear wavers between raging against the wind and rain and
         resigning himself to the shelter of the hovel which the disguised Kent persuades him to
         go into. The Fool keeps up a bitter cheerfulness.
              This scene and the preceding one are static, like the eye of the storm; Lear faces the
         elements.

2   *cataracts and hurricanoes:* downpours of rain and cloudbursts. – Lear's railing against the
         storm has been found by audiences over the centuries a specially memorable
         part of the play.
3   *drowned the cocks:* submerged the weathercocks [on the steeples].
4   *thought-executing fires:* lightning striking with the speed of thought. – Lightning was
         associated in men's minds with the burning of sulphur; cf. *Coriolanus* v.iii.151–3,
         where there are echoes of this passage:
                   To tear with thunder the wide cheeks o' the air
                   And yet to charge thy sulphur with a bolt
                   That should but rive an oak.
5   *Vaunt-couriers:* heralds, forerunners.
7   *rotundity . . . world –* i.e. the roundness of the earth's sphere.

To show their open banner. Now to you:*
If on my credit* you dare build* so far   35
To* make your speed to Dover, you shall find
Some that will thank you, making just report*
Of how* unnatural and bemadding sorrow
The King hath cause to plain.*
I am a gentleman of blood and breeding,   40
And from some knowledge and assurance* offer
This office* to you.

GENTLEMEN   I will talk further with you.

KENT   No, do not.
For confirmation that I am much more
Than my out-wall,* open this purse and take   45
What it contains. If you shall see Cordelia –
As fear not but you shall – show her this ring,
And she will tell you who your fellow* is
That yet you do not know. Fie on* this storm!
I will go seek the King.

GENTLEMAN   Give me your hand.   50
Have you no more to say?

KENT   Few words, but, to effect,* more than all yet:
That when we have found the King – in which your pain*
That way, I'll this – he that first lights on him
Holla* the other.

                              [*Exeunt in different directions*   55

scene ii

Another part of the heath. Storm still.

Enter LEAR *and* FOOL.

LEAR   Blow, winds, and crack your cheeks! rage! blow!
You cataracts and hurricanoes,* spout
Till you have drenched our steeples, drowned the cocks!*
You sulphurous and thought-executing fires,*
Vaunt-couriers* to oak-cleaving thunderbolts,   5
Singe my white head! And thou, all-shaking thunder,
Smite flat the thick rotundity* o' the world!

8   *Crack . . . man:* Break the moulds which nature uses, and destroy (*spill*) at once all the seeds of life (*germens*) which go to making ungrateful human beings. – The image of cracking the moulds carries with it the idea of utter destruction: if the mould is once broken, there is no hope of producing any more objects exactly according to its shape, and order and continuity are therefore lost.

10   *court holy-water:* flattery. – This is a set phrase evidently modelled on the French *eau bénite de cour*, which has the same meaning. The phrase refers literally to the holy water blessed by the priest and sprinkled on the faithful as a token of God's blessing. It contrasts neatly with *rain-water*, in the tradition of the Fool's clowning. Cf. *neither wise man nor fool* (line 12).

11   *out o' door:* outside [the house].

16   *tax:* accuse.

18   *subscription:* obedience.

21   *ministers:* agents. – In the preceding line the King puts in little space a realistic description of himself, and thus reaches a point of clarity and reason in the confusion of the storm. He 'taxes the elements' not for the wretchedness they bring but for being agents (*ministers*) of a worse evil, the unkindness of his daughters.

22   *joined . . . battles:* joined your battalions brought forth in the heavens.

25   *put 's:* put his.

25   *head-piece:* both 'helmet, a cover for the head', and 'brain'. – The word leads the Fool to think of armour and hence *cod-piece*, which begins the jingle.

26   *The . . . louse* (line 28): The man who seeks sexual satisfaction before he has a roof over his head will become infected with lice (*louse*) in head and body. – The *cod-piece* was the bag at the front of leg-armour or tight-fitting hose worn by men; here the meaning is transferred to the organ of the body which the cod-piece covered, and *house* means 'seek entry', i.e. seek to have intercourse. The transference follows the pattern of *headpiece* and brain (line 25). Here is another instance of passion (in this case the sex urge) dominating good sense (the provision of a roof over one's head).

29   *So . . . many:* Many beggars marry in this way.

30   *The man . . . wake* (line 33): The man who pays more attention to his toe (an unimportant part of his body) than to his heart (a vital part) will suffer grievously from a corn and will be kept awake when he wants to sleep (*turn his sleep to wake*, i.e. change his sleeping to wakefulness). – In more general terms, a man is misguided if he takes too much notice of a mean part of his body because that is where he is most likely to suffer physically. Lear has favoured his evil and worthless daughters and foolishly neglected the true and honest Cordelia. In saying this, the Fool is not changing the attitude he adopted in the first stanza; he is acknowledging the heart as a third element in human motivation, along with unbridled passion (the cod-piece) and cold reason (the head). This stanza implies that the heart should be supreme.

35   *there was . . . glass* – This is probably an irrelevant piece of nonsense thrown in to distract the attention from satire too bitter to be easily acceptable. All pretty women think of making themselves attractive by trying out new expressions in the mirror. Perhaps he means that even beautiful women are dissatisfied and worry about trivialities such as trying to make themselves look even prettier.

39   *grace and a cod-piece* – The Fool contrasts *grace*, the harmony of natural order, 'nature' intact and unblemished, and *cod-piece*, the image of the improvident man, overconcerned with physical gratification but without a roof over his head. It is left to the audience to decide which is the wise man and which the fool: *grace* suggests the King and *cod-piece* the Fool, but events suggest that they have exchanged their roles.

43   *Gallow:* terrify; *wanderers . . . dark:* wild beasts which roam in the night.

Crack nature's moulds,* all germens spill at once,
That make ingrateful man!

FOOL O nuncle, court holy-water* in a dry house is better than   10
this rain-water out o' door.* Good nuncle, in, and ask thy
daughters' blessing. Here 's a night pities neither wise man
nor fool.

LEAR Rumble thy bellyful! Spit, fire! spout, rain!
Nor rain, wind, thunder, fire, are my daughters;   15
I tax* not you, you elements, with unkindness;
I never gave you kingdom, called you children,
You owe me no subscription.* Then let fall
Your horrible pleasure. Here I stand, your slave,
A poor, infirm, weak and despised old man;   20
But yet I call you servile ministers,*
That have with two pernicious daughters joined
Your high-engendered battles* 'gainst a head
So old and white as this. O! ho! 'tis foul!

FOOL He that has a house to put 's* head in has a good head-piece.*   25

The cod-piece that will house
Before the head has any,
*The head and he shall louse;**
*So beggars marry many.**

The man that makes his toe   30
What he his heart should make
Shall of a corn cry woe,
*And turn his sleep to wake.**

For there was never yet fair woman but she made mouths in
a glass.*   35

LEAR No, I will be the pattern of all patience;
I will say nothing.

Enter KENT.

KENT Who's there?

FOOL Marry, here's grace* and a cod-piece; that's a wise man and
a fool.   40

KENT Alas, sir, are you here? Things that love night
Love not such nights as these. The wrathful skies
Gallow* the very wanderers of the dark,
And make them keep their caves. Since I was man,
Such sheets of fire, such bursts of horrid thunder,   45

47   *carry:* bear.
49   *dreadful pudder:* turmoil causing great fear.
50   *Find . . . now* – This is in the sense that those who offend the gods by their misdeeds will
      not be able to conceal their terror.
52   *of justice:* by the agents of justice.
53   *perjured:* perjurer, one who is perjured, who lies in a court of law.
53   *simular:* simulating, pretending to be virtuous.
54   *caitiff:* wretch.
55   *convenient seeming:* fair-seeming hypocrisy.
56   *practised on:* plotted against; *guilts:* crimes.
57   *Rive . . . grace:* burst open what holds you in (*continents*) and hides you (*concealing*), and
      cry for mercy (*cry . . . grace*) from these dreadful ministers of justice (*summoners*,
      literally the officers who called offenders before the ecclesiastical courts).
59   *I am . . . sinning* – Lear compares himself with the evil-doers he has just mentioned: they
      have crimes to conceal and must be warned that they will suffer in the end;
      he has few crimes to conceal and yet is being made to suffer now.
59   *Alack:* Alas; *bare-headed* suggests the lack in the physical sense of the protection which
      Lear has already spoken of in metaphorical terms in relation to the concealment
      of evil.
60   *hard by:* very near.
61   *lend:* provide.
64   *Which even . . . come in:* the dwellers in which a short time ago (*even but now*) refused to let
      me in when I asked for you. – Kent, unable to find the King in the storm,
      apparently went back to Gloucester's castle to look for him there.
65   *force . . . courtesy:* compel them to show the humane behaviour they withheld (*scanted*).
67   *dost* – i.e. *dost thou:* are you.
68   *straw* – i.e. the hovel, an open shelter thatched with straw (as also at III.iv.42).
69   *The art . . . precious.* Necessity produces a strange art that can turn base things into
      something precious. – Necessity makes the hovel entirely desirable; and there
      is also an allusion to the science (*art*) by which alchemists expected to turn
      base metals into gold (the *vile* into the *precious*).
73   *He that . . . –* This stanza sounds like a part of Feste's song in *Twelfth Night* v.i.369; the
      second and fourth lines are the same in general, and the theme is consistent:
      contentment comes from acceptance of one's fortunes and abilities. The song
      was probably a favourite with an actor in Shakespeare's company.
73   *and:* but, only – the main purpose of the word being to fill out the rhythm of the line.
75   *Must make . . . fit:* must make contentment match his fortunes – i.e. be content with his
      fortune.
77   *True* – Lear admits that the advice in the stanza of the song is true and suited to his own
      case.
77   *bring:* lead.
78   *brave:* fine. – He speaks sarcastically.
78   *a prophecy* – The lines which follow are not in Q and may be an interpolation by an actor.
      Pointing out an anachronism and making a joke of it (line 94: *I live before his
      time*) sounds un-Shakespearian. The prophetic lines are in the style of a set of
      verses printed in Puttenham's *Arte of English Poesie* (1589 – ed. Arber, p. 232)
      which finish with a couplet very similar to lines 90–1 of the text:
                  Than shal the londe of albyon
                  Be brought to great confusyon.
      The verses in Puttenham mention a number of customary practices in everyday
      life which would spell the country's ruin if they became widespread. The Fool's
      verses begin in the same vein, but for comic effect change direction (beginning
      line 84) and list *desirable* practices, thus becoming utopian instead of admoni-
      tory. The Fool's version therefore seems to be a parody of the Puttenham
      version.
80   *are . . . matter:* are more concerned with the words they use than with what they are talking
      about.

Such groans of roaring wind and rain, I never
Remember to have heard. Man's nature cannot carry*
The affliction nor the fear.

LEAR   Let the great gods,
That keep this dreadful pudder* o'er our heads,
Find out their enemies now.* Tremble, thou wretch,   50
That hast within thee undivulgéd crimes,
Unwhipped of justice;* hide thee, thou bloody hand;
Thou perjured,* and thou simular* man of virtue
That art incestuous; caitiff,* to pieces shake,
That under covert and convenient seeming*   55
Hast practised* on man's life; close pent-up guilts,
Rive your concealing continents* and cry
These dreadful summoners grace. I am a man
More sinned against than sinning.*

KENT   [Aside] Alack,* bare-headed!
[To LEAR] Gracious my lord, hard by* here is a hovel;   60
Some friendship will it lend* you 'gainst the tempest.
Repose you there, while I to this hard house –
More harder than the stones whereof 'tis raised,
Which even but now,* demanding after you,
Denied me to come in – return, and force*   65
Their scanted courtesy.

LEAR   My wits begin to turn.
Come on, my boy. How dost,* my boy? Art cold?
I am cold myself. Where is this straw,* my fellow?
The art* of our necessities is strange,
That can make vile things precious. Come, your hovel.   70
Poor fool and knave, I have one part in my heart
That's sorry yet for thee.

FOOL [Singing]   He that* has and* a little tiny wit –
                  With hey, ho, the wind and the rain
                  Must make* content with his fortunes fit, 75
                  For the rain it raineth every day.

LEAR True,* my good boy. Come, bring* us to this hovel.
                              [Exeunt LEAR and KENT

FOOL This is a brave* night to cool a courtesan. I'll speak a prophecy*
ere I go:

                  When priests are more in word than matter;* 80
                  When brewers mar their malt with water;

82	*their . . . tutors:* teach their tailors how to make clothes.
83	*but . . . suitors:* only men who get girls into trouble [are made to suffer].
87	*Nor . . . throngs:* and pickpockets do not move about among crowds.
88	*tell:* count; *i' the field* – i.e. in the open, not secretly for shame.
90	*Albion* – Britain, the ancient name used by the Greeks and Romans. Although the Romans associated the word with Latin *albus*, 'white', and took it as referring to the white cliffs of Dover, it may originate from a Celtic word unconnected with this.
93	*going . . . feet:* feet shall be used for walking (*going*).
94	*Merlin*, the wizard of the legends of King Arthur and his Knights. There are prophecies spoken by Merlin in Raphael Holinshed's *Chronicles of England, Scotland and Ireland* (1577), a source-book much used by Shakespeare. The Fool turns the reference into a joke by indicating that he cannot in fact quote Merlin because Merlin had not yet been born (at the time the action of *King Lear* is supposed to take place).

III.iii	Gloucester tells Edmund of his secret allegiance to the King, and has some foreboding of the consequences.
1	*Alack:* Alas.
1	*unnatural dealing:* unkind treatment. – Gloucester is referring to Regan's and Goneril's rejection of their father and refusal to help him.
2	*desired . . . pity him:* begged their permission to relieve his distress.
5	*sustain:* care for.
6	*unnatural* – The treacherous Edmund picks up this word from Gloucester (line 1) who as yet has no conception of how well it describes Edmund's own behaviour.
7	*Go to* – This phrase is used commonly in Shakespeare to express, among other attitudes, remonstrance: 'I beg you' or 'Have a care'. Gloucester shows by the series of short clauses in what follows that he is deeply perturbed at possessing such secret information. It is a disaster that he blurts it out to Edmund.
7	*division:* contention; *betwixt:* between.
8	*a worse matter* – i.e. the French invasion, which is much graver than the dispute between Cornwall and Albany.
10	*closet:* private cabinet for papers.
11	*home:* to the full – cf. driving a nail home.
11	*footed:* landed. – Cf. III.i.32.
12	*incline to:* side with.
13	*privily relieve:* secretly help.
13	*the duke* – This must be Cornwall, whom Gloucester was last in touch with at the end of Act II. In trying to help Lear, Gloucester will be going against Cornwall's advice: *'Tis best to give him way* (II.iv.294).
14	*of him:* by him.
17	*toward:* about to happen.

When nobles are their tailors' tutors;*
No heretics burned, but wenches' suitors* –

When every case in law is right;
No squire in debt, nor no poor knight;   85
When slanders do not live in tongues,
Nor cutpurses come not to throngs;*
When usurers tell* their gold i' the field,
And bawds and whores do churches build,
Then shall the realm of Albion*   90
Come to great confusion.
Then comes the time, who lives to see 't,
That going shall be used with feet.*

This prophecy Merlin* shall make; for I live before his time.

[*Exit*

scene iii

Gloucester's castle.

Enter GLOUCESTER *and* EDMUND.

GLOUCESTER Alack,* alack, Edmund, I like not this unnatural dealing.*
When I desired their leave* that I might pity him, they took
from me the use of mine own house; charged me, on pain of
their perpetual displeasure, neither to speak of him, entreat
for him, nor any way sustain* him.   5
EDMUND Most savage and unnatural!*
GLOUCESTER Go to;* say you nothing. There's a division* betwixt the
dukes. And a worse matter* than that: I have received a
letter this night; 'tis dangerous to be spoken; I have locked
the letter in my closet.* These injuries the King now bears will 10
be revenged home;* there is part of a power already footed;*
we must incline to* the King. I will seek him and privily
relieve* him. Go you, and maintain talk with the duke, that
my charity be not of him* perceived; if he ask for me, I am ill
and gone to bed. Though I die for it, as no less is threatened   15
me, the King my old master must be relieved. There is strange
things toward,* Edmund; pray you, be careful.   [*Exit*

18   *This courtesy, forbid thee:* This intended kindness [to the King], which has been forbidden [*thee:* to you].

20   *a fair deserving:* something which merits substantial reward; *draw me:* bring into my hands.

III.iv   Kent persuades Lear to take shelter in a hovel, but the Fool goes in first and finds Edgar inside, feigning madness as Poor Tom. Lear attributes Poor Tom's madness to the treatment of malicious daughters. Gloucester has already resolved to help him in secret, and now finds him exposing himself to the intensity of the storm. Gloucester is crazed with grief at his son's supposed treachery, and Edgar as Poor Tom is there to hear him.

This and scene vi together form the climax of the plot. Lear has become progressively calmer in speech and more deranged in mind (he persists in exposing himself to the storm) and the storm rages. In Lear and the storm are exemplified nature respectively with and without the morality which distinguishes humanity from the rest of creation. The two lines of plot converge with the entrance of Gloucester.

3   *nature:* human nature.

6   *'tis much:* it is a thing of great importance; *contentious:* warlike (apparently in the war of human nature against the elements). – The image is extended in *Invades* in the next line.

9   *Thou'dst:* You would.

11   *i' the mouth:* face to face; *free:* unworried.

12   *delicate:* sensitive.

13   *all . . . Save:* all other feeling except.

14   *beats:* (i) works laboriously, (ii) rages. – The storm outside and the storm in Lear's brain have converged so that he now speaks of the tempest in his mind and its domination of his senses. His mind is not *free*, and his body is not sensitive to the harshness of the tempest.

15   *as:* as if. – He indicates his own mouth and his own hand in this extreme case of 'biting the hand that feeds one'. The struggle is represented as between different parts of a single body.

16   *home:* fully. – One's natural thought in such a condition of pain and distraction is to punish those at whose hands one has suffered. He reverts to the theme of ingratitude, and then draws himself up: *that way madness lies* (line 21).

23   *ease:* comfort, protection.

EDMUND This courtesy,* forbid thee, shall the duke
        Instantly know, and of that letter too.
        This seems a fair deserving,* and must draw me   20
        That which my father loses: no less than all.
        The younger rises when the old doth fall.   [*Exit*

scene iv

The heath. In front of a hovel.

Enter LEAR, KENT, *and* FOOL.

KENT Here is the place, my lord. Good my lord, enter.
      The tyranny of the open night's too rough
      For nature* to endure.   [*Storm still*
LEAR   Let me alone.
KENT Good my lord, enter here.
LEAR   Wilt break my heart?
KENT I had rather break mine own. Good my lord, enter.   5
LEAR Thou think'st 'tis much* that this contentious storm
      Invades us to the skin. So 'tis to thee
      But where the greater malady is fixed
      The lesser is scarce felt. Thou'dst* shun a bear,
      But if thy flight lay toward the roaring sea   10
      Thou'dst meet the bear i' the mouth.* When the mind's free,*
      The body's delicate.* The tempest in my mind
      Doth from my senses take all feeling else
      Save* what beats* there. Filial ingratitude!
      Is it not as* this mouth should tear this hand   15
      For lifting food to 't? But I will punish home.*
      No, I will weep no more. In such a night
      To shut me out! [*To the storm*] Pour on; I will endure!
      In such a night as this! O Regan, Goneril!
      Your old kind father, whose frank heart gave you all –   20
      O, that way madness lies; let me shun that;
      No more of that.
KENT   Good my lord, enter here.
LEAR Prithee, go in thyself; seek thine own ease.*

25   *would:* that would.
26   *houseless poverty:* poor people without roofs over your heads.
27   *Nay . . . in* – The Fool hesitates, not at first believing that the King wants him to go in first, against the accepted order of precedence.
28   *Poor . . . wretches* – These are the *houseless poverty* he began to address in line 26.
29   *bide:* endure.
30   *houseless . . . raggedness* – It has been suggested that the two ideas of the house as shelter for the body and the body as shelter for the soul are fused together here; *sides:* stomachs (referring to the sides of the trunk of the body); *looped and windowed:* full of loopholes and openings (their ragged clothing letting in the wind and weather).
32   *seasons:* spells of bad weather.
33   *Take physic, pomp:* Take this medicine, you who live in a world of luxury and ceremony. – Pomp is especially associated with rich clothing.
35   *shake the superflux:* let the superfluity [of your riches] fall to them (like abundant fruit shaken down from a tree). Cf. what Gloucester says on the subject at IV.i.67:

> Let the superfluous and lust-dieted man
> . . . feel your [heaven's] power quickly;
> So distribution should undo excess
> And each man have enough.

36   *the heavens* – i.e. the gods.
37   *Fathom and half* – a depth of water suggested by the floods of rain.
38   *Poor Tom* – Cf. I.ii.125 and II.iii.20, and the notes to those lines.
42   *What:* Who.
44   *the foul fiend . . .* – Edgar talks in sententious outbursts to give the impression that his speech is made up of repeated set phrases, not original thought. In this line he uses alliteration, followed by a line from an old ballad concerning the harshness of nature.
45   *Go to . . . thee* – again a kind of proverbial saying; it occurs also in *The Taming of the Shrew*, Induction, i.10.
47   *Hast . . . daughters* – The sight of Edgar dressed as a madman has brought Lear near to the edge of madness himself; he begins to think that Edgar's madness, like his own, springs from the unkindness of daughters.
49   *gives* – Edgar catches up the idea from *given* in line 47. He goes on to talk of ways in which the devil has tried to make him commit suicide.
51   *that hath . . . pew* – In contemporary literature there are other references to the devil placing before his victim these instruments of self-destruction. There is a story depending on this idea in Harsnett's *Declaration of Egregious Popish Impostures*, in Marlowe's *Dr Faustus* (lines 632–4), and Greene and Lodge's *A Looking Glass for London.*
52   *halters:* ropes for hanging.
52   *pew:* gallery in a house. – The incident in Harsnett takes place in a gallery.
52   *rat's-bane:* rat poison.
53   *porridge:* soup, stew.
53   *a bay . . . bridges:* a reddish-brown (*bay*) horse, trained to trot in a stately fashion over bridges [only] four inches wide. – This illustrates the proverb: 'Pride comes before a fall.'
54   *course . . . traitor:* chase his own shadow believing it to be a traitor.
55   *five wits* – These were thought of as common sense, imagination, fantasy, estimation, and memory; they are not the same as the five senses. Edgar here and in the following line is, in the usual way of beggars, calling down blessings on a person who might give him alms.
56   *do . . . de* – the noise made by a person shivering.
57   *starblasting and taking:* withering away (*blasting*) under the evil influence of stars, and malignant influence (*taking*).

This tempest will not give me leave to ponder
On things would* hurt me more. But I'll go in.   25
[*To the* FOOL] In, boy; go first. You houseless poverty* –
Nay, get thee in.* I'll pray, and then I'll sleep. –

                                          [FOOL *goes in*

Poor naked wretches,* wheresoe'er you are,
That bide* the pelting of this pitiless storm,
How shall your houseless* heads and unfed sides,   30
Your looped and windowed raggedness, defend you
From seasons* such as these? O, I have ta'en
Too little care of this! Take physic,* pomp;
Expose thyself to feel what wretches feel,
That thou mayst shake the superflux* to them   35
And show the heavens* more just.

EDGAR [*Inside*] Fathom and half, fathom and half!*
       Poor Tom!*   [*The* FOOL *runs out from the hovel*
FOOL   Come not in here, nuncle; here's a spirit. Help me, help me!
KENT   Give me thy hand. Who's there?   40
FOOL   A spirit, a spirit; he says his name's poor Tom.
KENT   What* art thou that dost grumble there i' the straw?
       Come forth.

Enter EDGAR *disguised as a madman.*

EDGAR Away! the foul fiend* follows me! *Through the sharp haw-
       thorn blows the cold wind.* Humh! *Go to thy cold bed and*   45
       *warm thee.**
LEAR   Hast thou given all to thy two daughters?*
       And art thou come to this?
EDGAR Who gives* anything to poor Tom? whom the foul fiend
       hath led through fire and through flame, through ford and   50
       whirlpool, o'er bog and quagmire; that hath laid* knives
       under his pillow and halters* in his pew;* set rat's-bane* by
       his porridge;* made him proud of heart, to ride on a bay
       trotting-horse over four-inched bridges,* to course his own
       shadow for a traitor.* Bless thy five wits!* Tom's a-cold. O,   55
       do de, do de, do de.* Bless thee from whirlwinds, starblast-
       ing* and taking! Do poor Tom some charity, whom the foul
       fiend vexes. There could I have him now, and there, and
       there again, and there.   [*He strikes out at the air. Storm still*
LEAR   What, have his daughters brought him to this pass?   60
       [*To* EDGAR] Couldst thou save nothing? Wouldst thou give
       them all?

63   *else:* or else. – Edgar would have gone naked without a blanket.

64   *pendulous:* hanging overhead. – The idea seems to be an echo from Harsnett, but it is trans-
       ferred from the disasters hanging in the air to the air itself. The root of the word
       pendulous is the same as in *impending,* which gives the idea of hanging threaten-
       ingly overhead.

65   *fated o'er:* destined to fall on; *light:* fall, 'alight'.

67   *traitor* – Lear calls Kent this because he has dared to disagree with him. The idea is fixed
       in Lear's mind that Edgar has, like him, suffered from unkind treatment at the
       hands of his daughters.

67   *subdued nature . . . lowness . . . unkind* – The ideas in these words are closely linked; *sub-
       dued,* 'brought down', links with *lowness,* i.e. a degrading level of inhumane
       treatment. The word *unkind* here means 'unnatural', acting in a way which is
       not expected or fitting between people of the same *kind;* hence it links with
       nature in the preceding line. In Lear's mind, Edgar has become the prototype
       of *discarded fathers.*

70   *mercy . . . flesh* – referring presumably to Edgar's wretchedness and lack of proper protec-
       tion against the storm.

71   *Judicious:* (perhaps) Judicial, as meted out by a judge. – The hint may anticipate Lear's own
       sitting in judgement, IV.vi.107ff. At any rate, the punishment is 'just' since
       his own flesh was responsible for begetting such daughters.

72   *pelican* – A tradition widely current in Shakespeare's day was that the mother pelican
       feeds her young with blood from her breast, or revives them with it after she
       has killed them. She is therefore taken as a symbol of parents who love their
       children too much, giving more to them than they can reasonably expect,
       nothing less than life-blood. Some versions of the tradition suggest that the
       parent bird kills the young because they first strike out at their father or mother;
       Lear clearly carries this idea with his accusation against his daughters.

73   *Pillicock . . . -hill* – a line of an old rhyme, suggested by *pelican* in the preceding line.
       Pillicock was a flattering name for a youth. One version of the rhyme is:

> *Pillicock sat on Pillicock-hill;*
> *If he's not gone, he sits there still.*

       After quoting the first line, Edgar goes his own way, adding meaningless
       words such as might come from a madman.

77   *commit not:* do not commit adultery. – Edgar's speech, from *Obey . . .* (line 76) to *proud
       array* has many echoes of the Ten Commandments in the Bible (*Deuteronomy*
       5:6–21, *Exodus* 20:2–17).

78   *sweet heart:* yourself, your desires – and an affectionate form of address.

78   *proud array:* ostentatious clothes.

81   *serving-man* – What follows in this speech suggests that Edgar thinks of himself as both a
       servant and a lover, a man whose whole intent is to serve his mistress.

82   *gloves in my cap* – i.e. as a sign of his mistress's favour.

84   *in the sweet . . . heaven* – i.e. in the sight of heaven.

85   *contriving:* devising (evidently in his dreams).

87   *out-paramoured the Turk:* had more mistresses than the Grand Turk, the Sultan.

87   *light of ear* – ready to listen to, and believe, any accounts of evil.

87   *bloody of hand:* with hands ready to do any bloody deed.

88   *hog in sloth . . .* – The tradition of the bestiary (treatise on animals) gave each animal a
       typical quality or characteristic, and drew a moral from this and the animal's
       behaviour. Many ideas from these traditions survive today, e.g. *fox in stealth.*

89   *prey:* preying [on other animals].

89   *creaking of shoes* – It was apparently thought fashionable and enticing to wear shoes that
       creaked.

91   *plackets:* slits in petticoats.

92   *lenders* – i.e. moneylenders.

93   *Still . . . wind* – Edgar has already quoted another form of this line (line 44).

94   *suum, mun* – These are probably intended to represent the whistling and moaning of the
       wind. They lead into the meaningless words of a refrain, *hey, no, nonny,* as
       often used in one form or other in songs of the time.

95   *Dolphin . . .* – This line may be an echo of an old song, now lost. Essentially it seems to
       be an admonition to the devil to move away quickly. *Dolphin* is perhaps a
       common anglicised form of *Dauphin,* the name given to the eldest son of the

FOOL   Nay, he reserved a blanket, else* we had been all shamed.

LEAR   Now, all the plagues that in the pendulous* air

     Hang fated* o'er men's faults light on thy daughters!   65

KENT   He hath no daughters, sir.

LEAR   Death, traitor!* Nothing could have subdued nature*

     To such a lowness but his unkind daughters.

     Is it the fashion that discarded fathers

     Should have thus little mercy* on their flesh?   70

     Judicious* punishment! 'twas this flesh begot

     Those pelican* daughters.

EDGAR   *Pillicock* sat on Pillicock-hill;*

             Halloo, halloo, loo, loo!

FOOL   This cold night will turn us all to fools and madmen.   75

EDGAR   Take heed o' the foul fiend. Obey thy parents; keep thy word justly; swear not; commit not* with man's sworn spouse; set not thy sweet heart* on proud array.* Tom's a-cold.

LEAR   What hast thou been?   80

EDGAR   A serving-man,* proud in heart and mind, that curled my hair, wore gloves in my cap,* served the lust of my mistress' heart and did the act of darkness with her; swore as many oaths as I spake words and broke them in the sweet face of heaven;* one that slept in the contriving* of lust and waked   85
to do it. Wine loved I deeply, dice dearly, and in woman out-paramoured the Turk:* false of heart, light of ear,* bloody* of hand; hog in sloth,* fox in stealth, wolf in greediness, dog in madness, lion in prey.* Let not the creaking* of shoes nor the rustling of silks betray thy poor heart to woman; keep   90
thy foot out of brothels, thy hand out of plackets,* thy pen from lenders'* books, and defy the foul fiend.

     *Still through the hawthorn blows the cold wind.**

     Says suum, mun, hey, no, nonny.*

     Dolphin my boy, my boy, sessa! let him trot by.*   95

                        [Storm still

---

95 (*cont'd*)   French king, and taken as a name for the devil because of the traditional enmity between the English and the French; *sessa!* – a cry to make a horse move quickly.

96   *thou wert better:* it would be better for you to be.
96   *answer:* confront.
97   *extremity:* extreme rage – i.e. the storm. The theme of what follows is that most men cover
            their bodies with the products of animals: silk, hide, wool. But Edgar is a poor
            wretch without those trappings, and therefore an instance of man as he really is.
98   *Thou owest . . . silk* – in the sense: 'You are not wearing any silk which you have to thank
            the silk-worm for, etc.
99   *cat:* civet cat. – A gland in its body exudes a liquid which is used as a fixative for perfume.
100   *on 's:* of us.
100   *sophisticated:* impure – not *the thing itself* (because we are fully clothed).
101   *unaccommodated:* not provided with the necessities of civilisation (e.g. dress).
102   *forked* – i.e. two-legged.
102   *lendings:* non-essential belongings. – He is referring to his clothes, which are not essential
            parts of man. Lear now tears off his clothes because he wants to identify him-
            self with the naked beggars he has been thinking and speaking about.
104   *naughty:* nasty.
105   *a little fire* – A torch cannot do much to warm them in a storm, any more than the heart of
            an old libertine can impassion his whole body.
108   *Flibbertigibbet* – the name of a fiend, which, like many others in the play, comes from
            Harsnett's *Declaration* (cf. lines 131, 133–4). The name survives as a common
            noun for a restless, unstable person. Perhaps Edgar is reminded of it by the
            spluttering flame of the torch.
109   *the first cock* – The first cock-crow of the day was taken as a signal that dawn was breaking.
109   *the web and the pin* – a disease of the eye, cataract. Diseases and deformities were thought
            of as being caused by malignant spirits.
110   *white* – i.e. almost ripe.
111   *creature,* perhaps for *creatures.*
112   *'Saint Withold . . . aroint thee'* (line 116) – This stanza is thought to be a charm connected
            with St Vitalis, to be repeated as a protection against nightmares. Some points
            in it are however very obscure. The early editions have *Swithold* in place of
            Saint Withold as printed here; it is conjectured that *Saint Withold* may be an
            anglicised form of St Vitalis.
113   *nightmare:* demon of the night.
113   *nine-fold:* (perhaps) nine offspring, or nine attendant imps.
114   *Bid her . . . plight:* told her [the nightmare] to get down [off her horse] and promise on her
            honour [not to harm anyone].
116   *aroint thee:* away with you. – This seems to have been a phrase especially associated with
            witches. Cf. *Macbeth* I.iii.6:
                            'Aroint thee, witch!' the rump-fed ronyon cries.
122   *wall-newt:* lizard.
122   *water* – i.e. water-newt.
123   *sallets:* tasty morsels of food.
125   *green . . . pool:* scum on a stagnant pond.
125   *tithing:* district. – Vagrants could be whipped from parish to parish in an attempt to make
            them return to their place of origin. Their plight is remembered in a nursery
            rhyme beginning:
                            Hark, hark,
                            The dogs do bark,
                            The beggars are coming to town.
        One version ends:
                            Some gave them a good horse-whip,
                            And sent them out of town.
        but no early source for this is known.
126   *stock-punished:* punished by being put in the stocks.
126   *three suits* – Cf. II.ii.14, where *three-suited* is used in a series of epithets for a servant. The
            best that a wretched beggar could hope for was service under a good and
            honourable master.
128   *Horse . . . wear* – These words make a verse line which scans on the same pattern as the
            two following lines, and thus in a sense leads into them. A form of the French
            rhyming couplet appears in a popular metrical romance, *Sir Bevis of Hampton*,
            c. 1300.
129   *deer:* animals. – This usage is pre-Shakespearian and thus suggests the antiquity of the
            couplet.

LEAR   Why, thou wert better* in thy grave than to answer* with
         thy uncovered body this extremity* of the skies. Is man no
         more than this? Consider him well. Thou owest the worm no
         silk,* the beast no hide, the sheep no wool, the cat* no per-
         fume. Ha! here's three on 's* are sophisticated.* Thou art the   100
         thing itself; unaccommodated* man is no more but such a
         poor, bare, forked* animal as thou art. Off, off, you lendings!*
         Come, unbutton here.   [*Tearing off his clothes*
FOOL   Prithee, nuncle, be contented; 'tis a naughty* night to swim
         in. [*Sees a torch burning*]. Now a little fire* in a wild field were   105
         like an old lecher's heart – a small spark, all the rest on 's
         body cold. Look, here comes a walking fire.

         Enter GLOUCESTER, *with a torch.*

EDGAR This is the foul fiend Flibbertigibbet:* he begins at curfew
         and walks till the first cock;* he gives the web and the pin,*
         squints the eye and makes the hare-lip; mildews the white*   110
         wheat and hurts the poor creature* of earth.

                  Saint Withold footed thrice the old;
                  He met the nightmare* and her nine-fold;*
                       Bid her alight,
                       And her troth plight,*   115
                  And aroint* thee, witch, aroint thee!*

KENT   How fares your grace?
LEAR   What's he?
KENT   Who's there? What is 't you seek?
GLOUCESTER   What are you there? Your names?   120
EDGAR Poor Tom, that eats the swimming frog, the toad, the tadpole,
         the wall-newt* and the water;* that in the fury of his heart,
         when the foul fiend rages, eats cow-dung for sallets;* swallows
         the old rat and the ditch-dog; drinks the green mantle of the
         standing pool;* who is whipped from tithing* to tithing, and   125
         stock-punished,* and imprisoned; who hath had three suits*
         to his back, six shirts to his body,
         Horse to ride and wagon to wear;*
         But mice and rats and such small deer*
         Have been Tom's food for seven long year.

                                                                          130

131   *follower:* attendant spirit (in this case malignant).

131   *Smulkin* – evidently the name of the *follower*, taken from Harsnett, who gives it as *Smolkin.*

133   *a gentleman* – Edgar perhaps means that, despite what Gloucester has just said, Satan (*The prince of darkness*), in whose hands he now is, is a gentleman, and therefore fit company for a king. The use of *prince* here has a similar effect.

133   *Modo . . . Mahu* – These names come from Harsnett. It has been suggested that a passage in Horace's *Epistles* (II.i) is linked with the use of *Modo* here: . . . *magus . . . modo me Thebis, modo ponit Athenis*, which can be translated: 'the wise man sets me now in Thebes, now in Athens.' The reference is to the wise man (*magus*) who can by his skill transport one in imagination to Thebes or Athens. The use of *Modo* as a proper noun may have reminded Shakespeare of this passage in Horace, where *modo* appears twice to form an adverbial phrase ('sometimes . . . sometimes') and influenced him in what follows: Lear calls Edgar *philosopher* (lines 144, 166), a possible translation of *magus*, and *learned Theban* (147) and *good Athenian* (171).

135   *Our flesh and blood:* Our children; people in general.

136   *gets:* begets. – Gloucester is thinking, it seems, of Goneril and Regan as well as of his own son Edgar, whom Edmund has made appear a villain.

138   *Go in:* Come indoors (into the house mentioned in line 143 and by Kent in line 146); *suffer:* allow (me).

139   *in all:* completely.

144   *philosopher* – See note 133. The word can equally denote a natural scientist, who might well be asked about the nature of thunder.

149   *prevent:* avoid.

153   *good Kent* – Kent is in disguise and Gloucester does not recognise him. This permits the irony of Gloucester making a comment on Kent to his face.

157   *outlawed . . . blood:* disowned by me. – Outlawry, equivalent to a sentence of death, meant that the convicted person lost all right to inheritance.

161   *cry you mercy:* I beg for pardon. – Lear apologises to Gloucester as he interrupts him and returns to the conversation with his *Noble philosopher.*

166   *keep still:* stay.

Beware my follower.* Peace, Smulkin;* peace, thou fiend!

GLOUCESTER [*To* LEAR] What, hath your grace no better company?

EDGAR The prince of darkness is a gentleman;* Modo,* he's called,
and Mahu.

GLOUCESTER Our flesh and blood* is grown so vile, my lord,   135
That it doth hate what gets* it.

EDGAR Poor Tom's a-cold.

GLOUCESTER Go in* with me. My duty cannot suffer*
To obey in all* your daughters' hard commands.
Though their injunction be to bar my doors,   140
And let this tyrannous night take hold upon you,
Yet have I ventured to come seek you out
And bring you where both fire and food is ready.

LEAR First let me talk with this philosopher.*
[*To* EDGAR] What is the cause of thunder?   145

KENT Good my lord, take his offer; go into the house.

LEAR I'll talk a word with this same learned Theban.
[*To* EDGAR] What is your study?

EDGAR How to prevent* the fiend and to kill vermin.

LEAR Let me ask you one word in private.   150

KENT [*To* GLOUCESTER] Importune him once more to go, my lord;
His wits begin to unsettle.

GLOUCESTER   Canst thou blame him?
                                                    [*Storm still*
His daughters seek his death. Ah, that good Kent!*
He said it would be thus, poor banished man!
Thou say'st the King grows mad; I'll tell thee, friend,   155
I am almost mad myself. I had a son,
Now outlawed from my blood;* he sought my life,
But lately, very late. I loved him, friend,
No father his son dearer; truth to tell thee,
The grief hath crazed my wits. What a night's this!   160
I do beseech your grace –

LEAR   O, cry you mercy,* sir.
Noble philosopher, your company.

EDGAR Tom's a-cold.

GLOUCESTER In, fellow, there, into the hovel; keep thee warm.

LEAR Come, let's in all.

KENT   This way, my lord.

LEAR   With him;   165
I will keep still* with my philosopher.

167   *soothe:* humour.
169   *Take . . . on:* Take him [Edgar] along with you.
173   *Child Rowland . . .* – This appears to be a line from an old ballad, now lost. *Child:* a candidate for knighthood; *Rowland:* Roland, a hero in French legend; he was the nephew of Charlemagne, King of the Franks.
174   *His . . . still:* His motto was always.
174   *Fie . . . man* – These are the traditional words of the giant in the story of Jack the Giant-Killer, though the more common form ends *an Englishman.* Shakespeare, probably with proper regard for history, does not refer to England in the play, but rather Britain.

III.v   Edmund informs the fiery and impetuous Cornwall of Gloucester's loyalty to Lear. This loyalty is by implication treason, since Lear is supposedly aiming to link up with the French and Cordelia.
        This scene adds little to III.iii; it serves rather as a brief release from the tragic tension of the meeting-up of Lear and Gloucester.

1   *I will . . .* – The beginning of the scene gives the impression of an exchange between Cornwall and Edmund which is already in progress, and is consequently difficult to interpret in detail. The explanation given here assumes that the main reference is to Gloucester, in whose castle they are speaking.
1   *his* – i.e. Gloucester's. Cornwall, weak and easily led, is now persuaded that Gloucester is a traitor because of his allegiance to Lear, and must suffer accordingly.
2   *How, my lord . . . think of:* It rather frightens (*something fears*) me to think of what people will say about me (*I . . . censured*) for allowing my natural feelings [as a son] to be overcome by my sense of loyalty in this way.
5   *made him . . . death* – i.e. made Edgar seek Gloucester's death, according to the story put about by Edmund.
5   *a provoking . . . himself:* a feeling of positive merit aroused (*provoking*) and put into action by the culpable wickedness of [Gloucester] himself. – Edgar has been accused of wishing to take his father's life; since a case against Gloucester has now been made out, Edgar's supposed designs on his father have, by chance, some merit in them (for those who believe Edmund's stories).
7   *repent . . . just:* repent for being honest [about my father's treason].
9   *approves:* proves.
9   *an intelligent . . . France:* a spy (*intelligent party*) in the service of the King of France. – Intelligence is information useful to military services in wartime. The letter is that mentioned at III.iii.9 and 19.
10   *that this treason . . . detector:* how I wish that this treachery did not exist or that I were not the detector of it.
17   *ready . . . apprehension:* available for arrest by us.
18   *comforting:* supporting, giving assistance to.
19   *his suspicion:* people's suspicion of him.
19   *persever . . . loyalty:* continue to show my loyalty [to you].
21   *blood:* natural feelings [as a son].

KENT   [To GLOUCESTER] Good my lord, soothe* him; let him take the
        fellow.
GLOUCESTER   Take him you on.*
KENT   [To EDGAR] Sirrah, come on; go along with us.   170
LEAR   Come, good Athenian.
GLOUCESTER   No words, no words: hush.

EDGAR   Child Rowland* to the dark tower came;
               His word* was still 'Fie, foh, and fum,*
               I smell the blood of a British man'.   175

                                                        [Exeunt

scene v

A room in Gloucester's castle.

Enter CORNWALL *and* EDMUND.

CORNWALL   I will* have my revenge ere I depart his* house.
EDMUND   How, my lord,* I may be censured, that nature thus gives
        way to loyalty, something fears me to think of.
CORNWALL   I now perceive, it was not altogether your brother's evil
        disposition made him seek his death,* but a provoking*   5
        merit, set a-work by a reprovable badness in himself.
EDMUND   How malicious is my fortune, that I must repent to be just!*
        [Shows him a letter.] This is the letter he spoke of, which
        approves* him an intelligent party* to the advantages of
        France. O heavens! that this treason were not,* or not I the   10
        detector!
CORNWALL   Go with me to the duchess.
EDMUND   If the matter of this paper be certain, you have mighty busi-
        ness in hand.
CORNWALL   True or false, it hath made thee Earl of Gloucester. Seek out 15
        where thy father is, that he may be ready for our apprehen-
        sion.*
EDMUND   [Aside] If I find him comforting* the King, it will stuff his
        suspicion* more fully. [To CORNWALL] I will perséver* in my
        course of loyalty, though the conflict be sore between that   20
        and my blood.*
CORNWALL   I will lay trust upon thee, and thou shalt find a dearer father
        in my love.   [Exeunt

III.vi   With Edgar and the Fool as the judges uttering crazy irrelevancies and scathing comments, Lear gives flashes of a trial of his daughters which he imagines is taking place. His vindictive grief breaks out in vicious attacks on them. As Lear is borne away to Dover, Edgar muses on Lear's suffering and his own, but he sees the time coming when he can throw off his disguise and be reconciled with his father.

The imaginary trial furthers the consideration of the nature of humanity in III.iv. It explores the connection between Lear's new view of humanity, which depends on superfluities to distinguish it from animal nature, and the meting out of justice. In Poor Tom (Edgar) he sees a reflection of himself, and at the end of the scene, astride the two plots, Edgar observes 'He childed as I fathered' in a kind of valediction.

SD	This is the traditional location of the scene, but in view of III.iv.146, *go into the house,* the action may be placed more correctly in an outhouse of Gloucester's castle.
2	*piece out:* add to, improve. – This recalls the theme of superfluity and man's basic needs (II.iv.260ff.).
3	*from:* away from.
6	*Fraretto* – the name of a fiend, also appearing in Harsnett (cf. III.iv.108).
6	*Nero . . . darkness* – This passage may depend on various hints from Harsnett but is of course intended to be confused and inconsequent. Nero, the universally hated Roman emperor, passes his time fishing in the gloomy lake of hell.
7	*innocent:* idiot, simpleton (addressed to the Fool).
9	*gentleman . . . yeoman* – The contrast lies in the idea that a yeoman farmer would work on the land he owns, whereas a 'gentleman' would not.
10	*A king* – i.e. rather than be either, the madman is a king, after Lear's own experience.
11	*to his son:* for his son (the son having risen socially above his yeoman father).
13	*To have . . .* – Lear's mind continues to run on his own predicament by now devising punishments to inflict upon his daughters. He refers (following hints in Harsnett's description of the torments of hell) to devils with kitchen roasting *spits,* red-hot and hissing as they are brandished.
16	*a horse's health* – perhaps because horses were thought of as being delicate and prone to disease. Some have thought the phrase refers to the horse-trader's description of a horse, something that should not be taken at face value.
18	*arraign them straight:* bring them [his daughters] at once before a court for trial. – Lear abandons the idea of rash punishment and thinks instead of the orderly processes of law as a means of redressing his grievances. He summons Edgar and the Fool to sit in judgement as if they were court officers.
19	*justicer:* judge. – Q reads *Iustice;* this is usually amended as in the text here in order to maintain the rhythm of the line, and in the light of III.vi.53: *False justicer.*
22	*he stands . . .* – presumably a fiend, though the reference could be to Lear himself.
22	*Want'st . . . trial:* Do you want people looking at you during your trial. – Edgar, pretending that he is addressing one of the evil daughters, apparently thinks of a fiend staring at her and asks whether this is the kind of admiration she wants.
24	*Come . . . me* – This is the first line of a popular song in which the lover calls the loved one to come to him across a stream (*bourn*). Taking this as his cue, the Fool makes up three lines in the rhythm of the refrain of the song. The song was imitated by William Birch (*c.* 1560) in a 'Songe betwene the Quenes Majestie and Englande', in which England, personified, addresses Queen Elizabeth, but there is nothing to suggest that this is the form referred to in the text.
26	*speak:* say.
28	*The foul . . . nightingale* – The singing suggests to Edgar the idea that the fiend haunting poor Tom (himself) has the qualities of a nightingale.
29	*Hoppedance* – the name of a dancing devil, the *black angel,* evil spiritual being, of the following line; it appears in Harsnett in a slightly different form, *Hoberdidance,* plainly from the rhythm of the popular dance, considered by some to be a source of wickedness. *Hobbididence* appears at IV.i.60. The voice of this devil is the rumbling in his empty stomach.
29	*white herring* – Herring were cheap food. They were preserved by smoking or by pickling in various ways; *white* herring were either fresh (unsmoked) or pickled with salt.
30	*Croak not:* Do not rumble.
31	*amazed:* bewildered, struck dumb.
33	*their evidence:* the evidence (witnesses) against them (such as would be called in the trial of his daughters, which his mind now reverts to).

scene vi

A room in a farmhouse adjoining the castle.

Enter GLOUCESTER, LEAR, KENT, FOOL, *and* EDGAR.

GLOUCESTER Here is better than the open air; take it thankfully.
I will piece out* the comfort with what addition I can.
I will not be long from* you.

KENT [*Aside to* GLOUCESTER] All the power of his wits have given
way to his impatience. The gods reward your kindness!   5
[*Exit* GLOUCESTER

EDGAR Frateretto* calls me, and tells me Nero is an angler in the lake
of darkness.* Pray, innocent,* and beware the foul fiend.

FOOL Prithee, nuncle, tell me whether a madman be a gentleman or
a yeoman.*

LEAR A king,* a king.   10

FOOL No, he's a yeoman that has a gentleman to his son;* for he's
a mad yeoman that sees his son a gentleman before him.

LEAR To have* a thousand with red burning spits*
Come hissing in upon 'em –

EDGAR The foul fiend bites my back.   15

FOOL He's mad that trusts in the tameness of a wolf, a horse's
health,* a boy's love, or a whore's oath.

LEAR It shall be done; I will arraign* them straight.
[*To* EDGAR] Come, sit thou here, most learned justicer;*
[*To the* FOOL] Thou, sapient sir, sit here. Now, you she-foxes!   20

EDGAR Look, where he stands* and glares! Want'st thou eyes at
trial,* madam?

*Come o'er the bourn, Bessy, to me.**

FOOL [*Singing*]   *Her boat hath a leak,*   25
*And she must not speak**
Why she dares not come over to thee.

EDGAR The foul fiend* haunts poor Tom in the voice of a nightingale.
Hoppedance* cries in Tom's belly for two white herring.*
Croak not,* black angel; I have no food for thee.   30

KENT How do you, sir? Stand you not so amazed.*
Will you lie down and rest upon the cushions?

LEAR I'll see their trial first. Bring in their evidence.*
[*To* EDGAR] Thou robèd man of justice, take thy place.

35	*yoke-fellow of equity:* partner in the administration of justice. – In the violent change of roles, the Fool, so long totally subjected to the whims of royal authority, is himself suddenly promoted to a position of power.
36	*Bench:* sit (as a judge).
36	*o' the commission:* of the justices (i.e. of the group of people charged with this particular office).
39	*Sleepest or wakest . . .* – Edgar breaks out into another song; it means: 'Are you asleep or awake, carefree shepherd? Your sheep are in the cornfield, and will not come to harm if you give just one blast [of the horn] from your pretty (*minikin*) mouth.' The song seems to have no particular relevance to the context, even ironically, and it is to be taken as a further display of Edgar's feigned madness. It is very likely associated with a popular nursery rhyme beginning:

> Little Boy Blue, come blow your horn;
> The sheep's in the meadow, the cow's in the corn.
> But where is the boy who looks after the sheep?
> He's under a haycock, fast asleep.

In both versions the fear expressed is that the animals will be molested for damaging the crops. The interpretation of *blast* in the text here is taken from the nursery rhyme.

43	*Purr* – either the name of a devil (as *Purre* in Harsnett) or simply the noise made by a cat.
43	*the cat is grey* – This is perhaps an allusion to the proverb: 'All cats are grey in the dark.'
49	*Cry you . . . stool:* Please forgive me, I mistook you for a stool. – This was a saying used jokingly as an apology for not noticing a person. The Fool is making fun of the routine of the law courts, in which everyone appearing before the court is asked his name, without regard to whether he is well known or not.
50	*warped:* perverse.
51	*store:* stuff. – Many editors suggest that *store* is a mistake for *stone* here. Regan is the sister who finally let Lear go his own way into the storm (end of II.iv).
51	*Stop her* – The fading of her image, as in a dream, seems to Lear like her escape from trial.
52	*place:* high place, the seat of justice.
54	*five wits:* senses, mind. – Cf. III.iv.55.
57	*take his part:* be in sympathy with him.
58	*mar my counterfeiting:* spoil my pretence [of madness].
59	*little dogs* – Even the dogs, usually friendly, turn against him.
61	*throw his head:* (probably) direct his gaze, his attention (cf. line 68).
61	*Avaunt:* Get away.
62	*Be thy mouth . . .* – The passage is in the form of a ritual imprecation or curse: such-and-such will happen to the object of the curse, whatever particular variety of that object may be in question, whatever its shape or form. *Be thy mouth . . . white:* Whether your mouth is black or white. There is some alliteration in the piece (*greyhound, mongrel grim . . . tike and trundle-tail . . . weep and wail*) which gives it the tone of an incantation.
65	*brach* – a kind of hound with a keen scent for the trail (as in I.iv.100); *lym* – a kind of bloodhound, associated with a special lead called a *leam.*
66	*tike:* common dog, cur; *trundle-tail:* dog with a dragging tail.
69	*leap the hatch:* (literally) jump out over the hatch, the bottom half of a door or gate divided into two. The phrase means 'get out quickly'.
70	*Do de* – He is shivering with the cold. Cf. III.iv.56.
70	*Sessa* – See III.iv.95.
70	*wakes:* merrymaking connected with the holy day to celebrate the dedication of a church. – The call *Come, march . . . market-towns* is perhaps that of a beggar to a companion to go to places where the begging will be the most profitable because there will be plenty of people in the streets.
71	*thy horn is dry* – Beggars wore a horn hanging around their necks. They blew blasts on it to announce their approach, and filled it with the drink they were given as alms. As this point marks the end of Edgar's feigned madness, some commentators have thought it also means, 'You have no more resources left [to play your part].'
72	*anatomize:* dissect (as an exercise in anatomy).
74	*entertain:* take into my service (*my hundred*) – i.e. the hundred knights he wanted to keep as his retinue (I.i.128).

[*To the* FOOL] And thou, his yoke-fellow of equity,*   35
Bench* by his side. [*To* KENT] You are o' the commission;*
sit you too.

EDGAR   Let us deal justly.

> Sleepest or wakest* thou, jolly shepherd?
> Thy sheep be in the corn,   40
> And for one blast of thy minikin mouth,
> Thy sheep shall take no harm.

Purr!* the cat is grey.*

LEAR   Arraign her first; 'tis Goneril. I here take my oath before
this honourable assembly, she kicked the poor King her   45
father.

FOOL   Come hither, mistress. Is your name Goneril?

LEAR   She cannot deny it.

FOOL   Cry you mercy, I took you for a joint-stool.*

LEAR   And here's another, whose warped* looks proclaim   50
What store* her heart is made on. Stop her* there!
Arms, arms, sword, fire! Corruption in the place!*
False justicer, why hast thou let her 'scape?

EDGAR   Bless thy five wits!*

KENT   O pity! Sir, where is the patience now,   55
That you so oft have boasted to retain?

EDGAR   [*Aside*] My tears begin to take his part* so much,
They'll mar my counterfeiting.*

LEAR   The little dogs* and all,
Tray, Blanch, and Sweetheart, see, they bark at me.   60

EDGAR   Tom will throw his head at them.* Avaunt,* you curs!

> Be thy mouth* or black or white,
> Tooth that poisons if it bite;
> Mastiff, greyhound, mongrel grim,
> Hound or spaniel, brach* or lym,   65
> Or bobtail tike* or trundle-tail,
> Tom will make them weep and wail;
> For, with throwing thus my head,
> Dogs leap the hatch,* and all are fled.

Do de, de, de.* Sessa!* Come, march to wakes* and fairs and   70
market-towns. Poor Tom, thy horn is dry.*

LEAR   Then let them anatomize* Regan; see what breeds about her
heart. Is there any cause in nature that makes these hard
hearts? [*To* EDGAR] You, sir, I entertain* for one of my

75   *fashion:* style, cut.

76   *Persian* – used (as the Latin *persicus*) of gorgeous, 'oriental' dress.

78   *curtains* – i.e. the curtains round his own bed, where he now imagines he is.

79   *supper . . . morning* – because he is going to rest without any supper now.

80   *go to . . . noon* – The Fool in saying this seems to be capping what Lear has just said about supper. With these words the Fool has completed his part and disappears from the play except where he does Kent's bidding at 95 below; some commentators see in his words a reference to this fact. As Lear, at his nadir, begins to question human nature itself, the Fool with all his own confusions of that state of nature leaves him, and Lear is persuaded to rest.

84   *upon:* against. – Armed forces are ready in the region of Dover to fight the Dukes of Albany and Cornwall on behalf of the King, as Oswald reports more fully in the next scene (III.vii.14ff.).

86   *drive:* hurry. – The King is to be carried there on a portable bed (*litter*).

89   *offer:* dare.

90   *Stand . . . loss:* are sure to be lost.

93   *yet have . . . sinews:* possibly [in spite of the advanced state of the mental breakdown] have soothed your tortured nerves. – Kent remains tender and thoughtful in all he says and does.

94   *Which . . . cure:* which, if no provision is made [for him], can hardly be cured.

98   *When we our betters . . .* – Edgar's speech, which closes this scene, is flat and commonplace in both matter and manner. He soliloquises on the conventional lines of the lightening of suffering when it is shared with another; the poetry is uninspiring, in some places descending to the level of doggerel. But the audience is at least aware from this sharp change of style in what Edgar says that he has entirely thrown off his pose of madness and speaks again with true feeling.

98   *bearing our woes* – i.e. bearing the same woes as we have to bear.

100   *alone* – i.e. by himself.

101   *free:* carefree, free from suffering.

101   *shows:* visions.

102   *sufferance:* suffering.

103   *mates:* [other griefs as] companions – i.e. other people to share grief; *bearing:* endurance.

104   *portable:* bearable.

105   *makes . . . bow* – i.e. whatever my own suffering, I am only bending with it, whereas the King is bowed down to the earth with his.

106   *He childed . . . fathered:* he had his children [to make him suffer] and I had my father. – Cruelty from a father, Edgar suggests, is more bearable than cruelty from one's children.

107   *Mark . . . noises:* (perhaps) Watch out for the forthcoming great events. – Some have thought the phrase means, 'Watch out for signs of discord among the great.'

107   *thyself . . . reconciles thee* (line 109): reveal (*bewray*) yourself, when your reputation (*opinion*), which falsely and mistakenly soils your good name (*defile thee*) calls you back (*repeals*) and brings you again into favour and honour (*reconciles thee*) on proof of your integrity (*just proof*).

110   *What:* Whatever: *safe . . . King:* may the King escape in safety.

111   *Lurk* – He is evidently telling himself to lie hidden and in wait.

        hundred; only I do not like the fashion* of your garments. 75
        You will say they are Persian* attire, but let them be changed.

KENT Now, good my lord, lie here and rest awhile.

LEAR Make no noise, make no noise; draw the curtains;* so, so, so.
        We'll go to supper i' the morning.* So, so, so.

FOOL And I'll go to bed at noon.* 80

      Re-enter GLOUCESTER

GLOUCESTER Come hither, friend. Where is the King my master?

KENT Here, sir; but trouble him not; his wits are gone.

GLOUCESTER Good friend, I prithee, take him in thy arms.
        I have o'erheard a plot of death upon* him.
        There is a litter ready; lay him in 't, 85
        And drive* toward Dover, friend, where thou shalt meet
        Both welcome and protection. Take up thy master.
        If thou shouldst dally half an hour, his life,
        With thine and all that offer* to defend him,
        Stand in assured loss.* Take up, take up, 90
        And follow me, that will to some provision
        Give thee quick conduct.

KENT   Oppressèd nature sleeps.
        This rest might yet have balmed* thy broken sinews
        Which, if convenience will not allow,
        Stand in hard cure.* [*To the* FOOL] Come, help to bear thy 95
        master;
        Thou must not stay behind.

GLOUCESTER   Come, come, away.
                    [*Exeunt all but* EDGAR

EDGAR When we our betters* see bearing our woes,*
        We scarcely think our miseries our foes.
        Who alone* suffers, suffers most in the mind, 100
        Leaving free* things and happy shows* behind.
        But then the mind much sufferance* doth o'erskip,
        When grief hath mates,* and bearing fellowship.
        How light and portable* my pain seems now,
        When that which makes me bend makes the King bow.* 105
        He childed as I fathered!* Tom, away!
        Mark the high noises,* and thyself bewray,*
        When false opinion, whose wrong thoughts defile thee,
        In thy just proof repeals and reconciles thee.
        What* will hap more tonight, safe 'scape the King!* 110
        Lurk, lurk.*   [*Exit*

III.vii   Reports have arrived that the French army has landed; Gloucester is now believed to be
in sympathy with the French. He is sent for and quickly brought in, and finds the opposite
faction now assembling in his own castle. Gloucester's expressions of sympathy for Lear
are in vain, and he is blinded for his loyalty to the King. A servant intervenes, Cornwall is
injured in a scuffle with him, and the servant dies. Gloucester realises that Edmund, not
Edgar, has brought him to this pass.

The Gloucester plot here reaches its climax in a terrible deed against the guiltless
Gloucester himself. Yet, having seen the destitution and madness of Lear, we need in the
style of the play to experience as actually as possible the more terrible physical suffering
of Gloucester. Gloucester is unwittingly moving into the care of the son he has banished,
as Lear is to the daughter he cut off.

1	*Post:* Go [with a message].
2	*letter* – the one Edmund showed to Cornwall (III.v.8). In it Gloucester appears to be addressed as a collaborator of the French king.
6	*our sister* – i.e. Goneril, his sister-in-law, who is to take the letter to her husband Albany.
7	*are bound:* intend.
7	*for your beholding:* for you to see.
9	*festinate:* speedy.
10	*bound . . . like:* ready to do the same – i.e. make *preparation* for war with France.
10	*posts:* messengers.
11	*intelligent:* well provided with information.
13	*where's the King* – Oswald has evidently been sent on a mission to find the King, perhaps as part of the *plot of death upon him* (III.vi.84).
14	*My lord . . . Dover* (line 18): The Earl of Gloucester has taken [the King] away; some 35 or 36 of [Gloucester's] knights, swift riders (*Hot questrists*) after him, met him on the way (*at gate*), and they (*Who*), with some other followers of Gloucester, have gone with the King towards Dover. – The meanings of *questrists* and *at gate* are uncertain, but the explanation given here seems to make good sense; *questrist* is taken to be associated with *equestrian*, though the word is not known elsewhere and may have been invented by Shakespeare.
23	*pass . . . life:* pass the death sentence upon him. – The law of the time is imagined as not permitting a sentence being passed without the full process of law.
25	*do a courtesy to:* oblige. – On this occasion he will allow his power, which should control his anger, to submit to it instead – 'oblige' it. Cornwall's power is of course very strong in any case; people may object to it (*blame*) but cannot bring it under control. Alternatively, *do a courtesy* may mean 'yield to some extent'; in this case he is saying he cannot pass a sentence of death without a trial, but his power can to some extent yield to his anger in a way which people can disapprove of but cannot legally stop, i.e. he can inflict suffering short of death on Gloucester.

scene vii

Gloucester's castle.

Enter CORNWALL, REGAN, GONERIL, EDMUND, *and* SERVANTS.

CORNWALL [*To* GONERIL] Post* speedily to my lord your husband; show
him this letter:* the army of France is landed. Seek out the
traitor Gloucester.
                              [*Exeunt some of the* SERVANTS

REGAN Hang him instantly.

GONERIL Pluck out his eyes.   5

CORNWALL Leave him to my displeasure. Edmund, keep you our sister*
company. The revenges we are bound* to take upon your
traitorous father are not fit for your beholding.* Advise the
duke, where you are going, to a most festinate* preparation;
we are bound* to the like. Our posts* shall be swift and   10
intelligent* betwixt us. Farewell, dear sister! farewell, my
Lord of Gloucester.

Enter OSWALD

How now! where's the King?*

OSWALD My lord of Gloucester* hath conveyed him hence;
Some five or six and thirty of his knights,   15
Hot questrists after him, met him at gate;
Who, with some other of the lord's dependants,
Are gone with him toward Dover, where they boast
To have well-arméd friends.

CORNWALL   Get horses for your mistress.

GONERIL Farewell, sweet lord, and sister.   20

CORNWALL Edmund, farewell.
                         [*Exeunt* GONERIL, EDMUND, *and* OSWALD
                         Go seek the traitor Gloucester.
Pinion him like a thief; bring him before us.
                              [*Exeunt other* SERVANTS
Though well we may not pass upon his life*
Without the form of justice, yet our power
Shall do a courtesy* to our wrath, which men   25
May blame but not control. Who's there? The traitor?

Enter GLOUCESTER, *brought in by two or three* SERVANTS.

REGAN Ingrateful fox! 'tis he.

28   *corky:* withered, like dry cork.

32   *none –* i.e. not a traitor.

SD   *plucks his beard –* This was a gesture of the grossest insult, especially to old age.

36   *white –* of his beard, in contrast to what she takes to be the blackness of his deed.

36   *Naughty:* Wicked.

37   *ravish:* pull out.

38   *quicken:* come to life.

39   *my hospitable favours:* my features in my role as your host. – To abuse another's hospitality is an unforgivable crime.

40   *ruffle:* treat violently, abuse. – Gloucester's fears increase in intensity as he asks the question which follows.

42   *Be simple answerer:* (apparently) give a direct answer. – F has *answer'd* here.

43   *confederacy:* conspiracy.

44   *Late footed:* recently landed. – Cf. III.iii.11, where Gloucester uses *footed* in connection with this force.

47   *guessingly set down:* written as the result of guessing. – This phrase and the claim about the writer's neutrality which follows are Gloucester's attempts to play down the importance of the letter.

51   *at peril:* on peril of death. – Gloucester tells of these orders at the beginning of III.iii.

53   *I am tied . . . course –* The metaphor is of a chained animal baited by dogs. Bear-baiting as a sport continued in England until after Shakespeare's time. A *course* was one 'round' of attacks by the dogs. Gloucester's reference to this cruel sport anticipates the cruelty that he himself is to suffer.

55   *cruel nails . . . eyes –* This is a more specific reference to cruelty; unwittingly it anticipates what he is himself to suffer, as Goneril has already hinted (III.vii.5).

57   *anointed:* sanctfied – since the King, like a priest, is anointed with holy oil to show that he is appointed by God to his office.

57   *stick –* This is the F reading. Q reads *rash,* 'dash, strike sideways', as a boar does with its tusk; this is a more technical word and may have been abandoned because of its obscurity and because the resultant three adjacent words with the *-sh* sound in them would have given an inharmonious effect.

59   *buoyed up:* risen up – apparently on the analogy of a buoy rising to the surface of turbulent water, though the metaphor applied to the sea itself is hardly convincing.

60   *stelléd fires:* stars. – *stelléd* seems to mean both (i) starry (Latin *stella*) and (ii) fixed, as elsewhere in Shakespeare. Stars proper were thought of as 'fixed', while planets were 'wandering'. Storms of thunder and lightning came from the sky; the storm Lear suffered was so terrible that, Gloucester says, the sea would have risen up and in the process have put the stars out.

61   *holp:* helped. – The rain and his tears fell together.

62   *dearn:* dreadful.

63   *Thou shouldst:* you would; *porter:* gate-keeper.

CORNWALL Bind fast his corky* arms.
GLOUCESTER What mean your graces? Good my friends, consider
You are my guests; do me no foul play, friends.   30
CORNWALL Bind him, I say.   [SERVANTS *bind him*
REGAN   Hard, hard. O filthy traitor!
GLOUCESTER Unmerciful lady as you are, I'm none.*
CORNWALL To this chair bind him. Villain, thou shalt find –
                              [REGAN *plucks his beard*
GLOUCESTER By the kind gods, 'tis most ignobly done
To pluck me by the beard.   35
REGAN So white,* and such a traitor!
GLOUCESTER   Naughty* lady,
These hairs which thou dost ravish* from my chin
Will quicken* and accuse thee. I am your host;
With robbers' hands my hospitable favours*
You should not ruffle* thus. What will you do?   40
CORNWALL Come, sir, what letters had you late from France?
REGAN Be simple answerer,* for we know the truth.
CORNWALL And what confederacy* have you with the traitors
Late footed* in the kingdom?
REGAN To whose hands have you sent the lunatic King?   45
Speak.
GLOUCESTER I have a letter, guessingly set down,*
Which came from one that's of a neutral heart,
And not from one opposed.
CORNWALL   Cunning.
REGAN   And false.
CORNWALL Where hast thou sent the King?
GLOUCESTER   To Dover.   50
REGAN Wherefore to Dover? Wast thou not charged at peril* –
CORNWALL Wherefore to Dover? Let him first answer that.
GLOUCESTER I am tied to the stake,* and I must stand the course.
REGAN Wherefore to Dover, sir?
GLOUCESTER Because I would not see thy cruel nails*   55
Pluck out his poor old eyes, nor thy fierce sister
In his anointed* flesh stick* boarish fangs.
The sea, with such a storm as his bare head
In hell-black night endured, would have buoyed up,*
And quenched the stelléd fires;*   60
Yet, poor old heart, he holp* the heavens to rain.
If wolves had at thy gate howled that dearn* time,
Thou shouldst* have said, 'Good porter, turn the key,'

64   *All cruels else subscribed:* (perhaps) all other cruel creatures having yielded [to compas-
        sionate treatment]. — F has *subscribe* for *subscribed* here; if this reading is
        correct, the meaning is perhaps: 'all other cruel creatures yield [to feelings of
        compassion in conditions such as these]'. Gloucester is apparently imagining
        Regan admitting that she has treated her father more cruelly than she would a
        pack of wolves.

65   *wingéd vengeance:* vengeance from above. — This may refer to an avenging angel, a bird
        of prey, or even lightning. Gloucester says he will see vengeance descend from
        heaven on Regan and Goneril. But his use of the word *see* leads dramatically to
        the moment when he is to pay an appalling price for his loyalty to the King.

68   *will think:* hopes, expects. — In their own interests they should stop Cornwall and Regan,
        whose ruthlessness will only grow worse, and who will certainly want to
        silence any witnesses.

70   *One side . . . too* – i.e. the side of Gloucester's face which still has an eye will mock the
        other; so Regan urges Cornwall to tear out the second eye too.

71   *If . . . vengeance* – referring back to line 65. Cornwall, who has up to now been dominating
        the stage, is interrupted by a servant who attempts unsuccessfully to hold him
        back. Cornwall is about to say something to the effect that he will not have
        done what he resolves to do if Gloucester is to see vengeance – or to see any-
        thing else.

71   *Hold:* Hold back.

74   *How now:* What is this.

76   *shake it* – Cf. lines 34–8.

76   *What . . . mean* – The text printed here is as in the Fs and Qs, but these words should
        probably be attributed to Regan, taken aback by the outrageousness of the
        servant's words. If they are part of the servant's utterance, however, they
        mean: 'What are you trying to do?' and must be addressed to Cornwall as well
        as Regan.

77   *My villain* – Cornwall is perhaps using the word to mean both 'serf', lowest order of ser-
        vant, as the possessive *My* suggests, and also 'evil-doer'.

78   *take . . . anger:* risk a fight in deadly earnest – not just a friendly fencing match.

79   *A peasant . . . thus:* How disgraceful that a peasant should stand up in opposition [to you]
        like this. – Regan uses the servant's low social status as an excuse for killing
        him by running her sword into him from behind.

81   *some mischief on him:* some harm come to him [Cornwall].

        The simulation on the stage of the blinding of Gloucester moves the audience
        with intense terror. Commentators have over the years objected to the crudity
        of the device. Directors place Gloucester in the chair with his back to the
        audience; an earlier style was for Gloucester to be taken off the stage or into
        the inner stage over which the curtains were then drawn. In this way the
        audience would experience only his cries; the deed of blinding was left
        entirely to the imagination. But Shakespeare's audience would have reacted
        to it with less sensitivity than we do now. For them a public hanging, which
        normally included the mutilation of the body, was a spectacle drawing large
        crowds.

85   *enkindle . . . nature* – The *sparks* of light refer back to the blinding and the *lustre* of the eye-
        ball; *nature* recalls the 'natural' bond of kinship which should join father and
        son.

86   *quit:* pay back, requite. – To add to Gloucester's desolation, Regan shows him how
        Edmund, the son in whom his hopes of revenge momentarily rested, is the
        source of all his pain and sorrow.

86   *Out* – an interjection expressing reproach or intense dislike; perhaps near to 'No!'

88   *made the overture:* revealed, made open.

89   *Who:* and he.

90   *abused:* wronged. – As soon as Gloucester loses his sight he begins to 'see' how he has been
        deceived and to perceive his sons' true natures.

93   *how look you:* how are you, what is wrong with you.

97   *Untimely:* at an unfortunate time [in view of the impending attack].

	All cruels else subscribed.* But I shall see
	The wingéd vengeance* overtake such children.	65
CORNWALL	See 't shalt thou never. Fellows, hold the chair.
	Upon these eyes of thine I'll set my foot.
GLOUCESTER	He that will think* to live till he be old,
	Give me some help! O cruel! [CORNWALL *tears one eye out.*]
	O you gods!
REGAN	One side will mock another; the other too.*	70
CORNWALL	If you see vengeance* –
FIRST SERVANT	Hold* your hand, my lord.
	I have served you ever since I was a child;
	But better service have I never done you
	Than now to bid you hold.
REGAN	How now,* you dog!
FIRST SERVANT	If you did wear a beard upon your chin,	75
	I'd shake it* on this quarrel. What do you mean?*
CORNWALL	My villain!* [*They draw swords and fight*
FIRST SERVANT	Nay, then, come on, and take the chance of anger.*
REGAN	[*To a* SERVANT] Give me thy sword. A peasant* stand
	up thus! [*Takes a sword and runs at him from behind*
FIRST SERVANT	O, I am slain! [*To* GLOUCESTER] My lord, you have one eye
	left	80
	To see some mischief* on him. O! [*He dies*
CORNWALL	Lest it see more, prevent it. Out, vile jelly!
	Where is thy lustre now?
GLOUCESTER	All dark and comfortless. Where's my son Edmund?
	Edmund, enkindle all the sparks of nature,*	85
	To quit* this horrid act.
REGAN	Out,* treacherous villain!
	Thou call'st on him that hates thee. It was he
	That made the overture* of thy treasons to us,
	Who* is too good to pity thee.
GLOUCESTER	O my follies! Then Edgar was abused.*	90
	Kind gods, forgive me that, and prosper him!
REGAN	Go thrust him out at gates, and let him smell
	His way to Dover. [*Exit a* SERVANT *with* GLOUCESTER]
	[*To* CORNWALL] How is 't, my lord, how look you?*
CORNWALL	I have received a hurt. Follow me, lady.
	Turn out that eyeless villain; throw this slave	95
	Upon the dunghill. Regan, I bleed apace;
	Untimely* comes this hurt; give me your arm.
	[*Exit* CORNWALL, *led by* REGAN

100　*old:* usual, natural – not death by murder.
101　*Women . . . monsters* – They will become unnatural beasts of cruelty because they will see that Regan's evil deeds have gone unpunished.
102　*the Bedlam* – This term refers to Edgar, though it is odd they should think of him as a well-known figure when he has only recently assumed the guise of a mad beggar.
103　*he would:* he [Gloucester] wishes to go.
104　*Allows . . . anything:* makes it possible for him to do whatever he wants. – Gloucester will now want to join the French faction in Dover, and the mad beggar leading the blind man through the country will cause no surprise and draw no attention.
105　*flax . . . eggs* – to make plasters for the eye-sockets.

SECOND SERVANT   I'll never care what wickedness I do,
                  If this man come to good.
 THIRD SERVANT   If she live long,
                  And in the end meet the old* course of death,   100
                  Women will all turn monsters.*
SECOND SERVANT   Let's follow the old earl, and get the Bedlam*
                  To lead him where he would.* His roguish madness
                  Allows* itself to anything.
 THIRD SERVANT   Go thou. I'll fetch some flax and whites of eggs*   105
                  To apply to his bleeding face. Now, heaven help him!
                                      [*Exeunt in different directions*

Edgar, as poor Tom, leading the blinded Gloucester (Act IV, Scene i).

The confrontation between Goneril and her husband Albany (Act IV, Scene ii).

IV.i   Gloucester has evidently been put into the care of an aged, loyal tenant. He dismisses him
and puts himself into the hands of Edgar, whom they have met by chance as the poor
Bedlam. Gloucester's wish is to go to Dover so that, by throwing himself over the cliffs
there, he can end his misery by taking his own life.

As Gloucester did not know Edgar for his true worth when his family was undivided,
so now he does not recognise him, despite his clearer view of the malevolence of Edmund,
since in accordance with the convention of the theatre his disguised voice is impenetrable.
The two plots now intermesh closely. Gloucester avers it is 'the gods' who kill for their
sport, but his suffering has been at men's hands; Lear's suffering looks more as if its origin
lies in the inscrutable workings of fate. At the end of the scene the more beneficent tone
is marred by Gloucester's hint of suicide.

1   *contemned:* despised. – *known* perhaps implies 'known to oneself'.
2   *still:* always, and at the same time. – The early editions complete the clause at the end of
        the line; the full stop after *flattered* is as amended by Pope and makes the two
        sentences simpler to interpret. The meaning is: 'Yet it is better like this, to be
        fully aware of being despised rather than to be at the same time despised and
        flattered (so that one is unaware of people's scorn).'
3   *most dejected . . . fortune:* creature most humbled (*dejected*) by fortune.
4   *Stands . . . esperance:* is always in a condition of hope.
5   *The lamentable . . . laughter:* The change to be deplored is a change from what is better
        (or best); the change from the worst must inevitably be for the better. –
        Thoughts on what is 'worst' in the degrees of human condition pervade this
        scene; see especially lines 26–9.
7   *unsubstantial* – i.e. that cannot be detected as substance, cannot be touched. The action
        shows him cast out into the open, and his invocation to the open air indicates
        to the audience the nature of the stage setting.
10   *poorly led:* led like a beggar. – The reading of this phrase in F is *poorly, led* (perhaps mean-
        ing: 'dressed in rags, and being led'),. The corrected Q sheet has *parti, eyd,*
        which makes no sense but suggests that in the original play there was some
        reference here to Gloucester's blindness.
11   *But that . . . age:* If it were not that your inexplicable changes make us hate you, we would
        not submit our lives so readily to old age [and death]. – The old man is a retainer
        of Gloucester's and is leading him away from the castle, even though Edgar as
        the Bedlam (III.vii.102) was to have done this.
16   *comforts:* attempts to help.
19   *want:* need, lack. – This, followed by the paradoxical statement in the following line,
        leads to a philosophical generalisation, *Full oft* (very often) *'tis seen . . . ,* in a
        characteristic Shakespearian manner. Humanity errs through failure to reason
        from the evidence of its senses; when he had eyes, he allowed himself to be
        deceived by Edmund.
21   *Our means . . . commodities:* the advantages we enjoy make us careless (*secure us,* i.e. give
        us a sense of safety which is not justified), while our very deficiencies turn out
        to be advantageous to us.
23   *food:* object [on which his anger fed]; *abuséd:* deceived.
24   *Might I . . . touch:* If only I could live on to perceive your presence by touching you. – He
        can no longer *see* him because he is blind.
26   *Who . . . can say . . .* – He is referring to his speech at the beginning of the scene.
28   *the worst is not* – i.e. we have not reached the worst.

ACT IV scene i

The heath.

Enter EDGAR.

EDGAR   Yet better thus, and known to be contemned,*
Than still* contemned and flattered. To be worst,
The lowest and most dejected* thing of fortune,
Stands still in esperance,* lives not in fear.
The lamentable* change is from the best;   5
The worst returns to laughter. Welcome then,
Thou unsubstantial* air that I embrace!
The wretch that thou hast blown unto the worst
Owes nothing to thy blasts. But who comes here?

Enter GLOUCESTER, *led by an* OLD MAN.

My father, poorly led?* World, world, O world!   10
But that thy strange mutations* make us hate thee,
Life would not yield to age.

OLD MAN   [*To* GLOUCESTER]   O, my good lord,
I have been your tenant, and your father's tenant,
These fourscore years.

GLOUCESTER   Away, get thee away; good friend, be gone.   15
Thy comforts* can do me no good at all;
Thee they may hurt.

OLD MAN   Alack, sir, you cannot see your way.

GLOUCESTER   I have no way and therefore want* no eyes;
I stumbled when I saw. Full oft 'tis seen,   20
Our means* secure us, and our mere defects
Prove our commodities. Ah, dear son Edgar,
The food* of thy abuséd father's wrath!
Might I but live to see thee in my touch,*
I'd say I had eyes again!

OLD MAN   How now! Who's there?   25

EDGAR   [*Aside*] O gods! Who is 't can say* 'I am at the worst'?
I am worse than e'er I was.

OLD MAN   'Tis poor mad Tom.

EDGAR   [*Aside*] And worse I may be yet; the worst is not*
So long as we can say 'This is the worst.'

32   *reason:* intelligence.
34   *worm:* weak, vulnerable creature.
36   *scarce friends with him:* by no means well disposed towards him [my son].
37   *As flies . . . sport:* The gods kill us for their amusement (*sport*) just as playful (*wanton*) boys
            kill flies. – The fatalism of these lines rounds off Gloucester's statement of his
            own despair. Yet this despair is not complete; we quickly see that Gloucester
            is to exercise a free choice in his determination to take his own life. He is saved
            by the intervention, not of some blind agent of fate, but of his own son, Edgar,
            who wishes him well. And Edgar's view of his father's fate is very different
            (v.iii.170–3: *The gods are just . . .*).
38   *How . . . be:* What has happened to make this come about? – Edgar is probably wondering
            how his father came to lose his eyes.
39   *Bad . . . others:* It is a bad business when you have to play the fool for someone who is
            in great sorrow; you anger yourself, and others too [by acting in this way].
42   *get thee gone:* get on your way.
43   *o'ertake us:* catch us up. – Gloucester will get the *naked fellow* (Edgar) to lead him while
            the old man finds some clothes.
43   *twain:* two.
44   *ancient:* former. – Gloucester does not expect his old retainer to love him now.
45   *soul:* person – i.e. Edgar disguised as a beggar.
47   *madmen . . . blind* – Gloucester speaks of his own predicament as a symbol of state corrup-
            tion: the blind, the helpless, are led along by rulers who are mad.
48   *do thy pleasure:* do as you wish. – Gloucester cannot order the old man about any more.
49   *the rest:* all.
50   *'parel* for *apparel:* clothing.
51   *Come . . . will:* whatever the consequences may be; *on:* of. – The pretext of the old man's
            departure is an important dramatic device. The stage is now left clear for
            Gloucester and Edgar to be alone together, and for the revelation of Edgar to
            his father to begin.
53   *daub it:* deceive (*daub:* cover up with an exterior designed to deceive).
57   *Both stile . . .* – Edgar uses the names and characteristics of evil spirits, taken from some
            sort of traditional demonology, which he thinks of as having entered into him.
            Shakespeare used Harsnett as a source for their names.
58   *Bless thee:* May God preserve you. – Beggars expected alms in return for the blessings they
            gave; hence Gloucester gives Edgar his purse (line 64).
60   *as:* in the person of. – The devils are associated with particular evils in the way that patron
            saints are looked to for particular kinds of help.
62   *mopping and mowing:* making faces and grimacing. – Harsnett has 'mow and mop like an
            Ape', of a woman possessed with evil spirits.
62   *possesses:* takes possession of. – There is again the perversion of the patron saint idea.
65   *to all strokes:* to accept the cruellest strokes [of fortune].

OLD MAN   Fellow, where goest?

GLOUCESTER   Is it a beggar-man?   30

OLD MAN   Madman and beggar too.

GLOUCESTER   He has some reason,* else he could not beg.
I' the last night's storm I such a fellow saw,
Which made me think a man a worm.* My son
Came then into my mind; and yet my mind   35
Was then scarce friends* with him. I have heard more since.
As flies to wanton boys* are we to the gods;
They kill us for their sport.

EDGAR   [Aside]   How should this be?*
Bad is the trade* that must play fool to sorrow,
Angering itself and others. [Aloud, in country dialect] Bless
thee, master!   40

GLOUCESTER   Is that the naked fellow?

OLD MAN   Ay, my lord.

GLOUCESTER   [To the OLD MAN] Then, prithee, get thee gone.* If for my
sake
Thou wilt o'ertake* us hence a mile or twain*
I' the way toward Dover, do it for ancient* love;
And bring some covering for this naked soul,*   45
Who I'll entreat to lead me.

OLD MAN   Alack, sir, he is mad.

GLOUCESTER   'Tis the times' plague, when madmen lead the blind.*
Do as I bid thee, or rather do thy pleasure;*
Above the rest,* be gone.

OLD MAN   I'll bring him the best 'parel* that I have,   50
Come on 't what will.*   [Exit

GLOUCESTER   Sirrah, naked fellow –

EDGAR   Poor Tom's a-cold. [Aside] I cannot daub* it further.

GLOUCESTER   Come hither, fellow.

EDGAR   [Aside] And yet I must. – Bless thy sweet eyes, they bleed.   55

GLOUCESTER   Know'st thou the way to Dover?

EDGAR   Both stile* and gate, horse-way and foot-path. Poor Tom hath
been scared out of his good wits. Bless thee,* good man's son,
from the foul fiend! Five fiends have been in poor Tom at
once: of lust, as* Obidicut; Hobbididence, prince of dumb-   60
ness; Mahu, of stealing; Modo, of murder; Flibbertigibbet,
of mopping and mowing;* who since possesses* chamber-
maids and waiting-women. So, bless thee, master.

GLOUCESTER   Here, take this purse, thou whom the heavens' plagues
Have humbled to all strokes.* That I am wretched   65

66   *Heavens . . . still:* O heavens, deal always this way [with mortals]. – The invocation to the
      heavens continues in the lines that follow.

67   *Let . . . ordinance:* Let the man who has more than enough (*superfluous*) and satisfies all his
      desires (*lust-dieted*), who makes the system you have ordained (*ordinance*) his
      slave [to do whatever he has a desire for] . . .

69   *see . . . feel –* This clearly refers to Gloucester's blindness, but the idea of *feel* is extended to
      'feel sympathy for', in this case for those less fortunate than the *lust-dieted man.*

70   *undo:* prevent, be a bar to.

73   *a cliff –* There is a cliff near Dover called Shakespeare's Cliff in reference to this incident.
      The demands of the plot call for Gloucester and Lear to meet at Dover. Dover
      has high white cliffs which everyone in southern England would know about.
      In the play Dover has by now become almost a symbolic goal for comfort and
      redress of grievance.

73   *bending:* overhanging.

74   *fearfully in:* frighteningly into; *confinéd deep:* sea hemmed in [by cliffs]. – The sea is
      especially turbulent because it is confined in a small area. Shakespeare is
      perhaps thinking of the narrowness (21 miles) of the Straits of Dover.

76   *repair:* do something to repair, alleviate (with a reward, *something rich about me*).

IV.ii   Goneril and Edmund, who had set out from Gloucester's castle in III.vii, now arrive at
        Albany's palace; Goneril finds she is sexually attracted to Edmund. Oswald, who has
        already reported the latest news to Albany, says that Albany is a changed man, and is now
        vehemently loyal to the King. Goneril, in this changed situation, sends Edmund back to
        Cornwall, and then confronts Albany, taunting him for cowardice. Cornwall's death is
        reported; Goneril realises that Regan is therefore a widow and jealously worries that
        Edmund will soon be with her.

        Edmund now takes Gloucester's place as the link between the two plots. Albany thinks
        the intervention of fate, natural justice, is inevitable. However, the servant's killing of
        Cornwall is more a triumph of human decency than evidence of a just universe; the
        universe seems just because it is sometimes kind. The movement of both Regan and Goneril
        towards emotional involvement with Edmund is foreboding, but looks more like a device
        for the plot than the inevitable working of fate. The complexity of movement in this scene,
        however, reflects the impossibly difficult task of attributing outcomes to either divine
        disposition or human contrivance.

1   *Welcome –* i.e. to my palace. Goneril and Edmund have completed together the journey
      from Gloucester's castle which Cornwall told them to undertake at the begin-
      ning of III.vii.

2   *Not met:* has not met.

3   *within:* indoors.

6   *The worse:* So much the worse [for them]. – Albany's attitude is hardening; he is no longer
      the *mild husband* Goneril thinks him to be (line 1).

8   *sot:* idiot.

9   *the wrong side out –* on the analogy of turning clothes 'inside-out', when the wrong side of
      the garment is, as it were, treated as the right side: it is Edmund who is the
      traitor, not Gloucester.

11   *What like offensive –* i.e. what he should like seems offensive to him.

12   *cowish:* cowardly.

Makes thee the happier. Heavens, deal so still!*
Let the superfluous* and lust-dieted man,
That slaves your ordinance, that will not see
Because he does not feel,* feel your power quickly;
So distribution should undo* excess   70
And each man have enough. Dost thou know Dover?
EDGAR   Ay, master.
GLOUCESTER   There is a cliff* whose high and bending* head
Looks fearfully* in the confinéd deep.
Bring me but to the very brim of it,   75
And I'll repair* the misery thou dost bear
With something rich about me. From that place
I shall no leading need.
EDGAR   Give me thy arm;
Poor Tom shall lead thee.
                                                       [*Exeunt*

scene ii

In front of the Duke of Albany's palace.

Enter GONERIL *and* EDMUND.

GONERIL   Welcome,* my lord. I marvel our mild husband
Not met* us on the way.

Enter OSWALD.

                                Now, where's your master?
OSWALD   Madam, within;* but never man so changed.
I told him of the army that was landed;
He smiled at it. I told him you were coming;   5
His answer was, 'The worse'.* Of Gloucester's treachery
And of the loyal service of his son
When I informed him, then he called me sot,*
And told me I had turned the wrong side out.*
What most he should dislike seems pleasant to him;   10
What like, offensive.*
GONERIL   [*To* EDMUND]   Then shall you go no further.
It is the cowish* terror of his spirit

13	*undertake:* embark on a venture, make an attempt.
13	*He'll . . . answer:* He will not take any notice of abuses which would [if he did notice them] force him to react against them.
14	*Our wishes . . . effects:* The wishes we expressed to one another on our journey here may be realised. – They have been talking about getting Albany out of their way and fulfilling their love for one another.
15	*my brother* – i.e. Cornwall (her sister's husband).
16	*Hasten . . . powers:* hasten the enrolment of his troops and take over the leadership of (*conduct*) his military forces (*powers*).
17	*change arms:* exchange the symbols [of our sexes]. – In normal circumstances the man has the sword, the wife the distaff. But now Goneril is going to join the fight, taking on a man's role.
19	*pass:* carry messages; *like:* likely.
20	*in your own behalf:* on your own part.
21	*mistress's* – evidently a pun: as commander-in-chief of the army (if she is to *change arms* with Albany, line 17), she is going to 'order' Edmund like the mistress of a household and she is also going to be his mistress, i.e. lover.
SD	*favour:* mark of favour, perhaps a jewel on a chain, or a glove.
22	*Decline:* Bend – for the kiss or the placing of the *favour*.
24	*Conceive:* Take the meaning of this.
27	*due:* fitting, appropriate – i.e. Edmund is worthy of a woman's services.
28	*My fool* – i.e. Albany, her husband. Instead of *body* in this line, a Q reading has *bed*.
29	*I have . . . whistle:* There was a time when you thought me worth taking notice of. – This is an adaptation of a proverbial expression: 'It is a poor dog that is not worth the whistling', meaning 'The dog is worth the bother of whistling for.'
30	*rude:* rough. – The mention of *wind* is an immense transformation of Goneril's ironically joking *whistle*.
31	*fear:* have fears about.
32	*That nature . . . itself:* the type of human nature (*That nature*) which despises its (*it*) origin cannot be firmly restrained within itself. – He goes on to expand this point.
34	*herself . . . sap:* will tear herself off (*sliver*) and sever herself [like the branch of a tree, *disbranch*] from the sap which is the essential, life-giving substance (*material*). – The image is of a family tree, the branches of which spring from the same roots.
36	*come . . . use:* be used as dead wood [for burning].
37	*text:* (mockingly) the parable, imagery you have been using to preach at me.
39	*Filths . . . themselves:* filths have a taste only for themselves – i.e. to the filthy all things are filthy.
42	*head-lugged:* dragged along by the head – said of a performing bear which would have little respect for ordinary humans.
43	*madded:* maddened. – The object is *A father* in line 41.
44	*Could . . . do it* – I am amazed, he is saying, that Cornwall, who was a man of noble blood and who owed so much to the King, should have allowed you to do it; *suffer:* allow.
46	*visible:* in visible form – and therefore the more convincing and terrible.

That dares not undertake.* He'll* not feel wrongs
Which tie him to an answer. Our wishes* on the way
May prove effects. Back, Edmund, to my brother;*   15
Hasten* his musters and conduct his powers.
I must change arms* at home and give the distaff
Into my husband's hands. This trusty servant
Shall pass* between us. Ere long you are like to hear,
If you dare venture in your own behalf,*   20
A mistress's* command. Wear this; spare speech.
                         [*Giving him a favour*
Decline* your head. This kiss, if it durst speak,
Would stretch thy spirits up into the air.
Conceive,* and fare thee well.

EDMUND   Yours in the ranks of death.

GONERIL   My most dear Gloucester!   25
                         [*Exit* EDMUND
O, the difference of man and man!
To thee a woman's services are due;*
My fool* usurps my body.

OSWALD   Madam, here comes my lord.
                         [*Exit*

Enter ALBANY.

GONERIL I have been worth the whistle.*
ALBANY   O Goneril!
You are not worth the dust which the rude* wind   30
Blows in your face. I fear* your disposition:
That nature* which contemns it origin
Cannot be bordered certain in itself;
She that herself will sliver* and disbranch
From her material sap, perforce must wither   35
And come to deadly use.*
GONERIL No more; the text* is foolish.
ALBANY Wisdom and goodness to the vile seem vile;
Filths savour but themselves.* What have you done?
Tigers, not daughters, what have you performed?   40
A father, and a gracious aged man,
Whose reverence even the head-lugged* bear would lick,
Most barbarous, most degenerate! have you madded.*
Could* my good brother suffer you to do it!
A man, a prince, by him so benefited!   45
If that the heavens do not their visible* spirits

47   *vile* – The older spellings of this word, *vild* or *vilde*, are used in Q and, since they look like *wild*, suggest a concealed play on the contrast with *tame* in the same line here.

49   *Humanity . . . deep:* human beings will inevitably (*must perforce*) devour one another like sea monsters. – The crime is so monstrous, so upsetting to the natural order, that without divine intervention it will surely lead to cannibalism, the final stage of savagery (*Most barbarous, most degenerate*, line 43). There are many references in older literature to big fish preying on little fish.

50   *Milk-livered:* Cowardly – cf. II.ii.15.

51   *That bear'st . . . wrongs:* You who have a cheek ready to take blows and a head ready to suffer injustices. – He is in Goneril's eyes weakly submissive to the malevolence of others, and does not put up a fight. The mention of *cheek* recalls a text from the Bible; Jesus said:
> But I say unto you, That ye resist not evil: but whosoever shall smite thee on thy right cheek, turn to him the other also. (*Matthew* 5:39).

52   *discerning . . . suffering:* which distinguishes what can honourably be borne from what should be resisted.

53   *that not know'st:* you who do not know that . . .

54   *Fools . . . mischief:* only fools are sorry for evil-doers who are punished before they have committed their crimes. – She is apparently referring to Lear, who has been prevented so far from linking up with the French forces; the same applies to Gloucester, but she does not yet know of this. Her thoughts turn to the French military threat and its manifestations; there is no counter-demonstration on Albany's side.

56   *noiseless* – i.e. without the noise of preparation for war, such as the beating of drums.

57   *With . . . . threat:* [the King of France] begins to threaten your power (*state*) with plumed helmets. – The helmet with a plume was a symbol of proud defiance. The line as given here is in the version usually accepted; it is very imperfect in Q.

58   *Whiles:* whilst; *moral:* moralising.

60   *Proper . . . woman:* The deformity natural (*Proper*) to a devil does not appear (*seems not*) so horrible in a fiend as it does in a woman.

62   *changéd:* transformed (as woman into devil); *self-covered thing:* object which has disguised its nature – most probably, woman with the outward appearance of a devil, though possibly the other way about; clearly, from what follows, her face has taken on a look of fiendish fury.

63   *Be-monster . . . feature:* do not change your whole appearance (*feature*) into a monster's.

63   *Were 't my fitness:* If it were fitting for me. – He cannot bring himself to do what his emotions call for because he still sees Goneril as a woman.

64   *blood:* passion.

65   *apt:* ready; *tear:* tear apart.

66   *howe'er:* but although.

68   *Marry:* By the Virgin Mary – an oath.

68   *your manhood* – This presumably refers in a roundabout way to Albany's *my fitness* (line 63), or possibly to Albany's allusion to her *woman's shape* in line 67.

68   *mew:* make a noise like a cat – traditionally a feminine creature.

73   *bred:* kept; *thrilled with remorse:* moved by compassion.

74   *bending:* directing.

76   *felled:* they felled [the servant]. – The idea of the subject comes from *amongst them.*

78   *plucked him after:* taken him the same way. – In the scuffle Cornwall was mortally wounded. The retribution which the tragedy calls for is beginning to be worked out; the use of *plucked* recalls the blinding of Gloucester; see also line 85.

79   *justicers:* [heavenly] judges – as at III.vi.19, 53.

79   *nether:* [committed] here below.

80   *venge:* take vengeance on, punish.

Send quickly down to tame these vile* offences,
It will come,
Humanity must perforce* prey on itself,
Like monsters of the deep.

GONERIL   Milk-livered* man!   50
That bear'st a cheek for blows, a head for wrongs;*
Who hast not in thy brows an eye discerning*
Thine honour from thy suffering; that not know'st*
Fools* do those villains pity who are punished
Ere they have done their mischief.* Where's thy drum?   55
France speads his banners in our noiseless* land,
With pluméd helm thy state begins to threat,*
Whiles* thou, a moral fool, sit'st still and criest
'Alack, why does he so?'

ALBANY   See thyself, devil!
Proper deformity* seems not in the fiend   60
So horrid as in woman.

GONERIL   O vain fool!

ALBANY Thou changéd* and self-covered thing, for shame,
Bemonster* not thy feature. Were 't my fitness*
To let these hands obey my blood,*
They are apt* enough to dislocate and tear   65
Thy flesh and bones; howe'er* thou art a fiend,
A woman's shape doth shield thee.

GONERIL Marry,* your manhood!* mew!*

Enter a MESSENGER.

ALBANY What news?

MESSENGER O, my good lord, the Duke of Cornwall's dead,   70
Slain by his servant, going to put out
The other eye of Gloucester.

ALBANY   Gloucester's eyes!

MESSENGER A servant that he bred,* thrilled with remorse,
Opposed against the act, bending* his sword
To his great master; who thereat enraged   75
Flew on him and amongst them felled* him dead,
But not without that harmful stroke which since
Hath plucked him after.*

ALBANY   This shows you are above,
You justicers,* that these our nether* crimes
So speedily can venge.* But, O poor Gloucester!   80
Lost he his other eye?

84   *widow* – She is referring to Regan.
84   *my Gloucester* – i.e. Edmund, now Earl himself. Her ambition is to leave her husband for
         him.
85   *May all . . . life:* may bring down upon me, making my life hateful, all my ambitions, my
         castles in the air (*building in my fancy*).
87   *tart:* bitter.
90   *back:* on his way back.

IV.iii   This conversation between Kent and a Gentleman reveals that the French King has left his
         forces near Dover and returned to France, that Cordelia is overwhelmed by feelings of
         patient sorrow at her father's distress, and that the forces of Albany and Cornwall are
         afoot. Kent is to put Lear in the Gentleman's care for a while.
              Although this scene does not appear at all in the Folio it is integral to the play since it not
         only explains the action at some doubtful points but highlights the patient, reasoned
         sorrow of Cordelia as the corresponding virtue to the vice of petulant anger in Lear. The
         French King's return to his own country is dramatically desirable since his stay in Britain
         would make his force appear alien and confuse the audience's loyalty to Cordelia's cause.

2   *the reason* – The King of France is not with his troops in Britain at this time. His absence
                 makes Cordelia's actions all the purer; she is now able, when the occasion
                 arises, to use the troops in her father's cause, and the audience is undisturbed
                 by the consideration that Britain is being invaded by a foreign power, possibly
                 with expansionist intentions.
4   *imports:* involves [as a consequence].
7   *general:* as general.
9   *pierce:* move. – The *letters* are evidently ones taken by the Gentleman from Kent to
                 Cordelia, showing what needs to be done.

MESSENGER   Both, both, my lord.
         This letter, madam, craves a speedy answer;
         'Tis from your sister.   [*Hands her a letter*
GONERIL [*Aside*]   One way I like this well.
         But being widow,* and my Gloucester* with her,
         May all the building in my fancy* pluck   85
         Upon my hateful life; another way,
         The news is not so tart.* – [*Aloud*] I'll read, and answer.
                                                        [*Exit*
ALBANY   Where was his son when they did take his eyes?
MESSENGER Come with my lady hither.
ALBANY   He is not here.
MESSENGER No, my good lord; I met him back* again.   90
ALBANY   Knows he the wickedness?
MESSENGER Ay, my good lord; 'twas he informed against him,
         And quit the house on purpose, that their punishment
         Might have the freer course.
ALBANY   [*Aside*]   Gloucester, I live
         To thank thee for the love thou show'dst the King,   95
         And to revenge thine eyes. [*To the* MESSENGER] Come
         hither, friend.
         Tell me what more thou know'st.
                                                        [*Exeunt*

scene iii

The French camp near Dover.

Enter KENT *and a* GENTLEMAN.

KENT Why the King of France is so suddenly gone back know you
      the reason?*
GENTLEMAN Something he left imperfect in the state which since his
      coming forth is thought of, which imports* to the kingdom
      so much fear and danger that his personal return was most   5
      required and necessary.
KENT Who hath he left behind him general?*
GENTLEMAN The Marshal of France, Monsieur La Far.
KENT Did your letters pierce* the Queen to any demonstration of
      grief?   10

12 *ample:* full, large; *trilled:* trickled.

13 *she was . . . o'er her* (line 15): she controlled, as Queen, her emotions (*passions*), which (*who*), tried (*Sought*) to impose their rule as king over her. – This self-control is the *patience* the Gentleman refers to in line 16.

17 *Who . . . goodliest:* [to decide] which of them would express her emotion more fittingly. – Here the idea is not so much struggle to control the emotions as struggle to decide which of them should appear paramount.

18 *at once:* together.

19 *Were . . . way:* like this, but in a more beautiful fashion. – The similes of *sun/smiles* and *rain/tears* are common in English literature, especially in the courtly styles of Shakespeare's own age. The speeches of the courtly Gentleman are suitable for the use of this style, and with their wide range of imagery introduce it newly to the play.

19 *smilets:* little smiles.

20 *ripe:* red and beautiful, like ripe fruit.

21 *guests* – i.e. the tears which accompanied the smiles.

21 *which parted thence:* and they [the tears] left there (*parted*, 'departed', continuing the idea of tears being *guests*).

22 *pearls from diamonds* – i.e. her eyes shone like diamonds as the tears dropped like pearls.

24 *If all . . . it:* if everyone made it look as beautiful as she did; *become:* adorn.

24 *verbal question* – i.e. communication in words; *question:* speech, communication.

25 *Faith:* By my faith – an oath.

25 *heaved:* uttered like a groan.

29 *Let . . . believed* – Perhaps both (i) 'Let pity be believed not to exist at all' (since such cruel treatment is possible), and (ii) 'Let the pity [of the bringer of this report] not be believed' (because he must surely have been exaggerated).

29 *There:* At this point.

31 *clamour moistened:* (perhaps) drowned her outcry with her tears. – This seems the least unsatisfactory explanation, but the text is probably faulty at this point. Elucidation is made more difficult by the courtly style which the Gentleman continues to use, e.g. with the religious imagery of the *holy* water and Cordelia's *heavenly* eyes. See note on III.ii.10 for the implications of *holy water.*

33 *govern:* which govern; *conditions:* essential qualities. – The only explanation of such different qualities in people of the same descent must be that fate, the conjunction of the stars, decrees it so.

34 *Else . . . issues:* otherwise one and the same (*self*) marriage and partner in marriage (*mate and make*) could not produce offspring of such different qualities. – Fate must be a stronger influence than the inheritance of family characteristics.

37 *the King returned* – i.e. the King [of France] returned to France.

39 *sometime . . . tune:* sometimes, in his more lucid moments.

41 *yield:* consent.

42 *A sovereign . . . him:* An overmastering (*sovereign*) shame jostles him to such an extent. – He wants to approach her, but the shame he feels at the way he has treated her prevents him from doing so. Kent's speech shows that Lear is now ripe for reconciliation. The mood in common between Kent and the Gentleman is mirrored in the similarity of their poetic styles.

43 *stripped . . . benediction:* deprived her of paternal blessing, i.e. the love she should have enjoyed.

43 *turned . . . casualties:* turned her out to face the chances of life (*casualties*) away from home (*foreign*).

44 *dear:* much-prized, precious.

47 *Detains him:* keeps him away.

GENTLEMAN	Ay, sir; she took them, read them in my presence,
	And now and then an ample* tear trilled down
	Her delicate cheek. It seemed she was a queen*
	Over her passion, who most rebel-like
	Sought to be king o'er her.
KENT	O, then it moved her.	15
GENTLEMAN	Not to a rage; patience and sorrow strove
	Who should express her goodliest.* You have seen
	Sunshine and rain at once;* her smiles and tears
	Were like, a better way.* Those happy smilets*
	That played on her ripe* lip seemed not to know	20
	What guests* were in her eyes; which parted* thence
	As pearls from diamonds* dropped. In brief,
	Sorrow would be a rarity most beloved
	If all could so become* it.
KENT	Made she no verbal* question?
GENTLEMAN	Faith,* once or twice she heaved* the name of 'father'	25
	Pantingly forth, as if it pressed her heart;
	Cried 'Sisters! sisters! Shame of ladies! sisters!
	Kent! father! sisters! What, i' the storm! i' the night?
	Let pity not be believed!'* There* she shook
	The holy water from her heavenly eyes,	30
	And clamour moistened.* Then away she started
	To deal with grief alone.
KENT	It is the stars,
	The stars above us, govern* our conditions;
	Else one self mate and make could not beget
	Such different issues.* You spoke not with her since?	35
GENTLEMAN	No.
KENT	Was this before the King* returned?
GENTLEMAN	No, since.
KENT	Well, sir, the poor distressèd Lear's i' the town;
	Who sometime* in his better tune remembers
	What we are come about, and by no means	40
	Will yield* to see his daughter.
GENTLEMAN	Why, good sir?
KENT	A sovereign shame* so elbows him: his own unkindness
	That stripped her from his benediction,* turned her
	To foreign casualties,* gave her dear* rights
	To his dog-hearted daughters. These things sting	45
	His mind so venomously that burning shame
	Detains* him from Cordelia.

49   *afoot:* on the march. – The quiet conversation which this scene comprises, having given a
        résumé of the current position, leads up to this point; a clash of forces is now
        inevitable.

51   *dear cause:* important matter. – There is some dramatic fitness in the disguised Kent with-
        drawing for a while before he reveals himself.

53   *grieve . . . acquaintance:* regret having become acquainted with me.

IV.iv.   Cordelia prepares for her meeting with her father by consulting a doctor and by resolving
          for herself the conflict of loyalties: should she support Lear even though this means siding
          with the French against her own countrymen.

SD   *colours:* military ensigns.

1   *even now:* just now.

2   *vexed:* turbulent, tossed by the wind.

3   *Crowned . . . corn* (line 6) – The detailing of the noxious and other weeds which Lear used
          to crown his head may seem unnecessary. It is perhaps designed to bring home
          the idea that his crown was a travesty of the wreath of flowers or laurel tradi-
          tionally associated with the hero or leader. And the series of names gives a
          pleasing passage of poetry, with strong rhythms and some alliteration (*fumiter,
          furrow; hardocks, hemlock*). *rank fumiter:* coarse fumitory, a weed with a
          bitter smell; *furrow-weeds:* weeds that grow in the furrows of ploughed land;
          hardocks: presumably a kind of dock, a weed with large coarse leaves; *hemlock:*
          a weed used as a drug; *cuckoo-flowers:* wild flowers of the spring, when the
          cuckoo sings; *Darnel:* tares, kinds of weed which grow among the corn and
          take the moisture from it.

5   *idle:* useless – contrasting with *sustaining:* nourishing, in line 6.

6   *century:* troop of a hundred men.

8   *What . . . wisdom:* What skill can human knowledge have. – Doctors are often confident
          about cures for the body but much less sure of how to cure diseased minds.
          For *wisdom,* 'knowledge', cf. *wisdom of nature* I.ii.97.

9   *restoring:* restoring of; *bereavéd:* impaired, diseased.

10   *He that . . . worth:* Let anyone who cures (*helps*) him take all my worldly possessions. – The
          meaning of *outward* is uncertain, but is perhaps 'physical, material', i.e. not
          the riches of the mind.

11   *is,* for *are.* – The doctor's prescription for the cure of insanity is impressive, and far in
          advance of the usual practices of Shakespeare's time. Then, many kinds of
          violent and inhumane treatment were administered to the mentally ill, such
          as chaining up and shaving of the scalp.

12   *Our foster-nurse . . . repose* – i.e. mother nature employs rest (*repose*) as the source (the
          foster-nurse supplying nourishment) of restored strength.

13   *that to . . . him:* and to induce this [rest and sleep] in him.

14   *Are . . . operative:* there are many effective medicinal herbs (*simples*). – Doctors of the time
          were looked upon as trading in the special knowledge of the effect of herbal
          medicines on the human body; these are the *blest secrets* referred to in the next
          line, and the *unpublished virtues* (i.e. hidden powers which the earth puts forth)
          in line 16.

17   *Spring . . . tears* – The concept of tears falling to the earth and engendering or encouraging
          the growth of plants is of classical origin and common in literature.

17   *aidant and remediate:* helpful and healing.

19   *ungoverned rage:* ungovernable madness.

20   *wants:* lacks; *it* – i.e. itself, the life, and therefore the *means* must be his reason.

GENTLEMAN   Alack, poor gentleman!
    KENT Of Albany's and Cornwall's powers you heard not?
GENTLEMAN 'Tis so; they are afoot.*
    KENT Well, sir, I'll bring you to our master Lear,   50
And leave you to attend him. Some dear cause*
Will in concealment wrap me up awhile.
When I am known aright, you shall not grieve*
Lending me this acquaintance. I pray you, go
Along with me.   55

                                       [*Exeunt*

scene iv

The French camp; a tent showing.

*Enter, with drum and colours,** CORDELIA, DOCTOR, *and*
SOLDIERS.

CORDELIA Alack, 'tis he. Why, he was met even now*
As mad as the vexed* sea: singing aloud;
Crowned* with rank fumiter* and furrow-weeds,*
With hardocks,* hemlock,* nettles, cuckoo-flowers,*
Darnel,* and all the idle* weeds that grow   5
In our sustaining corn. A century* send forth;
Search every acre in the high-grown field,
And bring him to our eye. [*Exit an* OFFICER.] What can
man's wisdom*
In the restoring* his bereavéd sense?
He that helps him, take all my outward worth.*   10
  DOCTOR There is* means, madam:
Our foster-nurse of nature* is repose,
The which he lacks; that to provoke* in him
Are many simples* operative, whose power
Will close the eye of anguish.
CORDELIA   All blest secrets,   15
All you unpublished virtues of the earth,
Spring with my tears!* be aidant and remediate*
In the good man's distress! Seek, seek for him,
Lest his ungoverned* rage dissolve the life
That wants* the means to lead it.

21   *hitherward:* in this direction.
22   *before:* already; *preparation:* army in battle array.
25   *Therefore . . . pitied:* it is for this (*Therefore*) that the powerful King of France has taken pity
     on my lamenting and importunate (*important*) tears.
27   *blown:* inflated, pretentious.

IV.v   Regan confides in Oswald her ambition to marry Edmund despite Goneril's interest in him,
       and her regret that Gloucester lives on.

1   *my brother's* – i.e. Albany's, those of her sister Goneril's husband. Oswald is on an errand
     for his mistress Goneril.
2   *with much ado:* after much hesitation – both because he is uncertain where his allegiance
     lies and because he is less powerful in military affairs than his wife.
6   *What . . . letter:* What message does my sister's letter bring. – They have apparently been
     talking before the scene opened about the letter Oswald is carrying; it is
     addressed to Edmund.
8   *posted:* gone with haste; *serious matter:* important business.
9   *ignorance:* Foolishness.
12   *In pity . . . misery* – The real reason is not pity but fear that Gloucester will attract public
     support.
13   *nighted:* darkened [Gloucester being blind].
15   *must needs after:* must follow.
16   *Stay with us* – Regan wants to prevent Edmund from getting Goneril's letter because she is
     in love with him herself, and is jealous of her sister. Her fear that Edmund and
     Goneril are lovers is now evident.
18   *charged my duty:* gave me particular instructions.

Enter a MESSENGER.

MESSENGER   News, madam: 20
          The British powers are marching hitherward.*
CORDELIA 'Tis known before;* our preparation stands
          In expectation of them. O dear father,
          It is thy business that I go about;
          Therefore great France*   25
          My mourning and important tears hath pitied.
          No blown* ambition doth our arms incite,
          But love, dear love, and our aged father's right.
          Soon may I hear and see him!

                                                     [*Exeunt*

scene v

Inside Gloucester's castle.

Enter REGAN *and* OSWALD.

REGAN   But are my brother's* powers set forth?
OSWALD   Ay, madam.
REGAN   Himself in person there?
OSWALD   Madam, with much ado.*
          Your sister is the better soldier.
REGAN   Lord Edmund spake not with your lord at home?
OSWALD   No, madam.   5
REGAN   What might import* my sister's letter to him?
OSWALD   I know not, lady.
REGAN   Faith, he is posted* hence on serious matter.
          It was great ignorance,* Gloucester's eyes being out,
          To let him live; where he arrives he moves   10
          All hearts against us. Edmund, I think, is gone,
          In pity of his misery,* to dispatch
          His nighted* life; moreover, to descry
          The strength o' the enemy.
OSWALD   I must needs after* him, madam, with my letter.   15
REGAN   Our troops set forth tomorrow. Stay with us;*
          The ways are dangerous.
OSWALD   I may not, madam:
          My lady charged my duty* in this business.

19 *Might not . . . word* – i.e. could Goneril not have given Oswald an oral message?
20 *Belike:* Probably. – She hesitates before suggesting that she should see the letter herself.
24 *at her . . . here:* when she was here recently.
25 *oeillades:* amorous glances. – This must be the word indicated by various spellings in the early editions: *aliads* in Q; *Eliads* in F.1.
26 *of her bosom:* in her close confidence.
29 *take this note:* take note of what I say. – Regan in this speech snaps out short clauses in a peremptory style, designed to scare Oswald into conniving with her.
30 *talked:* come to an understanding.
31 *convenient:* fitting.
32 *gather more:* deduce more (i.e. the rest) for yourself. – She has virtually revealed that she is in love with Edmund.
33 *this* – apparently a token of her passion for Edmund (as suggested by the SD in this text), not a letter, since only Goneril's letter is found on Oswald after he is killed (IV.vi); letters in the plural are mentioned (IV.vi.241), but as often in Shakespeare the word refers to a single communication.
34 *thus much:* what I have told you.
35 *call . . . to her:* to see sense, to be reasonable.
38 *Preferment . . . off:* advancement (*Preferment*) will come to anyone who puts him [Gloucester] to death. – This offer appeals to Oswald, who uses the opportunity to reassert his loyalty.

IV.vi Gloucester, determined to take his own life, is deceived by Edgar into thinking that he has been brought to the cliff edge near Dover. When he throws himself on the ground, Edgar in another guise tries to convince him that he has been miraculously saved. Now Lear enters, and shows himself far gone in madness – he cannot follow any line of reasoning and is distracted by hallucinations – even though he and Gloucester manage to recognise one another. When people come looking for Lear he runs off and they chase after him. As the battle is about to begin, Oswald enters and prepares to kill Gloucester, who is still puzzled by Edgar's identity. Edgar intervenes and kills Oswald. Oswald is found to have been carrying a letter from Goneril to Edmund plotting the murder of her husband Albany.

This is the first scene of Act IV to have expansive treatment of a series of incidents squarely within the frame of the plots. The first five scenes have been little more than short interludes filling in details in preparation for the catastrophe; they each contain hints of humane influences at work to counter the effects of unregenerate nature (Edgar's tender treatment of his father, Albany's change of attitude, Cordelia's patient sorrow, etc.), but none has the broad development of a full scene. The present scene and vii show the regenerative influences themselves at work, and these centre on Edgar. In his dominance he begins to reflect a divine order of things, realised most clearly in the cruel play-acting of Gloucester's attempt at suicide and also in the bringing together of Gloucester and Lear. Lear's total madness and the unseemly chase after him are a set-back. It is Edgar too who kills Oswald and so brings to an end his evil missions.

REGAN   Why should she write to Edmund? Might not* you
        Transport her purposes by word? Belike,*   20
        Something – I know not what. I'll love thee much;
        Let me unseal the letter.
OSWALD   Madam, I had rather –
REGAN   I know your lady does not love her husband;
        I am sure of that. And at her late being here*
        She gave strange oeillades* and most speaking looks   25
        To noble Edmund. I know you are of her bosom.*
OSWALD   I, madam?
REGAN   I speak in understanding; you are; I know 't.
        Therefore I do advise you, take this note:*
        My lord is dead; Edmund and I have talked;*   30
        And more convenient* is he for my hand
        Than for your lady's. You may gather more.*
        If you do find him, pray you, give him this;*
                        [*Hands him a token*]
        And when your mistress hears thus much* from you,
        I pray, desire her call* her wisdom to her.   35
        So, fare you well.
        If you do chance to hear of that blind traitor,
        Preferment* falls on him that cuts him off.
OSWALD   Would I could meet him, madam! I should show
        What party I do follow.
REGAN   Fare thee well.   40
                              [*Exeunt*

scene vi

Fields near Dover.

Enter GLOUCESTER, *and* EDGAR *dressed like a peasant.*

GLOUCESTER   When shall we come to the top of that same hill?
EDGAR   You do climb up it now. Look, how we labour.
GLOUCESTER   Methinks the ground is even.
EDGAR   Horrible steep.
        Hark, do you hear the sea?
GLOUCESTER   No, truly.

6   *By . . . anguish:* because of the pain of your eyes. – The doctor uses the phrase *the eye of anguish* at IV.iv.15.

7   *thy voice is altered* – Edgar's change of style into one more fitting his origins is marked also by a change from prose to verse. The change is dramatically significant because later in the scene he is to break into a contrasting country style, part of his disguise as a peasant who intervenes between Gloucester and Oswald (lines 230ff.). Gloucester at first associates the change of dialect with the alleged imperfection of his own hearing which Edgar has deceived him over. But his doubts persist.

11   *here's the place* – Edgar deceives Gloucester into believing that they are standing on the edge of the high cliffs which face France across the Straits of Dover. The precise details in the description make it all sound very convincing.

13   *choughs:* birds of the crow family once common on rocky coasts.

14   *scarce so gross:* hardly as big. – The birds are imagined as flying below the feet of the observer, half-way up the cliff face (*the midway air*).

15   *sampire,* for *samphire:* an aromatic herb used for making pickles, and especially associated with Dover in Shakespeare's day. As it grows on the steep cliff face, the occupation of the man who gathers it is extremely dangerous (*dreadful trade*).

18   *yond:* that . . . over there.

19   *Diminished . . . cock:* reduced to the size of her ship's boat (*cock,* cock-boat).

21   *unnumbered idle pebble:* innumerable barren pebbles. – *pebble* is to be taken as plural in meaning, as *pearl* for *pearls,* in the English of the time.

23   *turn:* become dizzy. – The expression 'My head is turning' is modern English.

23   *the deficient . . . headlong:* and my failing (*deficient*) sight make me fall headlong.

27   *for all . . . upright:* I would not jump straight up in the air for anything in the world (*beneath the moon*). – He pretends to be so near the cliff edge that he would fall over even if he jumped straight up.

28   *another purse* – Gloucester has already given Edgar one purse, before he asked to be led to Dover (IV.i.64).

30   *Prosper it* – Gloucester is perhaps expressing a wish, according to a tradition of the time, that fairies should cause the riches in the purse to increase miraculously.

38   *fall:* begin, come. – This speech, in which Gloucester renounces life, turns naturally to the matter of fate, the inexorable will of the gods, which dominates the play. The will of the gods is *opposeless,* yet Gloucester believes he has, as he intended, acted in opposition to them.

40   *My snuff:* the smouldering wick of my candle of life, which is almost burnt out.

EDGAR   Why then your other senses grow imperfect   5
          By your eyes' anguish.*
GLOUCESTER   So may it be indeed.
          Methinks thy voice is altered,* and thou speak'st
          In better phrase and matter than thou didst.
EDGAR   You're much deceived; in nothing am I changed
          But in my garments.
GLOUCESTER   Methinks you're better spoken.   10
EDGAR   Come on, sir; here's the place.* Stand still. How fearful
          And dizzy 'tis to cast one's eyes so low!
          The crows and choughs* that wing the midway air
          Show scarce so gross* as beetles. Half way down
          Hangs one that gathers sampire,* dreadful trade!   15
          Methinks he seems no bigger than his head.
          The fishermen that walk upon the beach
          Appear like mice; and yond* tall anchoring bark
          Diminished to her cock;* her cock, a buoy
          Almost too small for sight. The murmuring surge   20
          That on the unnumbered idle pebble* chafes
          Cannot be heard so high. I'll look no more,
          Lest my brain turn* and the deficient sight*
          Topple down headlong.
GLOUCESTER   Set me where you stand.
EDGAR   Give me your hand. You are now within a foot   25
          Of the extreme verge; for all beneath the moon
          Would I not leap upright.*
GLOUCESTER   Let go my hand.
          Here, friend, 's another purse;* in it a jewel
          Well worth a poor man's taking. Fairies and gods
          Prosper* it with thee! Go thou further off;   30
          Bid me farewell, and let me hear thee going.
EDGAR   Now fare you well, good sir.
GLOUCESTER   With all my heart.
EDGAR   [Aside] Why I do trifle thus with his despair
          Is done to cure it.
GLOUCESTER [Kneeling] O you mighty gods!   35
          This world I do renounce, and in your sights
          Shake patiently my great affliction off.
          If I could bear it longer and not fall*
          To quarrel with your great opposeless wills,
          My snuff* and loathéd part of nature should   40
          Burn itself out. If Edgar live, O bless him!

43   *I know . . . theft* (line 45): I do not know how self-deception (*conceit*) can steal away the
     treasure of life, when life itself consents to the theft. – Edgar's strange debate
     with himself in this speech is not easily accounted for; it may serve principally
     to emphasise the fantasy of the whole situation. Here his argument seems to be
     that self-deception, imagination, is barely necessary in a man so ready to give
     up his life; the shock of Gloucester's imagined fall may kill him since he is so
     ready to die.

46   *By this . . . past* – i.e. he would now be dead, past thinking about anything (with the not
     altogether serious play on *thought*).

48   *pass:* die.

51   *fathom,* for *fathoms.*

52   *Thou'dst shivered:* you would have smashed to pieces.

54   *at each:* fastened end to end.

55   *fell,* for *fallen.*

58   *bourn:* boundary (of the sea, i.e. the cliff).

59   *a-height:* on high.

59   *shrill-gorged:* shrill-voiced (*gorge:* throat). – The skylark flies high above the earth with a
     shrill, sharp twitter as it soars.

62   *that benefit* – The *benefit* is what follows: to end itself.

63   *yet:* still.

64   *beguile . . . rage:* disappoint the tyrant's rage – by killing oneself and not waiting for the
     tyrant to kill one.

72   *welked:* twisted; *enridgèd:* furrowed. – Edgar is pretending that Gloucester's companion
     at the top of the cliff was not himself but a demon. If he can persuade Gloucester
     that there was supernatural intervention, he hopes his father will abandon the
     idea of suicide as being clearly against the will of the gods.

73   *father:* old man.

74   *the clearest . . . impossibilities:* the purest, most righteous gods, who win honour for them-
     selves by achieving things that men think impossible. – The explanation of
     clearest given here is the usual one; perhaps, however, it means rather 'evident,
     apparent to all', since it is part of Edgar's purpose to emphasise the work of fate
     in its beneficence.

Now, fellow, fare thee well.

EDGAR   Gone, sir; farewell.

[GLOUCESTER *throws himself forward and falls*

[*Aside*] And yet I know not* how conceit may rob

The treasury of life, when life itself

Yields to the theft. Had he been where he thought,   45

By this had thought been past.* Alive or dead?

[*To* GLOUCESTER] Ho, you sir! friend! Hear you, sir! speak!

[*Aside*] Thus might he pass* indeed; yet he revives.

[*To* GLOUCESTER] What are you, sir?

GLOUCESTER   Away, and let me die.

EDGAR   Hadst thou been aught but gossamer, feathers, air,   50

So many fathom* down precipitating,

Thou'dst shivered* like an egg. But thou dost breathe;

Hast heavy substance; bleed'st not; speak'st; art sound.

Ten masts at each* make not the altitude

Which thou hast perpendicularly fell.*   55

Thy life's a miracle. Speak yet again.

GLOUCESTER   But have I fall'n, or no?

EDGAR   From the dread summit of this chalky bourn.*

Look up a-height;* the shrill-gorged* lark so far

Cannot be seen or heard. Do but look up.   60

GLOUCESTER   Alack, I have no eyes.

Is wretchedness deprived that benefit,*

To end itself by death? 'Twas yet* some comfort,

When misery could beguile the tyrant's rage*

And frustrate his proud will.

EDGAR   Give me your arm.   65

Up; so. How is 't? Feel you your legs? You stand.

GLOUCESTER   Too well, too well.

EDGAR   This is above all strangeness.

Upon the crown o' the cliff, what thing was that

Which parted from you?

GLOUCESTER   A poor unfortunate beggar.

EDGAR   As I stood here below, methought his eyes   70

Were two full moons; he had a thousand noses,

Horns welked* and waved like the enridgéd sea.

It was some fiend; therefore, thou happy father,*

Think that the clearest* gods, who make them honours

Of men's impossibilities, have preserved thee.   75

GLOUCESTER   I do remember now. Henceforth I'll bear

Affliction till it do cry out itself

78   *die* – Affliction (personified) is thought of as dying when it has taken sufficient toll of the sufferer. Until it does so, Gloucester vows he will bear life patiently.

81   *free:* innocent – i.e. free from evil thoughts of despair.

82   *The safer . . . thus:* No one in possession of his senses (*The safer sense*) would dress himself up like this. – Man is thought of as master of his senses so long as he is in his right mind.

84   *touch . . . coining:* punish me for making coins. – Being a king, he has a right to make coins as currency for his realm. The word *coining* has a second meaning: it can be used euphemistically for the procreation of children; hence perhaps the turn of Lear's thoughts to *Nature* in line 86. Lear evidently has money in his hand and thinks he can use it to press Edgar or Gloucester into military service (*press-money*); this was the method used for forcing a man to serve in the army; if he took the money he was legally bound to serve. Lear's thoughts run on from this point in short inconsequential phrases, lacking mental control but having a train of connecting links which give a semblance of meaning. The *press-money* reminds him of recruits practising with the bow and arrow; this suggests a living target, a mouse, and a contest arising from a challenge (*There's my gauntlet*); he goes on to supporting forces of men (*brown bills*) and *bills* reminds him of *bird*. By the next speech (line 96ff.) his mind has clarified and the drift of the sense is fully logical.

85   *side-piercing:* agonising.

87   *crow-keeper:* one who shoots at crows (to keep them away from growing crops); possibly a scarecrow fitted out with a bow.

88   *a clothier's yard:* a full yard, as used by clothiers in measuring cloth; *me:* for me. – He wants the recruit to draw his bow down to the head of the arrow, the full length of which was a yard.

90   *gauntlet:* a glove armour-plated with steel. – Throwing down a gauntlet was a signal for challenging an enemy to combat.

90   *prove it:* try it out [in combat].

90   *brown bills:* bills or halberds painted brown to keep off the rust. – He is referring to a troop of halberdiers or billmen.

91   *bird* – i.e. the arrow, imagined as shot by the recruit, and flying with the use of tail-feathers, like a bird.

91   *i' the clout:* on the mark shot at – a bull's eye.

91   *hewgh* – a whistling sound, imitating the flight of an arrow.

92   *the word:* the password. – Cf. *Pass* (line 94).

93   *Sweet marjoram:* a herb said to be helpful in treating diseases of the brain. – Edgar uses as a password the first one that comes into his head; he is thinking of possible cures for madness.

96   *Goneril . . . beard* – Lear takes Gloucester for Goneril because his mind is running on her and her inhumanity. (But it has also been suggested that Lear is actually addressing Goneril in her absence, asking her how she could have treated her white-bearded father as she has done.)

96   *They flattered . . .* – His flatterers told him he had the wisdom of age even before he had a beard.

97   *like a dog:* as a dog fawns on its master.

98   *'ay' and 'no'* – i.e. short answers agreeing with what he said so as to please him, and regardless of whether he was right or wrong.

99   *'Ay' . . . divinity:* (perhaps) It was not good Christian behaviour to say both 'yes' and 'no' [to the same proposition in order to please the speaker]. – There may be a reference here to the Bible, *James* 5:12: 'let your yea be yea; and your nay, nay; lest ye fall into condemnation'.

101   *peace:* be still.

102   *'em:* them – i.e. the flatterers, those who were not true friends.

102   *Go to* – an expression of disapprobation, implying: 'I do not want to hear any argument to the contrary.'

103   *was everything* – i.e. had every desirable quality.

104   *ague-proof:* immune from catching a fever.

105   *trick:* turn, particular tone.

106   *a king* – Lear acts momentarily the part of a king, but his thoughts run on to more personal matters and the ambiguous role of woman, at once the enticer and the help-meet. In his madness he begins to universalise his own suffering and to pene-

'Enough, enough,' and die.* That thing you speak of,
I took it for a man; often 'twould say
'The fiend, the fiend'; he led me to that place.   80

EDGAR Bear free* and patient thoughts. But who comes here?

Enter LEAR, *fantastically dressed with wild flowers.*

The safer sense* will ne'er accommodate
His master thus.

LEAR No, they cannot touch me for coining;* I am the King himself.

EDGAR O thou side-piercing* sight!   85

LEAR Nature's above art in that respect. There's your press-
money. That fellow handles his bow like a crow-keeper;*
draw me a clothier's yard.* Look, look, a mouse! Peace,
peace; this piece of toasted cheese will do 't. There's my
gauntlet;* I'll prove it* on a giant. Bring up the brown bills.*   90
O, well flown, bird!* i' the clout;* i' the clout; hewgh!* Give
the word.*

EDGAR Sweet marjoram.*

LEAR Pass.

GLOUCESTER I know that voice.   95

LEAR Ha! Goneril, with a white beard!* They flattered* me like a
dog,* and told me I had white hairs in my beard ere the black
ones were there. To say 'ay' and 'no' to everything that I
said! 'Ay' and 'no' too was no good divinity.* When the
rain came to wet me once and the wind to make me chatter;   100
when the thunder would not peace* at my bidding; there I
found 'em,* there I smelt 'em out. Go to,* they are not men o'
their words. They told me I was everything;* 'tis a lie, I am
not ague-proof.*

GLOUCESTER The trick* of that voice I do well remember.   105
Is 't not the King?

LEAR   Ay, every inch a king:*
When I do stare, see how the subject quakes!*
I pardon that man's life. What was thy cause?*
Adultery?

---

106 (*cont'd*)   trate its sources much more profoundly than he was able to do in his apparent
sanity. His theme turns on the frailty of the human condition.

107   *When . . . quakes:* when I glare at one of my subjects, see how he shakes with fear.

108   *cause:* offence, charge [against you].

112   *lecher:* have sexual intercourse.
115   *Got:* begotten. – But Gloucester already knows that Edmund has been anything but kind
         to him (III.vii.85).
115   *To 't . . . pell-mell:* Get to work, lust (*luxury*), and do it promiscuously. – He invokes lust
         and calls on it to pursue its desires outside the confines of the marriage vow.
         Lear continues to pursue the subject of sex relations in impassioned detail.
116   *Behold . . . dame:* Look at that woman over there with the silly, self-conscious smile. –
         Lear is thinking of women who act coyly in order to conceal their real desires.
         His concern with women's hypocrisy springs from his daughters' behaviour.
117   *Whose . . . snow:* (perhaps) the look on whose face suggests frigid chastity between her
         legs (*forks*). – A human being he calls *forked animal* (III.iv.102).
118   *minces virtue:* affects the coyness of chastity.
118   *shake the head* – i.e. in shocked surprise.
119   *pleasure's name:* the very name of [sexual] pleasure.
120   *The fitchew . . . horse:* Neither the polecat nor the horse heated with rich green fodder
         (*soiled*).
122   *centaurs* – imaginary creatures in Greek mythology, half man and half horse, i.e. animal
         from the waist down.
124   *But to:* Only as far as.
124   *inherit:* possess, rule. – The upper part of the body is thought of as sanctified, the lower
         as given over to the devil because it is associated with fleshly lusts.
126   *There* – i.e. in that place, below the girdle.
128   *civet:* a strong-smelling perfume extracted from the glands of the civet-cat. (Cf. III.iv.99.).
131   *mortality* – The sense is that the hand, which Gloucester wants to kiss as a gesture of
         devotion, is flesh and therefore corruptible.
132   *This great world* – i.e. the universe. As Lear's former greatness has come to nothing, so
         must the universe pass away. This phrase, and the mention of *nature*, show
         Gloucester mystically sensing the universal implications of Lear's condition.
133   *Dost thou know me:* Do you recognise me. – Q reads *Do you* here. The present reading is
         preferred, since it gives the right tone of warm sympathy and affection,
         reciprocating Lear's own approach (*There's money for thee*, line 129, etc.).
134   *I remember . . . enough* – The dramatic irony of this passage springs from the notion of
         recognising a person most readily by looking into his eyes. Lear's madness
         prevents him from realising the implication of Gloucester's blindness. His
         thoughts revert to sexual love, possibly because prostitutes glance sidelong
         (*squiny*) at men they wish to entice. Cupid was pictured as the blind, or rather
         blindfold, god of love who aimed his arrows at the hearts of men and gods,
         causing them to fall in love. Like Fate, his arrows could strike anyone and at
         any time; hence the blindfold. Here *blind Cupid* may refer to the street sign of
         a brothel rather than to the god himself.
136   *mark . . . of it:* just notice how it is written. – The *challenge* may refer back to the *gauntlet*
         of line 90, but Lear's train of thought is by no means clear. It has perhaps
         something to do with a challenge by a bowman against the archery of Cupid
         (i.e. love). Dramatically the action re-emphasises Gloucester's blindness, since
         the challenge is meant to be in writing, and he therefore cannot see what it says.
138   *I would . . . it is:* If this [scene that I am now witnessing] were reported to me, I would
         not believe it, yet it exists.
141   *the case of eyes:* the sockets where the eyes have been.
142   *are you . . . me:* is that what you mean.
143   *in a heavy case:* in a sad state. – He puns on *case* in line 141, and continues to play on
         words in what follows: *light* ('light in weight', 'the light of day'); the comments
         on *eyes* and *purse* are in a rhetorical turn of phrase; *see* ('understand', 'see by
         the eyes'). Gloucester himself catches up the tone of the word-play in *feelingly*
         (line 145). All this word-play sounds to our ears grossly incongruous at this
         highly-charged point in the tragedy, but there are parallels to it elsewhere in
         Shakespeare, and we must assume that contemporary audiences did not find
         it distasteful.
145   *feelingly:* (i) with emotion; (ii) through my sense of touch.
147   *yond:* that . . . over there. – The scene is, of course, only in Lear's imagination. By calling
         up situations where appearances deceive (e.g. powerful but corrupt officials
         who look honourable because of their fine clothing) he tries to prove that
         Gloucester's blindness is a positive advantage.

Thou shalt not die. Die for adultery? No.   110
The wren goes to 't, and the small gilded fly
Does lecher* in my sight. Let copulation thrive;
For Gloucester's bastard son
Was kinder to his father than my daughters
Got* 'tween the lawful sheets. To 't, luxury, pell-mell,*   115
For I lack soldiers! Behold yond simpering dame,*
Whose face between her forks presages snow;*
That minces virtue,* and does shake the head*
To hear of pleasure's name.*
The fitchew* nor the soiled horse* goes to 't   120
With a more riotous appetite.
Down from the waist they are centaurs,*
Though women all above.
But to* the girdle do the gods inherit,*
Beneath is all the fiend's.   125
There's* hell, there's darkness, there 's the sulphurous pit,
Burning, scalding, stench, consumption; fie, fie, fie! pah,
pah! Give me an ounce of civet,* good apothecary, to sweeten
my imagination. There's money for thee.

GLOUCESTER O, let me kiss that hand!   130

LEAR Let me wipe it first; it smells of mortality.*

GLOUCESTER [Aside] O ruined piece of nature! This great world*
Shall so wear out to nought. [To LEAR] Dost thou* know me?

LEAR I remember thine eyes well enough.* Dost thou squiny* at
me? No, do thy worst, blind Cupid; I'll not love. Read thou   135
this challenge; mark but the penning of it.*

GLOUCESTER Were all the letters suns, I could not see one.

EDGAR [Aside] I would not take this from report; it is,*
And my heart breaks at it.

LEAR Read.   140

GLOUCESTER What, with the case of eyes?*

LEAR O, ho, are you there with me?* No eyes in your head, nor no
money in your purse? Your eyes are in a heavy case,* your
purse in a light. Yet you see how this world goes?

GLOUCESTER I see it feelingly.*   145

LEAR What, art mad? A man may see how this world goes with no
eyes. Look with thine ears; see how yond* justice rails upon

148   *simple:* poor, humble.
148   *change places* – i.e. get them to change places.
149   *handy-dandy:* take your choice. – The words are used in a children's game and mean
           literally, 'Which hand will you have?'
152   *creature* – i.e. the beggar, one of God's creatures.
153   *in office:* in a position of authority.
154   *beadle:* constable, parish officer with authority to punish small offences.
154   *hold:* hold back.
156   *kind:* way.
157   *The usurer . . . cozener:* The money-lender condemns the petty offender to hang – i.e. the
           greater criminal condemns the lesser. To *cozen* is to cheat.
159   *Robes* – i.e. robes of office, outward signs of authority, especially in judges.
160   *the strong . . . breaks:* the strong weapon of the law breaks without causing any hurt. –
           Plate in the previous line sparks off the image of mortal combat between men
           dressed in plate armour. The *gold*, i.e. riches, offers sufficient protection for
           the person being attacked. The imagery is extended to *Arm* in the following
           line.
162   *None does offend* – i.e. No one commits any offence from now on, in the sense that there
           can be no accusation if there is no honest person to act as accuser. Lear is in his
           imagination reverting to the role of sovereign over his people; he mentions
           his *power* in the next line.
162   *able 'em:* vouch for them.
165   *scurvy politician:* contemptible trickster. – *Politician* was a term used pejoratively to refer
           to a cunning trickster seeking his own advantage by any means, good or bad.
167   *pull off my boots* – The raving of Lear is brought down to earth by this homely remark
           about his clothing. Cf. III.iv.103, v.iii.309. The simplicity of these trifling con-
           cerns with clothing recalls the impatience of a child being dressed or undressed.
           As a quieter frame of mind returns, he becomes conscious that it is Gloucester
           he is talking to (line 171).
168   *matter and impertinency:* sense and nonsense.
172   *hither* – i.e. into this world.
174   *wawl:* wail (cf. modern English *caterwaul*).
177   *great . . . fools* – i.e. the world, thought of as a theatre. Shakespeare makes use of this symbol
           elsewhere; the most famous instance is perhaps in *As You Like It*, II.vii.138:
                           All the world's a stage,
                           And all the men and women merely players.
           There are many aspects to the pertinence of the symbol; the most striking here
           is perhaps that of the theatrical play being worked out in advance, like fate
           ordaining what is to happen during the life of a human being.
177   *This',* for *This is.*
177   *block:* (literally) a wooden mould which hats are made on. – The sense which links this
           word to the context here is unclear. Perhaps a property representing a mound
           or tree-stump on the stage reminds him of a block used to mount on horseback,
           a block on which felt is shaped in hat-making, and an execution block. This
           might lead his thoughts to (i) the *troop of horse*, (ii) *felt*, and (iii) judicial murder
           (*kill, kill, kill* . . . –line 181).
178   *were:* would be; *delicate:* neat.
179   *in proof:* to the test.
180   *stol'n upon:* crept silently up to – like the horses shod in felt.
183   *daughter* – i.e. Cordelia; the Gentleman knows of her essential goodness (lines 200–2),
           since he attends her and has evidently been sent by her to bring Lear in.
185   *The natural . . . fortune:* born to be the sport of fortune.

yond simple* thief. Hark, in thine ear; change places,* and,
handy-dandy,* which is the justice, which is the thief? Thou
hast seen a farmer's dog bark at a beggar?   150
GLOUCESTER Ay, sir.
        LEAR And the creature* run from the cur? There thou mightst
behold the great image of authority: a dog's obeyed in office.*
Thou rascal beadle,* hold* thy bloody hand! Why dost thou
lash that whore? Strip thine own back. Thou hotly lusts to   155
use her in that kind* for which thou whipp'st her. The
usurer hangs the cozener.*
Through tattered clothes small vices do appear;
Robes* and furred gowns hide all. Plate sin with gold
And the strong lance of justice hurtless breaks;*   160
Arm* it in rags, a pygmy's straw does pierce it.
None does offend,* none, I say, none; I'll able* 'em:
Take that of me, my friend, who have the power
To seal the accuser's lips. Get thee glass eyes,
And, like a scurvy politician,* seem   165
To see the things thou dost not.
Now, now, now, now; pull off my boots;* harder, harder;
so.
      EDGAR [Aside] O, matter and impertinency* mixed!
Reason in madness!
        LEAR If thou wilt weep my fortunes, take my eyes.   170
I know thee well enough; thy name is Gloucester.
Thou must be patient. We came crying hither;*
Thou know'st, the first time that we smell the air,
We wawl* and cry. I will preach to thee; mark.
GLOUCESTER Alack, alack the day!   175
        LEAR When we are born, we cry that we are come
To this great stage of fools.* This'* a good block.*
It were* a delicate stratagem, to shoe
A troop of horse with felt. I'll put 't in proof;*
And when I have stol'n upon* these sons-in-law,   180
Then, kill, kill, kill, kill, kill, kill!

Enter a GENTLEMAN, with ATTENDANTS.

GENTLEMAN O, here he is; lay hand upon him. Sir
Your most dear daughter* –
        LEAR No rescue? What, a prisoner? I am even
The natural fool of fortune.* Use me well;   185
You shall have ransom. Let me have surgeons;

187 *cut to the brains:* both (i) mentally disturbed (cf. 'cut to the heart') and (ii) suffering from a brain injury (as he supposes) – and therefore in need of a surgeon.

188 *No seconds:* [Have I] no supporters [in my fight against imprisonment]?

189 *salt* – i.e. salt tears, bitter tears of grief.

193 *bravely;* (i) with courage (believing he is being taken prisoner), and (ii) decked out in fine clothes (like a *smug bridegroom*); *smug:* neatly dressed; *die* is used here metaphorically in relation to sexual intercourse as well as in its normal sense.

197 *there's life in 't:* the case is not hopeless – punning on *die* (line 193) and on the general theme of the passage.

197 *and you get it:* if you catch your quarry (i.e. Lear himself). – As he runs out he utters the hunting cry *Sa, sa,* as a gesture of challenge and defiance.

201 *general:* universal. – The *general curse* must be 'original sin' which all mankind has inherited since the fall of Adam and Eve from the innocence of paradise.

202 *twain:* two – apparently Adam and Eve; some think the reference is to Goneril and Regan, but they can hardly be said to have brought nature to the *general curse.*

203 *gentle* – a polite form of address, 'good, honourable', as in *gentleman.*

203 *speed you,* for 'May God speed you' – i.e. prosper your undertakings.

204 *toward:* impending, about to take place. – The forthcoming battle is between the French and British forces.

205 *sure and vulgar:* certain and common knowledge.

206 *Which . . . sound:* who is able to hear sounds – i.e. who isn't deaf. The Gentleman is being very condescending to Edgar in disguise.

208 *the main . . . thought:* we expect to see the main body of the army any hour now.

210 *Though that:* Although; *the Queen* – Cordelia is looking for her father, and has left the advancing French army.

212 *You ever-gentle . . . from me* – He asks fate, the gods, to take his life when the time comes, and vows he will make no more attempts at suicide. What he has now learnt of Lear's desperate plight has brought him to this resolve.

213 *worser spirit:* evil angel.

216 *tame:* ready to submit. – This is another way of saying what Gloucester has prayed should happen to him, i.e. acceptance of the will of fate (*fortune's blows*).

217 *the art . . . sorrows:* the lessons of the heart-felt (*feeling*) sorrows I have experienced (*known*).

218 *pregnant . . . pity:* well disposed to feel pity for others.

219 *biding:* lodging place.

220 *benison:* blessing.

	I am cut to the brains.*	
GENTLEMAN	You shall have anything.	
LEAR	No seconds?* all myself?	
	Why, this would make a man a man of salt,*	
	To use his eyes for garden water-pots,	190
	Aye, and laying autumn's dust.	
GENTLEMAN	Good sir –	
LEAR	I will die bravely,* like a smug bridegroom. What!	
	I will be jovial: come, come; I am a king.	
	My masters, know you that.	195
GENTLEMAN	You are a royal one, and we obey you.	
LEAR	Then there's life in 't.* Nay, and you get it,* you shall get it	
	by running. Sa, sa, sa, sa.	

[Exit running; ATTENDANTS *follow*

GENTLEMAN	A sight most pitiful in the meanest wretch.	
	Past speaking of in a king! Thou hast one daughter	200
	Who redeems nature from the general* curse	
	Which twain* have brought her to.	
EDGAR	Hail, gentle* sir.	
GENTLEMAN	Sir, speed* you; what's your will?	
EDGAR	Do you hear aught, sir, of a battle toward?*	
GENTLEMAN	Most sure and vulgar;* every one hears that,	205
	Which can distinguish sound.*	
EDGAR	But, by your favour.	
	How near's the other army?	
GENTLEMAN	Near and on speedy foot; the main* descry	
	Stands on the hourly thought.	
EDGAR	I thank you, sir; that's all.	
GENTLEMAN	Though that* the Queen on special cause is here,	210
	Her army is moved on.	
EDGAR	I thank you, sir. *[Exit* GENTLEMAN	
GLOUCESTER	You ever-gentle gods, take my breath from me;*	
	Let not my worser spirit* tempt me again	
	To die before you please!	
EDGAR	Well pray you, father.	
GLOUCESTER	Now, good sir, what are you?	215
EDGAR	A most poor man, made tame* to fortune's blows;	
	Who, by the art of known and feeling sorrows,*	
	Am pregnant to* good pity. Give me your hand,	
	I'll lead you to some biding.*	
GLOUCESTER	Hearty thanks;	
	The bounty and the benison* of heaven	220

221   *To boot, and boot:* in addition [to my thanks] and as an extra reward. – The two meanings of *boot* in effect merge into one, and Gloucester's repetition is in the nature of innocent word-play.

221   *A próclaimed prize* – A public proclamation has gone out that Gloucester should be hunted down and killed as a traitor. Coming upon him in this way, Oswald thinks it will be to his own advantage if he can take his life.

222   *framed:* made.

224   *Briefly . . . remember:* quickly call to mind your past life [so that you can pray for forgiveness of your sins before you die].

225   *friendly* – Gloucester thinks of the hand as friendly because it will bring him the death he still desires, despite his resolve not to attempt again to take his own life.

226   *Wherefore:* To what purpose.

227   *published:* proclaimed.

228   *Lest that . . . thee:* in case the disease that his fortune is suffering from infects you in the same way – i.e. in case I kill you too; *Like:* similar, the same.

230   *Chill not . . .* – Edgar here begins to talk in a West Country dialect so as to make his disguise completely convincing. The chief features of the dialect are that the consonants usually pronounced [s] and [f] generally become voiced, [z] and [v]; forms arising from *ich*, Middle English for *I* (1st person singular pronoun), are retained: *chill*, 'I will'; *chud*, 'I could'.

230   *without . . . 'casion:* without more reason [than your telling me to let go]; *'casion,* for *occasion:* reason, cause.

232   *go your gait:* go on your way.

233   *An chud . . . vortnight:* If I could (*An chud*) have been bullied into giving up my life, it would have been a fortnight shorter than it is.

233   *zwaggered,* for *swaggered:* bullied, blustered.

235   *che vor ye:* I warn you.

235   *I'se try . . . harder:* I shall test whether your head (*costard,* literally a kind of apple) or my cudgel (*ballow*) is the harder. – Both this and the sentence beginning at line 232 have an aphoristic ring about them, as of a countryman speaking more wisely or in more shapely sentences than he is consciously aware of.

237   *dunghill:* rascal, 'born on a dunghill'.

238   *no matter . . . foins:* your thrusts (*foins*) are of no account to me.

239   *Villain:* Serf.

240   *If ever . . . thrive:* (literally) If you wish to prosper in life – i.e. if you want to avoid a curse, whatever you do.

241   *the letters* – This is the letter referred to in IV.v.

243   *Upon . . . party:* among the British forces.

245   *serviceable:* diligent in service.

250   *May be my friends* – might help me.

251   *deathsman:* executioner.

252   *Leave:* By your leave – asking permission of the wax to break it because the letter is not addressed to him.

252   *manners:* proper social behaviour, common decency. – He goes on to excuse his own behaviour by saying that we can go to any lengths to get information about enemies, even to the extent of opening letters addressed to them.

254   *Their papers* – i.e. to rip open their papers.

To boot,* and boot!

Enter OSWALD.

OSWALD   A próclaimed prize!* Most happy!
That eyeless head of thine was first framed* flesh
To raise my fortunes. [*He draws his sword.*] Thou old
unhappy traitor,
Briefly thyself remember;* the sword is out
That must destroy thee.

GLOUCESTER   Now let thy friendly* hand   225
Put strength enough to 't.   [EDGAR *interposes*

OSWALD   Wherefore,* bold peasant,
Dar'st thou support a published* traitor? Hence!
Lest that the infection* of his fortune take
Like hold on thee. Let go his arm.

EDGAR   Chill* not let go, zir, without vurther 'casion.*   230

OSWALD   Let go, slave, or thou diest!

EDGAR   Good gentleman, go your gait,* and let poor volk pass. An
chud* ha' been zwaggered* out of my life, 'twould not ha'
been zo long as 'tis by a vortnight. Nay, come not near th'
old man; keep out, che vor ye,* or I'se try* whether your   235
costard or my ballow be the harder. Chill be plain with you.

OSWALD   Out, dunghill!*   [*They fight*

EDGAR   Chill pick your teeth, zir. Come; no matter vor your foins.*
                                                [OSWALD *falls*

OSWALD   Slave, thou hast slain me. Villain,* take my purse.
If ever thou wilt thrive,* bury my body;   240
And give the letters* which thou find'st about me
To Edmund Earl of Gloucester; seek him out
Upon the British party.* O, untimely death!
Death!   [*Dies*

EDGAR   I know thee well; a serviceable* villain,   245
As duteous to the vices of thy mistress
As badness would desire.

GLOUCESTER   What, is he dead?

EDGAR   Sit you down, father; rest you.
Let's see these pockets; the letters that he speaks of
May be my friends.* He's dead; I am only sorry   250
He had no other deathsman.* Let us see:
Leave,* gentle wax; and, manners,* blame us not;
To know our enemies' minds, we'd rip their hearts;
Their papers* is more lawful.

256   *him* – i.e. Goneril's husband, Albany.

256   *if your will want not:* if your will is not lacking [in strength].

257   *fruitfully:* abundantly – balancing *want not* in the previous clause.

260   *supply . . . labour:* take his place as a reward for your labour.

264   *undistinguished . . . will:* unbounded range of woman's lust.

266   *in the sands* – It has been pointed out that only Gloucester thinks they are on the beach. Edgar doubtless refers to *sands* here as part of his attempt to reassure his father.

267   *rake up:* cover up [by raking sand over the body].

267   *post:* messenger; *unsanctified* – because he is an unholy messenger and will therefore be buried in unconsecrated (*unsanctified*) ground.

268   *in the . . . time:* when the time is ripe.

269   *ungracious:* wicked.

270   *death-practised duke:* the duke whose death is plotted – i.e. Albany.

272   *How stiff . . . sorrows!* (line 274): How unassailable (*stiff*) my own rude mental vigour (*vile sense*) is, that I am not bowed down (*stand up*) and have conscious awareness (*ingenious feeling*) of my immense grief! – All this is of course in contrast to the madness of the King.

274   *distract:* mad.

276   *wrong imaginations:* illusions.

279   *bestow:* lodge.

IV.vii   Cordelia acknowledges Kent's goodness, and Kent begs to be allowed to maintain his disguise. Lear is brought in, and on the doctor's advice Cordelia, with quiet talk and music, brings him back to consciousness. As he is carried away, Kent and the Gentleman mention the impending battle.

    The scene begins with a careful preparation for Lear's return to sanity and quiet by glimpsing the harmony of Kent's and Cordelia's relationship. Lear's appearance is short, but what he says shows in its style that his invective has given place to a cooler view of his predicament; he keeps within his soul the bitter resentment of one who has suffered abuse at the hands of fate, yet the 'reason' for this still bewilders him. When he has gone, the scene relaxes its tension and tails off into an almost casual mention of the impending battle.

    A new sense of recovery has now developed, as if by natural processes, like Lear's curative sleep. His recognition of Cordelia, her own contact with Kent, the battle to be fought, are all converging at a point where humanity will, if all goes well, be lifted up again above the crude necessities of survival in a natural world.

1   *work:* strive.

3   *every . . . me:* every measure of my own goodness will fall short in comparison with yours. – Kent's goodness is immeasurable.

5   *All my . . . truth:* What I have reported to you [about Lear] is a truthful and moderate (*modest*) account.

6   *nor more nor clipped:* neither exaggerated nor understated; *so:* exactly as I have said.

[*Reads*] *Let our reciprocal vows be remembered. You have*   255
many opportunities to cut him* off; if your will want not*,
time and place will be fruitfully* offered. There is nothing
done if he return the conqueror; then am I the prisoner, and
his bed my gaol; from the loathed warmth whereof deliver
me, and supply the place for your labour.*   260
                    Your – wife, so I would say –
                    affectionate servant,
                            GONERIL.

O undistinguished space of woman's will!*
A plot upon her virtuous husband's life;   265
And the exchange my brother! Here, in the sands,*
Thee I'll rake up,* the post* unsanctified
Of murderous lechers; and in the máture time*
With this ungracious* paper strike the sight
Of the death-practised* duke; for him 'tis well   270
That of thy death and business I can tell.
GLOUCESTER The King is mad. How stiff* is my vile sense,
That I stand up, and have ingenious feeling
Of my huge sorrows! Better I were distract.*
So should my thoughts be severed from my griefs,   275
And woes by wrong imaginations* lose
The knowledge of themselves.   [*Drum far off*
EDGAR   Give me your hand.
Far off, methinks, I hear the beaten drum.
Come, father, I'll bestow* you with a friend.
                                    [*Exeunt*

scene vii

A tent in the French camp.

Enter CORDELIA, KENT, GENTLEMAN, *and* DOCTOR.

CORDELIA O thou good Kent, how shall I live and work*
To match thy goodness? My life will be too short,
And every measure* fail me.
KENT To be acknowledged, madam, is o'erpaid.
All my reports go with the modest truth;*   5
Nor more nor clipped,* but so.

6   *suited:* clothed.

7   *weeds:* garments.

9   *Yet . . . intent:* to make myself known now would interfere with the plan I intend to carry out. – He wants to stay disguised a little longer.

10   *boon:* request.

11   *meet:* fitting. – It is never quite clear why Kent persists in his disguise, since no profit now comes of it.

16   *abuséd:* violated, wronged.

17   *The untuned . . . up:* O tune up the out-of-tune and inharmonious senses. – The metaphor is from tuning the strings of a stringed instrument by winding the pegs to tighten them up and thus revitalising them. This metaphor exists in a number of forms in modern English, e.g. 'keyed up'. Music and sleep are symbols of restoration through the harmonising of the senses.

18   *child-changéd:* perhaps both (i) changed into a child, and (ii) changed by the conduct of his children.

18   *So please:* Would it please.

21   *sway:* rule. – She asks him to be ruled by his own will, i.e. do whatever he decides. Since she is Queen of France he recognises her own rule by addressing her as *your majesty.*

25   *doubt . . . temperance:* have no fears about his sanity, the harmony of his senses – perhaps linking with the musical metaphor in line 17. The stage music has both a therapeutic effect and dramatic significance in emphasising this climax in the play.

28   *Thy medicine:* the medicine you need. – *Restoration* and *Repair* recall the *great breach* in line 16.

31   *these white . . . them:* your white hair would undoubtedly have claimed (*challenged*) their pity. – *flakes* must refer to snow, a common metaphor for the white hair of old age. His pitiful old age should have been enough to win anyone's sympathy, regardless of family relationship.

33   *opposed against:* exposed to.

34   *deep dread-bolted:* deep-sounding and bringing with it the terrible thunderbolt.

36   *perdu:* (literally) lost, lost one. – The word is from the French *sentinelle perdue,* 'sentry placed in a forward position', *perdue* giving the idea that his position is hopeless and he is therefore lost; cf. 'forlorn hope' and *rogues forlorn* in line 40. Cordelia, by using *watch,* 'stand on guard', shows she is thinking of a sentry, but the idea of his being 'lost' is also present.

37   *thin helm* – the *white flakes* of line 31 instead of a sentry's helmet.

39   *Against:* by; *fain:* obliged.

40   *To hovel thee:* to take shelter in a hovel; *rogues:* vagrants.

41   *short:* broken up (through long use).

CORDELIA   Be better suited;*
          These weeds* are memories of those worser hours.
          I prithee, put them off.
    KENT   Pardon me, dear madam;
          Yet to be known shortens my made intent.*
          My boon* I make it that you know me not   10
          Till time and I think meet.*
CORDELIA Then be 't so, my good lord. [*To the* DOCTOR] How
          does the King?
  DOCTOR Madam, sleeps still.
CORDELIA O you kind gods,   15
          Cure this great breach in his abuséd* nature!
          The untuned* and jarring senses, O wind up
          Of this child-changéd* father!
  DOCTOR   So please* your majesty
          That we may wake the King. He hath slept long.
CORDELIA Be governed by your knowledge, and proceed   20
          I' the sway* of your own will. Is he arrayed?

          Enter LEAR *in a chair carried by* SERVANTS.

GENTLEMAN Ay, madam; in the heaviness of his sleep
          We put fresh garments on him.
  DOCTOR Be by, good madam, when we do awake him;
          I doubt not of his temperance.*
CORDELIA   Very well.   [*Soft music*   25
  DOCTOR Please you, draw near. Louder the music there!
CORDELIA O my dear father! Restoration hang
          Thy medicine* on my lips, and let this kiss
          Repair those violent harms that my two sisters
          Have in thy reverence made!
    KENT   Kind and dear princess!   30
CORDELIA Had you not been their father, these white flakes*
          Had challenged pity of them. Was this a face
          To be opposed* against the warring winds?
          To stand against the deep dread-bolted* thunder?
          In the most terrible and nimble stroke   35
          Of quick, cross lightning? to watch – poor perdu!* –
          With this thin helm?* Mine enemy's dog,
          Though he had bit me, should have stood that night
          Against* my fire. And wast thou fain,* poor father,
          To hovel* thee with swine and rogues forlorn,   40
          In short* and musty straw? Alack, alack!

43	*concluded all:* ended altogether – i.e. his life along with his wits.
47	*in bliss* – i.e. in the blessedness of heaven. Lear's hints of experience in another world suggest that he is 'resurrected' from a remote past of suffering.
48	*a wheel of fire* – one of the torments of hell, where Lear thinks he is. The victim was thought of as being bound to a flaming wheel and revolved. But Lear can at least contemplate for a brief moment the heavenly harmony of a *soul in bliss.*
48	*that:* so that.
51	*far wide:* wandering far away [in his mind].
54	*abused:* deceived – with some element of 'ill-used' also. He thinks he is deceived because although he believes he is in hell he sees a heavenly spirit, Cordelia. The next sentence he speaks, however, touches more on the aspect 'ill-used' (cf. line 78). The simplicity and directness of the speech which follows marks Lear's gradual return to sanity.
55	*another thus:* someone else in this condition.
57	*Would I:* I wish.
61	*fond:* in my dotage.
62	*Fourscore and upward:* Eighty years of age and more.
63	*deal plainly:* speak frankly with you.
66	*mainly:* entirely.
72	*tears wet* – i.e. not the scalding leaden tears of hell (lines 48–9).
72	*faith:* by my faith.

'Tis wonder that thy life and wits at once
Had not concluded all.* [*To the* DOCTOR] He wakes; speak
to him.

DOCTOR   Madam, do you; 'tis fittest.

CORDELIA   How does my royal lord? How fares your Majesty?   45

LEAR   You do me wrong to take me out o' the grave.
Thou art a soul in bliss;* but I am bound
Upon a wheel of fire,* that* mine own tears
Do scald like molten lead.

CORDELIA   Sir, do you know me?

LEAR   You are a spirit, I know; when did you die?   50

CORDELIA   Still, still, far wide!*

DOCTOR   He's scarce awake; let him alone awhile.

LEAR   Where have I been? Where am I? Fair daylight?
I am mightily abused.* I should e'en die with pity
To see another thus.* I know not what to say.   55
I will not swear these are my hands. Let's see;
I feel this pin prick. Would I* were assured
Of my condition!

CORDELIA   O, look upon me, sir,
And hold your hands in benediction o'er me.
No, sir, you must not kneel.

LEAR   Pray, do not mock me: 60
I am a very foolish fond* old man.
Fourscore and upward,* not an hour more nor less;
And, to deal plainly,*
I fear I am not in my perfect mind.
Methinks I should know you and know this man;   65
Yet I am doubtful; for I am mainly* ignorant
What place this is, and all the skill I have
Remembers not these garments, nor I know not
Where I did lodge last night. Do not laugh at me;
For, as I am a man, I think this lady   70
To be my child Cordelia.

CORDELIA   And so I am, I am.

LEAR   Be your tears wet?* Yes, faith.* I pray, weep not.
If you have poison for me, I will drink it.
I know you do not love me; for your sisters
Have, as I do remember, done me wrong.   75
You have some cause, they have not.

CORDELIA   No cause, no cause.

LEAR   Am I in France?

79   *rage:* delirium.

81   *even o'er* – The meaning is doubtful; 'fill in, in his memory' gives good sense. It is then a warning to Cordelia not to encourage Lear to think back on all he has suffered since his mind became unbalanced.

83   *Till further settling:* until his mind is more settled, calmer.

84   *walk:* withdraw.

SD   After Lear has left the stage, the scene does little more than convey the news that the Duke of Cornwall is dead. Cf. III.vii.97–104, where the injured Cornwall is led away by Regan, and the servants are left to comment like a chorus on the juncture the action has reached.

86   *Holds it true:* Is it still accepted as true.

88   *conductor:* leader.

94   *arbitrement:* decisive encounter; *like:* likely.

95   *My point . . . ill:* The object and end of my life will be fully established, either for good or for bad; *period:* full stop. – Kent's concluding couplet, delivered when he is alone on the stage, seems to look forward to further action in the disguise he would not abandon; but nothing comes of it, at least in the play as we now know it.

KENT   In your own kingdom, sir.

LEAR   Do not abuse me.

DOCTOR   Be comforted, good madam: the great rage,*
You see, is killed in him. And yet it is danger   80
To make him even o'er* the time he has lost.
Desire him to go in; trouble him no more
Till further settling.*

CORDELIA   Will 't please your highness walk?*

LEAR   You must bear with me.
Pray you now, forget and forgive; I am old and foolish.   85

[*Exeunt all but* KENT *and* GENTLEMAN.

GENTLEMAN   Holds it true,* sir, that the Duke of Cornwall was so slain?

KENT   Most certain, sir.

GENTLEMAN   Who is conductor* of his people?

KENT   As 'tis said, the bastard son of Gloucester.

GENTLEMAN   They say Edgar, his banished son, is with the Earl of Kent   90
in Germany.

KENT   Report is changeable. 'Tis time to look about; the powers of
the kingdom approach apace.

GENTLEMAN   The arbitrement* is like to be bloody. Fare you well, sir.

[*Exit*

KENT   My point* and period will be throughly wrought,   95
Or well or ill, as this day's battle 's fought.

[*Exit*

Edgar 'aiding' Gloucester's attempted suicide at Dover (Act IV, Scene vi).

Cordelia comforting Lear with the Doctor looking on (Act IV, Scene vii).

v.i   Regan suspects that Edmund is associating with Goneril as well as with herself. Albany
      and Goneril enter with forces and Albany, confused over loyalties, determines to fight
      against the French, i.e. to honour his alliance with Cornwall's forces, now commanded by
      Edmund. Edgar is able to hand to Albany in secret Goneril's letter, taken from the dead
      Oswald. Edmund, alone, thinks over his relations with the two sisters, and plots to use
      Albany for the battle before his known sympathies for Lear and Cordelia can bear fruit.
        This is one of the 'summary scenes' packed with information for the furtherance of the
      plots, all of it treated perfunctorily especially that relating to the battle, which is about to
      start. The cursory treatment of the battle is in proportion to its own small significance;
      this scene shows how the battle reflects the complexity of Albany's choice of loyalties
      (which side is right, which wrong?), the wrongful passions of Goneril and Regan, and
      Edmund's altogether reprehensible plotting. The tone of relief and restoration at the end
      of Act IV is largely maintained; even Edmund's scheming looks as if it cannot succeed
      against the upright Albany.

1   *Know of . . . course* (line 3): Find out from the duke [of Albany] if he intends to keep to
             his recent decision (*last purpose*), or whether since then he has been persuaded
             by anything (*advised by aught*) to change his course of action. – All this refers
             to Albany's reluctance to fight on the British side while Lear is with the French.
             Ostensibly Edmund and Albany are to take joint command of the British forces,
             but Edmund is preoccupied with his evil designs on Regan and Goneril, and
             Albany does not feel fully committed to the fight against the invading army
             because it supports Lear's faction.
3   *alteration:* hesitation [as to which course to take].
4   *constant pleasure:* fixed purpose. – Edmund asks for information to be brought on what
             Albany has finally decided to do.
5   *Our sister's man* – i.e. Oswald; *miscarried:* come to harm.
6   *doubted:* feared.
7   *goodness . . . you:* good thing I intend to grant you.
8   *but then* – i.e. even if this truth is unwelcome to me.
9   *honoured:* honourable – i.e. with no evil intentions.
10   *brother's* – i.e. brother-in-law's.
11   *forfended place:* forbidden place – i.e. Goneril's bed.
11   *abuses:* disgraces. – But he does not answer the question.
12   *am doubtful:* fear; *conjunct And bosomed:* in close contact and embracing, intimate.
13   *as far . . . hers:* to the utmost point [of intimacy with her].
15   *I never . . . her* – This is evidently a cry of hatred and jealousy at the thought that Goneril
             may win Edmund from her. Cf. Goneril's words in lines 18–19.
16   *Fear me not:* Do not have any fears about me.
17   *She . . . husband:* Here they come, she and her husband.
19   *loosen:* loosen the ties between – with evidently a pun on *lose* in the previous line.
20   *well be-met:* it is good that we have met one another.
22   *the rigour . . . out:* the harshness of our rule (*state*) forced to rebel [against us].
23   *Where:* In cases where. – Albany now begins to reveal how far his loyalties have been
             strained, torn in opposite directions.
24   *For:* As for.
25   *touches:* concerns; *as France:* because the King of France.

ACT V scene i

The British camp near Dover.

Enter, with drum and colours, EDMUND, REGAN, GENTLEMEN, *and* SOLDIERS.

EDMUND   [*To a* GENTLEMAN] Know of* the duke if his last purpose hold,
Or whether since he is advised by aught
To change the course. He's full of alteration*
And self-reproving. Bring his constant pleasure.*

                                            [*Exit* GENTLEMAN

REGAN   Our sister's man* is certainly miscarried.   5
EDMUND   'Tis to be doubted,* madam.
REGAN   Now, sweet lord,
You know the goodness I intend upon you.*
Tell me, but truly, but then* speak the truth,
Do you not love my sister?
EDMUND   In honoured* love.
REGAN   But have you never found my brother's* way   10
To the forfended* place?
EDMUND   That thought abuses* you.
REGAN   I am doubtful* that you have been conjunct
And bosomed with her, as far as we call hers.*
EDMUND   No, by mine honour, madam.
REGAN   I never shall endure her.* Dear my lord,   15
Be not familiar with her.
EDMUND   Fear me not.* –
She and the duke her husband!*

Enter, with drum and colours, ALBANY, GONERIL, *and* SOLDIERS.

GONERIL   [*Aside*] I had rather lose the battle than that sister
Should loosen* him and me.
ALBANY   Our very loving sister, well be-met.*   20
Sir, this I hear: the King is come to his daughter,
With others whom the rigour* of our state
Forced to cry out. Where* I could not be honest,
I never yet was valiant. For* this business,
It touches* us, as France invades our land,   25

173

26   *Not bolds . . . oppose:* not because it emboldens (*bolds*) the King [i.e. Lear], whom, along with others, most justifiable and weighty reasons (*just and heavy causes*) have induced to contend against us. – This appears to be the drift of the passage, although literal interpretation is hard and the text is very likely corrupt. Albany's scruples, he is saying, are partly outweighed by the invasion being led by the French King, whom he is willing to fight. Even though Lear and his followers (for many good reasons) are siding with the French in the forthcoming battle, Albany's resistance is not directed at them, and he is determined to make this clear.

28   *reasoned:* argued out. – Regan wants to know why Albany is spending time reasoning out his attitude to the impending struggle. Goneril supports her.

30   *particular broils:* private quarrels.

32   *ancient of war:* veterans, experienced officers; *proceedings:* plan of campaign.

36   *convenient:* proper. – Regan does not want Goneril to be alone with Edmund, but it is not clear whether Regan herself is to attend the council of war in Albany's tent. Assuming that she is, we must take it that she does not want to leave her sister alone with Edmund even for a moment when she and her husband go out. This is Regan's *riddle*, i.e. ruse. In the upshot Albany is waylaid by Edgar and the two sisters go off with Edmund. Or perhaps Goneril guesses that Regan wants to observe how she and Edmund behave when together.

39   *overtake you:* catch you up.

42   *let . . . brought it:* have a trumpet sounded to call me (the bringer of this letter).

43   *a champion* – Edgar seems to be concerned to prove that he comes in good faith despite his shabby appearance, and asserts that he has a *champion*, a fighting man ready to take up causes single-handed on someone else's behalf, to vouch for him.

44   *avouchéd:* asserted; *miscarry:* come to grief.

45   *of:* as regards; *so:* in this way.

46   *love:* favour, smile on.

50   *o'erlook:* read through.

52   *guess:* estimate.

53   *By diligent discovery:* arrived at by careful reconnoitring.

54   *greet the time:* meet the eventuality.

55   *To both these sisters . . .* – Edmund plans to exploit Albany's authority until the battle is over, and then leave it to Goneril to kill him.

56   *jealous:* suspicious.

           Not bolds* the King, with others, whom, I fear,
           Most just and heavy causes make oppose.

EDMUND Sir, you speak nobly.

REGAN   Why is this reasoned?*

GONERIL Combine together 'gainst the enemy,
           For these domestic and particular broils*   30
           Are not the question here.

ALBANY   Let's then determine
           With the ancient of war* on our proceedings.

EDMUND I shall attend you presently at your tent.

REGAN Sister, you'll go with us?

GONERIL No.   35

REGAN 'Tis most convenient;* pray you, go with us.

GONERIL [*Aside*] O, ho, I know the riddle. – I will go.

As they are going out, enter EDGAR *disguised.*

EDGAR If e'er your grace had speech with man so poor,
           Hear me one word.

ALBANY   [*To the others*] I'll overtake* you. [*To* EDGAR] Speak.
                    [*Exeunt all but* ALBANY *and* EDGAR.

EDGAR Before you fight the battle, ope this letter.   40
           If you have victory, let the trumpet sound
           For him that brought it.* Wretched though I seem,
           I can produce a champion* that will prove
           What is avouchéd* there. If you miscarry,
           Your business of* the world hath so an end,   45
           And machination ceases. Fortune love* you!

ALBANY Stay till I have read the letter.

EDGAR   I was forbid it.
           When time shall serve, let but the herald cry,
           And I'll appear again.

ALBANY Why, fare thee well; I will o'erlook* thy paper.   50
                            [*Exit* EDGAR

Re-enter EDMUND.

EDMUND The enemy's in view; draw up your powers.
           Here is the guess* of their true strength and forces
           By diligent discovery;* but your haste
           Is now urged on you.

ALBANY   We will greet the time.*   [*Exit

EDMUND To both these sisters* have I sworn my love;   55
           Each jealous* of the other, as the stung

60   *Exasperates, makes mad:* would infuriate, make mad.
61   *carry . . . side:* fulfil my ambition.
63   *countenance:* authority. – Albany's authority would be much greater than that of Edmund, an earl's bastard son.
65   *taking off:* killing.
68   *Shall:* they shall. – Lear and Cordelia will never see any pardon from Albany at the end of the battle because Edmund will see to it that they are killed. Without them, his chances of becoming king of a reunited kingdom are strong.
68   *my state . . . debate:* my main concern is to defend my position (*state*), not debate it [within myself or with others].

v.ii   While Gloucester rests under a tree, Edgar joins the battle, off-stage, in which the forces of Lear and Cordelia are defeated. Edgar returns to hearten Gloucester.
       Ripeness, i.e. full maturity in a man, the readiness to accept what nature dispenses, here emerges as the essential virtue. Without it, the disappointment of the military defeat would be scarcely endurable. This defeat of the forces of good when the audience might expect victory and relief is the first of the play's apparent approaches to resolution which come to nothing.

SD   This is the nearest that the play gets to representation on the stage of battle action. Off-stage sound of armies in conflict (*Alarm*) would continue through the first speech of this scene.
1   *father* – Edgar calls him *father* presumably with deliberate ambiguity, but Gloucester takes him to mean only 'old man'. Cf. IV.vi.73, 214, and 248, where only the second meaning seems to be implied.
2   *For your good host:* as a good innkeeper. – Edgar recommends Gloucester to accept the place under the tree as a source of hospitality or shelter.
2   *thrive:* succeed.
4   *comfort:* consolation. – Edgar is ready to go off to join in the battle.
4   *Grace:* The grace of God.
9   *In ill thoughts:* Despondent.
11   *Ripeness is all:* maturity, readiness for death, is all-important. – Edgar is saying that we should not anticipate our death (as Gloucester proposes to do by staying there) but wait until the time is 'ripe' for it. We must accept the time laid down for our *going hence* as we have accepted the time of our *coming hither*.

Are of the adder. Which of them shall I take?
Both? one? or neither? Neither can be enjoyed
If both remain alive: to take the widow
Exasperates, makes mad* her sister Goneril;   60
And hardly shall I carry out my side,*
Her husband being alive. Now then we'll use
His countenance* for the battle; which being done,
Let her who would be rid of him devise
His speedy taking off.* As for the mercy   65
Which he intends to Lear and to Cordelia –
The battle done, and they within our power,
Shall* never see his pardon. For my state*
Stands on me to defend, not to debate.

scene ii

A field between the two camps.

Alarm within. Enter, with drum and colours, LEAR, CORDELIA,
and SOLDIERS, *over the stage; and exeunt.*

Enter EDGAR *and* GLOUCESTER.

EDGAR   Here, father,* take the shadow of this tree
For your good host;* pray that the right may thrive.*
If ever I return to you again,
I'll bring you comfort.*

GLOUCESTER   Grace* go with you, sir!

                                              [*Exit* EDGAR

Alarm and retreat within. Re-enter EDGAR.

EDGAR   Away, old man; give me thy hand; away!   5
King Lear hath lost, he and his daughter ta'en.
Give me thy hand; come on.

GLOUCESTER   No further, sir; a man may rot even here.

EDGAR   What! In ill thoughts* again? Men must endure
Their going hence, even as their coming hither.   10
Ripeness is all;* come on.

GLOUCESTER   And that's true too.

                                              [*Exeunt*

v.iii   In a dispute with Albany, Edmund has his way: Lear and Cordelia are kept in captivity. Albany challenges Edmund on the question of his loyalty, and a champion appears on Albany's side; this is Edgar, who brings down Edmund and reveals himself, telling how Gloucester died of a broken heart when he learned who his guide really was.

In jealousy over Edmund, Goneril has poisoned Regan, and later stabbed herself. Edmund recalls his association with them when their bodies are brought in. His dying act is a vain attempt to save Cordelia, whom he has secretly condemned to be hanged.

Lear brings in the dead Cordelia, and Kent reveals himself to him. Albany says the power of kingship will revert to the aged Lear, but this is a vain hope; Lear's life now ebbs away. Kent too is passing, and Albany calls on Edgar to take over the kingdom.

Up to the end of Act IV the audience has been able to detect a partial upsurge of hope in the qualified triumph of traditional values, such as pity and justice, despite persistent set-backs. Scenes i and ii in this last act contain indications here and there of impending triumphs of good over evil, indications of a type very familiar to Shakespeare's audiences from the substantiated touches of optimism in other plays, e.g. *Hamlet*. This final scene of *King Lear* is different; it is a series of advances and repudiations of visions of hope, a see-saw of comfort and disaster: Goneril and Regan both die, but nothing good comes of it; Edmund's dying wish is to save Cordelia's life, but it comes too late; Albany resolves to restore to Lear his kingly rights, but Lear dies; Albany wants Kent to share in the rule of the kingdom, but Kent too passes away.

There is also a reversion to the expository and summary modes of the first scene of the play and a few other scenes; there is much ground to cover, and many threads need to be caught up.

The two plots are now so closely intermingled that there is little point in trying to separate them. Yet the treatment of the Gloucester plot – the confronting of Edgar and Edmund and the death of Gloucester – retains in language and method of exposition the characteristics of allegory and the Morality play (Gloucester's 'fault' in the begetting of Edmund). Such treatment exposes the naturalness of the Lear plot, its calculated refusal to fit into some grand order of things ruled by a just supernature. Instead, it is Edmund's 'The wheel is come full circle' (174) which is nearer to reality. Lear's approaching death does not lead him to reconciliation; to the end, hints of resignation in what he says are interspersed with words of defiance and vindictiveness.

1   *Good guard:* Guard them well.
2   *their greater pleasures:* the wishes of those with greater authority.
3   *censure:* pass sentence on.
4   *meaning:* intention.
5   *cast down:* distressed.
6   *Myself . . . frown:* I could otherwise (*else*) have outfaced this evil turn in our fortunes.
9   *i' the cage* – Apart from its literal meaning, the phrase meant 'in prison' and is therefore a pun here. Lear is almost jubilant at the prospect because prison with his daughter will give him all he now wishes, an opportunity to reconcile himself to her and wipe away the blot of his imperceptive treatment of her.
12   *old tales:* stories of long ago.
13   *gilded butterflies:* (perhaps) brightly-dressed courtiers (not the literal meaning).
13   *poor rogues:* wretched people – presumably the people they will have contact with in prison.
15   *who's . . . out:* who is in favour, who out.
16   *And take . . . things:* and undertake to explain the mysterious ways of the world. – This covers the subject which so baffles Lear and dominates the play:
       Who is it that can tell me who I am?
                                                              (I.iv.213)
17   *God's spies:* beings who observe the course of the world and report on it to God. – Lear thinks he and Cordelia could probe deeply into the mysteries of the world without the restraint they might have to exercise if they did it for other men. Yet again, the drama turns to the puzzlement at the workings of fate, and man's power over his destiny.
17   *wear out:* outlast – with perhaps a nuance of the sense 'weary'.
18   *packs . . . moon:* cliques and factions of powerful people who go down and up in the world like tides controlled by the moon. – The rhythm of the tide is nothing of the sea's

scene iii

The British camp near Dover.

Enter, in conquest, with drum and colours, EDMUND; LEAR *and*
CORDELIA, *as prisoners;* CAPTAIN, SOLDIERS, *etc.*

EDMUND Some officers take them away. Good guard,*
Until their greater pleasures* first be known
That are to censure* them.

CORDELIA   We are not the first
Who with best meaning* have incurred the worst.
[*To* LEAR] For thee, oppresséd King, am I cast down;*   5
Myself* could else outfrown false fortune's frown.
Shall we not see these daughters and these sisters?

LEAR No, no, no, no! Come, let's away to prison.
We two alone will sing like birds i' the cage.*
When thou dost ask me blessing, I'll kneel down   10
And ask of thee forgiveness. So we'll live,
And pray, and sing, and tell old tales,* and laugh
At gilded butterflies,* and hear poor rogues*
Talk of court news; and we'll talk with them too,
Who loses and who wins, who's in,* who's out;   15
And take* upon 's the mystery of things,
As if we were God's spies;* and we'll wear out,*
In a walled prison, packs and sects* of great ones
That ebb and flow by the moon.

EDMUND   Take them away.

----

8 (*cont'd*)   doing, any more than the rise and fall of great men is in their own hands. The
phrase *by the moon* suggests also 'under the moon', i.e. free, at large, and therefore in contrast to *In a walled prison.*

20 *such sacrifices* – He is probably referring to Cordelia's return to Britain, by which she has deliberately put her own life in danger. The mention of *incense* in the following line indicates the intensity of the *sacrifices* image.

21 *Have . . . thee?:* Have I you back? – This extends the idea of *birds i' the cage* (line 9) and is in fact a quotation from Sidney, *Astrophel and Stella* (second song), though this identity may have no significance here.

22 *shall:* must. – Nothing that man can contrive, but only a firebrand from heaven can drive them apart.

23 *like foxes* – Foxes can be driven from their holes by fire and smoke.

24 *The good-years . . . weep* – While *good-years* has not been satisfactorily explained, the context suggests a nameless force of evil; *What the good-year!* ('What the devil!') occurs three times in Shakespeare. If this explanation is correct, the passage must mean: They [presumably Goneril and Regan] will not make us weep before the devils have eaten them up entirely, flesh and skin (*fell:* skin).

29 *One step . . . .* – Edmund's wickedness gives him an efficiency which characterises other Shakespeare villains, e.g. Claudius, Macbeth; they all quickly turn from one matter to another, showing how they are to all appearances in command of the situation. The paper gives directions for the murder of Lear and Cordelia and follows swiftly upon their departure from the stage. Edmund anticipates some demur from the Captain, and promises him promotion if he does what he is asked.

32 *the time:* the world, things as they are. – As one would expect, Edmund's view of life is Machiavellian.

33 *become a sword:* befit a swordsman.

33 *Thy great . . . question:* This important task of yours is not open to argument. – Edmund perhaps wants the Captain not to take up the matter of the scruples he has himself raised. The task is delicate and is to be carried out quickly.

34 *'lt,* for *wilt.*

36 *About it:* Get to work; *write happy:* put yourself down as happy, in luck.

37 *carry it so:* manage it.

39 *I cannot . . . oats* – i.e. I am not a horse.

41 *valiant strain:* brave disposition. – The word *strain* carries with it also the idea of inherited characteristic, hence lineage, an important matter for Edmund as the bastard son of the Earl of Gloucester.

43 *opposites of:* opponents in.

44 *require . . . you:* want them from you; *so to use them:* in order to deal with them in such a way.

45 *merits:* deserts. – The treatment of Lear and Cordelia in this situation is dramatically calculated to open up a breach between Edmund and Albany.

48 *retention:* detention.

49 *Whose age . . . more:* because his age has a charm about it, and his title [of King] even more so.

50 *pluck . . . side:* win the hearts of the common people over to his side.

51 *turn . . . them:* turn the lances of our conscripted soldiers (*impressed lances*) into the faces of us who command them.

53 *all:* entirely, just.

LEAR   Upon such sacrifices,* my Cordelia,   20
            The gods themselves throw incense. Have I caught thee?*
            He that parts us shall* bring a brand from heaven,
            And fire us hence like foxes.* Wipe thine eyes;
            The good-years* shall devour them, flesh and fell,
            Ere they shall make us weep. We'll see 'em starve first.   25
            Come.

                                [Exeunt LEAR and CORDELIA, guarded

EDMUND Come hither, captain; hark.
            Take thou this note. [Gives him a paper.] Go follow them to
            prison.
            One step* I have advanced thee; if thou dost
            As this instructs thee, thou dost make thy way   30
            To noble fortunes. Know thou this, that men
            Are as the time* is; to be tender-minded
            Does not become a sword.* Thy great employment*
            Will not bear question; either say thou'lt* do 't,
            Or thrive by other means.

CAPTAIN   I'll do 't, my lord.   35

EDMUND About it;* and write happy when thou hast done.
            Mark. – I say, instantly, and carry it so*
            As I have set it down.

CAPTAIN I cannot draw a cart, nor eat dried oats;*
            If it be man's work, I'll do 't.   [Exit   40

            Flourish. Enter ALBANY, GONERIL, REGAN, another CAPTAIN,
            and SOLDIERS.

ALBANY [To EDMUND] Sir, you have shown today your valiant strain;*
            And fortune led you well. You have the captives
            That were the opposites* of this day's strife.
            We do require* them of you, so to use them
            As we shall find their merits* and our safety   45
            May equally determine.

EDMUND   Sir, I thought it fit
            To send the old and miserable King
            To some retention* and appointed guard;
            Whose age* has charms in it, whose title more,
            To pluck the common bosom on his side,*   50
            And turn our impressed lances* in our eyes
            Which do command them. With him I sent the Queen;
            My reason all* the same; and they are ready
            Tomorrow or at further space to appear

55   *session:* sitting of a court of justice – to try Lear and Cordelia for treason. Edmund goes on
            to imply that passions are at the moment running too high for them to be given
            a fair trial.
57   *best quarrels:* most well-established causes.
57   *in the heat* – i.e. in the heat of passion. Immediate trial is another way in which Lear and
            Cordelia may win over the public to their side.
60   *by your patience:* if you will allow me [to say it]. – This is said with ironic deference.
61   *hold you but . . . . :* consider you only as . . . – Albany is incensed at Edmund's attempt to
            control the situation by acting as if they are equals. This sparks off a quarrel
            over Edmund between Regan and Goneril.
62   *That's . . . him* – i.e. 'But it is precisely as your equal (*brother*) that I choose to honour him.'
            Regan uses *we* for the singular reference to herself, turning to *my* (line 65) when
            she wishes to be more specific.
63   *pleasure:* wishes; *demanded:* asked.
65   *place:* title. – Edmund had her warrant (*commission*) to act as commander-in-chief of Corn-
            wall's army, taking Regan's place in that command.
66   *immediacy:* immediate relationship in a position of authority. – Goneril is particularly
            jealous of this.
69   *your addition:* the honour you have conferred on him.
70   *compeers:* equals.
71   *were:* would be. – Goneril implies that her own hopes are better, i.e. that Edmund should
            be her husband, not Regan's.
72   *Jesters* – i.e. People who say things in jest.
73   *That eye . . . asquint* – There was a proverb: 'Love being jealous makes a good eye look
            a-squint.' Goneril probably means simply: 'You are wrong and you are not
            seeing straight', a case of the blind jealousy of love.
74   *else:* otherwise.
75   *a full-flowing stomach:* anger with a full tide of words. – The stomach was thought of as
            the seat of passion and anger in the body.
77   *the walls:* (probably) the walls of my heart, my all – on the analogy of a walled city under
            siege.
79   *Mean you:* Do you intend to. – Goneril has already contrived to poison Regan, and there-
            fore she knows Regan can never *enjoy him*.
80   *let-alone:* power to prevent it.
81   *Half-blooded:* Bastard; *fellow* is also pejorative.
84   *in thine attaint:* in accusing you I accuse also . . . – An *attaint* was an accusation, especially
            of a high-born person.
85   *gilded:* speciously beautiful, not pure gold but covered in gilt.
85   *For:* As for. – Albany now gives an almost comic version of the situation and his involve-
            ment in it; e.g. *sub-contracted*, meaning 'entered into a secondary marriage
            contract'.

	Where you shall hold your session.* At this time	55
	We sweat and bleed. The friend hath lost his friend;	
	And the best quarrels,* in the heat,* are cursed	
	By those that feel their sharpness.	
	The question of Cordelia and her father	
	Requires a fitter place.	

ALBANY   Sir, by your patience,*   60
I hold you but* a subject of this war,
Not as a brother.

REGAN   That's as we list* to grace him.
Methinks our pleasure* might have been demanded,
Ere you had spoke so far. He led our powers,
Bore the commission of my place* and person;   65
The which immediacy may well stand up
And call itself your brother.

GONERIL   Not so hot.
In his own grace he doth exalt himself
More than in your addition.*

REGAN   In my rights,
By me invested, he compeers* the best.   70

GONERIL   That were* the most, if he should husband you.

REGAN   Jesters* do oft prove prophets.

GONERIL   Holla, holla!
That eye that told you so looked but a-squint.*

REGAN   Lady, I am not well; else* I should answer
From a full-flowing stomach.* [To EDMUND] General,   75
Take thou my soldiers, prisoners, patrimony;
Dispose of them, of me; the walls* are thine.
Witness the world, that I create thee here
My lord and master.

GONERIL   Mean you* to enjoy him?

ALBANY   [To GONERIL] The let-alone* lies not in your good will.   80

EDMUND   Nor in thine, lord.

ALBANY   Half-blooded* fellow, yes.

REGAN   [To EDMUND] Let the drum strike, and prove my title thine.

ALBANY   Stay yet; hear reason. Edmund, I arrest thee
On capital treason; and in thine attaint*
This gilded* serpent [pointing to GONERIL]. For* your claim,
fair sister,   85
I bar it in the interest of my wife;
'Tis she is sub-contracted to this lord,
And I, her husband, contradict your banns.

90   *bespoke:* engaged, contracted already.

90   *interlude:* play – more precisely, the comedy or farce introduced as light relief between the acts of a long serious play (medieval Latin, *inter:* between; *ludus:* a play). By using this word Goneril shows that she has taken less than seriously Albany's bitter bantering about love between his sister-in-law Regan and himself.

94   *pledge:* surety, symbol of a challenge to fight. – According to the code of chivalric warfare, contestants in a quarrel, especially if they were nobles, would appoint or permit champions to fight in single combat on their behalf. Albany here says he will fight Edmund (whom he calls 'Gloucester') himself if no champion comes forward to fight on his behalf. Dramatically this is the cue for Edgar to come forward. The glove, or gage, was the traditional symbol of this pledge; Albany has accused Edmund of treachery and the glove is the symbol of a challenge to fight, with the aim of deciding the truth or otherwise of the accusation. The overriding implication is that if the contestant loses, he is guilty: . . . *prove upon thy person / Thy . . . treasons.*

95   *Ere . . . bread* – i.e. before I have another meal, before I eat any food again.

95   *in nothing:* in no way.

97   *medicine:* poison (a euphemism).

98   *exchange:* the glove thrown down as a symbol that the challenge is accepted. – *Exchange* and *pledge* (line 94) are the technical terms for these symbols.

98   *what:* whoever.

101   *maintain:* justify.

104   *thy single virtue:* your own bravery.

106   *took,* for *taken.*

110   *trumpet:* trumpeter – as in SD before line 118.

111   *quality or degree:* noble birth or position [in the army].

112   *maintain upon:* assert against.

113   *manifold traitor:* traitor in numerous respects.

114   *He is . . . defence* – Edmund maintains his innocence and will do battle with any champion. This sentence is perhaps a formula at the end of the call for a champion.

If you will marry, make your loves to me;
My lady is bespoke.*

GONERIL   An interlude!*   90

ALBANY Thou art armed, Gloucester. Let the trumpet sound:
If none appear to prove upon thy person
Thy heinous, manifest, and many treasons,
There is my pledge.* [*Throwing down a glove*] I'll prove it
on thy heart,
Ere I taste bread,* thou art in nothing* less   95
Than I have here proclaimed thee.

REGAN   Sick, O, sick!

GONERIL [*Aside*] If not, I'll ne'er trust medicine.*

EDMUND [*Throwing down a glove*] There's my exchange:* what* in
the world he is
That names me traitor, villain-like he lies.
Call by thy trumpet: he that dares approach,   100
On him, on you – who not? – I will maintain*
My truth and honour firmly.

ALBANY A herald, ho!

EDMUND   A herald, ho, a herald!

ALBANY Trust to thy single virtue;* for thy soldiers,
All levied in my name, have in my name   105
Took* their discharge.

REGAN   My sickness grows up on me.

ALBANY She is not well; convey her to my tent. [*Exit* REGAN, *led*

Enter a HERALD.

Come hither, herald – Let the trumpet sound –
And read out this.

CAPTAIN Sound, trumpet!*   [*A trumpet sounds*   110

HERALD [*Reads*] *If any man of quality or degree* within the lists of the
army will maintain upon* Edmund, supposed Earl of
Gloucester, that he is a manifold traitor,* let him appear by
the third sound of the trumpet. He is bold in his defence.*
Sound!   [*First trumpet*   115
Again!   [*Second trumpet*
Again!   [*Third trumpet*
                                [*Trumpet answers within*

Enter EDGAR, *at the third sound, armed, with a trumpet
sounding in front of him.*

ALBANY Ask him his purposes, why he appears

120   *quality:* birth or rank.
122   *canker-bit:* worm-eaten. – Edgar's reference to the treasonable acts which have caused his
          own suffering is appropriate here, since the accusation against Edmund is that
          he is a traitor.
124   *cope:* encounter.
127   *That:* so that.
129   *it is . . . profession:* it [drawing my sword against a traitor] is the privilege accorded to me
          by my rank as a knight (*honours*), my oath of honour, and my solemn under-
          taking (*profession*) as a knight. – All this is important because the laws of
          chivalry laid down that champions had to be properly matched in rank and
          skill. Edgar goes on to make a formal accusation.
130   *protest:* proclaim that.
131   *Maugre:* in spite of; *place:* station in life.
132   *victor:* victorious; *fire-new:* brand-new. – The *fortune* referred to must be the earldom of
          Gloucester, a title which would have incensed Edgar unbearably.
133   *heart:* courage.
135   *Conspirant:* conspirator; *prince* – i.e. Albany; cf. line 178 below.
136   *upward:* top.
137   *descent:* lowest part.
138   *toad-spotted:* stained with infamy, as a toad is spotted. – The toad was thought of as ugly
          and poisonous.
138   *Say thou 'No':* If you disagree – i.e. assert that my accusation is false.
139   *bent . . . liest* (line 141): intent upon proving on your heart, which I speak to now, that you
          lie. – The words *prove upon thy heart* have the ominous ring of carrying the
          combat to the death.
141   *In wisdom:* If I were wise. – Edmund knows that according to the laws of chivalry he is
          not bound to enter the lists against an adversary who is not his equal in rank.
          By asking Edgar his name, he would be able to ascertain his rank. But he does
          not do so, and as he is dying Goneril recalls this omission (lines 152–3).
142   *outside:* outward appearance.
143   *say:* indication. – Edmund has been able to get some impression of his family and upbring-
          ing from the way he speaks.
144   *safe and nicely:* by acting cautiously and in accordance with the precise letter of the law. –
          What here refers to the combat, but after *knighthood*, in the next line, the sen-
          tence changes direction: *disdain* and *spurn* refer to his right to refuse combat
          with an inferior.
147   *hell-hated:* as hateful as hell.
148   *Which . . . for ever* (line 150): and my sword shall open an immediate (*instant*) way into
          your heart for them [the accusations of treason], which at present (*yet*) glide off
          it and hardly hurt it, and they will stay there for ever. – In Edmund's metaphor
          his sword-stroke to the champion's heart will prove conclusively that the
          accusations were false.
SD   *Alarms:* Calls, signals to fight.
151   *Save him* – Perhaps Albany says this of Edmund because he wants to bring him to judicial
          trial. Edmund is indeed under arrest. Some have thought these words should
          be attributed to Goneril.
151   *practice:* trickery.
153   *opposite:* opponent.

Upon this call o' the trumpet.

HERALD   What are you?
Your name, your quality?* and why you answer   120
This present summons?

EDGAR   Know, my name is lost;
By treason's tooth bare-gnawn and canker-bit.*
Yet am I noble as the adversary
I come to cope.*

ALBANY   Which is that adversary?

EDGAR What's he that speaks for Edmund, Earl of Gloucester?   125

EDMUND Himself. What say'st thou to him?

EDGAR   Draw thy sword,
That* if my speech offend a noble heart,
Thy arm may do thee justice. Here is mine.
Behold, it is the privilege of mine honours,
My oath, and my profession.* I protest,*   130
Maugre* thy strength, youth, place and eminence,
Despite thy victor* sword and fire-new fortune,
Thy valour and thy heart,* thou art a traitor,
False to thy gods, thy brother and thy father,
Conspirant* 'gainst this high illustrious prince,   135
And from the extremest upward* of thy head
To the descent* and dust below thy foot,
A most toad-spotted* traitor. Say thou 'No,'*
This sword, this arm and my best spirits are bent*
To prove upon thy heart, whereto I speak,   140
Thou liest.*

EDMUND   In wisdom* I should ask thy name,
But since thy outside* looks so fair and warlike,
And that thy tongue some say* of breeding breathes,
What safe and nicely* I might well delay
By rule of knighthood, I disdain and spurn.   145
Back do I toss these treasons to thy head;
With the hell-hated* lie o'erwhelm thy heart;
Which,* for they yet glance by and scarcely bruise,
This sword of mine shall give them instant way,
Where they shall rest for ever. Trumpets, speak!   150

                    [Alarms.* They fight. EDMUND falls.

ALBANY Save him, save him!*

GONERIL   This is practice,* Gloucester.
By the law of arms thou wast not bound to answer
An unknown opposite;* thou art not vanquished,

154	*cozened and beguiled:* cheated and robbed of a fair trial [by combat].
155	*this paper* – i.e. Goneril's letter of enticement to Edmund, which Edgar took from Oswald (IV.vi.241–63) and gave to Albany (V.i.40–50).
155	*Hold:* Stop. – This is probably addressed to one of the men around Goneril who are ready to support her.
157	*No tearing.* Do not try to tear it up.
158	*Say:* What.
160	*Ask . . . know* – These words are assigned to Edmund in F but to Goneril in Q; the Q reading has been adopted here because it gives better sense and dramatic effect and leads directly to the angry exit of Goneril. (F marks the exit after *for 't,* line 159.)
161	*govern:* control.
164	*what art . . . on me:* who are you who have had the good luck to get the better of me.
166	*Let's . . . charity:* Let us deal with one another charitably. – Edgar has to forgive Edmund's crimes against him; Edmund has to forgive Edgar for wounding him mortally.
167	*less in blood:* lower in birth. – He goes on to say that if his rank turns out to be higher than Edmund's, Edmund has wronged him even more seriously. The reference is to Edgar's own legitimacy and seniority.
170	*pleasant:* pleasure-giving, indulgent. – The reference is to the adulterous conception of Edmund. The play is much concerned with fate, ruthless and inexorable; on the other hand, here at least Gloucester's suffering seems to be thought of as having arisen justly as a result of his misdeed. However, Gloucester himself could find no trace of justice in his sufferings: *As flies to wanton boys are we to the gods* (IV.i.37).
172	*place* – i.e. the bed of adultery; *got:* begot.
173	*'tis true* – Edmund thinks of the justice of the gods (line 170). But the image which follows is of Fortune's wheel, which has brought him up to a height of power and now down again to where he started.
181	*nursing them:* ministering to them, helping him to bear them.
181	*List:* Listen.
182	*my heart would burst* – Edgar longs for the relief from anguish which death brings, but recalls too the *lives' sweetness* (line 184) which makes man shun death as a release from his sufferings.
183	*proclamation* – The main verb of which this is the subject is *taught* in line 186. Edgar is referring to his half-brother Edmund's plot to drive him into exile (I.ii.139ff.).
184	*near:* closely.
186	*taught me to shift:* encouraged me to change.
188	*very:* even the; *habit:* clothing.

But cozened* and beguiled.
ALBANY   Shut your mouth, dame,
Or with this paper* shall I stop it. Hold,* sir;   155
Thou worse than any name, read thine own evil.
No tearing,* lady; I perceive you know it.
GONERIL Say* if I do, the laws are mine, not thine.
Who can arraign me for 't?
ALBANY   Most monstrous! O!
Know'st thou this paper?
GONERIL   Ask me not what I know.*   [Exit   160
ALBANY Go after her; she's desperate; govern* her.
                                  [Exeunt some ATTENDANTS
EDMUND What you have charged me with, that have I done;
And more, much more; the time will bring it out.
'Tis past, and so am I. But what art* thou
That hast this fortune on me? If thou'rt noble,   165
I do forgive thee.
EDGAR   Let's exchange charity.*
I am no less in blood* than thou art, Edmund;
If more, the more thou hast wronged me.
My name is Edgar, and thy father's son.
The gods are just, and of our pleasant* vices   170
Make instruments to plague us:
The dark and vicious place* where thee he got
Cost him his eyes.
EDMUND   Thou hast spoken right, 'tis true;*
The wheel is come full circle; I am here.
ALBANY [To EDGAR] Methought thy very gait did prophesy   175
A royal nobleness. I must embrace thee.
Let sorrow split my heart, if ever I
Did hate thee or thy father!
EDGAR   Worthy prince, I know 't.
ALBANY Where have you hid yourself?
How have you known the miseries of your father?   180
EDGAR By nursing them,* my lord. List* a brief tale;
And when 'tis told, O, that my heart would burst!*
The bloody proclamation* to escape
That followed me so near* – O, our lives' sweetness,
That we the pain of death would hourly die   185
Rather than die at once! – taught* me to shift
Into a madman's rags, t' assume a semblance
That very* dogs disdained. And in this habit

189   *rings*: i.e. eye-sockets; the *precious stones* were the jewels set in the rings, i.e. his eyes.
190   *new*: recently.
192   *fault*: mistake. – Some have thought the word may mean 'misfortune', as occasionally
         elsewhere in Shakespeare, but Edgar could now understandably think that he
         was mistaken in continuing with his disguise longer than was necessary, even
         though fear of his half-brother's malice justified the disguise at first.
194   *success*: result.
195   *from first . . . pilgrimage*: gave him an account of my pilgrimage from beginning to end.
196   *flawed*: cracked. – Sorrow at his affliction and joy at his reconciliation with Edgar caused
         Gloucester's heart, already cracked by suffering, to break.
201   *as*: as if.
202   *hold it in*: keep it back.
203   *dissolve* – i.e. in tears.
204   *period*: conclusion.
205   *but another . . . extremity* (line 207): just one more of such [sorrows] would, by enlarging on
         what is already too much, make 'much' into 'more', and exceed the extreme
         limit [of sorrow].
208   *big*: loud.
209   *estate*: condition. – The rest of Edgar's speech reintroduces a history of affliction in many
         ways parallel to his own.
212   *fastened . . . neck* – i.e. embraced me.
213   *As he'd*: as if he would; *him*: himself.
215   *which* – i.e. the tale.
216   *puissant*: powerful.
216   *strings . . . crack*: his heartstrings began to snap – i.e. his life began to pass away.
218   *tranced*: in a trance.
220   *enemy*: hostile – since Lear had banished him for taking Cordelia's part.
221   *Improper . . . slave*: unfitting even for a slave.

Met I my father with his bleeding rings,*
Their precious stones new* lost; became his guide,   190
Led him, begged for him, saved him from despair;
Never – O fault!* – revealed myself unto him,
Until some half-hour past, when I was armed;
Not sure, though hoping, of this good success,*
I asked his blessing, and from first to last   195
Told him my pilgrimage.* But his flawed* heart –
Alack, too weak the conflict to support! –
'Twixt two extremes of passion, joy and grief,
Burst smilingly.

EDMUND   This speech of yours hath moved me,
And shall perchance do good. But speak you on;   200
You look as* you had something more to say.

ALBANY   If there be more, more woeful, hold it in;*
For I am almost ready to dissolve,*
Hearing of this.

EDGAR   This would have seemed a period*
To such as love not sorrow; but another,*   205
To amplify too much, would make much more,
And top extremity.
Whilst I was big* in clamour, came there in a man,
Who, having seen me in my worst estate,*
Shunned my abhorred society; but then, finding   210
Who 'twas that so endured, with his strong arms
He fastened on my neck,* and bellowed out
As he'd* burst heaven; threw him on my father;
Told the most piteous tale of Lear and him
That ever ear received; which* in recounting,   215
His grief grew puissant,* and the strings* of life
Began to crack. Twice then the trumpet sounded,
And there I left him tranced.*

ALBANY   But who was this?

EDGAR   Kent, sir, the banished Kent; who in disguise
Followed his enemy* King, and did him service   220
Improper* for a slave.

Enter a GENTLEMAN, *with a blood-stained knife.*

GENTLEMAN   Help, help, O, help!

EDGAR   What kind of help?

ALBANY   Speak, man.

223   *smokes:* steams [with the fresh blood]. – The horrific detail is in keeping with the traditions of Senecan tragedy; the play now quickly moves to its denouement of blood and death.

228   *all three* – i.e. himself, since he is dying, and the two sisters, Goneril stabbed by her own hand (line 241) and Regan poisoned. The mention of marriage is a grim joke not thought out of keeping in such a moment.

230   *Produce:* Bring in.

231   *tremble* – i.e. with fear at the retribution of fate, not pity for its victim.

233   *The time . . . urges:* This present situation will not permit us to show the formal respect (*compliment*) that accepted good behaviour calls for; *manners* is thought of as singular, as the verb shows.

235   *aye:* for ever.

236   *Great . . . forgot:* [That is an] important matter we have forgotten.

238   *object:* sight.

241   *after:* afterwards.

242   *Even so:* Yes, that *is* what happened [although the explanation comes from a liar].

244   *Despite:* in spite.

245   *my writ:* the orders drawn up by me. – Edmund gave the captain these orders that Lear and Cordelia should be put to death (line 28).

248   *office:* commission [to carry out the orders].

250   *my sword* – The captain ordered to kill Lear and Cordelia will recognise Edmund's sword, and will know that the bearer of it is speaking with Edmund's authority.

EDGAR   What means this bloody knife?

GENTLEMAN   'Tis hot, it smokes;*
         It came even from the heart of – O, she's dead!

ALBANY   Who dead? speak, man.   225

GENTLEMAN   Your lady, sir, your lady. And her sister
         By her is poisoned; she hath confessed it.

EDMUND   I was contracted to them both; all three*
         Now marry in an instant.

EDGAR   Here comes Kent.

ALBANY   Produce the bodies,* be they alive or dead.   230

                                        [Exit GENTLEMAN
         This judgement of the heavens, that makes us tremble,*
         Touches us not with pity.

         Enter KENT.

                              O, is this he?
         The time* will not allow the compliment
         Which very manners urges.

KENT   I am come
         To bid my King and master aye* good night.   235
         Is he not here?

ALBANY   Great thing of us forgot!*
         Speak, Edmund, where's the King? and where's Cordelia?
         See'st thou this object,* Kent?

                         [*The bodies of* GONERIL *and* REGAN *are brought in.*

KENT   Alack, why thus?

EDMUND   Yet Edmund was beloved:
         The one the other poisoned for my sake,   240
         And after* slew herself.

ALBANY   [*To* KENT] Even so.* Cover their faces.

EDMUND   I pant for life. Some good I mean to do,
         Despite* of mine own nature. Quickly send,
         Be brief in it, to the castle; for my writ*   245
         Is on the life of Lear and on Cordelia.
         Nay, send in time.

ALBANY   Run, run, O, run!

EDGAR   To who, my lord? Who has the office?* send
         Thy token of reprieve.

EDMUND   Well thought on. Take my sword;*   250
         Give it the captain.

ALBANY   Haste thee, for thy life.

                                        [*Exit* EDGAR

255   *fordid:* destroyed. – The captain was to make it look as if Cordelia committed suicide.

SD   CORDELIA *dead* – For many years readers of Shakespeare found this high point of tragedy unbearable, and stage performances of the play made changes here to indicate that Cordelia was still alive. At the time of the Romantic Revival, when free and imaginative literature came to be admired in contrast to fixed classical styles, people wanted the honest and innocent to triumph in the end. (See Introduction, p. xi ff, for a more detailed discussion.)

257   *Howl* . . . – These cries of anguish and despair echo through the theatre as the storm did when Lear had to endure it without clothing or shelter.

259   *heaven's* . . . *crack:* a universal show of grief would make the sky crack and shatter. – Again there is the memory of the storm and the lightning which rent the sky.

262   *stone:* crystal [of the mirror].

263   *the promised end:* the end of the world, the Last Day. – Edgar thinks it might be a representation (*image*) of that Last Day.

264   *Fall and cease:* Let the universe fall in ruins and come to an end.

265   *This feather* . . . – He puts a feather near her mouth to test in another way whether she is still breathing, and imagines that it moves.

266   *chance:* piece of good luck. – Kent chooses this moment to try to make himself known to the King.

276   *falchion:* light sword with the point turned inward. – This special feature may explain why it is *biting.*

278   *these* . . . *spoil me:* such troubles as these (his age and poor eyesight, and the distresses he has suffered) spoil my skill [as a swordsman].

280   *If fortune* . . . *behold:* (perhaps) If Fortune can boast about two people whom she preeminently favoured and then turned against, we now see one of them. The implication is that Kent himself is the other.

       Since the fickleness of fortune is one of the themes of *King Lear*, and the fall of the great an important preoccupation of contemporary literature, this explanation has a good deal to recommend it. But some have thought that *One* refers only to *hated*; it has also been suggested that after *hated* the sentence goes off on a different tack, with *One* referring to Lear, who can serve as an example of both prosperity and adversity. It has also been suggested that Kent is deliberately talking in riddles – only one can be seen at a time: Kent is here; where is Caius? – in a desperate attempt to penetrate Lear's distraction.

282   *dull:* sad.

283   *Caius* – This is the name Kent has used in his disguise. Lear thinks his servant is dead.

EDMUND He hath commission from thy wife and me
　　　　To hang Cordelia in the prison, and
　　　　To lay the blame upon her own despair,
　　　　That she fordid* herself.   255
ALBANY The gods defend her! Bear him hence awhile.

　　　　　　　　　　　　　　[EDMUND *is borne off*

Re-enter LEAR, *with* CORDELIA *dead in his arms;* EDGAR,
CAPTAIN, *and others following.*

LEAR Howl,* howl, howl, howl! O, you are men of stones.
　　　Had I your tongues and eyes, I'd use them so
　　　That heaven's vault should crack.* She's gone for ever!
　　　I know when one is dead and when one lives;   260
　　　She's dead as earth. Lend me a looking-glass;
　　　If that her breath will mist or stain the stone,*
　　　Why, then she lives.
KENT   Is this the promised end?*
EDGAR Or image of that horror?
ALBANY   Fall and cease.*
LEAR This feather* stirs; she lives. If it be so,   265
　　　It is a chance* which does redeem all sorrows
　　　That ever I have felt.
KENT   [*Kneeling*] O my good master!
LEAR Prithee, away.
EDGAR   'Tis noble Kent, your friend.
LEAR A plague upon you, murderers, traitors all!
　　　I might have saved her; now she's gone for ever!   270
　　　Cordelia, Cordelia! stay a little. Ha!
　　　What is't thou say'st? Her voice was ever soft,
　　　Gentle and low, an excellent thing in woman.
　　　I killed the slave that was a-hanging thee.
CAPTAIN 'Tis true, my lords, he did.
LEAR   Did I not, fellow?   275
　　　I have seen the day, with my good biting falchion*
　　　I would have made them skip. I am old now,
　　　And these same crosses spoil me.* Who are you?
　　　Mine eyes are not o' the best; I'll tell you straight.
KENT If fortune brag* of two she loved and hated,   280
　　　One of them we behold.
LEAR This is a dull* sight. Are you not Kent?
KENT   The same,
　　　Your servant Kent. Where is your servant Caius?*

287   *see that straight:* see to that in a moment.

288   *your first . . . decay:* the beginning of your change and decline of fortune. – Despite this heartfelt account of his devotion, Kent gets only a conventional response from Lear.

290   *Nor . . . else:* No one else, but indeed that man. – This re-emphasises the assertion *I am the very man* in line 286. The punctuation in the text assumes that Kent's words from line 286 to this point form a single sentence, twice interrupted by Lear.

291   *fordone:* destroyed.

292   *desperately:* from despair.

294   *present us:* present ourselves, draw his attention to us.

294   *Very bootless:* Quite unavailing.

295   *a trifle* – So the matter of Edmund's death is laid aside. There follows a kind of policy statement by the commanding figure near the end of the play; it is paralleled in, for instance, *Macbeth* (v.ix.26–end), where Malcolm gives an outline of the way he will handle the situation.

297   *this great decay:* this ruin of a great man – i.e. Lear.

298   *resign:* assign, make over. – Lear dies a king after all.

300   *You . . . right:* You are restored to the positions which are yours by right.

301   *With boot . . . addition:* with such additional rights and titles; *boot:* advantage, profit.

304   *The cup* – something that must be received and undergone. The use of *cup* with this meaning is probably an echo from the Bible (*Matthew* 20:22 and 26:39).

305   *my poor fool* – i.e. Cordelia, *fool* being a term of endearment. Lear returns to his distraction, but there is a train of logic in citing Cordelia as an instance to disprove what has just been said: Cordelia, though a 'friend', has not tasted the wages of her virtue. It is clear from the speech which follows that he cannot be referring to the Fool.

309   *undo this button* – Lear feels death bearing down on him, and believes he is suffocating. The cosmic tragedy is heightened by this mundane reference to his clothing, the need to undo the button of the collar round his neck.

310   *her lips* – Lear dies believing that Cordelia still has breath on her lips.

313   *Break, heart* – Kent is evidently speaking of his own heart.

314   *ghost:* departing spirit.

315   *tough:* hard. – The *rack* referred to is an instrument of torture.

LEAR He's a good fellow, I can tell you that;
   He'll strike, and quickly too. He's dead and rotten.   285
KENT No, my good lord, I am the very man –
LEAR I'll see that straight.*
KENT That from your first of difference and decay*
   Have followed your sad steps –
LEAR   You are welcome hither.
KENT Nor no man else.* All's cheerless, dark and deadly.   290
   Your eldest daughters have fordone* themselves,
   And desperately* are dead.
LEAR   Ay, so I think.
ALBANY He knows not what he says, and vain is it
   That we present* us to him.
EDGAR   Very bootless.*

Enter a CAPTAIN.

CAPTAIN Edmund is dead, my lord,
ALBANY   That's but a trifle* here.   295
   You lords and nóble friends, know our intent.
   What comfort to this great decay* may come
   Shall be applied. For us, we will resign,*
   During the life of this old Majesty,
   To him our absolute power. [*To* EDGAR *and* KENT] You,
   to your rights;*   300
   With boot,* and such addition as your honours
   Have more than merited. All friends shall taste
   The wages of their virtue, and all foes
   The cup* of their deservings. O, see, see!
LEAR And my poor fool* is hanged! No, no, no life!   305
   Why should a dog, a horse, a rat, have life,
   And thou no breath at all? Thou'lt come no more,
   Never, never, never, never, never! –
   Pray you, undo this button;* thank you, sir.
   Do you see this? Look on her, look, her lips,*   310
   Look there, look there!   [*Dies*
EDGAR He faints. My lord, my lord!
KENT Break, heart;* I prithee, break!
EDGAR   Look up, my lord.
KENT Vex not his ghost.* O, let him pass! He hates him
   That would upon the rack of this tough* world   315
   Stretch him out longer.
EDGAR   He is gone indeed.

318   *He but . . . life:* He was merely holding on to life when it was no longer his.
320   *twain:* two.
321   *the gored . . . sustain:* care for this mutilated state. – The fugitive and .the banished are
          restored and elevated to positions of supreme authority. But Kent refuses the
          reinstatement because he knows he is dying. When he entered the present
          scene he said: *I am come/To bid my King and master aye good night* (line 234).
322   *journey* – i.e. into the next world.
323   *My master* – i.e. Lear.
324   *The weight . . .* – These final lines are given in Q to Albany, in F to Edgar. Edgar is the more
          likely speaker, since he should respond to Albany's delegation of power to
          him, and Albany can hardly be included among *we that are young* (line 326).
SD   *dead march:* march with solemn music when a dead person is carried along.

KENT The wonder is he hath endured so long.
   He but usurped his life.*
ALBANY Bear them from hence. Our present business
   Is general woe. [*To* KENT *and* EDGAR] Friends of my soul,
   you twain*   320
   Rule in this realm and the gored state sustain.*
KENT I have a journey,* sir, shortly to go;
   My master* calls me; I must not say no.
EDGAR The weight* of this sad time we must obey,
   Speak what we feel, not what we ought to say. 325
   The oldest hath borne most; we that are young
   Shall never see so much, nor live so long.

          Exeunt, with a dead march

Glossary

(S.D. = Stage direction)

A

abate, deprive II.iv.154
abatement, falling-off I.iv.52
able, vouch for IV.vi.162
about it, get to work V.iii.36
abroad, away from home I.ii.156
  going about II.i.6
abuse, wrong III.vii.90
  disgrace V.i.11
abused, deceived IV.i.23, IV.vii.54
  violated IV.vii.16
account, estimation I.i.17
act, do II.i.18
action-taking, litigious II,ii,15
addition, title, honour I.i.137, V.iii.69
  names, list of names II.ii.21
addition, additional rights V.iii.301
admiration, pretended surprise I.iv.220
ado, hesitation IV.v.2
advise, persuade V.i.2
advise oneself, think carefully II.i.27
affect, have affection for I.i.1
affected; ill affected intent on evil II.i.100
afoot, moving II.iv.211
  on the march IV.iii.49
after, according to I.ii.92
  afterwards V.iii.241
again, back II.iv.72
against, by IV.vii.33
ague, chattering fever IV.vi.104
aidant, helpful IV.iv.17
alack, alas III.ii.59, III.iii.1
alarm, sound of armies in conflict V.ii. S.D's
  call, signal to fight V.iii.150 S.D.
alarum, arouse (as to arms) II.i.55
Albion, Britain III.ii.90
all, entirely, only I.i.100, V.iii.53
  altogether IV.vii.43
all-licensed, permitted to take any liberty
  I.iv.182
allay, hold back I.ii.150
allow, approve of II.iv.187
allowance, approval I.iv.190, II.ii.98
alone, only I.i.289
alteration, hesitation V.i.3
amazed, bewildered III.vi.31
amity, tie of friendship I.ii.134
ample, large, full IV.iii.12
anatomize, dissect III.vi.72

ancient, old-fashioned (?) IV.i.44
ancient of war, veterans V.i.32
anger, deadly earnestness III.vii.78
anointed, sanctified III.vii.57
anon, shortly I.ii.162
answer, be responsible for I.iii.10, II.ii.137
  confront III.iv.96
antipathy, opposition II.ii.79
apish, silly I.iv.153
appertain to, concern I.i.280
apprehend, seize, arrest I.ii.72, II.i.110
apprehension, arrest III.v.16
approve, prove the validity of, show to be
  true I.i.180, II.ii.150, III.v.9
  confirm II.iv.179
apt, ready, willing II.iv.302, IV.ii.65
arbitrement, decisive encounter IV.vii.94
arch, chief II.i.61
argument, subject I.i.211
aroint, get away III.iv.116
art, experience III.ii.69
  lessons IV.vi.217
as, as if III.iv.15, V.iii.201, V.iii.213
aspect, look, glance II.ii.98
astronomical, astrological I.ii.138
attaint, accusation V.iii.84
attempt, set upon II.ii.113
attend, wait on I.i.329
  wait, await II.i.127, II.iii.5
a-twain, in two II.ii.66
aught, anything I.i.194
auricular, aural I.ii.85
avaunt, get away III.vi.61
avoid, depart from I.i.119
avouch, assert V.i.44
away, along II.ii.129
aye, for ever V.iii.235

B

ballow, cudgel IV.vi.236
balm, soothe III.vi.93
ban, curse II.iii.19
bandy, exchange, throw to and fro I.iv.73
barber-monger, fop II.ii.28
battle, battalion III.ii.23
bay, reddish-brown III.iv.53
beadle, constable IV.vi.154
bearing, endurance III.vi.103

201

Bedlam, Bethlehem Hospital (in London) I.ii.125, II.iii.14
　　mad beggar III.vii.102
become, befit II.iv.148, V.iii.33
　　adorn, look well on IV.iii.24
before, already IV.iv.22
beguile, disappoint IV.vi.64
behalf, part IV.ii.20
belike, probably IV.v.20
belly-pinched, starving III.i.13
bemadding, maddening III.i.38
be-meet, meet one another V.i.20
bending, overhanging IV.i.73
　　directing IV.ii.74
benison, blessing I.i.261, IV.vi.220
bent to, intent upon V.iii.139
bereaved, impaired IV.iv.9
besort, befit I.iv.234
bespoke, engaged V.iii.90
best; were best, had better I.iv.85
bestow, lodge II.iv.285, IV.vi.279
bethink (oneself), take thought, try to think I.ii.146
bethink, make up one's mind II.iii.6
betwixt, between I.i.134, III.iii.7
beweep, weep over I.iv.287
bewray, uncover, reveal II.i.109, III.vi.107
bias, 'bent', the way something normally tends to move I.ii.103
bide, endure III.iv.29
biding, lodging place IV.vi.219
bill, a weapon IV.vi.90
bitter, sarcastic I.iv.121
blame, object to III.vii.26
blank, spot at the centre of a target I.i.154
blast, wither II.iv.163
bliss, blessedness of heaven IV.vii.47
block, wooden block to shape hats on IV.vi.177
blood, natural feelings III.v.21
　　passion IV.ii.64
　　social rank V.iii.167
blown, inflated IV.iv.27
bold, embolden V.i.26
bolt, door-bolt II.iv.172
bond, duty, obligation I.i.89
boon, request IV.vii.10
boot, reward, advantage IV.vi.221
　　to boot, in addition IV.vi.221 [sic]
bootless, unavailing V.iii.294
bo-peep; play bo-peep, act stupidly I.iv.160
border, restrain IV.ii.33
bosomed, embracing V.i.13
bound, under obligation I.ii.2
　　ready III.vii.10
　　be bound, intend III.vii.7
bounds, territory I.i.59
bourn, stream III.vi.24
　　boundary IV.vi.58
brach, bitch I.iv.100
　　a kind of hound III.vi.65
brave, fine III.ii.78
bravely, decked out in fine clothes IV.vi.193

brazed, hardened I.i.9
breed, keep, support IV.ii.73
breeding, parentage I.i.8
　　(good) upbringing V.iii.143
briefness, speed II.i.18
bring, lead III.ii.77
broil, quarrel V.i.30
buoy, rise III.vii.59
business, plotting II.i.15
buzz, rumour I.iv.311

C

cadent, falling I.iv.270
cage, prison V.iii.9
caitiff, wretch II.i.64, III.ii.54
canker-bit, worm-eaten V.iii.122
capable, entitled to inherit II.i.87
carbonado, cut crosswise II.ii.32
care, concern I.i.98
care for, worry about I.iv.173
carp, complain I.iv.184
carry, bear, endure III.ii.47
　　manage V.iii.37
case, covering I.v.26
　　socket IV.vi.141
　　state IV.vi.143
casement, window I.ii.58
'casion for *occasion,* reason, cause IV.vi.230
cast down, distressed V.iii.5
casualty, chance IV.iii.44
cataract, downpour of rain III.ii.2
catastrophe, part of a play leading directly to the final event in it I.ii.123
cause, matter IV.iii.51
　　offence IV.vi.108
　　reason V.i.27
censure, pass sentence on V.iii.3
centaur, an imaginary creature, half man, half horse IV.vi.122
century, troop of a hundred men IV.iv.6
certain, firmly IV.ii.33
challenge, claim, lay claim to I.i.49, IV.vii.32
chamber, private apartment II.iv.114
champain, open plain I.i.60
chance (v.), come about, happen II.iv.61
chance (n.), lot I.i.252
　　piece of good luck V.iii.266
change, exchange IV.ii.17
changed, transformed IV.ii.62
character, handwriting I.ii.59, II.i.74
check (v.), reprove II.ii.132
check (n.), reproof I.iii.20
child, candidate for knighthood III.iv.173
child-changed, changed into a child; changed by the conduct of one's children IV.vii.18
chill, I will (dialect) IV.vi.230
choler, stomach bile, anger I.ii.23
chough, bird of the crow family IV.vi.13
chud, I could (dialect) IV.vi.233
civet, a strong-smelling perfume IV.vi.128

clap, stroke, moment I.iv.279
clear, pure, righteous IV.vi.74
clip, understate IV.vii.6
closet, private room I.ii.58
 private cabinet III.iii.10
clotpoll, idiot, 'clot' I.iv.43
clout, mark (in archery) IV.vi.91
clovest, past form of *cleave,* split I.iv.144
cock, weather-cock III.ii.3
 cock-crow III.iv.109
 cock-boat, ship's boat IV.vi.19
cockney, comic London woman II.iv.118
cod-piece, bag worn by men at the front of leg
 armour or tight hose III.ii.26
colour, kind II.ii.128
comfort (v.), support, assist III.v.18
 attempt to help IV.i.16
comfort (n.), consolation V.ii.4
comfortable, helpful I.iv.291, II.ii.154
commend, hand over, entrust II.iv.27, III.i.19
commodity, advantage IV.i.22
common, of the common people V.iii.50
compact, put together I.ii.7
 confirm I.iv.325
compeer, equal V.iii.70
compliment, ceremony, formality I.i.295
 formal respect V.iii.233
composition, consistency, physique, 'make-
 up' (see note) I.ii.12
compound, make terms I.ii.118
conceit, self-deception IV.vi.43
conceive, understand, take the meaning of
 I.i.10, IV.ii.24
conception, thoughts I.iv.58
condition, habits of mind I.i.290
 essential quality IV.iii.3
conduct, act as leader IV.ii.16
conductor, leader IV.vii.88
confederacy, conspiracy III.vii.43
confine, assigned limit II.ii.154
conjunct, closely in league II.ii.109
 in close contact V.i.12
conjure, call upon II.i.39
consideration, judgement I.i.145
consort, company II.i.199
conspirant, conspirator V.iii.135
constant, firm I.i.39
constrain, assume II.ii.89
contemn, despise IV.i.1, IV.ii.32
contentious, warlike III.iv.6
continent (n.), that which contains, holds in,
 something III.ii.57
continent (adj.), restraining I.ii.152
contrive, devise III.iv.85
convenience, provision III.vi.94
convenient, fitting, proper IV.v.31, V.i.36
converse, associate I.iv.13
convey, manage in secret I.ii.94
cope, encounter V.iii.124
corky, withered III.vii.28
costard, a kind of apple IV.vi.236
couch, lie hidden III.i.12

countenance, bearing I.iv.24
 authority V.i.63
counterfeiting, pretence III.vi.58
course, way of life I.i.183
 chase III.iv.54
 'round' in a fight III.vii.53
courtesy, humane behaviour III.ii.66, humane
 feeling III.iii.18
court holy-water, flattery III.ii.10
cowish, cowardly IV.ii.12
coxcomb, cap in the form of a cock's crest
 I.iv.85
cozener, petty offender IV.vi.157
crab, crab-apple I.v.15
crave, ask I.i.190
 demand, call for II.i.130
cross, trouble V.iii.278
cry you mercy, I beg your pardon III.iv.161,
 III.vi.49
cub-drawn, ferocious III.i.12
cue, hint as to how to act I.ii.124
cullionly, base II.ii.28
cunning, pretence II.i.29
curious, elaborate I.iv.29
curiosity, close examination I.i.5
 over-concern with detail I.ii.4
 preciseness I.iv.60
curst, fierce II.i.67
cutpurse, pick-pocket III.ii.87

D

dame, woman IV.vi.116
darkling, in the dark I.iv.199
darnel, tares (in corn) IV.iv.5
daub it, deceive IV.i.53
dead march, march in which a dead person is
 carried along V.iii.328 S.D.
deal, speak IV.vii.63
dealing, treatment III.iii.1
dear, loving I.i.178
 precious, much-prized IV.iii.51
dearn, dreadful III.vii.62
deathsman, executioner IV.vi.251
deboshed, depraved I.iv.225
decay, decline of fortune V.iii.288
decline, bend IV.ii.22
deed, essence, essential quality I.i.67
deer, animal(s) III.iv.129
defect, deficiency IV.i.21
deficient, failing IV.vi.23
defuse, diffuse, make unrecognisable I.iv.2
degree, rank, position, in the army V.iii.111
dejected, humbled IV.i.3
delicate, sensitive III.iv.12
 neat IV.vi.178
demand (v.), ask V.iii.63
demand (n.), question I.v.3
deny, refuse II.iv.84
departure, verbal manipulations I.v.44

depositary, trustee II.iv.247
deprive, keep one from one's rights I.ii.4
derogate, degraded I.iv.265
deserving, that which merits reward III.iii.20
desire, request I.iv.230
  beg, plead for III.iii.2
desperate, reckless II.iv.301
desperately, arising from despair V.iii.292
despite, in spite V.iii.244
detain, keep back I.ii.40
  keep away IV.iii.47
dialect, way of speaking II.ii.101
difference, distinction (e.g. of class) I.iv.78
  quarrel II.i.125, II.ii.45
  change V.iii.288
diffidence, suspicion I.ii.136
digest, amalgamate I.i.123
diligence, despatch I.v.3
diligent, careful v.i.53
dimension, bodily part I.ii.7
disbranch, sever IV.ii.34
discerning, power of discernment I.iv.211
disclaim in, disown II.ii.48
discommend, disapprove of II.ii.101
discover, expose II.i.68
discovery, reconnoitring V.i.53
discreet, sensible I.iv.195
disease, trouble I.i.170
dishonoured, dishonourable I.i.224
dismantle, strip off I.i.213
disnatured, unnatural, lacking in natural
  affection I.iv.268
disorder, disorderly practice I.ii.105
  misdemeanour II.iv.195
dispatch, quick putting-away I.ii.32
  kill II.i.60
display, behave ostentatiously II.iv.40
disposition, moody fit I.iv.204
  mood I.iv.277
disquantity, reduce the size or number of
  I.iv.232
dissipation, wastage of personnel (?) I.ii.136
dissuade, discourage, try to dissuade II.i.66
distaste, dislike I.iii.14
distract, mad IV.vi.274
division, embellished melodies in music
  I.ii.126
  contention III.iii.7
divorce, dissociate II.iv.126
Dolphin, (perhaps for) Dauphin III.iv.95
doom, judgement I.i.144
  sentence I.i.160
dost, for *doest thou,* do you fare II.i.91
doubt, fear V.i.6
doubtful, in fear V.i.12
dower (v.) endow I.i.200
dower (n.), dowry I.i.40
draw, bring into one's hands III.iii.20
dreadful, causing great fear III.ii.49
drive, hurry III.vi.86
due, fitting IV.ii.27
dull, sad V.iii.282

dullard, stupid fellow II.i.76
durst, dared I.i.165

E

each; at each, fastened end to end IV.vi.54
ear-kissing, passed around discreetly (of
  news, rumours, etc.) II.i.7
earnest, small payment as an instalment to
  secure a bargain I.iv.81
ease, comfort, protection III.iv.23
easy-borrowed, taken on without justification
  II.iv.181
effect, realisation II.iv.175
  realisation (of what is wished for) IV.ii.15
  to effect, in importance III.i.52
effects, realisation I.i.181
elbow, jostle IV.iii.42
election, choice I.i.202
element, proper place II.iv.56
elf, tangle II.iii.10
embossed, swollen II.iv.220
endeavour, encounter II.i.34
enemy, hostile V.iii.220
enforce, urge on II.iii.20
engine, instrument of torture I.iv.253
enguard, protect I.iv.312
enormous, disordered II.ii.160
enridged, furrowed IV.vi.72
entertain, treat I.iv.51
  take into service III.vi.74
entire, essential I.i.236
epicurism, riotous living I.iv.227
equality, share I.i.5
esperance, a condition of hope IV.i.4
essay, trial I.ii.44
estate, condition V.iii.209
even, just, exactly IV.iv.1, V.iii.242
ever, always I.i.286
evidence, witnesses III.vi.33
exasperate, infuriate V.i.60
exchange, symbol that a challenge is accepted
  V.iii.98
execution, exercise of powers I.i.132
exeunt, they go out S.D.
exhibition, allowance of money (for personal
  expenses) I.ii.25
exit, he/she goes out S.D.
extremity, extreme rage III.iv.97

F

faint, inactive, lazy I.iv.59
faintly, toned down I.ii.160
faith (v.), credit, believe in II.i.72
faith (n.), article of faith I.i.218
faith, by my faith (an oath) IV.iii.25, IV.vii.72
falchion, light sword V.iii.276
fall, begin, come IV.vi.38
fall into taint, decay I.i.217
fall off, weaken (in intensity) I.ii.99

fashion, style, cut III.vi.75
fa, sol, las, mi, names of notes in the musical
scale I.ii.126
fast, fixed I.i.34
fastened, hardened II.i.79
fated, destined III.iv.65
father, old man IV.vi.73
fault, sin, mistake I.i.13, V.iii.192
favour, mark of favour IV.ii.21, S.D.
favours, features III.vii.39
fear, frighten III.v.3
fear, have fears about IV.ii.31
fearful, afraid I.iv.187
fearfully, frighteningly IV.i.74
feature, appearance IV.ii.63
feel, try out I.ii.80
feeling (n.), awareness IV.vi.273
feeling (adj.), heart-felt IV.vi.217
felicitate, made happy I.i.71
fell (n.), skin V.iii.24
fell (adj.), fierce II.i.52
fellow, companion III.i.48
festinate, speedy III.vii.9
fetch, trick II.iv.85
find, experience I.i.55
find out, expose I.ii.106
fire-new, brand-new V.iii.132
fit (v.), agree, match III.ii.75
fit (n.), bout of illness II.iv.107
fit (adj.), fitting I.ii.169
fitchew, polecat IV.vi.120
fitly, at the right time I.i.154
flaw, fragment II.iv.281
flawed, cracked V.iii.196
flesh, initiate (with first experience of blood-
shed) II.ii.39
fleshment, contact of a sword with flesh
II.ii.114
flourish, passage of music on the trumpet
I.i.183, S.D., I.i.262, S.D.
foin, thrust IV.vi.238
fold, layer I.i.214
follow, attend II.iv.258
follower, attendant spirit III.iv.131
fond, foolish I.ii.47, I.iv.286
in one's dotage IV.vii.61
food, object IV.i.23
fool, foolishness I.iv.136
fop, fool I.ii.14
foppery, stupidity I.ii.109
foppish, foolish I.iv.151
foot, stride III.iv.112
footed, landed III.iii.11, III.vii.44
for, on account of II.iv.52
forbear, keep away from I.ii.147
fordo, destroy V.iii.255, V.iii.291
foreign, away from home IV.iii.44
fore-vouched, previously asserted I.i.216
forfended, forbidden V.i.11
fork, arrow I.i.139
forks, legs IV.vi.117
forsooth, indeed I.iv.176

foul fiend, the devil (used by Edgar during
his feigned madness) III.vi.7
fourscore, eighty IV.vii.62
frame, do, make, manage I.ii.92, IV.vi.222
fraught, filled, plentifully supplied I.iv.203
free, unworried, carefree III.iv.11, III.vi.101
innocent IV.vi.81
fret, wear I.iv.270
fretful, tempestuous III.i.4
from, away from II.i.126
front, forehead II.ii.100
frontlet, cloth worn across the forehead
I.iv.171
fruitfully, abundantly IV.vi.257
full, in full I.iv.323
very II.i.58
fumiter, fumitory, a weed IV.iv.3
furnishing, trimming, ornament III.i.29
furrow-weed, weed growing in the furrows of
ploughed-up land IV.iv.3
Fut, Pooh! I.ii.120

G

gad, sharp point I.ii.26
gait, way IV.vi.232
gall, sore I.iv.101
gallow, terrify III.ii.43
garb, manner II.ii.89
gasted, frightened II.i.57
gate, at gate, on the way (?) III.vii.16
gauntlet, armour-plated glove IV.vi.90
general, universal IV.vi.201
generation, kinsmen, 'flesh and blood' I.i.113
generous, gallant, high-born I.ii.8
gentle, good, honourable IV.vi.203
germen, seed of life III.ii.8
get, beget I.ii.15, III.iv.136
ghost, departing spirit V.iii.314
gilded, speciously beautiful V.iii.85
globe, the world II.ii.153
go, walk I.iv.108
goatish, lustful I.ii.117
good-year, a force of evil (?) V.iii.24
gored, mutilated V.iii.321
gorged, throated, voiced IV.vi.59
go to, away with you (an expression of disapprobation) I.iv.80, IV.vi.102
have a care III.iii.7
govern, control V.iii.161
grace, favour, patronage I.iv.150
honour V.iii.62
gross, big IV.vi.14
grossly, obviously I.i.285
ground, reason II.iv.139
grow, come, develop I.iii.24
grow out at heels, become threadbare II.ii.147
guardian, person who looks after property
II.iv.247
guess, estimate V.i.52
guessingly, as the result of guesswork III.vii.47
guilt, crime III.ii.56

H

habit, clothing v.iii.188
halcyon, kingfisher II.ii.70
half-blooded, bastard v.iii.81
handy-dandy, take your choice IV.vi.149
haply, perhaps I.i.96
happy, opportune II.iii.2
hard by, very near III.ii.60
hardocks, weed, a kind of dock (?) IV.iv.4
hatch, door, gate III.vi.69
head-lugged, dragged along by the head IV.ii.42
heart, courage v.iii.133
heave, utter like a groan IV.iii.25
heavy, sad IV.vi.143
hell-hated, as hateful as hell v.iii.147
hence, move away I.i.280
hereditary, descendants I.i.75
hewgh, a whistling sound IV.vi.91
hit, come to an agreement I.i.296
hitherward, in this direction IV.iv.21
hold, regard, esteem (as of a certain value) I.i.112, I.i.192
  hold back III.vii.71, IV.vi.154
  remain, be accepted IV.vii.86
  stand, continue without alteration (of e.g. a decision) v.i.1
  consider v.iii.61
  stop v.iii.155
hold in, keep back v.iii.202
holla, call out to III.i.55
hollowness, insincerity I.ii.104
holp, helped III.vii.61
home, to the full III.iii.11, III.iv.16
honours, rank as a knight v.iii.129
hospitable, in the role of host III.vii.39
hot, hot-tempered II.iv.100
hovel, take shelter in a hovel IV.vii.40
howe'er, but although IV.ii.66
how now, what is it (etc) I.ii.26
  what is this III.vii.74
hurricano, cloudburst III.ii.2

I

idle, unprofitable, unproductive I.ii.47, IV.iv.5, IV.vi.21
  foolish I.iii.16
ignorance, stupidity IV.v.9
ill, badly II.ii.51
image, indication II.iv.86
imagination; wrong imagination, illusion IV.vi.276
immediacy, close connection v.iii.66
impertinency, nonsense IV.vi.168
import, involve IV.iii.4
  bring by way of message IV.v.6
important, importunate IV.iv.26
impressed, levied v.iii.51
improper, unfitting v.iii.221

in-a-door, indoors I.iv.112
incense, incite II.iv.302
incline to, side with III.iii.12
indiscretion, inability to discern II.iv.192
infection, disease IV.vi.228
ingenious, conscious IV.vi.273
ingrateful, ungrateful II.iv.158, III.ii.9
inherit, possess, rule IV.vi.124
innocent, idiot III.vi.7
intelligent, giving information III.i.25
  well provided with information III.vii.11
intelligent party, spy III.v.9
interested (to), closely connected (with) I.i.81
interest, right of possession I.i.46
interlude, short play, comedy v.iii.90
intermission, delay II.iv.32
intrinse, entangled II.ii.67
invention, device I.ii.20
invest, endow I.i.125
issue, children, descendants I.i.62, I.ii.9
  consequence I.iv.3
it, its I.iv.198, IV.ii.32

J

jakes, water-closet II.ii.58
jealous, suspicious v.i.56
joint-stool, wooden stool III.vi.49
jot, moment I.iv.8
judicious, judicial, just (?) III.iv.71
Jug, (a nickname) I.iv.207
justicer, judge III.vi.19, IV.ii.79

K

kibe, chilblain I.v.7
kin, kind of people I.iv.165
kind, naturally loving I.i.119
  way IV.vi.156
knap, hit II.iv.119
knave, fellow I.i.17
  servant-boy I.iv.39
  rogue I.iv.84
knee, kneel before II.iv.210
know, find out v.i.1
known, experienced IV.vi.217

L

lag of, behind I.ii.6
lance (v.), pierce II.i.54
lance (n.), lancer v.iii.51
large, grand I.i.180
last, recent I.i.297, v.i.1
late, recent I.ii.96
learn, find out I.iv.215
leave, by your leave IV.vi.252
lecher, have sexual intercourse IV.vi.112
lend, provide III.ii.61
lender, moneylender III.iv.92
lending, non-essential belonging III.iv.102

oeillade, amorous glance IV.v.25
o'erlook, for *overlook*, read through I.ii.38, v.i.50
o'er-read, for *over-read*, read through I.ii.37
o'ertake, for *overtake*, catch up IV.i.43
o'er-watched, tired from keeping awake for too long II.ii.161
of, as regards v.i.45
    from v.iii.44
offend, harm I.i.298
offer, dare III.vi.89
office, service II.i.108
    duty II.iv.102, II.iv.174
    task III.i.42
    position of authority IV.vi.153
old, usual, natural III.vii.100
old, for *wold*, open country, downland (?) III.iv.112
on, of I.iv.90
on't, of it I.iv.138, IV.i.51
operative, effective IV.iv.14
opinion, reputation III.vi.108
oppose, draw (of a bolt to close a door) II.iv.172
    expose IV.vii.33
opposeless, irresistible IV.vi.39
opposite, opponent v.iii.43, v.iii.153
orb, heavenly body I.i.107
order, course I.i.16
ordinance, ordained system IV.i.68
or ere, before II.iv.282
or . . . or, either . . . or IV.vii.96
other, others I.v.183, III.iii.17
out, made public, ratified I.iv.138
out, abroad I.i.28
    an interjection III.vii.86
outside, outward appearance v.iii.142
out-wall, outward appearance III.i.45
outward, physical (?) IV.iv.10
overtake, catch up v.i.39
overture, revelation III.vii.88
owe, own, have I.i.198, I.iv.107

P

pack, pack up and go II.iv.76
packing, plotting III.i.26
pain, task III.i.53
pander, go-between II.ii.19
part (v.), divide I.i.134
part (n.), quality I.iv.248
partial, favourably disposed I.iv.297
particular (n.), smallest detail I.iv.249
    personal concern II.iv.288
particular (adj.), personal, own I.iv.323
    private v.i.30
pass, carry messages IV.ii.19
    pass away, die IV.vi.48
passion, emotion IV.iii.14
pass upon, pass judgement upon III.vii.23
pat, just at the right moment I.ii.123
pawn down, stake (in a wager) I.ii.80

pawn (n.), stake (in a wager) I.i.150
peace; hold one's peace, say nothing I.iv.167
peace, be still IV.vi.101
peascod, pea-pod I.iv.181
pell-mell, promiscuously IV.vi.115
pelting, petty II.iii.18
pendulous, hanging overhead III.iv.64
perdu, soldier placed in a particularly exposed position IV.vii.36
perdy, by God II.iv.81
perforce, by constraint I.v.33
    inevitably IV.ii.49
peril; at peril, on peril of death III.vii.51
period, full stop, end IV.vii.95
    conclusion v.iii.204
persever, persevere III.v.19
Persian, gorgeous III.vi.76
pew, gallery III.iv.52
Phoebus, the sun god II.ii.100
physic, medicine III.iv.33
pieced, in addition I.i.195
piece out, add to III.vi.2
pierce, move (emotionally) IV.iii.9
pight, determined II.i.67
pinfold, pound, enclosure for stray cattle II.ii.8
pity, relieve distress III.iii.2
place, high place III.vi.52
    title v.iii.65
placket, slit in petticoat III.iv.91
plain, complain of III.i.39
pleasant, pleasure-giving v.iii.170
pleasure, will, desire II.iii.142
    wishes v.iii.2, v.iii.63
pledge, surety v.iii.94
plight, promise I.i.97, III.iv.115
plighted, folded, (hence) concealed I.i.276
plot, plotting II.i.75
point; at point, ready I.iv.310, III.i.33
poise, weight II.i.122
politician, trickster IV.vi.165
poorly, dressed in rags (?) IV.i.10
porridge, soup, stew III.iv.53
port, gate II.i.82
    place of exit II.iii.3
portable, bearable III.vi.104
porter, gate-keeper III.vii.63
possess, take possession of IV.i.62
post (n.), messenger II.iv.29, III.vii.10, IV.vi.267
post (v.), go (with a message) III.vii.1
    go with haste IV.v.8
potency, power I.i.168
potential, powerful II.i.78
poverty, poor people III.iv.26
power, army III.i.30, III.iii.11
practice, evil design I.ii.167
    intrigue II.i.75
    cunning II.iv.111
practise on, plot against III.ii.56
practised, plotted IV.vi.270
prank, silly action I.iv.221

prefer, advance I.i.270
preferment, advancement IV.v.38
pregnant, ready II.i.78
    well disposed IV.vi.218
preparation, army in battle array IV.iv.22
present, immediate I.i.188
presented, exposed II.iii.11
presently, at once I.ii.94
press-money, money paid to a man when he
    is 'pressed' into military service IV.vi.86
pretence, intention I.ii.81, I.iv.60
pretty, fine I.iv.173
prevent, forestall I.i.41
    avoid III.iv.149
prick, skewer II.iii.16
prithee, (I) pray you, please I.iv.162, II.ii.5,
    III.vi.83
privily, secretly III.iii.12
prize, estimate I.i.66
proceedings, plan of campaign v.i.32
proclaim, publicly announce (a wanted per-
    son) II.iii.1, IV.vi.221
produce, bring in v.iii.230
profession, solemn undertaking v.iii.130
proof; in proof, to the test IV.vi.179
proper, fine I.i.15
    natural, to be IV.ii.60
property, complete identity I.i.110
propinquity, close relationship I.i.110
protect, condone I.iv.189
protest, proclaim v.iii.130
proud, ostentatious III.iv.78
prove, try out IV.vi.90
provision, board and lodging III.vi.91
provoke, induce IV.iv.13
publish, announce publicly I.i.39
published, proclaimed IV.vi.227
pudder, turmoil III.ii.49
puissant, powerful v.iii.216
purpose, intention, plans I.i.32, II.iv.3, v.i.1
purposed, resolved II.iv.289
put on, assume I.iii.12
    encourage I.iv.189
    incite to II.i.101
put up, put away, pocket I.ii.28
put upon (one), make oneself out to be II.ii.111

Q

quake, shake with fear IV.vi.107
qualify, moderate I.ii.148
quality, character II.iv.88
    manner II.iv.132
    rank, high rank in society v.iii.III,
    v.iii.120
quarrel, cause v.iii.57
queasy, difficult II.i.17
question, speech, communication IV.iii.24
question; bear question, be open to argument
    v.iii.34
questrist, seeker III.vii.16

quicken, come to life III.vii.38
quit, pay back, requite III.vii.86
    for *acquit,* acquit oneself, act, fight II.i.30

R

rage, madness IV.iv.19
    delirium IV.vii.79
raiment, clothes II.iv.151
rake up, cover up (with sand) IV.vi.267
rank, gross I.iv.185
rash, hot-headed I.i.288
rat's-bane, rat poison III.iv.52
raze, erase, wipe out I.iv.4
reason (v.), argue about II.iv.260
reason (n.), intelligence IV.i.32
reasoned, argued out v.i.28
reconcile, return to favour III.vi.109
recreant, traitor I.i.162
redress, measure to alleviate trouble I.iv.181
reek, sweat II.iv.29
regard, care, consideration I.i.235, I.iv.250
relieve, help III.iii.13
remediate, healing IV.iv.17
remorse, compassion IV.ii.73
remotion, remoteness II.iv.110
renege, deny II.ii.70
repair, alleviate IV.i.76
repeal, call back III.vi.109
reposure, placing II.i.70
require, want v.iii.44
reservation, retention, the reserving of some-
    thing for oneself I.i.128
    reserved right II.iv.248
resign, assign, make over v.iii.298
resolve, tell, inform II.iv.24
respect, consideration I.i.244
    liking I.i.251
respect; upon respect, deliberately II.iv.23
retention, detention v.iii.48
reverb, reverberate I.i.149
reverend, aged II.ii.117
reverse, go back on I.i.144
riched, enriched I.i.60
riddle, ruse v.i.37
rigour, harshness v.i.22
ripeness, maturity v.ii.11
rival, compete I.i.187
rive, burst open III.ii.57
rogue, vagrant IV.vii.40
    wretched person v.iii.13
rotundity, roundness III.ii.7
round, frank, blunt I.iv.48
rub, thwart II.ii.144
rude, rough IV.ii.30
ruffle, bluster II.iv.297
    abuse III.vii.40

S

safe (adj.), sure I.iv.187

safe (adv.), with due caution v.iii.144
sallet, tasty morsel of food III.iv.123
sampire, samphire, a herb IV.vi.15
Sarum, Salisbury II.ii.75
sa, sa, a hunting cry IV.vi.198
saucily, wantonly I.i.18
savour, kind, quality I.iv.220
say, indication v.iii.138
    what (with conditional) v.iii.143
scant, withhold I.i.274, III.ii.66
    cut down II.iv.171
'scape, for *escape* I.iv.191, III.vi.110
scattered, distracted III.i.31
scourge, afflict I.ii.98
scurvy, contemptible IV.vi.165
season, spell of bad weather III.iv.32
second, supporter IV.vi.188
sect, faction v.iii.18
sectary, student I.ii.138
secure, give a false sense of safety IV.i.21
seem, appear IV.ii.60
self, same I.i.65
sennet, fixed set of notes played on the trumpet I.i.29, S.D.
sense, mental vigour IV.vi.272
sequent, subsequent following I.ii.98
serious, important IV.v.8
serviceable, diligent in service IV.vi.245
sessa, a cry to urge a horse to move quickly III.iv.95
session, sitting of a court of justice v.iii.55
set, stake (in gambling) I.iv.110
    tie up, stable (of horses) II.ii.3
set at odds, cause strife among I.iii.5
set guard, send out a guard II.i.16
several, separate II.i.126
severally, separately II.ii. S.D.
shanks, legs II.ii.32
shealed, shelled I.iv.181
shift, change, v.iii.186
shiver, smash to pieces IV.vi.52
short, broken up IV.vii.41
show (v.), look I.iv.227
show (n.), vision III.vi.101
side-piercing, agonising IV.vi.85
simple (n.), medicinal herb IV.iv.14
simple (adj.), humble IV.vi.148
simular, simulating, counterfeit III.ii.53
single, one's own v.iii.104
sirrah, sir (a normal form of address used with inferiors) I.ii.72
sith that, since II.iv.235
size, allowance II.iv.171
slack (v.), be inattentive in one's duties to someone II.iv.241
slack (adj.), *come slack of*, fall short of I.iii.9
slenderly, superficially I.i.286
slip-shod, in slippers I.v.9
sliver, tear off IV.ii.34
smilet, little smile IV.iii.19
smooth, flatter II.ii.67
smug, neatly-dressed IV.vi.193

snuff, quarrel III.i.26
    smouldering wick (of a candle) IV.vi.40
soiled, fed with rich green fodder IV.vi.120
sojourn, stay I.i.43
something, somewhat, rather I.i.18, III.v.3
sometime, former I.i.116
soothe, humour III.iv.167
sophisticated, affected, artificial III.iv.100
sot, idiot IV.ii.8
soul, person IV.i.45
sound, approach (someone, for an opinion) I.ii.65
sovereign, overmastering IV.iii.42
sovereignty, supreme power I.iv.215
space, world of external appearances I.i.52
    range IV.vi.264
spake, spoke I.ii.141
speak, call out I.iv.229
    say III.vi.26
speculation, watcher III.i.24
speed, be successful, prosper I.ii.19, IV.vi.203
spherical, planetary I.ii.113
spill, destroy III.ii.8
spit, sharp-pointed rod (used for roasting meat) III.vi.13
spite, regardless II.iv.32
spleen, malice, I.iv.267
sport, pleasure IV.i.38
spy, look closely I.v.19
square, a symbol of perfection; see note to I.i.70
squiny, squint, look sideways IV.vi.134
squire, gentleman below the rank of a knight I.iv.224
    personal servant II.iv.210
stake, place of execution II.i.64
standing, stagnant III.iv.125
starblasting, withering away under the influence of the stars III.iv.56
start, impulse I.i.293
state, power IV.ii.57
    rule v.i.22
    position v.i.68
stay, wait I.iv.8
stelled, starry, fixed III.vii.60
stiff, unassailable IV.vi.272
still, always, for ever I.i.153, I.iv.315, III.iv.166
    at one and the same time IV.i.2
still-soliciting, constantly entreating I.i.227
stock, stocking II.iv.10
stock-punished, punished by being put in the stocks III.iv.126
store, stuff III.vi.51
straight, at once, in a moment I.iii.26, v.iii.279
strain, disposition v.iii.41
strained, excessive I.i.165
stranger, disown I.i.200
strip, deprive IV.iii.43
stubborn, rough II.ii.117
study, concern, endeavour I.i.272
subdue, bring down III.iv.67
subscribe, give up I.ii.24

subscription, obedience III.ii.18

success, result V.iii.194

sue, beg I.i.26

suffer, tolerate, allow I.ii.49, III.iv.138, IV.ii.44

sufferance, suffering III.vi.102

suggestion, wicked prompting II.i.75

suited, clothed IV.vii.6

summoner, officer who called offenders before an ecclesiastical court III.ii.58

sumpter, drudge II.iv.212

superfluous, having more than enough IV.i.67

superflux, superfluity III.iv.35

superserviceable, over-attentive II.ii.16

supply, take (the place of) IV.vi.260

surfeit, unhappy outcome I.ii.110

surrender, renunciation I.i.297

sustain, care for III.iii.5, V.iii.321
   maintain I.iv.318

sustaining, nourishing IV.iv.6

sway, control I.i.132

swear, swear by I.i.156

sword, swordsman V.iii.33

T

take, overtake I.iv.316
   strike with disease II.iv.159

taking, malignant influence III.iv.57

taking off, killing V.i.65

tame, ready to submit IV.vi.216

tardiness, holding-back I.i.231

tarry, wait I.iv.80, I.iv.302

tart, bitter, distasteful IV.ii.87

task; at task, open to criticism I.iv.329

taste, test I.ii.44

tax, accuse III.ii.16

teach, encourage, show how V.iii.186

tear, tear apart IV.ii.65

teem, bear children I.iv.266

tell, count, give an account of, reckon I.i.204, III.ii.88
   tell about V.iii.196

temper (v.), moisten I.iv.289

temper (n.), one's right mind I.v.39

temperance, sanity IV.vii.25

tender (v.) offer, put down I.i.191

tender (n.), earnest desire I.iv.192

tender-hefted, see II.iv.169 and II.iv.167

text, quotation, parable, imagery IV.ii.37

that, so that IV.vii.48, V.iii.127

therewithal, along with it I.i.290

things, the state of the world in general III.i.7

think, hope, expect III.vii.68

though, even though II.i.73

though that, although IV.vi.210

thrilled, moved IV.ii.73

thrive, succeed I.ii.20, V.ii.2

throughly, fully IV.vii.95

throw one's head, direct one's gaze (?) III.vi.68

thrusting-on, impulse I.ii.116

thwart, perverse I.iv.268

tike, common dog III.vi.66

time, eventuality V.i.48

time; the time, the world, things as they are V.iii.32

time, present situation V.iii.233

tithing, district III.iv.125

to, as to III.i.36

toad-spotted, stained with infamy V.iii.138

Tom o' Bedlam, madman I.ii.125

tonight, last night I.ii.24

top (v.), get the better of I.ii.21

top (n.), head II.iv.158

touch, punish IV.vi.84

tough, hard V.iii.315

toward, impending, about to take place II.i.10, III.iii.17, IV.vi.204

train, attendants I.iv.232

tranced, in a trance V.iii.218

treacher, traitor I.ii.113

trespass, crime II.iv.43

trice, moment I.i.212

trick, turn (of voice) IV.vi.105

trill, trickle IV.iii.12

troop with, follow in the train of I.i.127

troth, solemn undertaking III.iv.115

trow, believe, trust I.iv.109

true, well-proportioned I.ii.8

trundle-tail, dog with a dragging tail III.vi.66

trust; put in trust, entrust affairs to I.iv.13

tucket, trumpet call II.i.80, S.D., II.iv.178, S.D.

turn, become dizzy IV.vi.23

twain, two IV.i.43, IV.vi.202, V.iii.320

U

unaccommodated, without the necessities of life III.iv.101

unbolted, unsifted II.ii.57

unbonneted, with head uncovered III.i.14

undertake, embark on a venture IV.ii.13

undistinguished, unbounded IV.vi.264

undo, prevent IV.i.70

ungoverned, ungovernable IV.iv.19

ungracious, wicked IV.vi.269

unloose, unravel II.ii.67

unmannerly, disrespectful I.i.140

unpossessing, without possessions II.i.69

unprized, unappreciated I.i.255

unprovided, unprotected II.i.54

unpublished, hidden IV.iv.16

unstate, give up one's rank I.ii.93

unsubstantial, that cannot be detected by the senses IV.i.7

untented, (of wounds) (either) too deep to be cleaned, (or) not cleaned out I.iv.285

upon, against III.vi.84

use (v.), make a practice of I.i.155

use (n.), execution II.i.130, treat I.i.267

V

validity, value I.i.77

vantage, advantage II.ii.162
vassal, wretch I.i.156
vaunt-courier, herald III.ii.5
venge, punish IV.ii.80
vent, utter I.i.161
very, even, even the V.iii.188
vexed, turbulent IV.iv.2
victor, victorious V.iii.132
vile, rude, vigorous IV.vi.272
villain, servant, serf III.vii.77
vor, warn (dialect) IV.vi.235
vouchsafe, deign to give II.iv.151
vulgar, common knowledge IV.vi.205

W

wage, wager I.i.151
    contend II.iv.205
wake, merrymaking III.vi.70
walk, withdraw IV.vii.84
wall-newt, lizard III.iv.122
want (v.), lack, need I.i.226, IV.i.19, IV.iv.20
want (n.), lack I.i.226
wanton (n.), playful person II.iv.120
wanton (adj.), playful, unrestrained IV.i.37
warped, perverse III.vi.50
watch, go without sleep II.ii.145
waterish, (i) well-watered; (ii) poor in spirit
    I.i.254
wawl, wail IV.vi.174
weal, state I.iv.192
wear, use I.iv.152
wear out, outlast V.iii.17
web and the pin, cataract III.iv.109
weeds, garments IV.vii.7
weigh, balance I.i.5
welked, twisted IV.vi.72
well-favoured, pleasing II.iv.252
wench, girl, young woman III.ii.83
were, would be IV.vi.178, V.iii.71
what, whatever III.vi.110
    whoever V.iii.98
    who V.iii.164
where (n.), place elsewhere I.i.257
where (conj.), whereas I.ii.77
where (adv.), in cases where V.i.23
wherefore, why I.ii.2, II.iv.108
    to what purpose IV.vi.226

which, who V.iii.215
whiles, whilst II.iii.5, IV.ii.58
wholesome, healthy I.iv.192
    beneficial II.iv.139
whoreson (n.), fellow I.i.20
whoreson (adj.), an adjective intensifying the
    following noun, without separate meaning
    of its own I.iv.70, II.ii.56
wide-skirted, extensive I.i.61
wield, express I.i.51
wind, worm (one's way) I.ii.91
wisdom, common sense II.iv.303
    knowledge IV.iv.8
wit, cunning I.ii.168
    good sense I.iv.146, I.iv.169, II.iv.41
withal, with it I.ii.95
within, at the back of the stage II.i.80, S.D.
    indoors IV.ii.3
wont, used, accustomed to I.iv.52
work, strive IV.vii.1
worship, honour I.iv.251
worth; be worth, deserve I.i.275
worth, worthy of, earning, justifying II.iv.43
worthy, give a reputation for excellence
    II.ii.112
would, wish I.iv.202
writ (n.), written order V.iii.245
writ (v.), wrote I.ii.132
    written to I.iv.317
wrought, established IV.vii.95

Y

yeoman, working farmer, III.vi.9
yet, for the present, for the time being
    I.iv.38, IV.vii.9
    still III.vi.93, IV.vi.63
yield, consent IV.iii.41
yoke-fellow, partner III.vi.35
yond, that ... over there IV.vi.18, IV.vi.116,
    IV.vi.148

Z

zed, the letter Z II.ii.56
zwagger, for *swagger,* bully IV.vi.233